Florence Nightingale and
the Health of the Raj

The History of Medicine in Context

Series Editors: Andrew Cunningham and Ole Peter Grell

Department of History and Philosophy of Science
University of Cambridge

Department of History
The Open University

Titles in this series include:

*Health Care and Poor Relief in 18th and
19th Century Northern Europe*
Edited by Ole Peter Grell, Andrew Cunningham and Robert Jütte

*The Irritable Heart of Soldiers and the Origins of
Anglo-American Cardiology*
Charles F. Wooley

The Rise of Causal Concepts of Disease
K. Codell Carter

*A Cultural History of Medical Vitalism in
Enlightenment Montpellier*
Elizabeth A. Williams

To My Mother
Chinmoyee Torubala Sen

Plate 1   Florence Nightingale in 1856. (The Wellcome Library)

Florence Nightingale and the Health of the Raj

JHARNA GOURLAY

ASHGATE

Published by
Ashgate Publishing Limited
Gower House
Croft Road
Aldershot
Hants GU11 3HR
England

Ashgate Publishing Company
Suite 420
101 Cherry Street
Burlington, VT 05401-4405 USA

Ashgate website: http://www.ashgate.co.uk

British Library Cataloguing in Publication Data

Gourlay, Jharna
    Florence Nightingale and the health of the Raj. - (The
    history of medicine in context)
    l.Nightingale, Florence, 1820-1910 - Contributions in
    public health of India 2.East Indians - Health and hygiene
    - History - 19th century 3.Medical policy - India - History
    - 19th century 4.Sanitation - India - History - 19th
    century 5.India - Social conditions - 19th century 6.India
    - History - 19th century
    I.Title
    362 .1'092

Library of Congress Cataloging-in-Publication Data

Gourlay, Jharna, 1934-
    Florence Nightingale and the health of the Raj / Jharna Gourlay.
       p. cm. -- (The history of medicine in context)
    Includes bibliographical references and index.
    ISBN 0-7546-3364-0 (alk. paper)
       1. Nightingale, Florence, 1820-1910. 2. Nurses--Great Britain--Biography.
    3. Women social reformers--Great Britain--Biography. 4. Public health--
    India--History--19th century. 5. India--Relations--Great Britain. 6. Great
    Britain--Relations--India. I. Title. II. Series.

RT37.N5G68 2003
610.73'092--dc21
[B]
                                                              2003045331

ISBN 0 7546 3364 0 Hardback

The History of Medicine in Context

Typeset in Sabon by Bookcraft Ltd, Stroud, Gloucestershire, UK
Printed and bound in Great Britain by MPG Books Ltd, Bodmin, Cornwall.

Contents

List of Plates

Preface

Some years ago, when working for the BBC External Services, I was asked to produce a feature on Florence Nightingale. It was during my subsequent mini-research that I became aware of her involvement with India and my curiosity was roused. Many other commitments and interests meant that at that time further research was impossible, but I promised myself to return to it eventually. This book evolved from that initial curiosity and is the result of four years' research in Britain and India. It is a tribute to a woman much praised, more maligned, but hardly understood.

The life of Florence Nightingale is a much-trodden territory, but her involvement with India and Indians is relatively unknown and unresearched. Nightingale never went to India but instigated and inspired various sanitary and social reforms in India. She was involved with army sanitation, public health, famine, irrigation, land tenancy reform, nursing, female medical education and finally village sanitation. For almost forty years of her life, from 1857 to 1896, she worked and aspired for India.

The aim of this book is to present in some detail this aspect of her life and work, to show how she progressed from the narrow sphere of army sanitation to the socio-economic condition of the whole of India. I have tried to place this development in the context of events in India during that time, and to trace her political involvement and her growing awareness of Indian problems; how from an imperialist position she gradually changed into someone who not only approved but worked for the Indianisation of the administration. This is also the story of a woman in nineteenth-century patriarchal Britain who worked relentlessly to influence Government and public opinion over policy matters of value to her.

The book is based on primary sources in archives in Britain and India, focusing in particular on her letters and correspondence. I have made considerable use of her articles and pamphlets as well so that her story can be told directly through her own words. I have also referred to other secondary works principally to provide information on the necessary historical context to understand the events that moved her, and the situation in which she tried to work for India. In this matter, Sir Edward Cook's pioneering work *The Life of Florence Nightingale* (1913) is undoubtedly the most authentic source material. Unlike others, he did discuss Nightingale's Indian work, but largely from an official and British perspective. Moreover, as he covered the whole of Nightingale's life and work, he focused mainly on events in Britain and understandably he did not have space to consider her Indian activities in their proper historical context or devote much time to her association with various Indian leaders or Indian organisations. F.B. Smith's *Florence Nightingale – Reputation and Power* (1982) has one chapter on her Indian activities that is similarly limited to Britain but provides only a brief and one-sided assessment of her work that fails to do justice to the materials available. More recently, a number of well-researched books have been published on imperial health policies in nineteenth-century India. Unfortunately, most of these either totally ignore Nightingale's contributions or only mention her name in passing.

This book does not claim to be an exhaustive study of Nightingale's correspondence about India. Biographers of Nightingale know only too well how impossible that task would be considering the enormous volume of letters, notes and personal papers she left behind, and there is enough material for several aspiring PhD students. One major difficulty of dealing with Nightingale's letters is that she quite often wrote the same letter to more than one person and made several drafts of it and saved all, sometimes including a copy of the original. But they are not necessarily indexed in the same volume in the British Library. Sometimes she had put her thoughts in notes before drafting a letter and sometimes she left notes of her discussions with other people, not always mentioning who the person was. I have quoted them verbatim, remaining faithful to her punctuation as far as possible.

One particular problem concerning her Indian correspondence is that it is difficult to find. Correspondence with various British administrators, Viceroys, Sanitary Commissioners and other officials, and some non-official people, is easy to find. Letters to and from Indian correspondents on the other hand are conspicuous by their absence. There are few such letters in the Nightingale papers, nor are there drafts or copies of her many letters to Indians. Yet it is clear from cross-references in other letters and her correspondence published in contemporary Indian journals, or later, and the archives of prominent Indian leaders, that she carried on extensive correspondence with Indians throughout her involvement with India. It is quite possible that in her immense collection of private papers, in Britain and elsewhere, some Indian letters are still waiting to be discovered.

It should also be mentioned that this book is not only about Nightingale, it is also about India as she encountered it. Hence some events have been described in some length to put Nightingale's work in perspective. I have followed the nineteenth-century spelling of Indian names of places and individuals to maintain a parity with the quoted materials, hence Pune is spelled as Poona, Chennai as Madras, Mumbai as Bombay, and Kolkata as Calcutta.

The most valuable source of Nightingale's correspondence and private papers is of course the British Library and I am very fortunate to have been able to use that. My thanks to the British Library Staff for their cordial and efficient help. I am grateful to Radcliffes-LeBrasseur, the Administrators of the Henry Bonham Carter Will Trust for giving me the permission to publish selections of Nightingale's letters, to the National Archives of India and the Jawaharlal Nehru Memorial Library, New Delhi, and to the Gokhale Institute of Politics and Economics, Pune, for giving me permission to publish from Dadabhai Naoroji's correspondence with Nightingale and G.K. Gokhale's private papers. I also want to thank the Cama Oriental Institute and the State Archives of Mumbai, Jayakar Library, Pune, the West Bengal State Archives, the Centre for Social Studies, and Bethune College, Kolkata, for granting me access to papers and records in their possession. I am particularly grateful to the staff of these institutions who gave me every possible help in gathering materials within a very short time in my whirlwind tour of these places. I also want to thank Professor Martha Vicinus, Harvard University Press, and Oxford University Press for giving me permission to use printed materials from their published books. For illustrations, I want to thank the Wellcome Trust Medical Photographic Library and the British Library Reproductions, and particularly the Convocation Secretariat of the University of London for granting me a Convocation Trust Award towards the cost of using illustrations.

A book is never written alone. I am immensely lucky to have friends who have continuously supplied me with snippets of information, tapes and books relevant for the project. I am particularly grateful to Dr Ian Kerr and Dr Kaye Kerr for showing immense interest in my book from beginning to end and continuously providing me with references, contacts and valuable advice. I want to thank Anna Gourlay for typing the first draft of the manuscript and giving me much informative editorial advice. I want to thank specially Uttara Chakravarty of Bethune College in assisting me in collecting archival materials. I am grateful to Avijit Sen Gupta and Dr Alokananda Sen Gupta for providing me hospitality in Kolkata and to Mr Kunwar Narain and Mrs Bharati Narain for their hospitality in Delhi.

While travelling in India to gather materials for the book, I met many people whom I never knew before and had many experiences which I would not have had had I not been writing this book. One such interesting experience was to meet the descendants of Runchorelal Chotalall, the nineteenth-century Chairman of the Ahmedabad Municipality, with whom Florence Nightingale corresponded: my thanks to Radhika and Mr Achyut Chinubhai, who made my stay in Ahmedabad memorable, and to Mr Kirit Bhavsar who helped me to find them.

Lastly, I want to thank Dr Stephen Gourlay who, in spite of his own pressure of work, gave me his untiring endless help in every conceivable way, and without whom this book would not have been possible. But I have no qualms about it; as they say in modern marital vows, in sickness and in research.

Jharna Gourlay
December 2002
London

Abbreviations

BL	British Library.
BL Add. Mss	British Library, Additional Manuscripts collections
FN	Florence Nightingale.
NAI	National Archives of India, New Delhi.
NMML	Nehru Memorial Museum and Library, New Delhi.
OIOC	Oriental and India Office Collections, British Library, London.
WBSA	West Bengal State Archives, Calcutta.

CHAPTER ONE

Florence Nightingale and her Times (1820–1910)

Florence Nightingale's pioneering work in giving nursing a professional status, her self-sacrificing role in the battlefield of Crimea, her picture as the Lady with the Lamp by the bedside of a wounded soldier and her contribution to medical statistics are all well known. What is less well known is her interest and involvement with India. Very few people are aware that this nineteenth-century British woman took such an interest in India that it occupied the rest of her life after her return from Crimea in 1856. For almost 40 years she dedicated herself to the improvement of the health and sanitary conditions of ordinary Indians. In doing so she engaged herself with many other social and political issues that affected India at the time. After nursing, India was her greatest passion. Her empathy for Indians was in sharp contrast with the imperialistic and colonial attitudes of the period.

On her return from Crimea, Florence became involved with the Royal Commission, set up to investigate the health of the British Army.[1] During her work with this Commission she became aware of the high death rate of British soldiers in India and the appalling sanitary conditions in the army barracks. The mutiny of 1857 further drew her attention towards India. She realised that more soldiers died in India from preventable diseases and lack of sanitation than on the battlefield. At her instigation, a second Royal Commission was set up in 1859 to investigate and improve the sanitary state of the British Army in India.[2] While working with this Commission she came to appreciate the real situation that existed in India. She became aware of the poverty-stricken disease-ridden inhumane conditions of the ordinary Indian peasants, how they were decimated by famine and epidemics, how their conditions were exploited by money-lenders and *zemindars*, how the British system of justice had failed to help them, and how without improving the conditions of the masses of India it was futile to improve the sanitary conditions of the British soldiers in the barracks. This realisation finally moulded her perception of India, and led her to a lifelong involvement with the country. Once she realised that the problem of hygiene and sanitation in India was only one aspect of a complex problem, her attention soon moved from British soldiers to ordinary Indians and she started her fight to improve their conditions. She did this in a very unique way, by writing letters. To understand how this was possible and to appreciate the extent of her work for India, one needs to consider the historical context of her life and times.

Florence Nightingale was born at a time when social reform was an outstanding strong force in nineteenth-century Britain, one cause of which lay in industrialisation and economic transformation. It was the age of scientific discoveries, liberalism in politics, the flourishing of art, literature and philosophy, and of political expansion and imperialism. It was also the beginning of the feminist movement in the Western world.[3] Except for the first twenty years, Florence lived throughout the entire nineteenth century, plus a decade of the twentieth. During this long life, self-declared recluse and invalid though she was for much of it, she witnessed immense social changes that brought individual and collective freedom for many, as it did in her own life. The socio-political events and the economic changes of that period deeply influenced her thoughts and shaped her ideas.

When Florence undertook to solve the problem of Indian sanitation, India was also going through a radical change. The British presence on Indian soil for over a century forced Indian society to awake from its feudal slumber to a new self-awareness. The events that took place in Bengal and later in other parts of India at the time were also in a sense the consequences of the changes in Britain.[4] Whatever happened in Britain – social or political, good or bad, progressive or regressive – cast a long shadow in India. If there were war in Europe or a Russian threat, British military policy in India would change. If there were a change of government at Westminster, there would be changes in the internal policy in India. Whether or not new taxes were imposed, primary education introduced, newspaper freedom curtailed, or the age limit in the covenanted posts raised, was determined by who was in power in the British Parliament. India's fate sank or surfaced depending on the political alignments in Britain. Florence's working life was dominated by this period of social and political changes both in India and Britain.

Changes in British society in the nineteenth century

The two most influential forces in nineteenth-century Britain were industrialisation and the impact of the Benthamite vision of society. Florence was born in 1820, five years after the Battle of Waterloo had been fought and won, Napoleon had been defeated and Britain had emerged in Western Europe as a formidable power. By that time, the industrialisation of the country was well underway, with rapid growth of textile and wool industries, shipbuilding and coal mines, blast furnaces and other heavy industries. Railways were introduced in the 1830s, and together with trunk roads and canals reduced the distance from one place to another. The extensive change that was brought about by industrialisation and its impact on the rest of the world was completely unparalleled. Britain became the workshop of the world. 'The markets of the world lay wide open to her manufactured goods, and the undeveloped areas of the globe to her capital investments.'[5]

Industrialisation created immense wealth in certain sections of the British population such as mill owners and investors in the economic boom. The accumulated wealth in the hands of the entrepreneurs created a new class in British society, the middle class, which covered a broad spectrum of society. As Brock remarked, they had one thing in common: they shared the same irreverence towards the old system and the old masters of British society.[6] The power base gradually shifted from the aristocracy to these self-made men. It was they who were mostly influenced by the Benthamite philosophy and who effected immense changes in the social scene of Victorian Britain.

As industrialisation had created a class of socially mobile new rich, it had also created the working class, who were not so fortunate as the middle class. Pre-industrial Britain had mainly been an agricultural country. In the early part of the nineteenth century 22 per cent of the population was engaged in agriculture, but by the end of the century only 9 per cent remained so engaged. 'The old pattern of farmer and labourer, or of merchant and craftsman was largely replaced by a new pattern of factory owner and factory worker.'[7] With industrialisation, the population of Britain not only exploded, but also moved its habitation. At the beginning of the nineteenth century the population of Britain was about 13 million, but by the end it had risen to 29 million. A large section of this population left their rural homes and gathered in the periphery of the mills, factories and workshops in places like Glasgow, Manchester, Sheffield and Liverpool. They intensified a new type of social problem called urban poverty. Rural poverty was not unknown in pre-industrial Britain but industrialisation brought its own kind of deprivation and degradation. The number of slum dwellers increased in all industrial towns and big cities and they lived in appalling conditions, devoid of all social amenities. Housing was scarce, and rented accommodation and boarding houses were overcrowded and disease-ridden. A large section of the population lived on the streets, particularly unemployed men and destitute children. Sanitation and public facilities were practically non-existent, and provision for clean water and sewage removal was limited. In most of the big cities and towns, cesspools and dunghills were common sights. In London, the Thames was so polluted that it was described in newspaper cartoons as 'Monster Soup'.[8]

The poor housing conditions, unclean domestic water and unhygienic sanitary situation contributed to the ill health of the urban poor. Between

1831 and 1849 there were several cholera epidemics in England and Wales, but the number of victims in London was double the national figure. Apart from cholera, whooping cough, measles, smallpox and scarlet fever were rampant in London. The capital of the British Empire was considered as a 'gigantic sick house'.[9] There were few medical facilities and the rudimentary service provided by the Poor Law was selective.[10] People were afraid to go to the hospitals; the rich never went. Nurses were mostly from the bottom of the social ladder and were renowned for their drunkenness and socially unacceptable behaviour.

Education was a social privilege, mostly confined within the upper and wealthy classes and mainly for men. Working class children hardly went to school and primary education was not universal. The lower class women and children were a source of cheap labour for the mills and the factories. Although Britain from 1837 onwards was ruled by Queen Victoria, it was very much a patriarchal society. Men were considered superior in every respect and women, rich or poor, had no scope for a proper education, professional opportunity or vocational training. Most of the universities would not accept women. Many women considered marriage as an escape, but a married woman had even less status. She did not exist in the eyes of the law; she had no claim on property or the children. The lower class working women's conditions were equally bad. Their lives were oppressed by poverty and childbearing. There was an urgent need for social reform in nineteenth-century Britain in every sphere of life.

Reform came in the guise of a philosophical idea called utilitarianism. Like industrialisation, it touched every sphere of British life. The utility or usefulness of an idea, a measure or an institution to produce 'the greatest good for the greatest number', armed with 'free action for all', became the axiom of the day. Whether it was political or legal institutions, foreign policy or free trade, education or enfranchisement, the death penalty or trade union rights, all were influenced by the philosophy of 'utility' and 'greatest good'.

The earlier Benthamite version of utilitarianism, which prescribed free action for all in the pursuit of happiness, was unworkable for obvious reasons. It was gradually replaced, under the influence of James Mill and John Stuart Mill, by a more logical and pragmatic utilitarianism that did not rule out state intervention to remove social conflicts. It was understood that the pursuit of individual good would not necessarily lead to 'the greatest good for the greatest number' and the state's supervisory role was accepted both by the Tories and the Whigs, who alternately ruled the country. People from all spheres of life, landed aristocrats and *nouveau riche*, factory owners and trade union leaders, writers, philosophers, lawyers and journalists, philanthropists and missionaries, all accepted the need for social reform irrespective of their political allegiance.

The underlying themes of reforms in nineteenth-century Britain were humanitarianism and liberalism. The Reform Acts of 1832 and 1867, educational reforms of 1833 and 1880, factory legislation, the Poor Law, repeal of the Corn Laws, Public Health acts, and Municipal Reform acts were all aimed at eradicating ignorance, poverty and distress while providing new opportunities and securing individual rights. As the waves of reforms and philanthropy swept through the country, the question of women's political, legal and social rights received attention too, which subsequently led to changes in the divorce and property laws.[11]

Early years of Florence Nightingale

Florence was born and brought up in the climate of these reforms in British society. She was a true product of her time, a radical liberal. Her political lineage could be traced back to her maternal grandfather, William Smith, a Unitarian, liberal and freethinker. Florence's father, William Edward Nightingale, maintained the same tradition. He was also a Unitarian, a Benthamite and a Whig.[12] He stood as a parliamentary candidate for Andover in 1835, and Florence as a young girl had been excited by the prospect of her father becoming a Member of Parliament. He lost the election, however, and never went back to politics.[13]

William Nightingale's influence on Florence was profound. He not only educated her in literature, history and politics, he also ensured that she was proficient in a number of European languages. He opened the door for her to meet and befriend many of the influential politicians of the day. Lord Palmerston, the Whig Prime Minister, was a family friend and a neighbour. Apparently Florence supported his foreign policy in her formative years. When she was a little girl she even met Raja Ram Mohun Roy, the Indian social reformer, as she later recounted in a letter to Mary Carpenter.[14] Florence travelled widely in Europe with her parents, and met famous people such as the Italian leader Sismondi.[15] She spent time in Paris with a family friend, Mary Clarke, who was better known as Madame Mohl, and enjoyed the company of artists and intellectual rebels.

Although Florence was born into a wealthy family and spent her childhood and youth in luxury, she was well aware of the poverty and squalor that existed in the urban areas of Britain. She and her family regularly spent the 'season' in London. The slums of London were not far away from where she stayed. She was fully aware of the conditions of the working class in the big cities and the poor in the rural areas. She had also worked among the poor residents in her father's estate in Leahurst and knew the consequences of ignorance and poverty.

It was apparent from the letters she wrote at the time that in spite of her youth she was in no way a passive recipient of all the influences that she was exposed to.[16] She was articulate, well informed and a good participant in the intellectual discourse going on around her. She also had a strong practical sense and a logical mind that could clearly see through the confusions of unsound ideas. On top of that, she was good looking, a witty conversationalist, profoundly religious and a prodigious letter writer. Apparently she wrote more than 12 000 letters in her life, together with various notes, memoranda, reports, monographs, articles and books.[17] Men loved her company and throughout her working life she exerted immense influence on important people such as Sidney Herbert, Benjamin Jowett, Lord Lawrence, Lord Ripon, Dr William Farr, Dr Sutherland and many others.

Yet in spite of all her qualities and accomplishments, Florence's experience was no different from that of the rest of the British women of that period. She received a good education from her father, but it had not been aimed at achieving anything except being socially charming and a good companion to men. When, in her young days, Florence had wanted to study mathematics, she had been vehemently discouraged by her parents.[18] When she wanted to become a nurse, her family strongly opposed it.[19] Not only was nursing considered a socially unacceptable occupation for upper class women, but she was also trying to break the mould, which was considered dangerous. Florence had to fight for many years, risking depression and the possibility of a nervous breakdown before she could gain her freedom. She was almost 34 years old before she became a nurse.

Florence's Crimean experience, which put her in the international limelight in 1856, was also fraught with the difficulties that women often faced in a male-oriented environment such as the army. She was the first British woman to lead a group of nurses at the war front, where she faced immense hostility and antagonism from the chief medical officer, Dr Hall, and his protégés.[20] However, her experience in Crimea taught her how to enter an exclusive male zone and survive. It also gave her an insight into how important it is for women to achieve their potential, just like men, and inspired her at the very end of her Indian work to agitate for women's education in rural India.

Florence became seriously ill after her return from Crimea in 1856. Later, she often used her poor health as an excuse to fend off unwelcome visitors and devote her time and energy to more productive work. What her actual illness was has, in recent years, become a topic of much research.[21]

Florence's involvement with India occupied a period of her life when she considered herself an invalid and preferred to remain almost a recluse. In her early life she might have read and heard about India, but there was no reason to believe that before 1856–57 she was really interested in the country. The earliest indication of her interest in India can be found in her letter to Lady Charlotte Canning in 1856.[22] Lady Canning was residing in Barrackpore in Bengal with her husband, Lord Canning, the Viceroy of India. The letter was written when Florence had come back from Crimea and was involved with the Royal Commission, which was set up to inquire into the sanitary conditions of the British Army. As noted earlier, the information gathered by that Commission drew her attention for the first time to the appalling conditions in the British Army barracks in India, and the events of 1857 only reinforced her decision to get involved.

Changes in India in the nineteenth century

Florence's involvement with India covered almost four decades, from 1857 to 1897. These four decades were the most remarkable in India's history. They were marked by the gradual development of a political identity culminating in the formation of the Indian National Congress in 1885, leading to a change in British policy towards India. However, it must be said that the primary motive of the British administration in India, the consolidation and preservation of the Empire, remained practically unchanged until the third decade of the twentieth century.

In preserving the Empire, the British showed the same arrogance and sense of racial supremacy in India as they did in their other colonies, but in India's case with some sense of guilt. The plunder and exploitation that went on in the early days of the Company Raj made the philanthropic Victorians tearful. 'The Indians had a claim upon their conquerors and the claim was based on English misrule and tyranny. The English nation had to make restitution.'[23] The 'restitution' took the form of performing 'duties' to the people of India after the country had been pauperised by plunder and decimated by famines. The duty was, of course, done with the help of a very strong military force, stringent application of law and order[24] and keeping the Indians beyond the pale. It was not, therefore, surprising that throughout the period of Florence's involvement with India, Indians were continuously clamouring for a larger share of administrative power and equal rights as was guaranteed in the Charter Act of 1833 and the Queen's Proclamation of 1858: 'And it is our further will that, so far as may be, our subjects, of whatever race or creed, be freely and impartially admitted to offices in our service, the duties of which they may be qualified by their education, ability and integrity, duly to discharge.'[25] The guarantors, however, were not too keen to honour the guarantees, and the Indianisation of the Civil Service and the appointments of Indians to the covenanted posts remained a much-debated issue and a sore point almost throughout the century.[26] Florence herself often referred to the Queen's Proclamation when she supported the Indians' aspirations and throughout her life she remained committed to the Indianisation of the administrative structure in India.

Impact of Western education

The four decades of Florence's involvement with India also saw a growing opposition to British rule. It came mostly from the Indian elite, who later gave leadership to the national freedom movement in a more consolidated form. As happened in nineteenth-century Britain, there was the growth of an articulate middle class in India. This middle class was not the product of industrialisation, but owed its emergence to the so-called English education in India.

Almost from the beginning of the century, the trend to move away from more orthodox traditional teaching – in Sanskrit, Persian and Arabic – started in Bengal. A growing demand for modern secular education that would enable the people of India to rise to the same level of skill and competence as the Europeans arose first in Bengal and then spread to other presidencies. In 1817, the Hindu College in Calcutta was established by private enterprise of the Bengali middle class to provide such modern secular education. When the Government proposed to open the Sanskrit College in Calcutta for traditional Sanskrit studies, Raja Ram Mohun Roy sent his famous letter to Lord Amherst on 11 December 1823, urging him to spend government money on 'European gentlemen of talents and education to instruct natives of India in Mathematics, Natural philosophy, Chemistry, Anatomy and other useful sciences, which the Nations of Europe have carried to a degree of perfection that has raised them above the inhabitants of other parts of the world.'[27] The teachings of Henry Louis Vivian Derozio, a teacher in the Hindu College, also created a group of young Bengalis who were intellectually ready to challenge old ideas and to agitate for social and political reforms.[28] In Bombay, the Elphinstone Institution (College) was founded in 1827 after the fashion of the Hindu College, and also produced its own groups of unorthodox non-conformist social rebels.

The British were also keen to spread English education in India, but for their own interest. As a minority, they realised that without the help and support of the indigenous population, they would not be able to run an effective administration to maintain the Empire. The 'alien few' wanted to rule 'the native many'[29], for which they needed the services of Indian clerks and interpreters. 'We must at present do our best to form a class who may be interpreters between us and the millions whom we govern.'[30] Together with this imperial necessity was the missionary zeal to 'civilise' India, which led Lord William Bentinck, the Governor-General, to initiate secular English education of 'useful knowledge' in the Bengal Presidency in 1835.

Although there is a popular belief that the utilitarian ideas of the British administrators were behind the move,[31] it was obvious from the very nature of the system introduced that 'English education' was not meant for the 'greatest good' or for the 'moral and material progress' of the masses of India. It was meant only for the upper crust of society and the guiding principle was employment of the natives in the lower strata of the administrative structure. It was hoped that education would eventually 'filter down' from the English-educated elite classes of society to the masses. 'To that class we may leave it to refine the vernacular dialects of the country.'[32] Needless to say that English education in the medium of English had no roots in indigenous soil; it was completely alien to the masses of India. However, from time to time, concern for mass education through the vernacular languages was aired. In 1854, through Charles Wood's initiative, suggestions were made that the Government should support the spread of vernacular primary education.[33] But the Government did not have sufficient funds or the infrastructure to spread primary education among the masses of India.[34] The primary education of the ordinary people was left mostly in the hands of the missionaries, *pandits* and *moulavis*. Government resources were kept for higher education, where pupils would learn English language, literature and history, with mathematics and science. It was only later, when this English-educated elite demanded equal employment opportunities in accordance with their qualifications, that the authorities considered attending to primary education funded by transferring higher education to the private sector, a move which totally failed to achieve its aim.[35]

The speed with which English education was accepted and absorbed by the upper crust of Indian society surprised the British administrators and, in spite of its irrelevance for the masses of India, it gave rise to a vociferous middle class that subsequently formed the crest of an anti-imperial surge in India. The socio-political attitudes in India started to change from the beginning of the century, long before the educational reforms of 1835 had been introduced. As mentioned earlier, the influence of Bengali social reformers such as Ram Mohun Roy and Iswarchandra Vidyasagar, and the teachings of Henry Louis Vivian Derozio, were also behind the growing awareness of the impact of imperialism in the country and dissatisfaction with the rulers.[36] English education consolidated this dissatisfaction and created men who were well enough equipped with British ideas of justice and democracy to agitate for their own political rights. They fought the British with ideas imported into India through an alien elitist system of education. 'These men spoke highly of British justice, they asked God to bless the British Queen but they spoke of unBritishness of British rule in India.'[37]

When Florence tried to establish contact with Indians, these were the men with whom she got in touch. She witnessed the evolution of this elite class through her involvement with India and supported its endeavours and aspirations. Famous Indian leaders, like Dadabhai Naoroji, B.M. Malabari, Manmohun Ghose and G.K. Gokhale, were on her correspondence list. In 1885 she supported Allan Octavian Hume and William Wedderburn in the founding of the Indian National Congress. Although Florence worked with the Indian elite, she worked for the ordinary Indians. Her articles on education, written in the third quarter of the century, and her dedication to village education in the last quarter, carried the message that education should be relevant for the ordinary peasants of India so that they could conduct their lives in a better way. Reading Locke or John Stuart Mill was not enough, she said, the *ryots'* children should be able to read the *Kabuliyat* and the *Patta*.[38]

Agitation through associations

Another trend that characterised nineteenth-century India in a similar fashion to Britain was the growth of 'combination' through associations and organisations. This trend was not only limited to the middle class but also spread among the peasants. From the early part of the nineteenth century there was a rapid growth of associations and organisations, primarily in Bengal and spreading later to other presidencies. It was often said that nineteenth-century Bengal was a period of association, agitation and petition. Many of these middle class associations and organisations were initially debating societies or literary clubs. They were also regional and did not have an all-India basis. Their purpose was educational and for social reform. Many were founded by English philanthropists or missionaries. These associations were British-Indian collaborations and their members were often the same group of people overlapping from one to another. It would be difficult to find an association in Bengal in the middle of the century without the names of Peary Chund Mitra, Debendranath Tagore or Rev. James Long on its membership list. The Bengal Social Science Association, which Florence established contact with in 1870, was one such organisation. The members of this association collected statistical details on social issues, discussed and debated them, and wrote articles in the society's proceedings. But its activities did not extend beyond that and it exerted little pressure on the Government. Although Florence's initial contact was with a society like this, as the nature of the associations in India changed, the nature of her contacts also changed.

By the latter half of the nineteenth century there was an increase in the number of political organisations all over India. The most prominent of these was the British Indian Association, formed in Bengal in 1851. Its aim was to safeguard India's interests during the renewal of the Company's charter in the British Parliament, which came up for review in 1853. With similar intention, the Bombay Association was formed in 1852 and the Madras Native Association was formed in the Madras Presidency at about this time. There were other political organisations in Bengal before the founding of the British Indian Association, such as the Land-holder's Association or the Bengal British India Society, but they did not have an all-India profile and were mostly limited to within their class and local interest. The British Government, though initially distrustful, later took some of these organisations into its confidence and regarded them as representative bodies of Indian opinion on specific national issues. The proceedings of the British Indian Association show how often the Government sought its advice and how often the Association petitioned to the British Government on behalf of Indians.[39] In Bengal, however, the British Indian Association primarily represented land-owners and the *zemindars*. As a result, during the agitation over the Bengal Tenancy Bill in the late 1870s and early 1880s, most of the members of the association remained loyal to their class interests. The organisation that took the Indian peasants' side in this famous dispute was the Indian Association, founded in 1876. Its aim was clearly polit-ical and, under the leadership of Surendranath Banerjee, it not only agitated for the peasants of Bengal, but in the course of time it also played a significant role in the national struggle for freedom. Although Bengal based, it soon had branches all over northern India. It was not surprising that Florence found the Indian Association a compatriot in her fight for the rights of the peasants and considered it 'the people's Association'. During the land tenancy agitation in Bengal some members of the Association sent necessary information to Florence and she published articles that drew the attention of the British public to the tenancy issues in Bengal.

The two other political organisations Florence was in touch with were the Poona Sarvajanik Sabha and the Bombay Presidency Association. The Poona Sarvajanik Sabha was founded in 1870 and the Bombay Presidency Association in 1885. Both these associations, like the Indian Association of Bengal, occupied significant positions in India's national struggle for freedom. When, in 1885, the Poona Sarvajanik Sabha, the Bombay Presi-dency Association, the Madras Mahajan Sabha and the Indian Associa-tion jointly sent representatives to England to lobby the members of the British Parliament, all of them went to see Miss Nightingale.[40] In 1887, when Florence was involved with the Bombay Village Sanitation Bill, she sought support from the Poona Sarvajanik Sabha and the Bombay Presi-dency Association and acted with their collaboration. She also encour-aged the members of these two associations to come to London in 1891 to attend an international hygiene conference.

Role of the Indian press

Another important development in nineteenth-century India was the growth of the Indian press and the significant role it started to play in creating a national climate of political awareness. Educated Indians came to appreciate the importance of the press as a political weapon and almost from the beginning of the century the Indian press started to grind its journalistic axe as opportunity arose. The initial battle cry came from Bengal. The Bengali Baboos, as Lord Lytton, the Viceroy, called them, took to their pens to deliver unappetising criticisms of the Raj.[41] The Parsees of Bombay and the Brahmins of Deccan did not lag behind in brandishing their pens.

In the early days of the Company Raj, most of the press in India was under British management, but as modern journalism developed in India it became clearly divided between the English newspapers, managed by the British, and the English and vernacular newspapers, managed by Indians. From 1780, when Hickey's *Bengal Gazette*[42] first appeared, the press in India enjoyed considerable freedom. Occasionally this was curtailed by official displeasure, but the censorship imposed was often no more than the refusal of the Government-owned General Post Office to circulate their papers. In cases of so-called gross misrepresentation of news, the editor and the publisher-proprietor were penalised by 'immediate embarkation for Europe', which was possible because they were Europeans with permits for limited stay in India.[43] As the vernacular press started to exceed their limits by publishing seditious articles, the British administrators became more and more concerned, particularly as they could not read what was said in the paper and had to depend on others for translation.

During the Governor-Generalship of Lord Wellesley, some press censorship was imposed, but later Lord Bentinck's administration decided not to interfere with the press. Afterwards, in 1835, Sir Charles Metcalfe, during his Governor-Generalship, delivered almost total freedom to the press, both English and vernacular.[44] The Indian-owned vernacular press at the time was considered insignificant and incapable of any political mischief. Charles Metcalfe, in spite of the cautious advice of his administrators, refused to make any distinction between the English and the vernacular press. However, during the mutiny of 1857, Lord Canning, the Governor-General, started to suspect the vernacular press of instigating anti-British feelings.[45]

After the mutiny it was difficult for the Government to ignore the vernacular press. An office was soon established to keep the authorities informed about it so that the Government could keep track of which way the wind was blowing. Successive Governor-Generals after Canning were concerned about the press and some censorship was introduced at various times, but it was left to Lord Lytton to introduce an act to differentiate between the English and the vernacular press. The Vernacular Press Act of

1878 applied only to newspapers and journals published in vernacular languages; the English press was exempt. As opposition to the act grew in India, liberal-minded people in Britain, including Florence, supported the protest. The act was repealed by Gladstone in 1880. There is no doubt that from 1878 onwards the Indian press, vernacular and English, played a key role in establishing solidarity among the educated classes of India.[46]

Florence, a believer in the importance of the press and often a user of its publicity aspect, gave positive support to the need of the Indians in this area. In 1885, when William Wedderburn and Allan Octavian Hume were trying to establish an Indian telegraphic agency which would send news from India to be published in the British newspapers so that the British public could read an alternative version of what was happening in India other than the official one, Florence gave her advice and ideas about how to go about it. When the journal *India* emerged in Britain as the mouthpiece of the Indian National Congress, Florence supported it and made contributions.

It must be remembered, however, that Florence was not a politician but a sanitarian. Her main purpose was the improvement of the sanitary conditions of the ordinary people, their prosperity and good health. Indoctrinated by the ideals of utilitarianism, she wanted the 'greatest good' for the largest number of people in India. However much she supported the elitist groups and associations in India, she did not deviate from her goal, which was the end of the suffering of the poor peasants by helping to create a healthy environment for them. In achieving this goal, army sanitation was only a minor part of her work for India.

The phases of Florence's Indian work

As has been said before, Florence was involved with India for almost four decades. This prolonged period of her efforts to improve the conditions of the army and people of India can be divided into four phases:

1. Sanitation of the army and civilian population (1857 onwards).
2. Famines and irrigation (1870–78).
3. Land tenancy and the Indian peasants (1879–85).
4. Village sanitation and female education (1886–96).

Though these could be regarded as the main phases of Florence's Indian work, the dates are only approximate. She often did many things at the same time, and often the same thing throughout a period of time. For example, while working on army sanitation, she was also involved with female nursing in India and forming an Indian Army hospital corps. Her work with sanitation ran as a continuous theme from the beginning to the end of her Indian work. Similarly, when she worked for better land reform for the Indian peasants, she also agitated for their health and education. Sanitary education was another long-running theme in all her work for India. It should also be remembered that while she was working for India her work at home, in Britain, did not stop. She was equally busy with the nurses' training schools, hospital construction and administration and found time to write innumerable reports, articles and books on a multitude of subjects.

Sanitation

Florence took a wider logical approach towards the problem of sanitation in India. Between 1864 and 1869 we find her continuously pressing on the Secretary of State for India and the Viceroy that it would be futile to try to improve the sanitary conditions of the British Army without improving that of ordinary Indians; all should have an equal share in sanitary reforms and benefits. This sense of political liberalism and logical coherence often drove her into confrontation with the authorities. She did not want a top-heavy administration producing only reports. She wanted action, both for the military and the civilian population. When the Government failed to produce the desired result, she was not willing to accept their excuse of Indian apathy or the lack of funding.

As has been said before, Florence was deeply influenced by some of the reforms of her time that brought immense changes to British society, particularly among the urban poor. She knew that the 'Indian condition' was not unique. Such conditions existed in Britain before the reforms took place. She considered that the Indian sanitary problem was manageable, but only with the help of British expertise and engineering skills. She wanted to solve the problems of India with the knowledge, concepts and skills that had worked in Britain.

Florence's sanitary recommendations for the improvement of the health of the British Army and the people of India were very much based on the medical theories prevalent at the time. In the earlier part of the nineteenth century, medical research was still in its infancy and society had not yet benefited from Pasteur's research. Knowledge about viruses, bacteria, microbes and genes and their causal relation with illness was not available. The Victorian doctors and medical specialists were broadly divided into those who had started to support the germ theory of disease and those who did not. Florence and her friend Dr William Farr fell into the latter camp.

Dr William Farr, a medical practitioner and ardent statistician like Florence, collaborated with her in writing reports for the two Royal Commissions. Both were keen sanitarians and wanted to use statistics as a basis for planning social reforms. They saw the statistical evidence that existed of the correlation between illness and polluted environments. They were both supporters of the so-called miasmic theory of disease, according to which illness was caused by breathing in 'miasma' or foul air generated from decomposing organic matter such as human and animal excreta, sewage, household rubbish and stagnant polluted water.[47] The supporters of the theory believed that the environment in which people lived was largely responsible for the diseases they suffered from.

Florence was also influenced by Edwin Chadwick, another strong supporter of the miasmic theory of disease and urban pollution. Both Chadwick and Florence believed that cleanliness was the most necessary requirement for good health. Edwin Chadwick dedicated himself to the improvement of public health in Britain. He was responsible for the Poor Law Amendment Act of 1834, and later in 1842 for the *Report on the Conditions of the Labouring Population of England*. In this report, he insisted on proper drainage and supply of clean water for the towns and cities of England. Florence introduced all those ideas in her promotion of sanitation in India. In her report written for the Royal Commission in 1863, and in other articles published at the time or after, she continuously blamed the 'miasmic' environment of Lower Bengal for spreading diseases such as cholera and fever. Overcrowding in the army barracks, absence of sewage removal facilities and a lack of clean drinking water were all on her list of evils that had caused the high rate of mortality among the soldiers in peacetime. Like Chadwick, she also considered good drainage as essential for public health, and always insisted on not just 'engineers', but 'good sanitary engineers'[48] to do the groundwork. Although the miasmic theory of disease is now archaic, the element of holism in Florence's ideas is noteworthy, an approach which nowadays is increasingly appreciated with reference to environmental and occupational hazards in explaining human illness.[49]

Famines, irrigation and land policy

Florence's main contribution in her Indian work was of course her relentless fight to improve the conditions of the Indian peasants, the *ryots*. Her involvement with famine policy, land tenancy and irrigation was a logical consequence of her sanitary efforts in India. She was appalled by the devastation caused by successive famines and the decimation of the peasant population. It took a woman like Florence to point out that trying to improve Indian sanitary conditions was pointless if no one remained alive to benefit from them. She clearly saw that to counter famine, one needed to improve the conditions of the peasants by relieving their appalling poverty. This could only be done by increasing the yield of land by irrigation, ensuring peasants' rights to land, lessening the burden of taxation and, finally, ending the exploitation of the *zemindars* and the moneylenders. In this matter, she was very much impressed by the reforms undertaken in Britain to solve the Irish crisis in the second half of the nineteenth century. In a way, the Irish peasants' experience was very similar to that of Indian peasants. Irish peasants had also encountered famines, high taxation, eviction from the land and exploitation at the hands of the landowners who were a foreign power in Ireland.[50] In her fight to improve the conditions of the Indian peasants, Florence continuously referred to the Irish situation and the measures taken to achieve a better deal for the Irish peasants. During her involvement with the Bengal Rent Bill and the land tenancy dispute, she insisted that similar measures should be taken for the Bengali peasants, particularly fair rents and fixity of tenure, but she had her reservations about freedom of sale. She was afraid that given the choice, illiterate peasants would be under pressure to contract themselves out of their rights and would fail to see their own interests.

Throughout the 1870s and 1880s, Florence agitated for improvement of the conditions of the Indian peasants. First, she tried to impress on the Government that famines were expensive and, second, she tried to mobilise public opinion at home and in India by publicising India's deplorable famine conditions. She argued that the Government of India and the Secretaries of State always complained about lack of funds, but they should realise that they could curtail expenses by taking famine-preventive measures such as irrigation projects. This was the time when she became involved with the issue of railways versus canals in India. Florence was not anti-railway, but she saw the need for investment in irrigation and canals in India to avert repeated famines, and in the process of her agitation for irrigation she met a staunch opponent in the shape of Lord Salisbury as the Secretary of State for India.

During this period of her Indian work, Florence continuously published articles, supported progressive viceroys and put her weight behind their work. She also criticised Government efforts to please the *zemindars* and European planters by watering down the Bengal Land Tenancy Bill, which was finally passed as an act in 1885. It was in this context that she established rapport with progressive Indians and Indian associations to mobilise them to work for the peasants. She was truly the most loyal friend of the *ryots* – 'a faithful servant' – as she called herself.

It should be noted that although Britain never had a violent revolution as happened in France or elsewhere in Europe, the fight of the British working class for a better standard of living was not always without violence, nor did the leadership always come from the middle class. Nineteenth-century Britain not only saw the birth of a middle class and the shift of power from the landed aristocracy to this new social class, it also saw the growing power of the working class and the birth of socialism. Florence, socially aware as she was, could not possibly have missed the news of strikes, riots and other agitations that were going on in the country, and was wise enough to appreciate the message of such socio-political events. She was well aware that everywhere in Europe there was a growing awareness among peasants and the working class about their rights: 'In Europe we have been working up to this climax. Had it not been the emancipation of the peasants in Germany during Napoleon's time, would Germany ever have been what it is? Then there is the Russian emancipation of the serfs in 1861, though as yet it has not done all it ought.'[51] She also saw how reforms could pacify a volatile situation and applied this knowledge when she wrote about Indian peasants. Florence's writings on Indian peasants were marked with a timely warning: 'If reform does not begin from on high, it will begin from below.'[52] She had detailed knowledge of the Indigo revolt, the Pabna uprising and the Deccan riots, and warned the authorities that if something was not done the British Government would face unrest in India similar to that in Britain. When the authorities accused her of exaggeration, she advised them to read their own reports about the Indian situation.

The hallmark of Florence's writings about India was her clarity of thinking and the cogency of her argument. Whatever she tried to do for India, her political liberalism and the logical consistency of her thinking shone through. It was the same sense of liberalism that made her support Lord Ripon's political and social measures in India, and his attempt to remove some of the racial anomalies that existed in the laws of British India. When the Ilbert Bill almost brought about Ripon's downfall, she published articles supporting his measures and even wrote to Queen Victoria reminding her of her pledges given to the people of India. Her transition from 'exporting civilisation' to India to 'giving the Indians a chance of self-administration' was all part of the same liberal philosophy deeply embedded in her character and symptomatic of the age she was born in.

Village sanitation and female education

Like many other liberal reformers of her time, Florence was very much influenced by the ideas of 'self-help' and 'co-operation' and, however simplistic it may seem now in the context of nineteenth-century colonial India, she used these ideas to inspire Indians to work for themselves.[53] As a great believer in education, she realised that the root cause of the poverty and degradation of Indian peasants lay in their ignorance and helplessness to change their circumstances. They were resigned to their fate. If this ignorance and resignation could be changed by education, and more enlightened Indians could extend their co-operation by teaching the village population the skills of self-help, then they would be able to free themselves from their misery and suffering. This was the message all throughout her Indian work, especially in the last phase when she was involved with village sanitation and female education. At this stage we find her approaching various people and organisations to spread sanitary education and the notions of self-help and co-operation in Indian villages. She knew that the task was large, and no government alone could do it. The solution lay with the people: 'They must do it themselves.' Florence did not fail to recognise the 'inertia' of the Government officials in India. There was always the excuse of shortage of funds, reference to the difficulties due to the caste system and traditional values, and to 'Indian cosmogony'.[54] But those excuses did not fool Florence. If she failed to move the Government officials, she contacted Indians directly, urging them to help. Many of her Indian acquaintances were inspired by her, such as B.M. Malabari and Dayaram Gidumal in Bombay, and Runchorelal Chotalall of Ahmedabad, who launched themselves into village education and sanitary projects.

One important feature of Florence's later work was her attempt to use the *zenana* power that existed in India. Although she was never enthusiastic about women's right to vote, her personal experience and struggle for self-fulfilment helped her to understand the potential that lay with unutilised woman power in India. She felt that sanitary education should start at home with the helping hand of a mother. She wanted the educated middle class Indian women to extend their co-operation to their less fortunate rural sisters and educate them in sanitary matters. With this aim, Florence helped Lady Dufferin, the Vicereine, in her project for the promotion of female health care and education in India. Florence's task was to organise writers with Indian experience to write suitable health primers and sanitary tracts for training Indian women. In the course of time, the Dufferin project helped to produce a substantial number of female doctors, nurses, midwives and female hospital attendants in India, who in turn contributed significantly in providing medical and health care for women in purdah.

Florence's method of work

The immense horizon of Florence's involvement with India was marked by one curious factor; she never went to India. Whatever she did, she did it from her home in London. Many people found this so difficult to believe that in 1892 the *Amrita Bazar Patrika*, a Calcutta newspaper, even published the news of her visiting India: 'It will be remembered that Miss Florence Nightingale came to this country and was impressed with the idea that if India needed anything it was village sanitation. She collected masses of facts and has since been agitating in England.'[55]

One cannot help wondering how she worked from home covering such a vast range of enterprises. What was her *modus operandi*? Analysis of her work shows her method of work had several stages. She followed this method throughout her life whenever she tried to tackle a particular problem. Her starting point was always to get detailed facts of a situation from all possible sources. 'We do not want theory, we want facts,' she said. She gathered these facts from official records, memoranda and statements. Her contacts all over India, from viceroys to ordinary Indians, sent her information and copies of reports and despatches. She read the official Blue Books as regularly and thoroughly as she read the Bible. She often consulted retired Anglo-Indians who were only too happy to share their experience. As a result, Florence was always the most knowledgeable person on a given Indian issue such as irrigation, famine, land tenancy, the drainage system of Calcutta or the possibilities of navigating in a canal link in east Bengal. She always knew more than the Government officials.

Her organisational skill was extraordinary. She always planned out meticulously how a particular problem could be tackled and a solution achieved. In doing so, she would turn to the experts in the field and use their knowledge and expertise. Once a plan of work was drawn up she would remain convinced of her plan and would not change her mind easily.

The next stage of her work was to produce a written document, a memorandum, a report or a long letter on the subject, send it to people who were in a position to act, and lobby them intensely. She quite often did not remain satisfied with lobbying the officials involved. In case of delay, she also lobbied their bosses to put pressure on them, and achieved results in that way. Because of her depth of knowledge, organisational ability and clarity of thinking, the officials of the War Office and the India Office often used her skill and talent. We find her unfailingly telling viceroys and Secretaries of State what should be done and what could be achieved. She always wanted to start with a small project and proceed from there as she tried to do with female nursing in India. Where her plan did not work, it was because it was not followed.

Another important aspect of her work was insistence on written reports from India. Although she herself preferred 'action' to 'reports', she always wanted to know what was happening and what was achieved. Writing reports gave the officers in charge an opportunity to assess how much or how little had been achieved. Publishing articles in journals and sending copies of this to specific people in positions of power was another tactic she used. She mobilised public opinion in this way, as she did in the case of Indian famines and land tenancy in Bengal.

However, the most useful tactic Florence often applied had a modern flavour – leaking information to the press. She quietly passed information to journalists and asked them to write and raise questions about the problem concerned. Sometimes she even told them what, when and where to write. By leaking early information to the press, she quite often influenced opinions in higher circles before a decision had been taken. Finally, she supported people who believed in her cause and stood by them even if they fell from grace.

The question could be asked how it was possible for an individual like Florence without any official position to exert such influence on the policies in India. In sanitary matters of course her reputation at home played a significant part. She was the living authority on army sanitation. In non-sanitary matters it was possible for her to exert influence because of the way India was governed. During Florence's Indian work, India was governed by a Secretary of State in Council in London and a Governor-General in Council in India without any election or democratic representation of those who were being governed. The Governor-General, or the Viceroy as he was honoured after the Crown's takeover, was the supreme decision-maker. The Secretary of State normally did not interfere, and the British Parliament even less so. Personal friendship and alliance with the Governor-Generals therefore provided Florence with scope for exerting personal influence on the policies made. She made acquaintance with the viceroys, shared her knowledge with them, gave them advice, and introduced the new ones to the retired ones to secure a continuation of ideas. The same thing happened with the Secretaries of State. Many of them were her close acquaintances, many came to see her and many tapped her brain for wisdom. Lord Stanley, Sir Charles Wood, Lord de Grey (Ripon), Sir Stafford Northcote and Lord Cranbrook were all well known to her. Her position was such that when the Liberal Prime Minister Gladstone visited her once without an appointment she did not see him.

Florence was also fortunate to have the support of a Liberal government at home for most of the four decades of her involvement with India. Even when she was not politically aligned with the Government, many of them appreciated her simply because of who she was. Lord Salisbury, who belonged to the opposite political camp, did not hesitate to write to seek her advice. Exerting influence on Indian policy matters was also possible because Florence did not hold any official position. There was no tantalising promise of reward, promotion or recognition in the offing for which she could be held compromised. This was also the source of her 'Nightingale power'.

The interest she took in India from about the time of the mutiny lasted the rest of her life. The reforms she sought in India she tried to introduce by writing innumerable letters, memoranda, reports, articles and pamphlets, by corresponding with the Governor-Generals and officials in India to make sure they shared her ideas and interests, by cajoling, coercing, arguing and writing to ministers, Secretaries of State and public servants in London so that they did not delay the matter, and finally trying to establish a rapport with Indians, famous and not so famous, so that her ideas could be passed on to them. She did all this from her bedroom. This is a unique tale of an extraordinary effort by a very exceptional woman who never set foot in India. This book tells that story.

Notes

1. Royal Commission Appointed to Inquire into the Sanitary Condition of the Army (1858), *Report of the Commissioners Appointed to Inquire into the Regulations Affecting the Sanitary Condition of the Army, the Organization of Military Hospitals, and the Treatment of the Sick and Wounded: with Evidence and Appendix*, London: HMSO, 2 vols.
2. The Royal Commission on the Sanitary State of the Army in India (1863), *Report of the Commissioners*, London: HMSO, 2 vols.
3. Taylor, B. (1983), *Eve and the New Jerusalem, Socialism and Feminism in the Nineteenth Century*, London: Virago Press, pp. 9–15; Shiman, L.L. (1992), *Women and Leadership in Nineteenth Century England*, Basingstoke: Macmillan, pp. 121–150.
4. Dutt, R.C. (1897), *England and India. A Record of Progress During a Hundred Years 1785–1885*, London: Chatto and Windus, pp. ix–xii, 120–150.
5. Thomson, D. (1950), *England in the Nineteenth Century, 1815–1914*, Harmondsworth: Penguin Books, p. 26.
6. Brock, M. (1993), *The Great Reform Act*, London: Gregg Revivals, pp. 37–38.
7. Midwinter, E.C. (1968), *Victorian Social Reform*, London: Longman, p. 6.
8. Porter, R. (1994), *London: a Social History*, London: Hamish Hamilton, p. 258.
9. Porter (1994), pp. 258–9.
10. Flinn, M.W. (1976), 'Medical services under the new Poor Law', in Fraser, D. (ed.), *The New Poor Law in the Nineteenth Century*, London: MacMillan, p. 46.
11. Dennis, B. and Skilton, D. (1987), *Reform and Intellectual Debate in Victorian England*, London: Croom Helm, pp. 15–16.
12. Cook, E. (1913), *The Life of Florence Nightingale*, 2 vols, London: Macmillan, vol. 1, p. 6.
13. Woodham-Smith, C. (1950), *Florence Nightingale, 1820–1910*, London: Constable, p. 14.
14. FN to Carpenter, 3 August 1866, BL OIOC, Mss A 110. At the end of this letter Florence wrote 'I need hardly say that I should like much to see your book on Rajah Ram Mohun Roy (whom I knew as a child).'
15. Cook (1913), vol. 1, p. 17.
16. Cook (1913), vol. 1, p. 24.
17. Selanders, L.C. (1993), *Florence Nightingale: an Environmental Adaptation Theory*, London and Thousand Oaks, CA: Sage, p. ix.
18. Woodham-Smith (1950), pp. 37–38.
19. Woodham-Smith (1950), pp. 55–58.

20. Cook (1913), vol. 1, pp. 213–214; see also Mitra, S.M. (1911), *The Life and Letters of Sir John Hall*, London: Longman, Green & Co.
21. 'Throughout her lifetime she was diagnosed as having at least the following four illnesses: Crimean Fever, sciatica, rheumatism, and dilation of the heart. Each of the four had the potential for crippling side effects and for establishing a pattern of excessive bedrest.' Veith, S. (1990), 'The recluse: a retrospective health history of Florence Nightingale', in Bullough, V., Bullough, B., and Stanton, M.P. (eds), *Florence Nightingale and Her Era: a Collection of New Scholarship*, New York: Garland, pp. 75–83. See also Pickering, G. (1974), *Creative Malady*, London: George Allen & Unwin, pp. 164–177.
22. FN to Canning, 23 November 1856, as quoted in Vicinus, M. and Nergaard, B. (1989), *Ever Yours, Florence Nightingale. Selected Letters*, London: Virago, pp. 164–171.
23. Knorr, K.E. (1944), *British Colonial Theories 1570–1850*, Toronto: University of Toronto Press, p. 371.
24. For example, as late as January 1872, L. Cowan, Deputy Commissioner of Ludhiana, executed 55 Kuka insurgents by tying them to the mouth of a cannon to set an example to the natives. See Bajwa, F.S. (1965), *Kuka Movement*, New Delhi: Motilal Banarasidas, pp. 100–107.
25. The Queen's Proclamation Act of 1858 as quoted in Zaidi, A.M (ed.) (1988), *The Grand Little Man of India, Dadabhai Naoroji: Speeches and Writings*, New Delhi: Indian Institute of Applied Political Research, vol. 2, p. 40.
26. Zaidi (1988), vol. 2, pp. 22–96; Gopal, S. (1953), *The Viceroyalty of Lord Ripon, 1880–1884*, Oxford: Oxford University Press, pp. 167–171; Singh, H.L. (1982), *The British Policy in India*, New Delhi: Meenakshi Prakashan, pp. 13–74.
27. Sharp, H. (ed.) (1920), *Selections from Educational Records*, Part 1, 1781–1839, New Delhi: NAI, p. 99 (republished 1965).
28. Chattopadhyay, G. (ed.) (1978), *Bengal: Early Nineteenth Century. Selected Documents*, Calcutta: Research India Publication, pp. x–xiii.
29. Seal, A. (1968), *The Emergence of Indian Nationalism: Competition and Collaboration in the Late Nineteenth Century*, Cambridge: Cambridge University Press, p. 9.
30. T.B. Macaulay's Minute, 2 February 1835, in Sharp (1920), p. 116. Also see Trevelyan, C.E. (1838), *On the Education of the People of India*, London: Longman, Orme, Brown, Green, & Longmans, p. 158.
31. Acharya, S. (1992), *The Changing Pattern of Education in Early Nineteenth Century Bengal*, Calcutta: Puthipustak, pp. 1–26.
32. T.B. Macaulay's Minute, in Sharp (1920), p. 116.
33. Despatch from the Court of Directors of the East India Company to the Governor General of India in Council, No. 49, 19 July 1854, in Richey, J.A. (ed.) (1920), *Selections from Educational Records*, Part 2, 1840–1859, New Delhi: NAI, pp. 364–393 (republished 1965).
34. Acharya (1992), pp. 131–133.
35. Seal (1968), pp. 20–21.
36. Chattopadhyay (1978), pp. xii–xiii.
37. Seal (1968), p. 15.
38. FN (1879a), 'Can we educate education in India to educate men?', *Journal of the National Indian Association*, No. 105, September, p. 481. *Kabuliyat* and *Patta* are the contract documents between the landholder and the peasant.

39. See *Proceedings*, British Indian Association, Calcutta, 1853, 1861, 1864, 1866.

40. See Chapter 8.

41. ' ... the Baboos whom we have educated to write semi-seditious articles in the native Press and who really represent nothing but the social anomaly of their own position', Lytton to Salisbury, 11 May 1876, quoted in Seal (1968), p. 134.

42. *Bengal Gazette or Calcutta General Advertiser*, printed and edited by Hickey, J.A. (1780), Calcutta.

43. Chanda, M.K. (1987), *History of the English Press in Bengal*, Calcutta: K.P. Bagchi and Co., p. 416.

44. Chanda (1987), pp. 440–441.

45. Lord Canning's speech in the Proceedings of the Legislative Council of India, 1857, quoted in Barnes, M. (1940), *The Indian Press*, London: George Allen and Unwin, p. 250.

46. Mehrotra, S.R. (1971), *The Emergence of the Indian National Congress*, New Delhi: Vikas Publishing, pp. 36–37, 110–112, 280–286.

47. Eyler, J.M. (1979), *Victorian Social Medicine, the Ideas and Methods of William Farr*, Baltimore: John Hopkins University Press, pp. 97–122.

48. FN to Galton, 11 August 1889, BL Add. Mss 45766, fol. 263.

49. Selanders (1993), pp. 15–19.

50. Southgate, D. (1962), *The Passing of the Whigs, 1832–1886*, London: Macmillan, p. 186.

51. FN (1883a), *The Dumb Shall Speak and the Deaf Shall Hear, or the Ryot, the Zemindar and the Government*, London: East India Association, p. 6. Also published as FN (1883b), 'The Dumb shall speak and the Deaf shall hear, or the Ryot, the Zemindar and the Government', *Journal of the East India Association*, vol. XV, pp. 163–210. The page references are from the pamphlet.

52. FN (1883a), p. 32.

53. Booth, A.J. (1869), *Robert Owen – the Founder of Socialism in England*, London: Trübner & Co.; Stephens, M.D. and Roderick, G.W. (eds) (1983), *Samuel Smiles and Nineteenth Century Self-help in Education*, Nottingham: University of Nottingham, Department of Adult Education.

54. Cook (1913), vol. 2, p. 282.

55. *Amrita Bazar Patrika*, 29 June 1892, quoted in Cook (1913), vol. 2, p. 27. Unfortunately this issue of *Amrita Bazar Patrika* could not be found in the National Newspaper Library, Calcutta.

CHAPTER TWO

Hygiene as the Handmaid
of Civilization

In 1857 the British Government and the British public suddenly became aware that all was not well and peaceful in their distant Indian Empire. The Sepoy Mutiny, or the Great Revolt of 1857 as some present day Indian historians prefer to call it, caught the British people by surprise. Emotionally and militarily they were not prepared for such a violent awakening of the docile Indians.

The mutiny as a movement of liberation was not the first attempt on the British occupation of India. Between 1757 and 1857, from the Battle of Plassey to the mutiny, there were other small and not so small anti-British uprisings and acts of insurgence in India. To name a few, there was the *Sanyasi* and *Fakir* rebellion of 1763–73 in Northern and Western Bengal;[1] the Chuar Rebellion, which started in 1767 in the Bankura and Manbhum areas of Bengal and continued almost for three decades;[2] and the Santal Rebellion of 1855, which took place in Bengal and Bihar where the Santal tribes were dominant.[3] There were also the *Wahabi* and *Faraizi* movements in Bengal in the early part of the nineteenth century. Though essentially religious, these movements took a popular character in expressing anti-establishment feelings.[4] Anti-British uprisings were not limited to Bengal. In other parts of India there were sporadic uprisings and revolts against British domination. Most of the uprisings at this time were localised and often peasant or tribal in character. Some were not directly against the British but against exploitation and the tyranny of the *zemindars*, moneylenders and European planters. The revolt of 1857, however, was the most violent and widespread one. The atrocities committed by both sides, British and Indian, drew the attention of the liberal people of England to inquire as to the cause of such turbulent happenings. Florence Nightingale was one such person. She was not so much interested in the politics of India as she was in the plight of the British soldiers there, wounded and sick.

In 1857 Florence had been back from Crimea a year and was suffering from physical and mental exhaustion.[5] She was also busy with her work with the Royal Commission, which had been set up in 1857 to investigate and report on the mortality and sickness in the British Army. The investigation by the Royal Commission was necessitated by the catastrophic decimation of British soldiers in the Crimean War, not so much from actual fighting but from war wounds, disease and lack of medical care. While working for the Commission, Florence heard the news of the mutiny in India and her immediate reaction was to go there to nurse the wounded British soldiers. This was not at all surprising, as after her Crimean experience she always considered herself as one of them, 'a soldier in the ranks'.[6] In spite of her physical weakness, Florence was in earnest to go to India and serve as she had done in Crimea, if only someone would ask her to go. How sincere she was would be apparent from the fact that she wrote to Lady Charlotte Canning, who was at that time in Calcutta with her husband Lord Canning, the Governor-General of India.

Lady Canning and Florence had been good friends since the days of the Upper Harley Street Hospital where Florence had worked as a superintendent before going to Crimea.[7] The hospital was run by a ladies' committee, of which Charlotte Canning and Elizabeth Herbert, wife of Sidney Herbert, the War Minister, were two distinguished members. In fact, Charlotte Canning and Elizabeth Herbert had been instrumental in getting Florence the position of superintendent in the hospital, which had not only initiated her nursing career but also changed her life for ever.[8] During the Crimean War in 1854, Lady Canning helped Florence to recruit nurses for Scutari Hospital. She was also very impressed by Florence's personality: 'No one is so well fitted as she to do such work; she has such nerve and skill, and is so wise and quiet.'[9] Florence and Charlotte Canning corresponded frequently during the Crimean War, and continued to exchange letters after Charlotte Canning went to India as the Vicereine. When Florence thought of going to India she got in touch with her. 'Miss Nightingale has written to me,' wrote Charlotte Canning in a letter to her mother. 'She is out of health and at Malvern, but says she would come at twenty four hours' notice if I think there is anything for her to do in her "line of business".' Although Florence wanted to go, Lady Canning did not feel that it was the right time:

> I think there is not anything here, for there are few wounded men in want of actual nursing, and there are plenty of native servants and assistants who can do the dressings. Only one man, who was very ill of dysentery, has died since we went to the hospital a fortnight ago. The upcountry hospitals are too scattered for a nursing establishment and one could hardly yet send women up.[10]

Charlotte Canning was not the only person Florence wrote to. She also expressed her desire to go to India and help at this distressing time to Dr John McNeill and to Sidney Herbert. Florence had known Dr McNeill from her Crimean days and often sought his advice as she did during the time of the mutiny:

15 July 1857

... I don't think that you are at all more 'nervous' about the Indian affairs than the best informed here. I speak like a parrot. But my impression is from all I hear that this 'row' is but the beginning of things. As the revolution of '93 in France was but the beginning of what ended in the total overthrow of the Feudal System. So this affair in India must end in the entire doing away of the caste system or in the overthrow of the British power there. We may have to reconquer India. I should like much to go out; we shall have dreadful sickness there, but I have no one to advise me. I want to see you about this ... .[11]

Both McNeill and Sidney Herbert advised her against going to India. They felt that she was not physically strong enough, and that the work of the Royal Commission in London would suffer in her absence. Although Florence decided not to go to India in 1857 she always cherished the idea as she regarded India almost as her 'home'. Years later, in 1865, in reply to an invitation of Dr J. Pattison Walker, Secretary to the Bengal Sanitary Commission, she wrote about how much she had wanted to go to India:

January 3, 1865

There is nothing, really nothing – on this side of the grave which I long for so much as a visit to India – nothing which would interest me so much. While others try to run away from India, I would desire more than anything else which I do desire (I 'desire with desire', as the Hebrew says) to go to India. I have studied the country so much, I seemed to know so well what I want to do there, that it appears to me as if I would be going home, not going to a strange country. But alas for me, it is quite impossible. I shall never leave London, except for the grave. ... If there were even any hope of my reaching India alive, & of being able to go on working when there, as I do here, I believe I should be tempted to go. For my term of life cannot be much longer, wherever I am. But it is quite impossible ...

... I may tell you in confidence that, in 1857, that dreadful year for India, I offered to go out to India in the same way as to the Crimea. But Sidney Herbert, with whom I worked for 5 years, all but a week, in the War Office till his lamentable death, put a stop to it.[12]

As mentioned earlier, Florence's attention had been drawn towards India through her working with the first Royal Commission, set up after the Crimean crisis. That was probably the first time she became aware of the health situation of the British soldiers in India. The information that was gathered by the Royal Commission had revealed an extremely high death rate among the soldiers, which was due to preventable diseases and lack of sanitation rather than actual fighting. The events of the mutiny only emphasised what Florence already knew about the army in India. The memory of the appalling conditions of the common soldiers in the army hospitals of Crimea was still fresh in her mind and she knew that more lives could have been saved if hospital care and sanitation had been better. The British authorities' indifference towards army sanitation appalled her: 'What are the murders committed by these miserable Hindoos compared to the murders committed by an educated Englishman?'[13]

Earlier, in February 1857, when Lord Panmure, the Secretary of State for War, had asked Florence to comment on the information gathered by the Royal Commission, she prepared her *Notes on Matters Affecting the Health and Efficiency and Hospital Administration of the British Army*. The *Notes* consisted of a detailed analysis of the sanitary situation and organisation of the army in Britain, but in the postscript she referred to India and the mutiny:

> While the sheets were passing through the press, those lamentable occurrences took place in India which have led to an universal conviction that this vast Empire must henceforth be held by British troops. If we were to be led by past experience of the presumed effect of Indian climates on European constitutions, our country might almost despair of being able to supply men enough for the military occupation of so vast a region.[14]

Florence saw the events of the mutiny as an occasion to emphasise the need for reform in the army in India, which might require the intervention of another Royal Commission. The idea of setting up a second Royal Commission to inquire particularly into the conditions of the British Army in India had been gathering momentum in Florence's mind for quite some time: 'When all is done, the great subject of extending sanitary measures to India will be left untouched,' she wrote in January 1859. 'That subject must soon occupy the earnest attention of Her Majesty's government, and upon the spirit with which it is taken up will the ultimate fate of our Indian Empire to a great extent depend.'[15]

There is no denying the fact that Florence's initial approach to India was imperialistic and, until she became more seriously involved with India, she could not think of relinquishing the Empire. She saw sanitary reform of the army as a prerequisite for holding the Empire. There were not enough British soldiers in India to hold the country by force. The soldiers were dying not from war wounds but from preventable diseases such as cholera, hepatitis and typhoid, and the lack of sanitation. It was not possible to send sufficient soldiers from Britain to fill the vacancies and to maintain the strength of the army. The only way that it could be done was to have a healthy army by means of sanitary reform. 'That India will have to be occupied by British troops for several years, I suppose there is no question,' she wrote to Dr McNeill. 'And so far from the all absorbing interest of this Indian subject diminishing the necessity of immediately carrying out the reforms suggested by our Commission, I am sure you will agree that they are now the more vitally important to the very existence of an Army.'[16]

The absorbing question in Florence's mind at this stage was how to retain the Empire, as the events of the mutiny had shaken its foundations, and so she was primarily concerned with the health of the army. Nevertheless, even at this early stage, the idea of occupying India by another means, through the introduction of modern sanitation, was apparent in her thought: 'The observance of sanitary law should be as much part of the future regime of India as the holding of military positions or as civil government itself. It would be a noble beginning of a new order of things to use hygiene as the handmaid of civilization.'[17]

Such an idea was also suggested to her by her friend and advisor, Dr John Sutherland. In reply to her letter asking some medical advice for a relation of hers going to India, Sutherland echoed her thoughts:

> I am afraid we shall have a great deal of sickness among so many unacclimatized troops going to India. They will require great precaution to avoid disease. The whole sanitary work in India will require reconsideration in the altered state of matters. But I do not see why with our means we could not occupy India with British born troops at a much smaller loss than has hitherto taken place. It would be a beautiful thing to do it, and I am certain it could be done, and India be kept in hand effectually by the Anglo Saxon race. It would be a greater thing to do it than it was to capture Hindoostan.[18]

Setting up a Royal Commission for the British Army in India

There had been much concern about the mortality of British soldiers in India. India was considered the graveyard of white men, and everyone blamed the climate.[19] It was generally believed that almost 45 to 60 per 1000 soldiers died in India every year, although there were no accurate statistics of deaths. Florence and many others interested in the health of the army felt the need for a thorough investigation into the situation. Only a Royal Commission could do that, as had been the case following the Crimean War, but setting up a Royal Commission for the army in India was not an easy task. Florence started to work for a second Royal Commission even before she finished her work with the first one. This second Royal Commission, which is generally known as the Sanitary Commission for the Indian Army, was formed in 1859 and reported in 1863.

In order to hasten the process of appointing this second Royal Commission, Florence applied her well-known organisational skill and lobbying power in full force. She also used her influence in high places and her reputation as an army medical reformer. Florence never hesitated to use one particular modern tactic to achieve her goals, namely leaking information to journalists and asking them to write in favour of her cause. She repeatedly used Edwin Chadwick and Harriet Martineau for this purpose. When the question of army sanitation in India came up, Florence urged Chadwick, a keen sanitarian like herself, to write about it, supplying him with facts and figures: ' ... So little is known, and so much has to be done as to sanitary affairs in India that I think you must treat it from your own point of view. I know no one who can do it so well.'[20] This was not the first time that Florence had asked Chadwick to write on army sanitation. Earlier, when the first Royal Commission's report had been published, she not only asked Chadwick to write but also told him where to write:

> 11 February 1858
> You kindly said that we might call upon you for help whenever we wanted it. The Report of the Royal Commission on the Sanitary State of the army is printed, though not yet distributed.
>   We want a Review, and we want you to write it, and in the 'Westminster' (which is now most read) and for the next number if possible. But above al,l we want to be reviewed by no one but you.[21]

Florence also used Harriet Martineau, the leader writer of *The Daily News*, to publicise her cause and to pre-empt the bureaucrats by creating public opinion outside the corridors of power. How she worked was evident from her letter to Harriet Martineau when she was involved with the first Royal Commission:

> 30 November 1858
> I know that you have been interested about our Army matter & therefore, altho' an old story now, I venture to send you a copy of a certain 'Confidential Reports' of mine to the War Office. It is <u>really</u> confidential & no copy has been (or is to be) presented to the House of Commons. Therefore it is only for your own private reading that I send it, if you have still time, strength or inclination for this kind of subject. If not please put it in the fire – as the report is no sense public property ... .[22]

Needless to say Harriet Martineau, who wrote three leaders a week for *The Daily News*, was always delighted to have such information from the 'horse's mouth' as it were, and promised to make good use of it: 'I need not say that your wishes as to privacy shall be exactly observed. I suppose they do not preclude any use that I may be able to make of facts in the Report, <u>as facts</u> without citing you or the Report, or imputing blame to individuals.'[23]

Florence used similar tactics many times when she worked for the Sanitary Commission for the Indian Army. She frequently supplied materials to Harriet Martineau, who wrote the articles. The understanding and friendship that grew between these two women lasted more than twenty years. Whenever Florence felt the need to 'talk to a journalist', she got in touch with Harriet Martineau, whether it was about the delay of the Sanitary Commission's report or about female nursing in army hospitals in India.

By March 1858 it had been decided that a second Royal Commission should be formed especially to look into the sanitary and health conditions of the British Army in India. Lord Stanley, the Colonial Secretary, supported the idea.[24] But it took almost a year to finalise the decision and for the Queen to sign the warrant. 'I must tell you a secret,' a jubilant Florence wrote to Harriet Martineau, 'because I think it will please you. For eight long months now I have been "importunate-widowing" my "unjust judge" viz. Lord Stanley, to give us a Royal Sanitary Commission to do exactly the same thing for the Armies in India which the last did for the Army at home. We have just won it. The Queen has signed the Warrant. So it is safe.'[25]

The immediate task at hand was to select the members of the Commission. Any government appointments or the selection of committee members always involves stories of intrigue, manipulation and who knows who. Appointing the members of the Royal Commission for sanitary reform in the Indian Army was no exception. But Florence knew how to manipulate the bureaucrats in order to achieve her goals. The Commission was her brainchild, and she did not want to include anyone who was not committed to the cause of sanitary reform in India. As to the selection of the members for the Sanitary Commission for India, it was not too difficult for her to find committed people. Dr John Sutherland, Dr Ranald Martin and Dr Thomas Alexander, all friends of Florence, some from her Crimea days and all interested in sanitary reforms in Britain and abroad, became members of the Commission. So did Dr William Farr, the medical statistician. From the India Council, Sir R. Vivian and Sir Proby Cautley joined the group, and Colonel E.H. Greathed joined as a 'Queen's officer with acknowledged Indian experience'. Both Dr Ranald Martin and Sir Proby Cautley were old India hands. Dr Ranald Martin's name was associated with the Fever Hospital in Calcutta, and Proby Cautley's with the Ganges Irrigation Project in North India. How far Florence went to vet people before taking them in, and how much responsibility was left on her to select the members, was apparent from her letter to Dr McNeill:

9 May, 1859

... Sir E. Lugard has declined to serve on the Indian Sanitary Commission on account of the present pressure of business at the War Office. And we are again at our wit's end for a 'Queen's officer of acknowledged Indian experience' and again it is left to us to choose.

I mentioned Brigadier Greathed, now in England, the man of the wonderful march from Delhi, and Mr Herbert seems inclined to have him, merely because I cannot name any one else. But I know nothing of him but his reputation, nor do I know anyone to get his measure. In this dilemma, could you help us again both by saying what you think of Greathed and by mentioning any other Queen's officer now at home whom you think well for this purpose.[26]

Florence took great care in making sure that not only the right people were appointed as members of the Commission, but also that the Chairman of the Commission was a person she could rely on and work with. She wanted Sidney Herbert in the post. In a way, he was a natural choice as he had chaired the first Royal Commission and was devoted to the cause of army sanitation. But Sidney Herbert, overworked and in serious ill health at that time, wanted Lord Stanley to take over. Florence did not have much faith in Lord Stanley's enthusiasm or efficiency: 'Lord Stanley has neither the grasp of the subject nor the faculty that some men have of putting themselves into the right hand, as to detail and seeing who knows and who does not. I believe sanitary salvation of India depends upon Mr Herbert doing it.'[27]

Florence managed to get Sidney Herbert as Chairman, but only for a short while. Soon he moved to another post, and Lord Stanley took over. There was talk of including John Stuart Mill, the utilitarian philosopher, who at that time had retired from the East India Company, but that did not get universal approval.[28] Years later, Florence wrote a letter to Mill mentioning this: ' ... As you have had the kindness to let me address you, I cannot help putting in one more word on a subject very near my heart – the India Sanitary Service. I have worked very hard at this for six years. And during all those years my great wish has been: would it be possible to ask Mr. Mill for his help and influence? But you were so busy.'[29]

As the process of selecting members of the Sanitary Commission was going on, Florence, without wasting any time, launched herself into another massive task. With the assistance of Dr Sutherland and Dr Farr, she prepared a questionnaire to be sent to the barracks and army stations in India. This questionnaire had detailed queries about the sanitary state of the military bases in India. The idea was that the information gathered should be as exhaustive as possible so that the exact state of affairs could be known. Before finalising her questionnaire she sent it to Dr McNeill for his advice:

> 9 May 1859
> Would you look at the enclosed list of Heads for enquiries to be sent out to the stations in India and tell us your opinion as to the different queries therein? Would you also kindly give an opinion as to the general direction the Enquiry should take.[30]

Florence, being extremely methodical, wanted to tap every brain and gather all the relevant information from all possible sources. She sent Dr Sutherland to India House in London to study the Government reports for facts and figures and to incorporate them in the questionnaire and the report that followed. She put Dr William Farr onto drawing up statistical forms. 'We must, of course, have the most minute statistics – both for soldiers and officers in the Queen's, Company's and Native troops. These we should get by this method for 10 years.'[31]

One setback at the time was the death of Sidney Herbert in 1861. Both Sidney Herbert and Florence were deeply involved in the work of the Royal Commission. On his deathbed, he expressed his regret that his and Florence's joint work on Indian Army sanitation remained unfinished. This obviously had an effect on Florence: ' ... he perished in the midst of a great work which he knew himself to be unfinished and his last words were to recognize this.'[32] In Sidney Herbert's death, Florence not only lost a workmate, co-thinker and a friend, she also lost her master, her guru. She was also afraid that Herbert's untimely death might stop the reform work:

> ... before he was cold in his grave – Gladstone attends his funeral and then writes to me that he cannot pledge himself to give any assistance in carrying out his friend's reform – the reign of intelligence in the War Office is over – the reign of muffs has begun ... .[33]

Florence now launched herself with double enthusiasm to continue the work of the Sanitary Commission. Lord Stanley had taken over the chairmanship of the Royal Commission a little before Sidney Herbert's death, but he did not have the interest or enthusiasm of Sidney Herbert, and Florence more or less had to provide the energy and motivation to carry on the work of sanitary reforms in India. One consolation was that shortly after Sidney Herbert's death Lord de Grey, later Lord Ripon, was appointed Secretary of War. Although his power was limited, he was always sympathetic to Florence's cause.

In the meantime in London, old Anglo-Indians like John Lawrence, Dr Ranald Martin, Charles Trevelyan and many others had given evidence to the Royal Commission. The questionnaire as prepared by Florence, Dr Sutherland and Dr Farr had been sent to India, to the army, medical and engineering personnel. The army and medical officers working in India were co-operative, as many of them had already felt the need for sanitary reform. When the completed questionnaires came back from India, Florence, with the help of Dr Sutherland and Dr Farr, analysed them and prepared the report with the statistical analysis. Though Sutherland and Farr helped enormously, most of the work was done by Florence herself. 'I have written the greater part of the Indian Sanitary Report for Lord Stanley,' she wrote to Dr McNeill on 15 April 1862, 'and I am doing the digest of the stational reports. That for the Bombay Presidency is finished. Lord Stanley asked me to write answers to written questions under my own name. But these I have scarcely begun.'[34] The comments Florence made on the information gathered through the questionnaires created her famous *Observations*[35], which was submitted as a part of the Royal Commission's voluminous report on the sanitary state of the British Army in India.[36]

Florence's *Observations*

Florence's *Observations* was presented as a letter addressed to Lord Stanley, the Chairman of the Royal Commission, and dated 21 November 1862. It contained her comments on the evidence supplied and they were sarcastic, witty and highly readable. Her *Observations* revealed for the first time in an official document the true sanitary conditions that existed in army barracks and surrounding towns and villages in mid-nineteenth-century India. The picture was negative but based on facts. The commanding officers and army personnel responding to the questionnaire were honest enough in their answers, though many of them surely felt that too much candidness would bring blame on themselves for incompetence. It was therefore not surprising that some of the reports were ambivalent and indicated that the sanitary and health situation in the barracks and the townships was bad indeed, but not too bad to survive. Florence's powerful pen picked up just that. The *Observations* was written with such sarcasm and skill that it cannot be passed over without looking at it in some detail.

What Florence was going to say in her *Observations* was nothing new. It was already hinted at in the postscript of her *Notes* in 1857.[37] Now, five years later, in 1862, she presented a detailed picture of the sanitary situation in the army barracks in India by careful and painstaking analysis of every aspect of it. She claimed that the evidence presented by the reports sent from India showed beyond any doubt that the army barracks and camps in India were all subject to preventable diseases, and the causes of such diseases were bad water, bad drainage, filthy bazaars, lack of ventilation in the barracks and overcrowding in the barrack huts and sick ward. The effects of these conditions were intensified by the climatic condition of the country and the habits of the soldiers such as overeating and overdrinking. Florence did not present a general overall statement, but cited almost each and every station and cantonment individually, describing their sanitary situation by quoting their own words. She challenged those who would 'doubt whether this representation is true' to have a 'look at the stational reports for themselves'.[38]

Being a great believer in environmental hygiene and the miasmic theory of disease, she found everything wrong in the Indian army barracks and in their neighbourhood. First, she referred to the quality of drinking water:

> Where tests have been used the composition of the water reads like a very intricate prescription, containing nearly all the chlorides, sulphates, nitrates, and carbonates in the pharmacopoeia, besides silica and large quantities of organic matter (animal and vegetable), which the reports apparently consider to be nutritive, for few of them but 'consider' the water 'good' and 'wholesome'.

This situation existed not in one army station, but almost in all of them:

> Sealkote calls its water 'decidedly good' while containing a consider-
> able portion of sulphate of lime. Ghazeepore calls its water 'good' and
> 'sweet' and says that it 'does not seem contaminated by the amount of
> leaves that necessarily fall into open structures'. Chunar says that its
> water is clear, sweet and inodorous, 'if allowed to settle before it is
> drunk'. Agra's water is 'laxative' and 'apt to disagree at first'. Dinapore
> admits that 'its wells have been poisoned by infiltration from barrack
> privies'.[39]

Florence was equally scathing about the *modus operandi* for distributing
water in the barracks:

> The arrangements for raising and distributing water are everywhere,
> as Bombay Presidency remarks, the same as what they might have
> been '1000 years ago'. Belgaum has attained the maximum of civiliza-
> tion under this antique system. The water is there 'raised in leather
> skins by bullocks, emptied into troughs and thence conveyed by water
> carriers'.[40]

She referred to the Indian bheestiewallas, who carried water in an animal
skin to deliver it to the barracks, as the 'beginning' and 'end' of a water
pipe, and commented that these water pipes had a mind of their own and
they did not always do as they were told: 'These waterpipes with a will are
not always found to answer, for Fort William (which pays them 134l. per
annum) admits that they sometimes take the water from "nearer and
impurer sources". Would it not be better to try waterpipes without a
will?'[41] In order to clarify the point to the readers she supplied them with
woodcut pictures of the 'Indian waterpipes'.

After water, the drainage system of the barracks came into Florence's
firing line:

> This may be rendered no drainage whatever, in any sense in which we
> understand drainage. The reports speak of cesspits as if they were
> dressing rooms.
>   At Fort William it is stated that the fluid refuse is swept away by
> garrison sweepers and water carriers, with the aid of a fire engine ... .[42]

It was the same story everywhere, whether it was Umballa, Meean Meer,
Ferozepore, Sealkote, Berhampore or Allahabad: ' ... they draw water
from a well, not knowing whence it comes, and if there be any means to
drain off water it is into a cesspit, or into long open pervious drains, not
knowing whither it goes.'[43]

Overcrowding in the barracks and hospitals and lack of ventilation
also added to the ill health of the soldiers. In the barrack huts, 'Sometimes
there is no glass in the windows and when these are shut there is darkness
as well as foul air.'[44] In the summer heat, Florence considered 'the cooling

by tatties, i.e. air passing through damp vegetable matter, often tends to produce ague'.[45] It must be mentioned that Florence had no actual experience of Indian weather and she failed to understand the benefit of unglazed Venetian doors and windows, high ceilings, skylights, and keeping the room dark in summer. She also had no idea of the cooling power of the 'wet tatties'.[46] Her lack of experience in this matter later led to the dispute of 'doors vs. windows' between her and John Lawrence, the Viceroy of India.[47]

Just as Florence had disapproved of the use of the bheestiewallas for water carrying, she also disapproved of the use of cow dung for polishing the barrack room floors: 'At some stations, the floors are of earth, varnished over periodically with cow dung a practice borrowed from the natives. Like Mahomet and the mountain, if men won't go to the dunghill, the dunghill, it appears, comes to them.'[48]

Her next complaint was about the overeating and excessive drinking of the soldiers. The British soldiers drank too much and ate too much meat, on top of which they hardly did any physical exercise when they were not fighting. She gave an account of a soldier's day:

> bed till day break;
> drill for an hour;
> breakfast served to him by native servants;
> bed;
> dinner served to him by native servants;
> bed;
> tea served to him by native servants;
> drink;
> bed – and du capo.[49]

She concluded: ' ... everybody seems to believe that the way of making diseased livers in geese for Strasbourg pies is the best way of keeping men's livers sound, and of making efficient healthy soldiers for India.'[50]

In the 1860s the barracks and cantonments in India had no education or recreation facilities for the off-duty or incapacitated soldiers. Florence was always one for education. In her Crimea days she arranged for lessons and entertainment in Scutari Hospital. She suggested the same for Indian barracks: 'Learning the native languages in regimental schools would at once provide the men with interesting occupation and the prospect of future advantage.'[51] She also felt that the invalid British soldiers in the ill-equipped army hospitals would not behave so badly towards the Indian orderlies if they could speak the language and make themselves understood: 'To enable our soldiers to hold ordinary intercourse with the people among whom their lot is cast, is the first element of an useful and happy life for them in India. Every soldier should be required to learn something of the native language.'[52] The lack of proper nursing was another cause of the soldiers' ill health. The army hospitals in India, Florence commented, were overcrowded and 'full of rats, smell of gangrene, and infested with bed bugs', with no means of ablution. There were no professional nurses or trained orderlies, only 'a plentiful supply of ward coolies'.[53] Florence also drew attention to the complete lack of records of sickness and mortality in the Indian Army:

> The only way to keep a proper check over the sanitary condition of stations is to lay their sickness and mortality statistics annually before Parliament. This can be easily done by adopting the new statistical methods and forms at present in use for Queen's troops at home and on foreign service. These should be introduced over the whole of India and the result published every year together with those of the army at home.[54]

Although a large section of the *Observations* was devoted to the improvement of the health of the British soldiers, Florence did not ignore the plight of the Indian soldiers, the sepoys. A considerable part of her *Observations* also dealt with the conditions of the 'Native lines', 'Filthy bazaars', 'Native hospitals' and 'Native towns'. Florence recognised that the privileges available to some extent to the British soldiers were not available to the sepoys:

> Native troops have no barrack accommodation ... . They have hutting money (very little) and make their own huts, which are so badly built as to ensure thorough ventilation, being often indeed only open sheds in compartments. But little or no pains are taken to make them put up these huts in any regular order; they are crowded, or rather huddled together and without drainage of any kind. They are always damp, and the men always sleep in malaria. When they have families, the huts are too small, because the hutting money is too small.[55]

While the British soldiers overate and overdrank in the barracks, the Indian soldiers ' ... have no rations and stint themselves of proper food in order to hoard their pay. They are almost invariably temperate and have little or no liver disease ... .' But they suffered ' ... from quotidian, tertian, quartan, remittent and typhoid fevers ... from acute and chronic dysentery, from sporadic and epidemic cholera, from simple and confluent smallpox, and from acute and chronic rheumatism!'[56] The hospitals for the Indian soldiers were in an even worse condition than those for Europeans. They 'combine all the disadvantages of civilization without any of its advantages'.[57] They had no sanitation, no latrines, no washing facilities, no sweepers to clean them, and were always overflowing with patients. Outside the army barracks, Florence pointed out that the 'Native lines', 'Native bazaars', and 'Native towns' and settlements all had their share of insanitary conditions. As for the big cities like Bombay, Poona,

Peshawar, Madras or Calcutta, the sanitary conditions were equally appalling. She asked the inevitable question: 'Can it be possible that such a state of things exist after all these years of possession and unlimited authority?'[58]

The British administration in India always used the 'caste system' and the so-called 'Indian apathy' towards sanitation as excuses for their hesitation to introduce modern sanitary measures. From the start, Florence was not willing to accept such views. Talk about 'caste prejudices' was to her 'an excuse for European laziness'.[59] A year before writing her *Observations*, when Florence was analysing the reports sent from India, she was incensed to find out how little attention had been paid to the health and sanitation of the native army, the sepoys, and how stational replies continuously cited 'caste' as a barrier to the introduction of sanitary reforms: 'The "Replies" about the Native troops are sometimes disgraceful,' she wrote in disgust, 'disgraceful both to Commissions, and Medical and Engineering Officers. We look upon the Native troops ... much as Virginians look upon slaves.'[60] At that time, Florence wanted some positive feedback about the caste system in India. Perhaps the 'old Anglo-Indians', the retired British officers and army generals with Indian experience, would be able to tell her how far caste was 'an obstacle in the way of sanitary civilization', as she suggested to Dr Farr:

> Sept 28, 1861
>
> I think it would be very desirable ... to examine somebody who would give you evidence about <u>caste</u>, how far it is a religious & how far a social institution, how far it can be got over & how far you must bow to it – in civilizing and sanitarizing our native troops.
>
> As I have had everyone of the M.S. books of Replies to do nothing has stuck me so much as this: viz. that <u>caste</u> is made an excuse for
>
> not feeding
> not cooking for
> not cleansing or washing
> not housing
> not teaching
> not amusing
> not nursing them.
>
> The books of Replies differ widely as to the <u>right</u> of this – some say that nothing can be done, others show that a great deal <u>has</u> been done in some places. And others still, that it requires only a vigorous effort on the part of our Government to do it. I refer particularly to the absence of almost all sanitary civilization (or effort to introduce any) into the native parts of our stations or among our native lines.[61]

A year later, in her *Observations*, Florence equally refused to accept caste as a barrier to sanitary reforms in India: 'One remark, or rather inference, viz. native "caste" prejudices appear to have been made the excuse for European laziness, as far as regards our sanitary and hospital neglects of the natives. Recent railroad experience is a striking proof that "caste" in their minds, is no bar to intercommunication in arrangements tending to their benefit.' Florence realised from the beginning that without improving the health and sanitation of the Indian community, the health and sanitary conditions of the army could not be improved. Even if there was 'caste prejudice', such prejudice would have to give way to sanitary improvement. To her, such improvements would be 'an advance of civilization in India'.[62]

Publicising the Royal Commission's report

Once the Royal Commission's report had been written, Florence wanted to publicise it. Her aim was to put pressure on the Government so that the sanitary work in India could start, without delay, with the help of the technical knowledge and skill available in Britain. But the *Observations* was too critical of British complacency in India and raised many unpalatable questions. Needless to say, it did not make her popular with the War Office, the India Office, nor with the military or medical authorities in India. To mobilise the administration in London, Florence had to fight the same fight all over again against departmental bureaucracy and the apathy of the administrators, as she had done during and after the Crimean War.[63] In a way, the present fight was a more difficult one as it questioned the competency of the British colonial administration. It had been comparatively easy to create public awareness regarding the plight of the British soldiers in the Crimean War but it was not easy to evoke similar sentiments regarding the army in India, and Indians.

The first difficulty was the delay in releasing the report. Although Florence submitted her own comments, the *Observations*, in November 1862 and finished all the groundwork for the Royal Commission's voluminous report, the Government took time to release it. It did not come out until July 1863. The delay was partly caused by Dr Farr's failure to finish the statistical introduction in time. She wrote to Farr:

> I am miserably anxious about the Report (Indian Sanitary). There are so many (political) contingencies on the cards – not one favourable to us – that it would have been very important to have got the Reports presented this session – now to get it presented by next February to the House of Commons.
> ... If we could get your statistical introduction, our draft would be revised in two days and sent to press. ... What is really needed is the necessary statistical statement to precede the sanitary enquiry and conclusion in the Report. In your hands indeed is placed the question whether India is to have sanitary reform or not.[64]

Farr was not the only one who caused delay. The next hurdle came from the Treasury, which was not too keen to spend too much to print the Royal Commission's voluminous report with pictures and all. Florence first offered to publish it out of her own pocket, and then took a clever step to outwit the bureaucracy. As the printer, Mr Spottiswoode, was one of her personal acquaintances, she obtained a large number of printed copies of her *Observations* from him for her 'personal' use, which she was quite entitled to, and then distributed these among all her friends and whoever was slightly interested in Indian sanitation, including the Queen. 'I have sent (to the Athenaeum) a copy of my Indian paper (with wood-cuts) for you,' she wrote to Chadwick, 'and one for Mr Mill. Please remember and remind him (tho' it seems impertinent to say so to two such distinguished officials) that it <u>must be strictly confidential</u> till the Indian Blue Books is laid on the table of the Ho. of C.'[65]

When in July 1863 the report of the Royal Commission was finally published, Florence arranged through her journalist friends to get it reviewed as quickly as possible:

> By dint of sending three times a day to the printers and almost every half an hour to the lithographer, I have got a few copies of our Indian Army Sanitary Report, before it is issued.
> Can you do anything for us in the way of <u>publicizing</u> it? And, if so, where shall I send you a copy?[66]

On receipt of her letter, Chadwick promptly answered to let her know that he would do whatever he could to give the report suitable publicity and would also try to arrange a speech in the House of Lords to draw public attention to this Indian sanitary report.[67] Florence also complained about the delay in publishing the report to Harriet Martineau, and the difficulty that this would cause as she had sent her an early copy: 'We have lost five precious months of the session in getting it out. And I am now canvassing Ld de Grey and Sir C. Wood with all my might for the working commission.' Florence felt that had she been as strong as she was in 1857 with the first army sanitary report, she could have got it out in February when Parliament was in session, instead of in July. 'But with a chairman, for Lord Stanley does nothing for us, and without a secretary, what can a poor invalid woman do?'[68]

The speed with which Florence acted produced results. Reviews and notices appeared in most of the leading journals and newspapers.[69] But Florence wanted more, as she always believed that a 'Report is not self-executive and when a report is ended, the work begins'.[70] Florence wanted people to read the report, particularly influential people who would be able to create a climate of concern. To some extent she succeeded in achieving that. Her *Observations* in particular was highly praised for its lucidity, style and factual content by people like J.S. Mill and Charles

Trevelyan. Trevelyan, who was the Finance Member of the India Council, also promised to help: 'Did I tell you,' Florence wrote to Harriet Martineau, 'that I had heard from Sir C. Trevelyan that he has provided £300,000 in his budget for our building purposes etc. which he thinks is as much as can be expended in the first year. But he says if more is wanted it shall be forthcoming.'[71] Through Harriet Martineau, Florence was also able to send a copy of her report to Lord and Lady Elgin in India, where Lord Elgin was the Viceroy. Florence was pleased to announce that the report 'has made a great impression and all England is expecting to see it carried out'.[72] Florence had started her roller coaster of sanitation, and she was not willing to wait any longer.

However, the path of success is never smooth. The summer of 1863 was not an easy time for Florence. She wanted the recommendations of the report to be carried out at once. The working organisation she had in mind was first to appoint three Sanitary Commissions in India for the three presidencies, Bengal, Bombay and Madras, and a Home Commission in London. This Home Commission was to be attached either to the India Office or the War Office, or to both, with its function being consultative. It was to provide guidance to the Presidency Commissions in India until they could 'walk alone'. 'It is certain that without home influence, Indian improvement in the Sanitary line is hopeless,' she confided in Lord de Grey. 'But, if home assistance were given for a time, until the Presidency Commissions were able to walk alone, the improvements would go on.'

As to the structure and membership of the Home Commission, she had definite ideas:

> If your own Barrack and Hospital Improvement Commission is to be adopted as the basis, then Sir Proby Cautley and Sir Ranald Martin will have to be added on to it when Indian questions come before it. And Mr. Rawlinson C.E., when the great water supply and drainage question in India come on, will have to act upon it.
>   If an I.O. Commission were appointed its members should be
> Sir Proby Cautley
> Sir Ranald Martin
> Dr Sutherland
> Capt. Galton
> Mr. Rawlinson C.E. ...
>   Might I add that, for Sanitary Members of the Presidency Commissions, the documents point out none but Inspector General Dr MacPherson, Madras, Dr Norman Chevers, Calcutta, Dr Joseph Ewart who was at [ ],[73] and also Dr Dempster & Dr Macclellan. If you bid me look out for Engineers, I will do so (from the documents).[74]

Although Florence was eager to start, the Government machinery moved slowly. Departmental wrangles broke out between the War Office and the

India Office. Neither was willing to act unless they were specifically 'requested' by the other. Florence turned again in frustration to Harriet Martineau:

> I am so anxious about the results of the Indian Sanitary Report. No one but I who have been trying for 7 years 'come' August to work a War Office without being Sec. of State can tell how much cause for anxiety there is. Had Sidney Herbert been alive the thing would have been done directly. He never wanted anything but a reason to go himself straight to any minister and get it done. Lord Stanley wants a great deal besides a reason. He told me that he would not offer his services – but he would like to be asked. So I got Lord De Grey to ask Sir C. Wood to ask him. And on Monday there was a meeting of Sir C. Wood, Lord Stanley & Dr Sutherland at the I.O. But there is a most unfortunate hitch about the appointment of the home commission on the ground that there is no direct reference of plans from India to England, at present. Now such a reference is just what we want, as regards Sanitary works. And without it the R. Commission had better never have been.[75]

With the intervention of the Secretary of State, Sir Charles Wood, however, the misunderstanding between the War Office and the India Office cleared up shortly, but Florence faced another difficulty. This time the evidence presented in the Royal Commission's report was questioned. It was said that the facts and figures of the soldiers' death and sickness had been exaggerated and doubts were expressed about the relevance of introducing sanitary measures in India. Florence wrote to Martineau:

> I am in great tribulation about the I.O. We have found a more formidable enemy in Col. Baker there. … He has written a letter to Lord Stanley impugning our statistics. It is astounding how careless and superficial is the view which many clever men will take and accept on this subject.
> … His argument is that the War years give the highest death rates (not from wounds) and that therefore Peace, not sanitary measure is the remedy.[76]

The problem was that such criticisms from Government sources only made other Government officials hesitant to act: 'Lord De Grey says we had better stop arrangements for the Home Commission for the present as we should only irritate them.'[77] Colonel Baker was not alone. Colonel Norman, the Military Secretary to the Government of India, made 'a furious attack' on the report by pointing out some 'erroneous impressions and conclusions' in the report.[78] Further criticisms and complaints that facts were not truly represented later came from India.[79] 'The best things that can happen to us,' Florence wrote to Dr Farr, 'is that they should produce their complaints against us in the House of Commons.'[80]

In the meantime, earlier in the summer of 1863, more difficulties had arisen in submitting the report in its complete form to the House of Commons. The inept clerical staff produced an abridged version of the report, scrapped Florence's *Observations*, made a synopsis of the reports sent from Indian barracks and military stations, and submitted this shorter version of the report to the House of Commons. Florence was told that her *Observations* had been left out by 'a mistake', which could not be rectified as the typeface had already been broken. 'I cannot help connecting these "mistakes" now with the declaration of impugning our statistics from the I.O. They wanted to destroy our evidence.'[81] This certainly made Florence, Dr Farr and Dr Sutherland furious. As a counter-step to this so-called mistake, Florence's allies had her *Observations* privately printed, distributed and reviewed again.

Florence requested that the Government keep an unabridged copy of the Commission's report in the Hansard office, so that if people wanted to see the full report they could. When her request was granted, she asked her friends to go and see the full report in Hansard's office to make sure that it was actually there. Referring to her hard work for this report, she also got her request to write a shorter version herself granted, and this amended shorter version included both her *Observations* and the statistical evidence from the barracks. This revised edition came out in 1864, and got another press review.[82] Finally, exerting her personal prestige, she managed to secure an order from the Government for the distribution of the report among the British administrators, army officers, engineers and doctors working in India. Not only that, she managed to make the report obligatory reading for them. However, the Government of India did not receive an official copy until a year or so after it had been printed, because of bureaucratic mismanagement.[83]

The privately printed copy of Florence's *Observations* had a red cover, in contrast with the Royal Commission's official report, which, as usual, had a blue cover. This 'little red book' probably caused a stir among the nineteenth-century British administrators similar to that caused by another little red book in the twentieth century. A few years later, Sir Bartle Frere wrote in a letter to Florence:

> Your little red book on India, which made some of us so savage, did immense good to all of us, and … I have often wished you could embody in an appendix to it, a few pages on the right way to go with the work in India.[84]

How people may live and not die in India

About this time, in October 1863, Florence delivered her famous paper *How People May Live and Not Die in India* at the meeting of the National Social Science Association, held in Edinburgh.

> 'A meeting of the Social Science Association is surely the place to discuss one of the most important of social questions, viz., how the British race is to hold possession of India; and to bestow upon its vast populations the benefit of a higher civilization.[85]

Florence's paper was based on her *Observations* and was meant to publicise the predicament of the British soldiers in India. After her experience with the Royal Commission's report, presenting a written paper to a learned audience seemed to be the only channel left to her, and a very clever step to take. Then Florence was never hesitant to publicise her cause, though she never sought personal publicity. Her frustration was expressed in the footnote to the paper where she referred to the Government's handling of the Royal Commission's report: 'It is a pity that by mistake the complete report and evidence of the Commission (in two folio volumes) was not presented to Parliament, not distributed, not sold at the Parliamentary depots.'[86]

In a way, there was nothing new in this paper that Florence had not already said in her *Observations*. But this was the first time that she had presented her case directly to the British public about what was happening in India. The questions she raised sound totally imperialistic in the modern context but they did not conceal the fact that she was deeply concerned not only for the British soldiers, but also for Indians and India. In her mind, the sanitary question was never two different questions, one for the European soldiers only and another for the natives. For her, it was one problem and should be tackled as such: 'But it is not for the soldiers alone we speak. The report has a much deeper meaning and intent than this – it aims at nothing less than to bring the appliances of a higher civilization to the natives of India.' Florence pointed out that, as in the case of the soldiers, there were no statistics of how many Indians died every year from cholera, dysentery, fever and other epidemic diseases. 'The plague and pestilence is the ordinary state of things',[87] yet all of them were preventable.

Only a few years earlier, in 1857, Florence had been thinking of 'holding the Empire by British troops'. By 1863, although retaining the Empire was still very much in her mind, she had moved further beyond the sanitation and health of the army alone. India in its entirety with its millions of people started to fill her vision. She held the British Government to be morally responsible for the welfare of the Indians. 'The time has gone past when India was considered a mere appanage of British commerce. In holding India we must be able to show the moral right of our tenure.'[88]

Florence shared this idea of moral obligation towards the Indian Empire with many other liberals of that time. The British were in India, as she saw it, not just to rule, but also to implant seeds of a 'higher civilisation' – hygiene being its handmaid. But she did not make any claim to superiority. She knew that only a short while ago, similar insanitary conditions existed in Britain and London was considered as the Great Wen. ' ... I am sure it is not for us to talk of civilization,' she wrote to John Lawrence a year later, 'For I have seen, in our English workhouses, infirmaries, neglect, cruelty and malversation such as can scarcely be surpassed in some semi-barbarous countries.'[89] In her paper she emphasised that it was not possible for the ordinary Indians to prevent these catastrophic diseases that were decimating the population together with the British soldiers. It was the responsibility of the Indian Government to rectify the situation: ' ... till the Indian Government has fulfilled its vast responsibility towards those great multitudes who are no longer strangers and foreigners, but as much the subjects of our beloved Queen as any of us ... ',[90] the situation would remain as catastrophic as ever.

Presenting this paper to the Social Science Conference also gave Florence a chance to refute some of the criticisms made against the Royal Commission's report. Some British officials in India claimed that the insanitary conditions described in the report had changed during its compilation. Things were better, conditions in the barracks and neighbourhoods had improved and the mortality rate of the soldiers had fallen. But Florence was not to be fooled:

> It is difficult to see how India could have been freed from these causes of disease in three short years, which is about the average time since the Stational Reports were signed.
> We have also two printed documents of the Public Works Departments dated Calcutta June 26 and September 9, 1863 proving that the capital of India was in a much worse state than appeared from the Stational Report sent to the Royal Commission in June 1860.[91]

The concern caused by the Royal Commission's report finally led to the establishment of a working commission with representation from the India Office and the War Office. This was commonly known as the Barrack and Hospital Improvement Commission. Florence again wrote to Harriet Martineau:

> I cannot help telling you in the joy of my heart that the final meeting of the Indian Sanitary Commission was held today – that the report was signed – and that after a very tough battle lasting three days, to convince these people that a report was not self-executive, our

working commission was carried, not quite in the original form proposed, but in what may prove a better working form because drafted on what exists. This is the dawn of a new day for India in sanitary things, not only as regards our Army, but as regards the native population.[92]

Sir Charles Wood, the Secretary of State for India, also granted the appointment of Sanitary Commissions in India in August 1863,[93] and all that remained was for the work to begin. Florence's next efforts would be to mobilise the various authorities and departments at home and in India so that the Royal Commission's recommendations could be implemented. One can easily guess what an enormous task she had in front of her and the inactivity she would encounter. Florence was perceptive enough to foresee such delays: 'In India, as at home, no good will be done unless it be made some competent person's express business to look to these things.'[94] And as life gives to those who demand, almost by coincidence at this period of India's history, Florence found a friend who believed in her cause and was willing to carry out her ideas. That friend was John Lawrence, the Viceroy of India.

Notes

1. Ghose, J.M. (1930), *Sanyasi and Fakir Raiders in Bengal*, Calcutta: Bengal Secretariat Book Department.
2. Mazumdar, R.C. (1962), *The history of the Freedom Movement in India*, Calcutta: Firma K.L. Mukhopadhyay, vol. 1, pp. 106–127.
3. Datta, K.K. (1970), *Anti-British Plots and Movements before 1857*, Meerut: Meenkshi Prakashan, pp. 43–106.
4. Chaudhuri, S.B. (1955), *Civil Disturbances during the British Rule in India 1765–1857*, Calcutta: The World Press Ltd., pp. 95–97, 112.
5. The Crimean War, 1854–56, was fought between Russia on one side and Britain and France on the other, with Turkey in the middle. The Anglo-French effort was to prevent Russian expansion in Persia and the Balkans. The battles of Alma, Inkerman, and Balaclava, the famous Charge of the Light Brigade and the Siege of Sebastopol took place in the Crimean War. Florence went to Crimea with a group of nurses to care for the wounded soldiers in the midst of much difficulty, and encountered much hostility from male doctors. After Crimea, her dogged determination forced the British Government to set up a Royal Commission to investigate the army health and sickness question in 1857. See Coats, T. (ed.) (2000), *Florence Nightingale and the Crimea 1845–55*, London: The Stationery Office (abridged edition; first published, 1855).
6. Cook (1913), vol. 1, p. 371.
7. Institution for the Care of Sick Gentlewomen in Distressed Circumstances. Florence joined the Institution in 1853 after receiving some training in nursing in Kaiserwerth in Germany, and in Paris.
8. Woodham-Smith (1950), p. 110.
9. Cook (1913), vol. 1, p. 160.

10. Hare, A. (1893), *Story of Two Noble Lives*, London: George Allen, vol. II, p. 350. The letter was dated 14 November, and presumably was written in 1857 when the mutiny was happening. Florence offered her services to Lord Canning, once through Sidney Herbert and then in a personal letter carried by her cousin, Major Nicholson, who had been ordered to India.
11. FN to McNeill, 15 July 1857, BL Add. Mss 45768, fol. 60.
12. FN to Pattison Walker, 3 January 1865, BL Add. Mss 45781, fol. 260.
13. FN to McNeill, 10 October 1857, BL Add. Mss 45768, fol. 66. She referred to the indifference shown by Lord Panmure, Secretary for War.
14. FN (1858), 'Postscripts on Sanitary Matters in India', in FN (1858) *Notes on Matters Affecting the Health, Efficiency and Hospital Administration of the British Army founded chiefly on the Experience of the Late War*, London: Harrison & Sons, vol. 2, p. 565.
15. FN (1859), *A Contribution to the Sanitary History of the British Army during the Late War with Russia*, London, Harrison & Sons, p. 13.
16. FN to McNeill, 10 October 1857, BL Add. Mss 45768, fol. 66.
17. FN (1858), vol. 2, p. 567.
18. Sutherland to FN, 11 September 1857, BL Add. Mss 45751, fols 46–49.
19. Harrison, M. (1999), *Climate and Constitutions*, New Delhi: Oxford University Press, pp. 133–152.
20. FN to Chadwick, 7 October 1858, BL Add. Mss 45770, fols 50–51. See 'Lodging, food and dress of soldiers', *The Contemporary Review*, January 1859, vol. 105, pp. 155–176. Also see Smith, F.B. (1982), *Florence Nightingale. Reputation and Power*, London: Croom Helm, p. 114.
21. FN to Chadwick, 11 February 1858, BL Add. Mss 45770, fol. 8.
22. FN to Martineau, 30 November 1858, BL Add. Mss 45788, fols 1–2.
23. Martineau to FN, 3 December 1858, BL Add. Mss 45788, fol. 3.
24. Cook (1913), vol. 1, p. 379.
25. FN to Martineau, 19 May 1859, BL Add. Mss 45788, fol. 55.
26. FN to McNeill, 9 May 1859, BL Add. Mss 45768, fol. 98.
27. FN to McNeill, 11 June 1859, BL Add. Mss 45768, fols 104–5.
28. Cook (1913), vol. 2, p. 21.
29. FN to Mill, 11 August 1867, BL Add. Mss 39927, fol. 59, draft.
30. FN to McNeill, 9 May 1859, BL Add. Mss 45768, fol. 98. See also FN to McNeill, 11 June 1859, BL Add. Mss 45768, fols 104–5.
31. FN to Farr, 2 June 1859, in Cook (1913), vol. 2, p. 25.
32. FN to McNeill, 7 November 1861, BL Add. Mss 45768, fol. 162.
33. FN to Farr, 10 September 1861, BL Add. Mss 43399, fols 41–43.
34. FN to McNeill, 15 April 1862, BL Add. Mss 45768, fol. 170.
35. FN (1863a), *Observations on the Evidence Contained in the Stational Reports Submitted to her by the Royal Commission on the Sanitary State of the Army in India*, London: Edward Stanford. Reprinted from the Royal Commission's report.
36. Royal Commission on the Sanitary State of the Army in India, 1863, vol. 1, pp. 347–370.
37. FN (1858), vol. 2, p. 565–567.
38. FN (1863a), p. 2.
39. FN (1863a), pp. 3–4.
40. FN (1863a), pp. 5–6.
41. FN (1863a), p. 7.
42. FN (1863a), pp. 10, 15.

43. FN (1863a), pp. 18–19.
44. FN (1863a), p. 25.
45. FN (1863a), p. 24.
46. A screen made of the roots of fragrant grass (*khus khus*) to cover windows and doors during summer months.
47. See Chapter 3.
48. FN (1863a), p. 31.
49. FN (1863a), p. 42.
50. FN (1863a), p. 51.
51. FN (1863a), p. 49.
52. FN (1863a), p. 64, footnote.
53. FN (1863a), pp 52–63.
54. FN (1863a), p. 91.
55. FN (1863a), p. 72.
56. FN (1863a), p. 74.
57. FN (1863a), p. 75.
58. FN (1863a), p. 76.
59. FN to Farr, 5 October 1861, BL Add. Mss 43399, fols 56–57.
60. FN to Farr, 2 October 1861, BL Add. Mss 43399, fols 54–55.
61. FN to Farr, 28 September 1861, BL Add. Mss 43399, fols 50–53.
62. FN (1863a), pp. 81–82.
63. Cook (1913), vol. 1, pp. 334–361.
64. FN to Farr, 8 August 1862, BL Add. Mss 43399, fol. 70.
65. FN to Chadwick, 5 January 1863, BL Add. Mss 45771, fol. 27.
66. FN to Chadwick, 8 July 1863, BL Add. Mss 45771, fol. 28.
67. Chadwick to FN, 8 July 1863, BL Add. Mss 45771, fol. 29, and 22 July 1863, fol. 34.
68. FN to Martineau, 8 July 1863, BL Add. Mss 45788, fols 188–89.
69. Cook (1913), vol. 2, p. 35.
70. FN to McNeill, 9 July 1863, BL Add. Mss 45768, fol. 180.
71. FN to Martineau, 19 May 1863, BL Add. Mss 45788, fol. 187, draft.
72. FN to Martineau, 29 July 1863, BL Add. Mss 45788, fol. 194.
73. FN, and some of her correspondents, used both square brackets and parentheses in their letters. These are quoted as written. Italicised square brackets, or italicised text in square brackets, are used within quotations to indicate unreadable text, or interpolation or additional contextual information.
74. FN to de Grey, 8 July 1863, BL Add. Mss 43546, fols 60–63.
75. FN to Martineau, 22 July 1863, BL Add. Mss 45788, fols 190–193.
76. FN to Martineau, 1 August 1863, BL Add. Mss 45778, fol. 199.
77. FN to Martineau, 1 August 1863, BL Add. Mss 45778, fols 199–200.
78. Government of India, Military Despatch, No. 48, 5 February 1864, and No. 459, 8 December 1864, in *Memorandum on Measures Adopted for Sanitary Improvements in India up to the end of 1867*, 1868, London: Eyre and Spottiswoode, pp. 2–3 (hereafter referred to as *Memorandum, Sanitary Measures*). Also see FN to Farr, 10 December 1863, BL Add. Mss 43399 fols 159–160.
79. Leith, A.H. (1864), *Report on the General Sanitary Condition of the Bombay Army*, Bombay.
80. FN to Farr, 10 December 1863, BL Add. Mss 43399, fols 159–60.
81. FN to Martineau, 1 August 1863, BL Add. Mss 45788, fol. 201.
82. Cook (1913), vol. 2, p. 36.

83. Government of India, Military Despatch, No. 48, 5 February 1864, *Memorandum, Sanitary Measures*, 1867, p. 2
84. Frere to FN, 17 September 1867, BL Add. Mss 45780, fols 68–70.
85. FN (1863b), *How People May Live and Not Die in India*, London: Victoria Press, p. 3. Printed privately as a booklet in January 1864, dated 1863. It was reprinted in November 1864 with a preface where she acknowledged the work that had been done in India by Sir John Lawrence. See FN (1864b), *How People May Live and Not Die in India*, London: Longman, Green, Roberts, and Green.
86. FN (1863b), p. 3, footnote.
87. FN (1863b), p. 8.
88. FN (1863b), p. 9.
89. FN to Lawrence, 26 September 1864, BL Add. Mss 45777, fols 49–53.
90. FN (1863b), p. 10.
91. FN (1863b), postscript, p. 11.
92. FN to Martineau, 19 May 1863, BL Add. Mss 45788, fols 184–185.
93. Government of India, Military Despatch No. 297, 15 August 1863, *Memorandum, Sanitary Measures*, 1867, p. 1.
94. FN (1863a), p. 91.

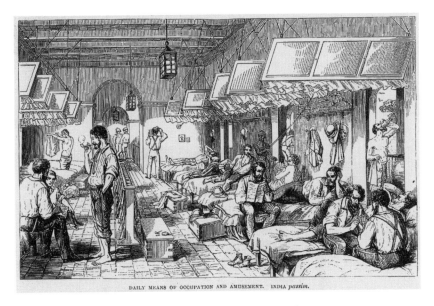

DAILY MEANS OF OCCUPATION AND AMUSEMENT. INDIA *passim.*

Plate 2   British soldiers' daily means of occupation and amusement.
(The Wellcome Library)

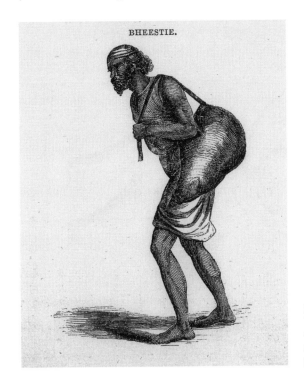

BHEESTIE.

Plate 3   Bheestiewalla.
The man who delivers
water in an animal
skin. (The Wellcome
Library)

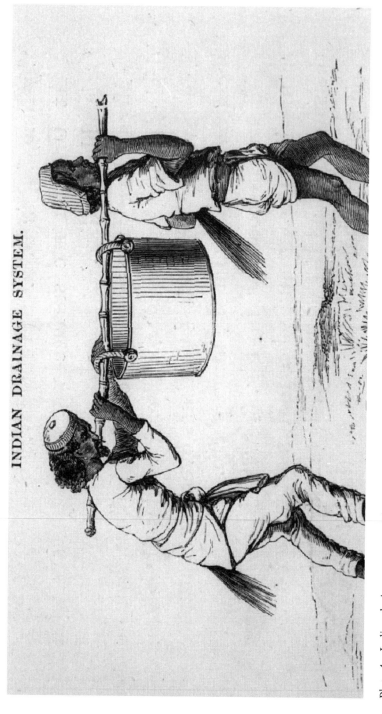

Plate 4   Indian drainage system. (The British Library)

CHAPTER THREE

The Governess of the Governors

'The Governess of the Governors of India' was what Benjamin Jowett, the Master of Balliol called her. But Florence preferred 'Maid of all (dirty) work or the Nuisances Removal Act'.[1]

Jowett was right. She was the Governess of the Governors in India; not only of one but of a succession of them, from the Governors-General to the Lieutenant-Governors, and to anyone else who was in a position to govern in India. Encompassing a period of almost forty years, from John Lawrence to Lord Lansdowne and even after, Florence wrote to the Governors-General and Governors, criticised them, praised them, encouraged them and supported them in their difficult days. 'When such officials came home on furlough, most of them came also to Miss Nightingale ... Miss Nightingale was never backward in filling the part of governess to those who in sanitary matters governed India.'[2] All these were for one single purpose, the improvement of the sanitary conditions in India. Sometimes she was successful, and sometimes she despaired and thought that she had failed. But over the years many of her ideas were gradually implemented as the Government machinery moved slowly. In her long list of correspondents in India one name stands out, and that was the name of John Lawrence.

John Laird Mair Lawrence, son of Colonel Alexander Lawrence, was born on 4 March 1811 and was nine years older than Florence. Lawrence was of Irish-Scottish descent and was related on his mother's side to the reformer John Knox. He went to India, with his brother Henry, in 1831 at the age of 20. Later, he became the Magistrate and Revenue Collector of Delhi, and afterwards the Chief Commissioner of Punjab. He and his brother Henry Lawrence showed courage and military skill during the mutiny in 1857, in which Henry died in Lucknow. John survived the ordeal of the mutiny and became known as the Saviour of Punjab.

In 1859, Lawrence resigned from the Governorship of Punjab and went back to England. By that time, he had achieved publicity and fame for his heroism in India and soon became a member of the India Council. When fighting broke out in the north-west of India in 1863, the British Government became anxious at the possibility of another mutiny. In the meantime, on the death of Lord Elgin, the post of Viceroy was lying vacant in India. Lawrence appeared to be a natural choice for the post, and public opinion was on his side. It was said that Florence's manipulation was also behind this; apparently she urged Lord Stanley, the head of the India Council at the time, to see that Lawrence got the post.[3] When Lawrence was appointed Viceroy of India, on 30 November 1863, Florence sent him a congratulatory note:

> Among the multitude of affairs and congratulations which will be pouring in upon you, there is no more fervent joy, there are no stronger good wishes, than those of one of the humblest of your servants. For there is no greater position for usefulness under heaven than that of the governing of the vast Empire you saved for us. And you are the only man to fill it … .

Florence's eulogy could not end without utilising the opportunity to further her cause:

> … In the midst of your pressure pray think of us, and of our sanitary things on which such millions of lives and health depend.[4]

A friendship began, and it seems that Florence was really bowled over by this man with unkempt hair, distant look and often 'boorish manners'.[5] To her, he was a hero: 'What would Homer have been if he had had such heroes as Lawrence to sing.'[6] In later years, it was said that a photograph of John Lawrence always hung in Florence's room,[7] and whenever she could she added a few lines of praise for Lawrence's good work in India.[8] When Lawrence died in 1879, Florence grieved deeply in a letter to Gladstone, who was the leader of the opposition in Parliament at that time.

> 6 July 1879
> … He was a man of iron; he had gone through 40 years of Indian life, in times of danger, toil and crisis; he had been brought sometimes to the brink of the grave; and had weathered it all … He had the blue eye and the expression in it (before his operation) of a girl of 16, and the massive brow and head of a General of Nations, rather than of Armies … .
> I received a letter from him, received it the day after his death – dictated, but signed by himself, sending me some recent Indian reports – private papers – which he had read and wished me to read – all marked and the page turned down where he had left off. This was his legacy. O that I could do something for India for which he lived and died.[9]

The friendship between Lawrence and Florence had its ups and downs, but stood the test of time with mutual appreciation. It was not true, as sometimes was suggested that Lawrence only paid lip service to Florence's 'overtures' and in fact did very little to follow her wishes, and that was only when it suited him.[10] The number of letters exchanged between these two outstanding persons showed that Lawrence was sincere and tried to do whatever was possible under the circumstances. This is well documented, which shows conclusively that Lawrence gave the 'go-ahead' to the sanitary reforms for the British Army in India as wished by 'Miss Nightingale'.

John Lawrence and Florence began to exchange letters long before he left for India as Viceroy. Between August 1862 and December 1863, they corresponded in London; afterwards Lawrence wrote to her from India. In 1869 when Lawrence retired and came back to England, they kept in touch. In later years, Florence often sent him papers concerning India or her own articles for his comments, and Lawrence without hesitation advised her. As a member of the India Council, Lawrence was well aware of the Royal Commission's report on the sanitary state of the Indian Army. He was also one of the main witnesses interviewed by the Royal Commission. He was familiar with Florence's ideas on sanitary matters as he had received a copy of her *Observations*, and mostly subscribed to her views. They both had the same empathy for the British soldiers in India. However, having been in India for many years, Lawrence had more practical experience of the country and did not hesitate to differ if the situation arose. There was considerable correspondence between Lawrence and Florence, exchanging ideas about the forthcoming Indian Sanitary Commission, sending each other reports, designs and diagrams of model barracks, and suggesting who to employ in the Indian Sanitary Commission and who would be the best person to lead. When Lawrence suggested the name of Dr Hathaway as a likely candidate for the head of the Indian health campaign, Florence was reluctant. She had read through the reports sent by the medical officers from India. She knew exactly who would or would not be the best person or persons to serve an Indian health campaign:

> 10 July 1863
>
> I had read Dr Hathaways report, but the impression produced by it is of a different kind. ... He is deficient in a much more rare talent, namely the choice of remedies for evils. His report contains principles on this point at variance with sound practice, even in the colder climate of England, and which if applied to India would leave matters there much as they are, in certain important points where reform is urgently wanted.[11]

Although Florence did not recommend Dr Hathaway as head of the Indian Sanitary Commission, later she corresponded regularly with him and Hathaway in turn furnished her with information about the progress of sanitary reforms in India.[12]

On 4 December 1863, before leaving for India, Lawrence went to see Florence and asked her for some guidelines and suggestions for sanitary reforms in India. Florence was so impressed by him that she wrote an exuberant letter to Dr Farr:

> 10 December 1863
>
> ... I have had the great joy of being in constant communication with Sir John Lawrence, and of receiving his commands to do what I had

almost lost the hope of being allowed to do – viz. of sending out full statements and schemes of what we want the Presidency Commissions to do.

I should be glad to submit to you copies of papers of mine which he desired me to write and which he took out with him, as to the constitution of the Presidency Commissions, if you care to see them. They are, of course, confidential. I have also seen Lord Stanley more than once during these busy days. And with Sir John Lawrence's command we feel ourselves empowered to begin the home commission and to further our plans upon it. Sir John Lawrence so far from considering our report exaggerated considers it under the mark.[13]

Florence had every reason to feel elated at John Lawrence's appointment. She saw new hope for her sanitation project in India, which was at a standstill because of departmental bickering and jealousy. She could see that Lawrence was keen to make army sanitation his 'express' business and she was not wrong. Lawrence reached Calcutta on 12 January 1864, and shortly afterwards wrote to Florence:

5 February 1864
We have commenced work by establishing the Sanitary Committees for Calcutta, Madras and Bombay. They are composed of 5 Members. A Civilian is at their head, and a Medical Officer as Secretary.

I hope that you will expedite the transmission to India of the codes and rules and plans which have been approved of for home and the Colonies. We shall then have some ideas in a practical shape of the main features of the sanitary system, and can readily adapt it to the peculiar circumstances of the Country. Without such a guide, we shall often be perhaps working in direct opposition to your views. Where we differ, it will become our duty to set forth the grounds for so doing, in sending our plans and reports home.[14]

Lawrence in India (1864–69)

Lawrence went to India in 1864 with a clear determination to improve the sanitary conditions of the British Army, but the energy he had shown during his Punjab days was not there any more. He was in his fifties and suffering from ill health. Fortunately for him, the period of his viceroyalty was relatively peaceful. The only two military encounters that took place during Lawrence's administration were the Bhutan War in 1864 and the Abyssinian War in 1867. Following the principles of non-interference in the native states and 'masterly inactivity'[15], he kept political and military turmoil under control, but his administration was continually plagued by budget deficits. This was a recurring source of anxiety for Lawrence, as was evident in his official memos and letters as well as in his private letters to Florence. Every decision he took, whether to reorganise the army, to improve the barracks, to introduce sanitary reforms, or to change the land tenure system in Oudh, was curtailed by lack of funds.

There is no doubt that Lawrence put army sanitary reform in India on a war footing, but it would be wrong to say that he was the father of Indian sanitary reforms. These started long before John Lawrence's viceroyalty, particularly in Calcutta, the capital, and in the Bengal Presidency. Later, similar reforms also took place in the Madras and Bombay Presidencies. Calcutta, however, was the main centre of British India and a large portion of the European population, official and non-official, lived there. There were powerful groups of British planters, landholders and traders in Calcutta, who controlled several associations such as the Indigo Planters' Association and newspapers such as *The Englishman*. These groups were vociferous and keenly motivated by self-interest. The British administration in India could not ignore them, as they had a powerful lobby in the British Parliament. As a result, any improvement introduced or any measures taken happened first in Calcutta where the Europeans lived. If they did not like the measures, the press would raise its voice and public meetings would overflow the town hall. Lawrence, in spite of his uncompromising attitude, could not altogether ignore the press.

Lawrence thoroughly disliked Calcutta. He did not like the people, he did not like the razzmatazz of the viceregal life and he did not like the climate: 'If I can only keep my health, I shall do very well. But Calcutta is a horrid place.'[16] At one stage he even threatened to quit unless Charles Wood, the Secretary of State, considered transferring the capital from Calcutta to Simla.[17] Similarly Florence, who never went to Calcutta, shared his views:

> 18 October 1865
> ... Anglo India has made its capital of a place where the Moguls used to send their state prisoners to die. And people fall ill in Calcutta and then say it's the climate. The R. Commission never told you all to live in Calcutta. But you abuse them for not having laid a sufficient stress on 'climatic influences'.[18]

There were, of course, plenty of reasons to dislike Calcutta in those days. It was situated in the marshy land of Lower Bengal on the bank of the Hooghly River with a huge salt-water lake to the east. The city was badly in need of a fresh water supply and proper drainage for all. The Europeans lived in the south of the city, in a reasonably clean enclave, whereas the Indians lived in the north with its open drains and complete lack of sanitation.[19] The city and its suburb were disease-ridden and miasmic. Cholera, malaria, hepatitis, fever, dysentery or typhoid – any disease that could flourish in waterlogged, insanitary conditions – was rife there. It was not surprising that the British soldiers died there at the rate of 69 per 1000 per year. There was no record of how many 'natives' died. The conditions in the mofussil or provincial areas in the Bengal Presidency were even worse. The infamous 'Burdwan fever' killed thousands of villagers and depopulated hundreds of villages. Apart from endemic fever, gastroenteritis and malaria, there were cholera and smallpox epidemics. Finally, there were biennial and triennial famines, droughts, floods, hurricanes and cyclones, which often completed the devastation and decimation of the population.

Attempts to improve the sanitary state of Calcutta and the suburbs started in the early days of the Company Raj. Records show that after 1704 there was some sort of rudimentary organisation to look after the town and the settlement. In 1803, Lord Wellesley, the Governor-General, initiated an organised effort to improve the sanitary conditions in the town. In 1817, a Lottery Committee was appointed to raise money for public works.[20] In 1836, the Government appointed a committee for the establishment of a Fever Hospital and for the management of Calcutta. This was at the initiative of Dr James Ranald Martin,[21] who later gave evidence to the Royal Commission and became a member of Florence's Sanitary Committee. The Fever Hospital Committee's voluminous reports pointed out that without improving the health and sanitation of the native quarters, the European areas could not be 'salubrious', an idea Florence emphasised in her *Observations*. This report led to the Municipal Act of 1856,[22] and schemes for water supply and a complete underground drainage system for Calcutta were sanctioned. This was the idea of a young town engineer called William Clark, who started to work on the scheme in 1859 and soon became acquainted with the authority of 'Miss Nightingale'. In 1861, the Seaton Karr Commission was appointed to look into 'the inefficient state of the municipal administration of Calcutta'.[23] In 1863, a Municipal Act was passed, putting the responsibility for the municipal administration of the town and suburbs into the hands of a corporation.[24] When Lawrence arrived in Calcutta, the city was already partly supplied with underground drainage, gaslight, metalled roads and scavenger carts.

Florence's groundwork for sanitary reforms

As soon as Lawrence arrived in India, he appointed Sanitary Commissions for Bengal, Madras and Bombay, as recommended by the Royal Commission. The order to set up such Commissions had already been sent by Charles Wood, the Secretary of State for India, on 15 August 1863. However, as noted earlier, the first Commission, in Bengal, was not appointed until Lawrence's arrival in Calcutta. The Commission was formed, as Florence wanted, with five members: a civilian as president, a secretary and three members from the judicial, military and engineering departments. The President of the Bengal Sanitary Commission was John Strachey, the Secretary was Dr J. Pattison Walker and the three members were Dr Gordon, Major Cooper, and Captain Williams. The Commission's function was partly consultative and partly administrative. Shortly afterwards, R.H. Ellis became the President of the Madras Sanitary Commission and Dr A.H. Leith of the Bombay Sanitary Commission.

John Strachey immediately approached the authorities in London for some ideas and suggestions as to the construction of barracks, hospitals and military buildings in India. He also asked advice for a new code of sanitary rules and regulations. In the meantime, Lawrence had already asked Florence for similar advice in his private letter. Now, being approached by the War Office, Florence started her work. In collaboration with Dr Sutherland, Dr Farr and the sanitary engineer Robert Rawlinson, she prepared a comprehensive list of suggestions that could be used to improve the sanitary conditions in the Indian barracks. This was later forwarded to India as *Suggestions ... prepared by the Barrack and Hospital Improvement Commission.*[25] In this Blue Book, recommendations and a scheme of work were put forward to tackle the sanitary situation of the Indian Army. It contained diagrams and plans with architectural details. The Barrack and Hospital Improvement Commission recommended that in order to improve the health of the army, it would be essential to introduce proper drainage, water supply, improved barrack accommodation and hospital facilities. The Commission also recommended similar improvements in the bazaars, native townships and dwellings surrounding the cantonment areas as well as the appointment of sanitary police and sanitary inspectors. Although the *Suggestions* was signed by the members of the Barrack and the Hospital Improvement Commission, Florence as usual wrote most of it. Bearing in mind the sensitivity of the military administrators, she also mentioned in the introduction that these suggestions were based on similar experience in Britain and the evidence gathered concerning conditions in India:

> They are in no sense intended to fetter the judgement of local authorities, either military or civil, in India. It would indeed be impossible, without careful local examination, to lay down precise measures and works required for abatement of causes of disease at any given station. Such an examination can be conducted only by persons on the spot; and suitable works can be best designed for India by engineers of Indian experience.[26]

It may seem that no time was wasted between Florence's preparing the *Suggestions* and sending it to India, but in practice it was just the opposite. Although she finished preparing the documents early in 1864, the

War Office delayed sending it to India for more than six months. Departmental rows broke out between the War Office and the India Office and no one would sign the documents.[27] In the meantime, in Calcutta, Lawrence became impatient waiting for the arrival of the *Suggestions*. He could not proceed with the construction of the barracks in case it was not what the Barracks and Hospital Improvement Commission had asked for. 'Our great want is your standard plans and rules,' he wrote to Florence from Simla on 6 May 1864, 'without which we are quite at sea, and so far from doing better than formerly I shall be in danger of doing worse.'[28]

As the War Office was delaying the matter unnecessarily the situation became extremely frustrating for Florence. She complained to her mentor, Dr John McNeill:

> 17 May 1864
>
> You will wish to hear how our sanitary affairs are going on.
>
> Sir John Lawrence's appointment gave us a most unexpected hold on India. He was so good as to see me during the short time between his appointment and departure. And he has carried out everything then suggested – a Commission of Health appointed for each Presidency, etc. etc.
>
> But few have had such extraordinary chances as I have had, twice a Secretary of State, and a Governor-General delivered, as it were into my hand. And few have seen such disappointment as I have … .
>
> And now no War Office has ever had such an opportunity with such a Governor-General actually asking, what would you have me do and has not used it.
>
> The instructions for his health commission, which he positively solicited, are still pending, as they were 5 months ago, and except my private suggestions he had nothing.[29]

While Florence tried to mobilise the War Office and the India Office to send the *Suggestions* quickly to India, she also tried to assure the officials in India that the *Suggestions* was on its way and there was no need to despair. 'They talk of Hindoos being slow,' she wrote to Pattison Walker, 'but War Offices and India Offices in England are slower. These plans are, however, nearly ready. And they will be sent out almost immediately with general suggestions.'[30] Then Florence did what she always did. She sent her private copies of the *Suggestions* to India without waiting for the Government to send them. By August 1864, the *Suggestions* was ready and signed, but not yet officially delivered to the Government of India. Florence again complained bitterly to McNeill:

> 4 August 1864
>
> … (Seven and a half months it has taken them to sign it, while Sir John Lawrence has been constantly writing home for it with his own hand.) It is expected that, in the course of the present century the I.O. will send it out to Sir John Lawrence officially. But in the meantime copies are speeding out to him direct from me by Her Majesty's Book Post.

You have no idea how heartbreaking much of my work is. Sidney Herbert has been dead three years on the 2nd, and these 3 years have been nothing but a slow undermining of all he has done. Sir John Lawrence writes discouraged; 'difficulties', he says to me (but this is quite confidential), he 'could scarcely understand or anticipate'. This I think breaks my heart more than anything.[31]

In the meantime, Florence sent a few more private copies to Dr Pattison Walker:

> August 10 1864
>
> These 'Suggestions' have now received the sanction of the Military Committee of the Council, and of the S. of S. of the India Office here. And they are about to be forwarded to you officially by the India Office.
>
> But our own people are so slow, that if I were not afraid of being profane, I should say that Sir John Lawrence is always a great deal more ready to hear than we are to pray. Therefore I forward you (by Book Post today) 4 more copies of the 'Suggestions' in case you may wish to apply them at once.[32]

The *Suggestions* was finally sent to India on 23 August 1864. As soon as it was received by the Government of India, the Sanitary Commission for Bengal started their work. They drew up a system of sanitary administration for the military cantonments in India, and then recommended a similar system for the civilian population. They proposed fourteen measures for civil sanitation that could be adopted by the Government of India. John Strachey emphasised in a letter the importance of sanitation for the native population in the midst of which the British soldiers lived: 'The interests of the community at large are as much concerned as those of the army.'[33] This simple fact, which Florence always pointed out, was of course understood and appreciated by everyone, but there was always a wide gulf between understanding and action. The official attitudes towards the two communities were poles apart. The gulf was not only of race and culture, but also between those who were governed and those who governed. This was most apparent in the contrast between what was done for the army and 'the community at large'.

As soon as Lawrence initiated the Sanitary Commission he launched himself into a pedantic confrontation with the Royal Commission at home in England. He was not happy about some of the things that were said in their report. As Governor-General of India, he accused the Commission of misrepresenting facts. He claimed that the situation in the Indian Army had changed, and the mortality rate of the European troops was no longer 69 per 1000 but 20 per 1000. As to the allegation in the Royal Commission's report that the barracks and cantonment sites were often chosen without care and were unhealthy, Lawrence claimed that 'such selections though made hurriedly at the end of a campaign during the last 25 years have, as a rule turned out well'.[34] Finally, the Government of India criticised the Royal Commission for not recognising the good work that had already been done in India to improve the health and general conditions of the soldiers.[35]

As a veteran 'Anglo-Indian', Lawrence had reasons to feel that the Royal Commission's report did not do justice to those who worked hard in India in difficult circumstances. During Lawrence's Punjab days, some sanitary measures had been adopted in the army barracks and prisons with the help of Dr Hathaway. Between 1859 and 1863, when the Royal Commission collected evidence and prepared their report, some army officers in India were busy putting their house in order. Lawrence was not alone in his protest. In October 1864, Dr A.H. Leith of the Bombay Sanitary Commission sent a similar protest to the Home Commission in London.[36]

Lawrence's despatch, sent on 8th December 1864, angered not only Florence, but other members of the Commission as well. Together with Lord Stanley, Dr Farr and Dr Sutherland, Florence prepared an answer, which was sent to Charles Wood, the Secretary of State, who in turn sent it to India as a despatch. In this, Florence pointed out that the Royal Commission's report was based on the evidence given by 48 people of the highest authority such as John Lawrence himself, Dr Ranald Martin, Dr Tulloch and Charles Trevelyan. The mortality statistics were compiled by two famous statisticians – Dr Farr and Dr Balgour. Evidence was sent by the Commanding Officers of various regiments that served in India. Dr Tulloch presented evidence from the documents of the War Office and the returns of the Royal Army in India during the years from 1817 to 1855. The annual casualty rolls of the East India Company's European troops were also taken into account. Therefore, what was reported was neither exaggeration nor untruth. Without surrendering the position held, Florence praised what had been achieved so far, especially after Lawrence's arrival in India, and said of the Royal Commission that ' ... while it was their painful duty to expose past and still existing abuses, they had the gratification of being able to point out remedies which, in their belief, were likely to prove effective and thus to hold out the prospect of a brighter future for the English soldiers in India.'[37]

Army sanitation

Throughout the years 1864 to 1869, considerable improvement and changes occurred in the barracks and cantonments in India. The initial sanitary reports of 1865, submitted in 1867, show that the work that John Lawrence's government planned for the soldiers was enormous, and it was believed that it would take four to five years to complete the task at an estimated cost of not less than £10 million, a great deal of money in 1865. The Government of India planned to build double-storeyed new barracks for the European soldiers with recreation rooms, day rooms and reading rooms, regimental workshops, gymnasia, swimming baths, cricket pitches and married quarters. There would be spacious sick-wards upstairs in the hospitals, the plans for which would be 'in all essential respects similar to those recommended by ... , the Barrack and Hospital Improvement Commission and especially by Miss Nightingale.'[38]

To improve sanitation in the barracks, a dry earth sewage system was introduced and drains were abolished. Barracks were provided with water filters and the soldiers' diet was improved. The issue of hard spirits from the mess hall was reduced and the illegal sale of alcohol and unwholesome food was banned in the cantonment areas. In order to check the spread of venereal disease among the soldiers, and two thirds of them were suffering from that, the Government of India passed a law, the Contagious Diseases Act of 1868, to control and inspect brothels in the neighbouring areas of the cantonments. The barracks and cantonment authorities were also asked to follow the preventive and precautionary measures prescribed by the Cholera Commission of 1861. Consequently, cholera epidemics among the soldiers were greatly reduced.

Great efforts were thus taken to protect British soldiers from an untimely death – and that paid dividends. The mortality rate for European soldiers was reduced from 69 per 1000 to 21.1 per 1000 in 1864. In 1865, however, it rose to 24.67 per 1000, then fell to 20.11 per 1000 in 1866. Subsequently, there was a gradual decrease and in 1911, a year after Florence's death, it went down to 5.04 per 1000.[39] John Lawrence kept his word to 'Miss Nightingale'. He introduced modern sanitary standards in the army barracks in India and set the sanitation ball rolling.

Dead bodies and burning *ghats*

One sanitary reform, achieved in Calcutta in 1864, of which Lawrence could have felt duly proud, was to put an end to throwing corpses into the Hooghly River.[40] There always was a feeling of revulsion among the European communities in India about the way Hindus cremated their dead in burning pyres. This was a custom that Hindus were not willing to give up in spite of the issues of 'conservancy' or 'decency' as Europeans saw it. Such cremation was mostly done on the bank of the Hooghly River in the north of Calcutta, where there were two burning *ghats* for that purpose.[41] If, however, some poor Hindus could not afford to pay for the pyre, they would throw the corpse into the river and hope for the

salvation of the departed soul. There was also the slaughtering and skinning of animals that went on by the river and the offal that was thrown
into it, including dead animals:

> ... more than 5000 corpses have been every year thrown from Calcutta
> into the river which supplies the greater part of the inhabitants with
> water for all domestic purposes, and which for several miles is covered
> with shipping as thickly as almost any river in the world. Fifteen
> hundred corpses have actually been thrown into the river in one year
> from the Government Hospitals alone. That such things should be true
> seems really to be hardly credible.[42]

Disposal of the dead was an important issue in Florence's mind. In her
Suggestions, she asked for a special investigation into this: 'The Officers
of Health should further examine into the state of burial-grounds,
burning-*ghats*, and generally into the manner of disposing of the dead,
and into the effect of this on public health.'[43] In her letter to Lawrence's
private secretary, Dr Hathaway, Florence also made a suggestion:

> 11 April 1864
> ... As regards the dead of Calcutta – they should either be disposed of
> below the city at high tide or in another branch of the river as
> suggested. There must be plenty of wood in the sunderbunds for
> cremation. And if you have to supply it to the poor, it would be
> nothing more than is done in England, where the parishes bury the
> dead poor at the public expense. Could you not contrive some
> machinery for stopping the dead descending from the Ganges, and
> either burning or burying them above Calcutta. Under a general
> system whereby the state found wood for the poor, the evils might
> perhaps best be remedied.[44]

The Municipal Act of 1863 was passed a little before Lawrence's arrival
as Viceroy. Empowered by this act, Cecil Beadon, the Lieutenant-
Governor of Bengal, wanted to put an immediate stop to the practice of
throwing corpses into the river. He also banned the skinning of animals
by the river bank. The sanitary report of 1864 mentioned that arrangements had been made to carry the offal and carcasses of animals daily
from Calcutta a distance of three miles and burn them.[45] Measures were
also taken to construct slaughterhouses in the suburbs of Calcutta
according to approved European standards. Beadon also wanted to ban
the practice of cremation within the limits of the town and on the banks of
the river on the grounds that the practice was 'a nuisance to a populous
neighbourhood'.[46]

> It is a reproach to a civilised Government that in a city like Calcutta,
> the practice of burning the dead at a public ghat, though sanctioned by
> long custom and possibly by religious sentiment, should have been

allowed to prevail so long to the detriment of general health of the community and public decency.[47]

Beadon asked the Justices of Peace for the Calcutta Municipal Corporation to consider the closure of two burning *ghats* on the grounds of conservation, and suggested that the *ghats* should be moved further south to Tolly's Nala, a side stream of the Hooghly, considered to be *Adi ganga*, or the original Ganges, by Hindus. At a meeting of the Corporation called on 7 March 1864, a heated debate took place among the members present, of which only a few were Indian. Ram Gopal Ghose presented the case for the Indians. In an eloquent and cogently argued speech, quoting from the Queen's Proclamation to honour the race, religion and culture of the Indians, he pointed out that the Government could not simply forbid the burning of bodies on the banks of the Hooghly alone; they would have to carry it out everywhere, all over India. Such an act would sow seeds of discontent everywhere throughout the Gangetic valley, the consequences of which would be unthinkable. 'Call it custom, or call it usage, or if you prefer, call it a superstitious prejudice, I submit you are equally bound to respect it.'[48]

As the Government through acts and pledges had made religious tolerance in India legally mandatory, they had no option but to concede. Besides, in 1864, the experience of the mutiny was still fresh in the mind of the British Government. Whatever it might do it could not possibly take the risk of firing another religious cartridge. The press was also against the Government's decision; *The Friend of India* wrote:

> The Hindoos have as much right to dispose of their dead in their own way as we have. The order which denies that right is most offensively worded – the language is needlessly strong and rude, and might become a fourth-rate newspaper, but is very much out of place when it proceeds from the Bengal Government, whose fault will it be if the order is understood to be a wholesale attack on the Hindoo faith. ... They have simply roused fanaticism of every shade over a simple question of sanitary reform, that might have been settled with the good will of all parties.[49]

Lawrence tried to evade his responsibility by reproaching Beadon,[50] but the reverberations of the debate reached the shores of England. Florence, in anxiety, wrote to Dr Pattison Walker on 23 April 1864:

> ... with regard to the very important question of disposing of the dead, would not the best plan be to confer with the different castes and ascertain what really constitutes religious burial. [This is what even old Indians at the India Office here seem not exactly to know.] Then the whole question would resolve itself into the best practicable and most wholesome method of doing the work.

> If cremation were adopted, suppose your Commission were to send a Minute home, desiring that the War and India Office Commission here [Barrack and Hospital Improvement Commission] should send them out the best plans of apparatus from this country, where the process has been applied to almost every purpose, except burning bodies [and even that has been considered].[51]

Lawrence was also criticised at home, in England, for interfering with the 'native' religious practices. Aggrieved, Lawrence wrote to Florence to give vent to his hurt feelings:

> Simlah 12 June 1864
>
> I am doing what I can to put things in order out here, but it is a very uphill task, and many influences here to be managed and overcome. I often think of the last visit I paid you before leaving England, and of your [ ] on that occasion. You will recollect how much I dwelt on the difficulties which met one on every side. These have been exemplified in a way I could scarcely understand or anticipate by the good folks [ ] of England really believing I had sanctioned an attack on the religion of the Hindoos, because I desired to improve the health of the people in Calcutta![52]

Meanwhile, the Justices of Peace for the Calcutta Municipal Corporation finally decided that the burning *ghats* should stay where they were, and instead of throwing paupers' dead bodies into the river the municipality should bear the cost of cremating them.

Florence's appreciation of Lawrence's work

Lawrence's speedy achievement in establishing Sanitary Commissions for the Bengal, Bombay and Madras Presidencies, and giving sanction to army sanitation projects, made Florence sing his praises loud and clear:

> 26 September 1864
>
> I always feel it a kind of presumption in me to write to you – and a kind of wonder at your permitting it. I always feel that you are the greatest figure in history, and yours the greatest work in history, in modern times. But that is my very reason. We have but one Sir John Lawrence.
>
> ... In India your work represents not only diminished Mortality, as with us, but increase of energy, increase of power, of the populations. I always feel as if God had said: mankind is to create mankind. In this sense, you are the greatest creator of mankind in modern history.
>
> ... you are conquering India anew by civilization, taking possession of the Empire for the first time by knowledge instead of by the sword.[53]

In her euphoria, Florence also rewrote the preface to her article, *How People May Live and Not Die in India*. The original version, which had been read at the Social Science Conference in Edinburgh in 1863, contained a scathing criticism of the British Government for failing to look after the welfare of the soldiers. Now she changed her preface to include Lawrence's praise.[54]

Loudly though she might have sung Lawrence's glory it did not, however, distract her from the essentials of the business at hand. The sanitary operation had just started, there was a long way to go, and she wanted to know what was happening. She wanted to know about 'the Police Hospitals (or state of Hospital accommodation) for sick poor at Calcutta', 'the condition of the Jails and Lunatic Asylums in India', 'the seamen at the Great Ports', the 'Sailor's Home', and what could be done about the inactivity of the Calcutta municipality. Not only did she want to know, she wanted to know before anyone else so that if necessary she could pre-empt her adversaries in the War and India Offices. Above all, she wanted the Sanitary Minutes of the Government of India to be referred back home, preferably to her. 'Would there be any impropriety in your Sanitary Commissions,' she wrote to Lawrence, 'sending copies of their printed Minutes to the Barrack and Hospital Improvement Commission here, through the India Office – merely for information?'[55]

Florence's intention was to get things done quickly, but bureaucratic wrangling would not let her. She had to manoeuvre intelligently and remove the obstacles to realise her objective. If a man did that it would have been called 'profound diplomacy', but in the case of a woman, she becomes the 'shrewd manipulator'.[56] In 1864, Florence was confined to her bed. The only contact she had with the outside world was through letters, memos and notes, and when people came to see her. Her strength came from her conviction and her determination to do the impossible. If Lawrence had had her conviction, things probably would have been different in India. But he believed in official procedures and rules and regulations, and certainly would not send papers home for Florence to look at first:

> Barrackpore
> 6 February, 1865
>
> I think that in your letter of 26th of Dec you attribute a great deal too much in the way of sanitary reform to me. I quite feel that I do not deserve these commendations, & that it is not honest in me accepting them in silence. All that I really do is to try and help you where I think that your plans & propositions are feasible. Few things are more difficult to accomplish in India than real sanitary improvements, & their expense is very large, & almost beyond our means. We must therefore of necessity progress but slowly.
>
> I am afraid you will consider me somewhat timid & perhaps even serving time but I do not like to answer your question regarding the papers which should go to the Sanitary Commission at home. All such papers should of course go home, but it must rest with the Secretary of State to say which should be sent on to the Sanitary Comm. I should be treading on his prerogative, if I did more.[57]

Female nursing in India

By the end of 1864, Lawrence decided to introduce female nursing to army hospitals. The system of using European women as nurses in Indian hospitals was already in its early stages. Female nurses had been employed on a limited scale in the General Hospital and the Medical College Hospital in Calcutta. The nurses working there were under the management of the Calcutta Hospital Nurses' Institution, which was a sort of Ladies' Committee initiated by Lady Charlotte Canning. This organisation was funded by private subscription with monthly donations from the Government and some income from private nursing. Only 27 female nurses were employed in 1864. Women nurses had also been introduced to Allahabad General Hospital in the autumn of 1858.[58]

The Sanitary Commission of Bengal now recommended that female nursing should be introduced to all large hospitals in India, including regimental hospitals, and for this the Supreme Government was willing to meet all expenses. The Commission sought 'to have the benefit of the advice of the highest living authority "Miss Nightingale"'.[59] Dr Pattison Walker, the Secretary of the Bengal Sanitary Commission, asked for Florence's help and advice:

> 21 November 1864
>
> Acknowledging you are the highest authority on the subject of hospital nursing, the Sanitary Commission for Bengal is solicitous of benefiting by any suggestions with which you might favour it, and I have therefore the honour, by the desire of the officiating President, to invite you to aid us with your esteemed advice ... .[60]

In 1864, Florence was truly 'the highest living authority on nursing'. No one else could provide better advice to the Government of India as to the organisation of female nursing. She had already founded a nurses' training school in St Thomas's Hospital in London. She had introduced trained nurses to hospitals in England. From her personal experience, she knew how appreciated female nursing had been by wounded soldiers in Crimea. Besides, she had written a number of articles, pamphlets and papers regarding nursing, and her work with two Royal Commissions made her the most knowledgeable person regarding the conditions in the barrack hospitals, both at home and abroad.

The conditions in the military hospitals in India and the standard of nursing there had occupied a large section of Florence's *Observations*.[61] At that time in India, there were neither trained orderlies nor female nurses in regimental hospitals, only a hospital surgeon and 'a plentiful supply of ward coolies'. In severe cases a comrade from the ranks provided care. The English soldiers never liked the ward coolies. 'The general impression as regards native attendants, is that they are in some sense kind, but as a rule very inattentive, and when there is any pressure of sick, they are "lazy" and apathetic, and the sick, it need hardly be said, neglected, and averse to be waited on by them.' The medical authorities, both civil and regimental, felt the need for trained nurses and orderlies in the hospitals. Doctors, and surgeons especially, were appreciative of the contribution already made by the female nurses in Calcutta and Allahabad General Hospitals.[62]

Female nursing was always a subject close to Florence's heart. She immediately set to work and submitted her first draft paper on nurses' training in India to her friend and ally Dr John McNeil:.

> 7 February 1865
> I always fly to you when in difficulty. I have had the most enormous order from Sir John Lawrence for Matrons and Nurses for India, of which a trifling item is
> 66 Head nurses
> 112 Assistants
> For Female Regimental Hospitals, these are already 'sanctioned'.
> He wishes, besides, to nurse all Military General Hospitals, of which 10 are named, and to establish Training Schools in all Civil Hospitals. He does not, like a wise man as he is, positively engage for or desire any particular specified thing. But he asks for advice on the largest scale and 'the Governor-General in Council' states that whatever expense is requisite must be met.
> (There is a private and most pressing invitation to me myself to go out.[63] If the doctor would give me six months there I would go. There is nothing in the whole world I should like better.)
> Of course, I lost no time in consulting our Training Schools as to what we could do. Of this more hereafter.
> But they in India ask for a printed paper. And I venture to submit to you the first rough Draft of one knowing that you, if you have time to glance at it, will help me more than any one … .[64]

McNeill was pleased to hear the news: 'It was pleasant to find that Sir John Lawrence is the man I believed him to be – to know that so much good is contemplated and likely to be accomplished … .' But he advised Florence against going to India: 'No wonder then that you should be ready to go to India six months if the Doctors would let you. But this is the true centre both of power and organization and even if the Doctors did not object to your going I must doubt whether at Calcutta you could do as much to promote the success of Sir John Lawrence's plans as you can do where you are.'[65]

However, training nurses was time-consuming, and there was already a great demand for them in Britain, which St Thomas's nursing school could hardly cope with. There was also a shortage of good matrons who would train the nurses. Above all, the cost of sending such nurses to India was something to consider. Florence understood all the difficulties but she was determined to help. She elaborated her plan to her journalist friend Harriet Martineau:

> 20 February 1865
>
> No, we don't aspire, altho' they are needed by the hundred and the thousand, to sending out nurses by the hundred or the thousand. What we want to do is to send a small staff of Trained Nurses and Trained Training Matrons, wherever we are asked, proper opportunities being guaranteed to us. But the material, especially for the latter [the Matrons] does not come to us.
>
> ... India would take from us any number of Trained Matrons and Nurses and pay highly. As it is ridiculous of us to think of sending them out by the shiploads, the more reason why we should send out a high stamp of Matrons and Head Nurses as nuclei, to form in India, a sort of 'Covenanted Service' of Nurses for India.[66]

In collaboration with Dr McNeill, Florence soon produced a comprehensive plan for female nursing for hospitals in India, which she sent to Dr Pattison Walker.

> It will be seen that our means of assisting India directly are at present very limited; and we are most anxious to send some seed. Good nursing does not grow of itself; it is the result of study, teaching, practice, ending in sound tradition which can be transferred elsewhere.[67]

In her letter she suggested training schools for nurses should be started either in England or in India, with competent teachers, and that ' ... if such teachers cannot at present be found in India they must be sent from England.' As far as matrons and head nurses were concerned, they should be trained in England for service in India. Nurses could be recruited in India, especially for the ranks:

> It is probable that in some parts of India persons, either born in this country or of English or Anglo-Indian parentage, and of suitable character and education, might desire to enter such a service, and some of them might rise in it. Such persons might be very useful from their knowledge of the native languages and of local circumstances of which persons arriving from England would necessarily be ignorant.[68]

At this stage Florence did not consider Indian women for nursing training. This was probably because at that time the upper and middle class Indian women were still not available as they were in *purdah*. Besides, nursing and midwifery was considered as a menial job and no middle class Indian woman would volunteer for that. Moreover, working class Indian women were mostly illiterate and did not have access to such training. Florence did not consider Eurasian women either, and kept her choice limited to Europeans only. There was a deep-rooted prejudice about the skill and efficiency of the Eurasian women among the Anglo-Indian community in

India and Florence was aware of that.[69] However, in twenty years time, Florence's attitude towards Indian nurses would completely change, to which we will return in due course.

Florence's letter to the Secretary of the Sanitary Commission of Bengal was accompanied by a list of suggestions of how to organise female nursing in Indian hospitals. It was written with the same foresight and sense of practicality as she had shown in her *Notes for Nursing* for nurses in England. The whole scheme was based on the rules and regulations that she and Mrs Wardroper, the matron of St Thomas's Hospital, had formulated for the employment and training of nurses in England. The list of suggestions contained almost every possible step in this matter, exhibiting her thoroughness and attention to detail; for example, how to recruit nurses, what the application form should look like, who would have the authority to discipline the nurses, how their day and night duties should be arranged and what sort of salaries they should get. The remuneration and prospects for such a service should be such that it would attract a 'competent and trustworthy class of people'.[70] Florence thought about every contingency that might occur, and her letter was an epitome of lateral thinking. She also suggested that female nursing should first be tried out in a single hospital as an experiment, and that hospital should be in Calcutta under the 'fostering care of the Governor-General'. 'If it succeeds,' she wrote, 'the experience acquired there will enable you to extend it, under less favourable circumstances, with a better prospect of success.'[71]

Florence spent a considerable time preparing these suggestions. She sent them with her cautionary statement that they were subject to modification in the Indian context if and when necessary. She also wrote that in St Thomas's and King's College training schools in London, 'every one is ready to help to the very utmost. If volunteers were asked for, we believe they could be had, but we have ventured only to raise the question with a view to its being considered by the authorities in India'.[72] She had to wait almost two years, however, before she knew the Government of India's decision on the fate of female nursing.

In the meantime, Mary Carpenter, the Unitarian philanthropist from Bristol, came to see Florence and tried to persuade her to send nurses to India: ' ... I am well aware that you have long turned your attention to India, and doubtless your efforts have produced valuable fruit. But I have seen no effort to train nurses in the hospitals etc.'[73] ' ... I consider that a few words from you will guide a movement which must spring up very soon for training nurses in India ... .'[74] Mary Carpenter had already visited India once and knew some prominent Indians in Bombay who were interested in introducing female nursing to Indian hospitals, more for the benefit of the women in *purdah* than for the general public.

Carpenter tried to impress upon Florence that if the Indian Government did not take action, 'the Natives' themselves would start such a venture. Carpenter's visit clearly made an impact on Florence as she recorded in her private notes:

> Miss Carpenter came here yesterday on very serious business. ... She says the Hospls are in most awful condition ... She described the state of the nursing in Bombay & Madras hospitals as something inconceivable ...
>
> She says if I wait for the action of the Government, I shall wait for ever. She wants to put me in communication with [ ] people at Madras & Bombay & she says if I don't do it, she shall ask Miss Edwards of Bristol.[75]

In the meantime, Carpenter wanted to introduce Florence to some Indian gentlemen who were in London and interested in female nursing. She wrote to Florence:

> 7 June 1867
> After my pleasant and I hope useful interview with you, I saw the Hindu and Parsee gentlemen who were very glad to hear of the possibility of a nurses' training institution at Bombay. They would much like to see that in London and would be most happy to have an interview on the subject with you before leaving for India.[76]

One of the Parsi gentlemen Mary Carpenter referred to was Dadabhai Naoroji, and the other was Naoroji Furdoonji. It is not clear whether Florence met Dadabhai Naoroji at that time.[77] In 1867 she was still relying on Government efforts to introduce female nursing, and did not want to get involved with private enterprise. There was also a tension between these two formidable women, which might have contributed to Florence's not following up Mary Carpenter's proposal directly. However, she was undoubtedly frustrated at the slow progress in introducing female nursing, and was still waiting for the final decision. On 10 June 1867, shortly after the meeting with Mary Carpenter, she wrote to Lawrence to emphasise her concerns:

> I have waited long and anxiously for some movement on your [ ] in India about trained nurses for your hospital.
>
> ... I do not wish to hurry you, & the reason of my writing at present is to say that events now a days appear to move so rapidly that established forms of procedure do not keep pace with them & I fear that unless we put the whole matter in train it will practically be taken out of our hands. I have just had such accounts of the nursing or rather nursing pretences of Indian hospitals as have shocked me greatly. I had no idea that things were in such a state. But they are described to me as they have been seen by intelligent & discerning eyes.
>
> ... the short and the long of it is that I have had a formal request made to me to place myself at the head of a nursing movement for India on the plea that it is no use to wait for the action of Government

and with a threat that if I dont [sic] act other parties will be found who will. It appears that not only Europeans but Native Indians would take the work up. Of course all I could do would be to offer them the same assistance that I have offered to you. That is, they to find the money & administer the funds and I to help in providing trained nurses and head nurses to train natives in India.

I have stated that at present I am in communication with you on the subject; and I am now very desirous that the work should be started as soon as possible, because it will take some time after I get your decision to prepare & send out the persons who are to take charge of the training.[78]

While Florence was conveying her thoughts to Lawrence about the use of private enterprise in introducing female nursing in India, the Governor-General in Council in India was taking a different decision. After deliberating for almost two years, Lawrence and his Council decided that the idea of female nursing in army hospitals was not a viable proposition after all, and should be shelved for the time being. What happened was that when Lawrence referred Florence's original scheme to his medical advisers, they elaborated on it and decided to apply it to seven hospitals at the same time. Consequently, the estimated cost was so high that the Governor-General in Council abandoned the idea of introducing the scheme and passed a resolution to that effect on 10 June 1867, the very day Florence wrote her letter. Two months later, Lawrence informed Florence:

> Simlah 16 August 1867
> Major Malleson tells me that he has sent to you a copy of the Resolution of the above date, deciding on not employing ladies or females of any kind in the Military Hospitals of India. We came to the conclusion after full enquiry and careful consideration.
>
> As to the General Hospitals in Calcutta, I enclose you a note which Dr Farquhar has prepared at my request. I do not think that we should import nurses from England for these Hospitals, and that those nurses who we procure in Calcutta do sufficiently well.
>
> I am afraid that this decision will not meet with your approval, but it has not been arrived at without due reflection. We have so little money in India, and so much to do with what we have that we have to weigh all proposals for additional outlay with a jealous eye.[79]

The note which Dr T. Farquhar prepared set out the reasons behind the decision. First, the military authorities did not think that there was enough work for such nurses to do, either in the female or male regimental hospitals. Second, the need for female nurses in the civil hospitals in Calcutta was satisfied by the Ladies' Committee that supplied them and the system did not cost the Government much, as it mostly ran on voluntary contributions. 'With this good work,' concluded Dr Farquhar, 'as long as it is carried on with heartiness, and comparative success, it would be surely unwise to interfere – should the Ladies however, find their difficulties, in procuring good nurses, increased, there is no source of help, to which the Government could turn for assistance, with greater confidence, than to Miss Nightingale.'[80] Lawrence was not willing to meet the expense of bringing matrons and head nurses from England to train nurses in India, and the possibility of retaining their services was also considered nil.

Lawrence's letter and Farquhar's note came to Florence as a bitter blow. She and Dr McNeill had both worked hard at the project of female nursing in India and both were upset by the decision. Florence wrote to McNeill, giving vent to her anger and frustration:

> You will see that they have constructed an immense scheme upon mine, or rather ours. And then they condemn this scheme, which is in some respects the opposite of mine, and call it mine, e.g., they propose to put nurses in all Regimental Hospitals, which is what we never would consent to, and never have consented to. And then they write that my scheme is condemned, when in fact I made no scheme, but simply pointed out methods of training and offered to begin ... .[81]

Florence had every reason to feel frustrated. She specifically asked Lawrence to start the project of female nursing on a small scale as an experiment, which would not have cost much. The Governor-General and his Council, however, planned it on a large scale, and then abandoned the project as 'too expensive'. In the meantime, she was planning to send a group of lady superintendents and head nurses to Sydney. She also received a similar application from the Madras Government and one from the Parsi community of Bombay. 'Now why cannot,' she asked, 'the Bengal people do the same, instead of making gigantic cut and dry systems on paper and then condemning them.'[82] Florence wanted to answer Lawrence's letter in strong language and asked for McNeill's advice. She felt the Government of India had made her work unnecessarily, and it had all been a 'fearful waste of time':

> I believe you hit on the right solution of the extraordinary proceeding, as it seems, of a Government taking and giving all this trouble not only to me, but to a number of its officers, for the pure pleasure of doing a great deal of utterly useless writing.
> But you can have no idea of the degree to which this has gone through in writing on the Public Health Service no one can tell, during these last 3½ years. I should think myself impatient and restless [though I am not a novice], did I not hear what Sir B. Frere says, which is much stronger than what I say. He thinks that this very kind of administration or no administration is bringing all Government in India to a deadlock.[83]

With McNeill's help, Florence made several drafts of a letter to Lawrence, and finally sent one on 26 September 1867:[84]

I have received your kind letter of August 16, with the M.S. note by Dr Farquhar enclosed; and I have also received from Major Malleson the voluminous printed papers, appended to the Resolutions of Government of June 10, deciding on not employing Female Nursing in the Military Hospitals in India.

I will now venture to remind you that I only gave my opinion when it was sought … .

The method proposed for giving effect to my recommendations & which the Government of India has rejected, was not mine – and indeed contained proposals to which I never could have agreed.

Having carefully perused the papers, M.S. & printed, which have been sent to me, I have not found in them anything that could lead me to change my opinions as to the benefits to be derived from Trained Nursing in India, & as to the manner in which it should have been introduced.

But it is for you, who are primarily responsible for the welfare of the British Army in India, and not for me, to determine what ought to be done with a view to improve the condition of the sick of that Army. If I can, at any future time, contribute to the promotion of so desirable an object, I shall be glad to have an opportunity of rendering such assistance as I may be able to give.[85]

Lawrence's answer was polite, but matter of fact:

Simlah 17 December 1867

… We move slowly out here, but we do move, which is something.

We do budget for such sanitary improvements as are resolved on; but as we have in the aggregate to spend something like 14 millions on Public Works of one kind or the other this year, exclusive of railways, we have not much to devote to sanitary matters. We shall however gradually do better.[86]

Although the idea of female nursing was abandoned by Lawrence, it was introduced on a limited scale shortly afterwards in the Madras Presidency by its Governor, Lord Napier. Napier was also a convert to Florence's sanitary cause. Before going to India, in 1866, he visited her and promised his sincere co-operation within the limits of his resources.[87] It was thus on Napier's initiative that female nursing and female medical education was established in Madras long before it was in Calcutta. Finally, in 1888, in Florence's lifetime, female nursing was introduced to Indian regimental hospitals by Lord Dufferin, then Viceroy of India, and his Commander-in-Chief Lord Roberts.[88] Both Roberts and Dufferin were eager to implement female nursing in the army hospitals. Roberts came to see Florence in 1885 before leaving for India. Florence was then 65 years old and still very keen on army health and welfare. One could easily imagine her joy and satisfaction when she heard of Roberts's and Dufferin's decision, and she played her usual role of advising and selecting the nurses.

Catherine Grace Loch, one of the two lady superintendents chosen, was trained in London's St Bartholomew's Hospital and was a highly efficient and dedicated person like Florence herself. She came to see Florence before leaving England and was in regular correspondence with her. She, like Florence, stressed the need for training hospital orderlies and, on her initiative, such a training scheme later started in the regimental hospitals in India. 'I have just been writing a long letter to Miss Nightingale in answer to one of hers,' Catherine Loch wrote to her sister from India on 28 January 1889. 'She does write such charming letters, full of encouragement and lots of questions about our work. When she wrote last it was immediately after receiving all the doctors' reports, etc., also several private and official letters to the India Office, which had all been sent for her to see, so you see, she is very well up in all that goes on.'[89] It is not surprising to find that even in 1889 Florence was still very much well informed about Indian hospitals. She had expended a great deal of effort to write *Suggestions on a System of Nursing for Hospitals in India* for John Lawrence.[90]

Doors versus windows

Female nursing was not the only dent in Florence's relationship with John Lawrence. Around this time, in 1867, another row brewed between them 'as to the relative merits of doors and windows for Barracks and Hospitals for European troops in India'.

As a staunch believer in the miasmic theory of disease, Florence was a great advocate of fresh air and proper ventilation. She once wrote in a private note, 'If for one fortnight from this time, I find all the doors shut and all the windows open (including those of the two water closets, which also must have the seats shut) I will give the servants a Doctor's fee, viz. one guinea.'[91] In her *Observations*, she spoke of bad ventilation in the army barracks and hospitals in India and, in her *Suggestions*, she recommended barrack and hospital construction with proper ventilation. Even when she spoke of 'native dwellings', she talked of 'overcrowding and bad ventilation'. However, she preferred windows rather than doors for ventilation. Therefore, when the Government of India substituted 'doors' for 'windows' in their barrack and hospital construction plan, a row broke out between her and Lawrence. 'A paper had been confidentially shown to me containing the decision of the Government of India on a subject which involves the entire question of Hospital and Barrack ventilation,' she wrote:

> I should have contented myself with reading & returning it, had it not been for the very serious nature of consequences likely to follow from it not only as regards the ventilation of the new Barracks but as regards the whole future of sanitary administration of India.[92]

The reason for her fury was that she thought that the new barracks would be ventilated only by doors, and to her an open door meant draughts, but if the doors were shut there would be neither light nor ventilation. The real reason, however, was that she did not like the way her *Suggestions* for barrack improvement had been flouted. If something as important as ventilation and light in the new barracks was ignored, there was no guarantee that other suggestions too would not be ignored, which meant the future of sanitary progress in India would be at risk.

Florence promptly accused Lawrence of ignoring the Royal Commission's recommendations. In reply, Lawrence wrote from Simla that he was taken aback by her letter: 'The fact is, that I was under the delusion that we were in essential acting in accordance with your views and those of the Royal Sanitary Commission.'[93] Lawrence also sent her a memorandum from Colonel Crommelin, who was in charge of barrack construction, and emphasised that he totally agreed with what Crommelin said. Crommelin, in his long explanatory note, tried to make Florence understand why 'doors' had been substituted for 'windows' and that she misunderstood the purpose of the Government of India's order. It was not a question of doors versus all other means of ventilation; sufficient measures were taken to provide other types of ventilation independently of open doors and windows. The Government of India did not ignore the Royal Commission's recommendations; they only substituted 'doors' for 'windows'. Crommelin's reply also referred to the introduction of the *Suggestions*, where it was said that suitable work for India could only be devised by engineers with Indian experience. Crommelin claimed that 'doors vs. windows' was such an issue that could only be settled by local authority with local experience, that is, the Government of India.

Crommelin's reply was obviously written under Lawrence's instruction. Lawrence was right to insist that the 'open' doors were a 'must' in the Indian climate, a point that Florence, never having been in India, failed to understand. There was, however, another issue that Florence raised and to which Lawrence objected. Florence had complained that nothing could get done in India without writing voluminous letters to various parties, some of who had no connection with the point at issue. She called this 'sanitary administration by universal suffrage' and for her 'doors vs. windows' was such an issue. It was referred to various authorities in India, military, medical and local, and finally sent back to London to the experts who had referred it in the first place and did not change their opinion. Florence knew that such procedures were time-consuming and only delayed action. Lawrence did not take this kindly and protested through Crommelin's memorandum that Florence was wrong to think that such matters were referred to a 'vote' in India:

> It is certainly usual for the Government of India to consult all local Governments and authorities regarding general measures in which they may be concerned and which they may have to carry out, and to collect evidence just in the same way that a special Commission would do.
>
> ... I believe that the course that has been followed in this respect has in a great degree assisted in the progress that has been made during the last few years with our barracks and hospitals and general sanitary measures.[94]

Lawrence's response through Crommelin's memorandum silenced Florence on the 'doors vs. windows' issue, but she was impatient and angry at the slow pace of sanitary progress in India. She wanted immediate action, but Lawrence sanctified the delay by reference to office procedures, and the government machinery moved at a snail's pace through volumes of memoranda and despatches. The year 1867 was one of disillusionment for Florence. About this time, as previously mentioned, her plan for female nursing in India had also been scrapped by the Governor-General in Council. The frustration Florence experienced at this time was evident in her letter to Dr John McNeill:

> Any foolscap is sent all over India to see how many fools heads it will fit. Of course, it fits a good many. Then there comes home to us a mass of papers, incredible to any who did not see them. And we have to answer them all seriously. Then answers come back from India. It is so easy to answer if you don't want to act. Latterly, a proposition about doors versus windows in Barracks was sent round to every British Department, 6 in every British Province in India, only one of which Departments knew anything about it at all, and then came home to us with the opinions of all the Cooks printed.[95]

Civil sanitation and John Lawrence

The euphoria with which Florence congratulated Lawrence in 1864 for 'bringing civilization to India' did not last long. By 1867, she realised that the Government of India would not win the race for sanitation, nor did they have the desire to win it. This was particularly true when the question of civil sanitation came up. The speed with which Lawrence launched his army sanitation project, in 1864, diminished considerably when the question of civil sanitation arose. Then finance, as usual, became his main concern.

John Strachey, the President of the Bengal Sanitary Commission, had recommended that there should be a comprehensive system of sanitary administration in the country. He suggested that there should be a central organisation with controlling power, funded by the Supreme Government and municipal boards at local level. These local boards and municipalities should look after the sanitary improvements in their own areas and provide their own funds.[96] In 1864 there were already some municipal organisations in existence in the mofussil towns of the Bengal Presidency. In addition, there were *Chowkeedari* Unions for policing, and the village *panchayat* system. The need was to revitalise them and introduce a better administrative system with proper funding. The local municipalities did not have the finance required to carry out sanitary reforms at local level. The only way to raise funds would have been to levy taxes, which the poor people of India could not have paid. Lawrence himself was very much against new taxes. The large-scale work in army barracks was going to cost him almost £10 000 000 and there were also war expenses. In May 1864, Lawrence wrote to Charles Wood, the Secretary of State: 'I greatly deprecate additional taxation, for I know the complications which are likely to ensue. The minds of the Natives are unsettled. It is far better to reduce expenditure than to increase taxation.'[97] Furthermore, he was unwilling to share his central funds with local governments for public works.

In October 1865, Lawrence sent a memorandum informing local Commissioners and the Lieutenant-Governor of Bengal that there was no prospect of funding civil sanitary measures from the general revenues. However, ' ... much may be done even without the special machinery proposed by the Sanitary Commission, if the local Government and Administrations can induce District Officers and their Assistants and also the Medical Officers of the Government to take a real interest in the matter and to obtain the co-operation of influential Natives.'[98] In response, the local administrators were unanimous in their opinion that without central funding, no sanitary reform was possible. The Commissioner of Rajshahi, for instance, claimed: 'In Bengalee villages, the clearing of jungle and filling up filthy holes will always be looked on as acts of oppression by the natives; for other improvements there will be a want of funds ... .' The Commissioner of Assam declared: 'No funds can be raised locally in Assam ... the Government should bear the cost of all sanitary improvements and employ its own officers.' The Commissioner of Chittagong wrote that: 'No comprehensive and really efficient system of sanitary administration can be established without cost to the Government.' The Lieutenant-Governor of Bengal also reacted in the same way, claiming that 'the want of local funds are at present effectual barriers to the adoption of the elaborate scheme of sanitation'.[99] The Government of India was only too happy to pass the bulk of the costs of civil sanitation to the district and local authorities, but none would take the responsibility. Between 1864 and 1869, many memoranda were written, despatches, minutes, reports and letters sent to and fro, new laws passed, and old laws changed. Lawrence tackled his financial difficulties by continuous reorganisation and curtailment of administrative expenses. One such effort was the reorganisation of the Sanitary Commission, much to the annoyance of Florence.

Restructuring the Sanitary Commission

In as early as 1865, Lawrence had wanted to restructure the Sanitary Commission on the grounds of expense, disagreement between departments and the questionable utility of some members. He wanted to replace the five-member Commission with two members to make it more compact.[100] In March 1866, Strachey vacated the post of President of the Sanitary Commission for Bengal, and Lawrence took the opportunity to reduce the salary of this post and implement his new proposals. He proposed that the Inspector-General of Prisons in each province should be the principal health officer, responsible for the supervision of sanitary improvements among the civilian population and advisor to local governments on sanitary matters. In addition, the civil surgeon in each district would be a health officer. In exceptional cases, a separate health officer could be appointed, depending on the availability of local funds. The Public Health Department would be under the Home Department of the Government of India.[101]

Lawrence's proposal that the Inspector-General of Prisons should be the principal health officer was met with strong disapproval. Since Indian prisons had an appalling mortality and sanitation record, doubt was expressed whether such a person was the right one for the post. The efficiency of the Indian prison authorities was already in question. Florence did not approve the idea at all as it was too far removed from what she envisaged.[102] To put the Sanitary Department under the jurisdiction of the prison authorities would mean the department would lose its importance and influence. Florence wanted the Sanitary and Public Health Department to be an independent body, not subsidiary to another department or a sub-head under the Prison Department.

In spite of Florence's disapproval, the Secretary of State approved Lawrence's proposal, but suggested that instead of the Inspector-General of Prisons, the Inspector-General of Hospitals should become the principal health officer. A compromise was reached in that specially selected medical officers were to be appointed as the principal health officers.[103] Florence was happy that the Public Health Department would not be swept aside under the carpet of the Prison Department, but she was far from satisfied about the way civil sanitation was going in India. She could see that more time and energy was spent on deciding the status and the responsibility of the sanitary administrators than on the question of sanitation itself; and when it came to report writing there was no end to that. Florence, a non-believer in the efficacy of report writing, had to read through masses of reports and sort them out.[104] But it was she who asked for annual sanitary reports from India, and the Government of India did its best to satisfy her. In spite of Lawrence's deficit budget, sanitary reports were scrupulously compiled to show the amount of work done or undertaken, and sent to the Secretary of State year after year. They always took a year or more to arrive in London. 'I consider it very desirable,' wrote Lord Argyle, the Secretary of State, 'that this Annual Report should, if possible, be sent to this country at an earlier date than at present is the case … .'[105] The annual sanitary reports were not only late, but also bulky. 'An octavo volume is not wanted,' commented Florence, 'a dozen lines may be made to hold much wisdom.'[106]

It would appear from such voluminous reports that enormous changes were taking place both in the military and in the civil sectors. In the case of the army, changes did happen; the new barracks were built. But essential progress, both in the military and public sectors, was very slow for Florence's liking. Apart from annual sanitary reports, volumes were produced on theoretical discussion of the origins and possible causes of cholera, and they were done at Government expense.[107] Such discussion and analysis contributed almost nothing to the sanitation problems of the country. Florence caused some anger when she asked a few pertinent questions:

> … has not some uncertainty been thrown over the whole subject of Indian public health question by intruding into it theories of disease? … The public health question is not a question of opinion. It is a question
> 1) of what is fact,
> 2) of what is practicable and expedient …
>   However ingenious a theory may be, the wisest thing is never to expend public money on it.
>   Are not the theories we have had, too, not of Indian produce, but of European manufacture? And have they in reality anything whatever to do with public health problem?[108]

Florence was criticised for her outspoken comments, but she was not to be thwarted.[109] She wanted action, not reports: 'Reports are not self-executive'.

Sanitary progress in India

In 1870, Florence wrote a paper called *The Sanitary Progress in India*, which was included in the official Blue Book containing sanitary reports from the last phase of Lawrence's administration in India. In this paper she openly criticised the Government of India for failing to follow the Royal Commission's recommendations. She said changes and more changes were made, and the work done so far was 'to a large extent inspectional and reporting'. However, out of such voluminous reporting one truth came out:

> The Inspectors are gradually bringing to light what is the real social state of the mass of the Indian peoples.
> Their reports have removed any veil of romance woven by poets over Hindoostan and show us peoples to be numbered by tens of millions living under social and domestic conditions quite other than paradisiacal.[110]

She criticised the costly way the barracks had been built without paying attention to proper drainage or clean drinking water: 'No improvement in barrack or hospital accommodation will compensate for a malarious subsoil, or for bad water.' Besides, the new barracks were not free from diseases as they were still close to unhealthy 'native towns and bazaars' and 'there is no reference to cleansing measures for filthy native towns near stations except such reference as shows how excessively filthy these towns are'.[111] In short, Florence refused to be hoodwinked by the glitter of the new barracks.

Florence also criticised the Government for not applying sanitary engineering skills that were already familiar in the West to improve public health in India. She wanted progress reports from all over India, from stations, cities and villages. She could also see through the verbosity of the reports how little had actually been done for the general public: 'However extensive the stational improvements required may be, they are but a small matter when compared with those required for the civil population.'[112] She admitted that some sanitary progress was made in the big cities like Calcutta or Bombay, but the villages were still in dire need of reform where the Government's initiative did not reach, a claim supported by the evidence in the annual sanitary reports.

The sanitary reports of 1864–66 showed that the actual achievement in the case of civil sanitation was lamentably poor. Most of the essential reforms were either 'under consideration' or 'recommended', and did not quite materialise even two or three years later. For instance, the establishment of local boards in all districts of Bengal was recommended by the Sanitary Commission in 1864, but was still 'under consideration' when the report was submitted in 1867.[113] Funding was always a problem. Florence's comment was that the Government spent its funds on unnecessarily costly plans, 'Hence there is no balance at the Bankers'.[114] Registration of deaths of civilians was recommended by the Royal Commission, but the 1865 report spoke of 'no reliable results' being obtained.[115] In the meantime, the mortality rate of the civilian population in Calcutta alone reached 58.08 per 1000 due to preventable diseases such as cholera, smallpox and Bengal fever. Sickness and mortality in jails were as high as before. In 1864, a special committee was appointed to report on the appalling condition of Indian jails, and the committee reported 'overcrowding' and 'insanitary conditions' as the main causes of high mortality. There was some success in vaccinating the population, but the 1865 sanitary report also spoke of the public lack of faith in vaccination as it had little effect in checking smallpox.[116]

The Royal Commission had recommended a pure water supply for the barracks and for civilians. The barracks were provided with filters, and a number of reports were written on potable and aerated water. But no provision was made for the public, whose water continued to be drawn from polluted ponds, tanks and rivers. When it came to the conservancy of Calcutta, the capital of British India, the reports showed a deplorable state of affairs. A Calcutta municipality report, included in the 1869–70 sanitary reports, stated that 'pipe sewers had been laid in some of the narrowest and most tortuous lanes of Calcutta, without the slightest damage to any house or property'. But the so-called drainage project of Calcutta, which Florence called 'an unnecessary costly project', remained confined to within a 2–3 mile radius of the European settlement.[117]

In 1865, the sanitary report 'promised' to supply clean water for the town, and the work started. But in 1866 the authorities decided that another two or three years would be needed for the project. By 1870, the reports proudly said that '137 miles of pipe started to distribute 6,000,000 gallons of pure water to the households',[118] but it was not every household that got the water. It remained limited to within one particular area of the town, as Beverley's Census Report of 1876 showed:

> In the European Quarter perhaps little now remains to be done; this portion of Calcutta indeed may fitly compare with any other city in the world; but the native town is still far from being in that state in which one desires to see it. There are large areas as yet unconnected with main drainage; the cleansing of bustees and the filling up of filthy tanks will be a work of time and patience. The supply of filtered water needs enlargement and extension.[119]

There was no denying that between 1864 and 1869 some sanitary progress was made, but, as Florence said, it was without any overall planning or proper organisation and was mostly in the towns. From 1865 onwards, Lawrence repeatedly wrote to Florence about the difficulties of raising taxes to fund sanitary reforms, particularly, as he thought, in the context of people's lack of interest in the matter. He often blamed lack of funds, and more often the people of India:

> Calcutta, 7 April 1865
> The Natives themselves are ignorant, apathetic, or even opposed to sanitary improvements. They will not expend money on such matters. We have no easy job in raising the necessary income to meet the public demands. Then the very reforms in themselves are difficult of execution, & are very expensive. The Water supply for Calcutta alone is

estimated to cost 3/4 of a million, & though Calcutta is the richest place in India, the inhabitants grudge the expense, & I doubt much if they will consent to incur it.[120]

Simlah, 17 June 1866

The drainage of cities & above all of the Country generally, must take time, & must depend on our carrying the people with us, & inducing them to make improvements. But the people of India though docile and intelligent in many ways are *[fond]* of their money, & have no idea of the real *[return]* of sanitary arrangements. The great body also of them are really very poor, and nothing is more disliked by all classes than new modes of taxation ... .[121]

Simlah, 9 July 1867

We are however on the whole doing as much as our means will admit. For military [ ] our machinery is very complete, in other places it is in truth defective. But we have not the means of doing much more at any rate for the present. Until the people are better educated, & until they see the results of such as are taking place, they will not appreciate the work; & above all they are not willing to be taxed further for such purposes ... .[122]

Lawrence was not alone. Many British administrators were convinced that Indians were apathetic towards sanitary improvements; some thought they were hostile and uncooperative.[123] The argument that rich influential Indians were not interested was repeatedly presented in the sanitary reports.[124] The fantasy that Indians were indifferent towards sanitation was contagious. It even affected Florence to some extent:

Habits of cleanliness are inculcated as matters of doctrine by most Eastern religions. Have these habits degenerated in India into mere 'washing of cups and platters and such like things', while all the weightier precepts of the laws of health are passed over with little or no notice?[125]

However, from the very beginning, Florence resisted succumbing to the theory of Indian apathy towards sanitary reforms and using this as an excuse for inaction. She wrote to Lawrence:

It is a mistake to suppose that Natives take little interest or would object to pay for improvements.

The cost of the sanitary service at Conjeveram was gladly borne by the Natives. The Pilgrims at Hurdwar gladly paid a tax to help the expenses incurred by Government for the Sanitary arrangements and one of the officials argued from this that they would gladly pay for the town & village improvements.

Lately a severe Marsh fever due to want of drainage & bad agriculture broke out in villages near Calcutta. It was pointed out to some of them that they might improve the public health by cultivating the ground. They *[snatched]* at the idea & began immediately ... .

Then she added the inevitable comment which probably annoyed the Government to no small extent:

> The Central government must lead the way in all these improvements.
> [ ] there is nothing to show that the Natives would not readily follow.[126]

In spite of Florence's trust in the natives' common sense, she was unable to move the British administrators. Here she faced a rigid colonial attitude, which predefined a problem as unsolvable and then declared that it was impossible to solve. The question of sanitary reform in India was not only a question of funding; it was also a question of beliefs, not of the Indians but of the British administrators. A fantasy was certainly woven about Indian attitudes towards sanitation and it was not at all difficult to understand why. It was easy for the British administrators to say that the people for whom the reforms were meant did not care for them, and then do nothing or the absolute minimum. How easy it was for them to argue that the reforms were for the people and they had to pay for it. As the people could not pay, the status quo was maintained. On the other hand, ample funds were found, more than £10 000 000, for building barracks, as well as to pay for the Abyssinian War. It was of little importance if the peasant in Bengal did not have clean water to drink.

The attitude of the British administrators prompted Florence to look deeper into the problem of sanitation and reform in India: 'For many ages the people of India were more civilized and more clean than almost any nations of Europe. Why has this condition of things been in later days reversed?'[127] As she went along with her reform work, she found her answer. She realised that the problem was not one but had many facets. She began to appreciate the complexity of the problem and the wider context in which the question of sanitation should be placed and judged. This appreciation ultimately led her to inquire into the conditions of the Indian peasants, promote land reforms and to establish direct contact with Indians. This was also the time when she started to realise that the focus of any reform should be the ordinary people of India. She began to appreciate the significant role the Indians themselves could play in this matter. They needed education and social awareness. They should be made aware of their rights and obligations. Although she was critical of the British policies in India, she had the foresight to understand that a lot depended on the people of the country:

> Bearing in mind the enormous number of villages in India, we may say that no Government could do the work required, although no people could do it without the Government. All that a Government can do in such circumstances is to collect and make known the facts; to bring them and their consequences to the knowledge of the people; to help them with advice and encourage their efforts by examples. But the people themselves will have to do the work.[128]

In the context of official apathy, the concept of 'self-help' became the key issue in her mind and it remained a focal point right up to the end of her involvement with India. She realised that sanitary reform in India could not be achieved simply through governmental effort. The Government would be either indifferent or hesitant to spend money, or nestle in the cosiness of its own theory of Indian apathy. It was the people themselves who would have to take an active interest in their problems, and she with them.

Towards the end of 1868, Lawrence wrote a couple of letters to her from Simla:

> 25 October 1868
> I am doing what I can to press forward sanitary matters, & will I hope leave them in a tolerably satisfactory state. The matter requires delicate handling in every way. ... It may seem to you, with your great earnestness & [ ] of mind, that we are doing very little, & yet in truth, I already see great improvements, more particularly in the Military Cantonments, & doubtless we shall from year to year do better. But the extension of sanitary arrangements through the Country & among the people must be a matter of time, especially if we wish to carry them with us.[129]

> 31 October 1868
> ... I believe that we are now doing as much as it is safe & reasonable to do in the way of sanitary arrangements. After a while we may go faster. But at present we have to show the people, & make them understand that they will benefit by the changes we may introduce. The money question is also a great difficulty. The [ ] funds which are raised from the masses of the people are very limited, & are already overburdened, & the Govt. have no surplus reserves, & cannot raise more by new taxation without causing discontent. The rich people like to keep their riches for themselves, to spend them on their own pleasures.
> I am sorry that I can do more [sic] in furtherance of your objects & wishes. My time in India is now limited to a few weeks; & I am looking out with pleasure to the prospect of being soon relieved ... .[130]

In 1869, John Lawrence left India and returned to England bearing the gift of a Tibetan goat hair shawl for Florence.[131] The admiration Florence had for him, however, never died out and she kept regular contact with him until his death. She often exchanged ideas, sought his advice or sent her papers to him for his opinion, and their relationship remained amicable. Although often in disagreement with Lawrence's ideas, she appreciated the difficulties he was working under and never held him personally responsible for the slow progress of sanitary reform in India.

One must not forget that Florence did not have any official position. She was not even a member of the Royal Commission that was investigating the sanitary state of the army in India. It was easy for her to write open letters, ask controversial questions and give expression to her doubts and indignation without fearing censorship or reprimand. But John Lawrence, the Viceroy and the Governor-General of India, was not in the same position. He could only write what was officially judicious. It was easy for her to become impatient and impetuous, but Lawrence had to tread cautiously and the five years' tenure of a Viceroy was not long enough to clean the Augean stable that was India.

Florence continued her sanitary efforts long after Lawrence left India. She pursued her dream with equal vigour through other Viceroys like Mayo, Ripon, Dufferin and Lansdowne. Many a Governor-General or Governor came and went, many a Secretary of State disagreed with her. But the 'Governess of the Governors' kept up her vigil and never allowed her grip to slacken. However, at the end of Lawrence's administration, for the first time in her life she reached out to the Indians.

Notes

1. Cook (1913), vol. 2, p. 169.
2. Cook (1913), vol. 2, p. 178.
3. Cook (1913), vol. 2, p. 43.
4. Bosworth Smith, R. (1883), *Life of Lord Lawrence*, London: Smith, Elder and Co., vol. 2, p. 394.
5. Saint Clair, W. (1887), *John Laird Mair Lawrence, A Viceroy of India*, London: Hamilton, Adams & Co., p. 2. 'In court he was very irascible and violent to natives, often excessively passionate; a blow, a kick and native language, that was not choice, were liberally bestowed in every direction. Shokiram, the native judicial officer, often had to replace his turban on his head' (p. 44).
6. FN to Martineau, 2 February 1865, in Cook (1913), vol. 2, p. 43.
7. Cook (1913), vol. 2, p. 43.
8. FN (1879b), 'A missionary health officer in India', *Good Words*, August, pp. 639–40.
9. FN to Gladstone, 6 July 1879, BL Add. Mss 44460, fols 234–236.
10. Smith (1982), p. 121.
11. FN to Lawrence 10 July 1863, BL Add. Mss 45777, fol. 20.
12. Hathaway to FN, 31 August 1864, BL Add. Mss 45782, fols 156–161.
13. FN to Farr, 10 December 1863, BL Add. Mss 43399, fols 159–160.
14. Lawrence to FN, 5 February 1864, BL Add. Mss 45777, fol. 31.
15. A phrase used by John Willie in an article, 'The foreign policy of Sir John Lawrence', *Edinburgh Review*, January 1867, no. 255, p. 44. The phrase became instantly popular.
16. Lawrence to Eastwick, 18 February 1864, in Bosworth Smith (1883), vol. 2, p. 416.
17. Lawrence to Wood, 30 May 1864, in Bosworth Smith (1883), vol. 2, p. 424.
18. FN to Pattison Walker, 18 October 1865, BL Add. Mss 45781, fol. 296. Apparently Job Charnok, the British trader, was at liberty to choose either side of the River Hooghly for his trading post, but chose the east, the most unhealthy place, for the sake of a shady tree. See Martin, J.R. (1847), *A Brief Topographical and Historical Notice of Calcutta with a Sketch of the Rise and Progress of Sanitary Improvement in the East Indies*, London, pp. 6–10.

19. Beverley, H. (1876), *Report on the Census of the Town of Calcutta, 1876 taken on the 6th April 1876*, Calcutta: Bengal Secretariat Press, p. 39. This report gives a vivid picture of how Calcutta was then and previously.
20. Beverley (1876), p. 46.
21. Beverley (1876), p. 50.
22. Beverley (1876), p. 53.
23. Government of Bengal, Judicial Proceedings, Nos 55–60, Nov. 1861, pp. 63–123; Report of the Seaton Karr Commission, 1861, WBSA.
24. Beverley (1876), p. 53.
25. FN (1864a), *Suggestions in Regard to Sanitary Works Required for Improving Indian Stations; Prepared by the Barrack and Hospital Improvement Commission, 1 July 1864*, London, Eyre and Spottiswoode (hereafter referred to as *Suggestions*). The *Suggestions* in printed form were signed by Richard Airey, Quartermaster General and President; Douglas Galton, Assistant Under-Secretary of State for War; John Sutherland; T.G. Logan, Inspector-General of Hospitals; Edward Belfield, Deputy Director of Works, War Office; Proby T. Cautley, Member of the Council of India; J. Ranald Martin; Robert Rawlinson, Local Government Act Office; J.J. Frederick, Secretary, Barrack and Hospital Improvement Commission, War Office. There was no mention of Florence's name although it was mainly her work.
26. FN (1864a), Introduction, p. 1.
27. Cook (1913), vol. 2, pp. 46–9.
28. Lawrence to FN, 6 May 1864, BL Add. Mss 45777, fol. 33.
29. FN to McNeill, 17 May 1864, BL Add. Mss 45768, fol. 183.
30. FN to Pattison Walker, 3 June 1864, BL Add. Mss 45781, fols 219–222.
31. FN to McNeill, 4 August 1864, BL Add. Mss 45768, fol. 188.
32. FN to Pattison Walker, 10 August 1864, BL Add. Mss 45781, fol. 233.
33. Government of Bengal, Judicial Proceedings, Nos 36–38, October 1865, p. 31; Strachey, to the Secretary, Government of India, 5 September 1864, WBSA.
34. Government of India, Military Despatch, No. 103, 8 March 1864, *Memorandum, Sanitary Measures*, 1867, p. 2.
35. *Memorandum, Sanitary Measures*, 1867, p. 4.
36. Leith (1864).
37. *Memorandum, Sanitary Measures*, 1867, pp. 4–9.
38. *Memorandum, Sanitary Measures*, 1867, p. 37.
39. Cook (1913), vol. 2, p. 55, footnote.
40. *Memorandum, Sanitary Measures*, 1867, p. 41.
41. Nimtala Ghat and Kashimitra's Ghat. They still exist.
42. Minute by John Strachey, 5 March 1864, in Buckland, C.E. (1901), *Bengal under the Lieutenant Governors*, Calcutta, S.K. Lahiri & Co., vol. 1, p. 281.
43. FN (1864a), p. 34.
44. FN to Hathaway, 11 April 1864, BL Add. Mss 45782, fol. 142.
45. *Memorandum, Sanitary Measures*, 1867, p. 41.
46. Buckland (1901), vol. 1, p. 297.
47. *Proceedings of an Ordinary Meeting of the Municipal Corporation of Calcutta held on 7 March 1864*, Calcutta 1864, p. 1.
48. *Proceedings of an Ordinary Meeting of the Municipal Corporation of Calcutta held on 7 March 1864*, Calcutta 1864, pp. 5–7. Ram Gopal Ghose was a leading member of the British Indian Association and a great orator. Apparently he was approached by Iswarchandra Vidyasagar to

oppose the Government proposal – see Mitra, S.C. (1902), *Iswar Chandra Vidyasagar, a Story of his Life and Work*, Calcutta: New Bengal Press, pp. 493–495.

49. *Proceedings of an Ordinary Meeting of the Municipal Corporation of Calcutta held on 7 March 1864*, Calcutta 1864, pp. 13–14.
50. Lawrence Papers, BL OIOC, Mss Eur F90/51.
51. FN to Pattison Walker, 23 April 1864, BL Add. Mss 45781, fol. 219. By 'old Indians' she meant retired British administrators.
52. Lawrence to FN, 12 June 1864, BL Add. Mss 45777, fol. 35.
53. FN to Lawrence, 26 September 1864, BL Add. Mss. 45777, fols 49–53.
54. FN (1864b), pp. vi, 18.
55. FN to Lawrence, 26 September 1864, BL Add. Mss. 45777, fols 49–53; FN to Lawrence, 26 December 1864, BL Add. Mss 45777, fol. 58.
56. Smith (1982), p. 114.
57. Lawrence to FN, 6 February 1865, BL Add. Mss 45777, fol. 62.
58. Extracts from the *Proceedings of the Sanitary Commission for Bengal*, 7 July 1864, Minute No. 151, BL Add. Mss 45781, fol. 252.
59. *Memorandum, Sanitary Measures*, 1867, pp. 38–9.
60. Pattison Walker to FN, 21 November 1864, BL Add. Mss 45781, fol. 251.
61. FN (1863a), pp. 52–63.
62. The report submitted by Dr Chevers of Calcutta Medical College, 1863, p. 9, BL Add. Mss 45781, fol. 255.
63. She probably meant the invitation she received from Dr Pattison Walker. There was no evidence of John Lawrence ever inviting her to India. Dr Farquhar did once sarcastically suggest that she should pay 'a flying visit' to India – see 'Dr. T. Farquhar's Notes on Miss Nightingale's questions relative to sanitation in Algeria and India', Calcutta, 20 April 1867, p. 1, BL, Miscellaneous Papers of Florence Nightingale, 1866–1879.
64. FN to McNeill, 7 February 1865, BL Add. Mss 45768, fols 190–192.
65. McNeill to FN, 9 February 1865, BL Add. Mss 45768, fols 193–4.
66. FN to Martineau, 20 February 1865, BL Add. Mss 45788, fols 284–90.
67. FN to Pattison Walker, 24 February 1865, in FN (1865), *Suggestions on a System of Nursing for Hospitals in India*, London: Eyre and Spottiswoode, p. 4; BL, Miscellaneous papers of Florence Nightingale, 1866–1879.
68. FN (1865), p. 1.
69. 'Eurasian women as a class be most unacceptable as nurses to European soldiers. Because they are lazy, have native servants waiting on them – have no physical stamina of body and mind – to lift a heavy European soldier. They do not know what a real day's work means.' Memorandum of the Controller General of Military Expenditure, Military No. 47, 11 April 1867, BL Add. Mss 45782, fols 249–251.
70. FN (1865), p. 1.
71. FN (1865), p. 2.
72. FN (1865), p. 10.
73. Carpenter to FN, undated, BL Add. Mss 45789, fol. 104.
74. Carpenter to FN, 6 June 1867, BL Add. Mss 45789, fol. 108.
75. FN, private notes, 7 June 1867, BL Add. Mss 45752, fol. 177.
76. Carpenter to FN, 7 June 1867, BL Add. Mss 45789, fol. 108.
77. In July 1867 Dadabhai Naoroji wrote to Florence to arrange a meeting between her and Naoroji Furdoonji, and her private notes contain the names of four Indian men with comments about their interest in female

nursing, but there is no confirmation that she actually met them. See Naoroji to FN, 29 July 1867, BL Add. Mss 45800, fols 129–130, and fols 131–132.

78. FN to Lawrence, 10 June 1867, BL Add. Mss 45777, fol. 97, draft.
79. Lawrence to FN, 16 August 1867, BL Add. Mss 45777, fol. 120.
80. BL Add. Mss 45777, fol. 123. This was probably enclosed with Lawrence's letter (BL Add. Mss 45777, fol. 120).
81. FN to McNeill, 10 September 1867, BL Add. Mss 45768, fol. 202.
82. FN to McNeill, 10 September 1867, BL Add. Mss 45768, fol. 204.
83. FN to McNeill, 21 September 1867, BL Add. Mss 45768, fol. 216.
84. It is not clear from her private papers which version she finally sent to Lawrence. Vicinus and Nergaard quoted one that seems to be a draft letter (Vicinus and Nergaard, 1989, pp. 292–4; see also BL Add. Mss 45777, fols 149–155). The letter that this author thinks Florence finally wrote to Lawrence (BL Add. Mss 45777, fols 156–157, 26 September 1867) was much subdued in tone and lacked the thunder and lightning of the letter Vicinus and Nergaard quoted.
85. FN to Lawrence, 26 September 1867, BL Add. Mss 45777, fols 156–7. Fol. 158 gives an alternative ending: '... I shall be glad to have an opportunity of rendering such assistance as I may be able to give believing, as I still do, that much progress in the right direction might be made at a cost so moderate that the Govt. of New South Wales have not hesitated to undertake it – and the Parsees of Bombay are desirous to pursue a similar course.'
86. Lawrence to FN, 17 December 1867, BL Add. Mss 45777, fol. 159.
87. Cook (1913), vol. 2, p. 112.
88. Lord Roberts (1905), 'Introduction', in Bradshaw, A.P. (ed.), *Catherine Grace Loch – a Memoir*, London: Henry Frowde, pp. v–vii.
89. Bradshaw (1905), p. 36.
90. FN (1865). Although female nursing in army hospitals in India started in 1888, it was still in its infancy. The system expanded during the 1914–18 World War, when Indian nurses were recruited for the first time. They were attached to the Queen Alexandra's Military Nursing Service for India. The service was made permanent in 1926, and in 1927 received the title of Indian Military Nursing Service [I.M.N.S.]. In 1923, the Lady Reading Fund provided the opportunity for the first two Indian nurses, Miss Lavinia Mewa and Miss Yaula Bukhsh to go to England for training. The service really came of age during the Second World War of 1939–45, to meet the demands of the Eastern War Front, and emerged as a properly constituted service. See: Wilkinson, A. (1958), *A Brief History of Nursing in India and Pakistan*, Madras: Trained Nurses Association, p. 11.
91. FN, Private note, 16 August 1860, BL Add. Mss 43402, fols 189–190.
92. FN to Lawrence, 26 June 1867, BL Add. Mss 45777, fols 98–101; also FN to Stanley, 10 July 1867, BL Add. Mss 45781, fol. 198, draft.
93. Lawrence to FN, 3 August 1867, BL Add. Mss 45777, fol. 106.
94. Memorandum, Crommelin to Blanc, no date, copy to FN, BL Add. Mss, 45777, fols 110–119.
95. FN to McNeill, BL Add. Mss 45768, fol. 217.
96. Government of Bengal, Judicial Proceedings, Nos 37–38, October 1865; Strachey to the Secretary, Government of India, Home Dept., No. 620, 5 September 1864, WBSA.
97. Bosworth Smith (1883), vol. 2, p. 461.

98. Government of Bengal, Judicial Proceedings, No. 36, 11 October 1865, p. 31. The lack of cooperation from 'influential Natives' was always a sore point for Lawrence's administration.

99. Government of Bengal, Judicial Proceedings, Nos 145–146, 9 November 1865, pp. 108–16.

100. Military Despatch, Nos 462–63, 21 October 1865, *Memorandum, Sanitary Measures*, 1867, p. 9.

101. Government of India, Home Public Proceedings, A88-101, 9 January 1866, Consultation Paper.

102. Cook (1913), vol. 2, pp. 153–154.

103. *Memorandum, Sanitary Measures*, 1867, p. 12.

104. 'Her constant work was in helping to edit and in contributing to the Annual Blue-Book containing reports of "measures adopted for sanitary improvements in India ... ".' Cook (1913), vol. 2, pp. 179–80.

105. *Report on Measures Adopted for Sanitary Improvements in India, from June 1869 to June 1870*, 1870, London, Eyre & Spottiswoode, p. 3 (hereafter referred to as *Report, Sanitary Measures*).

106. FN (1869–70), 'Remarks on the present aspect of the sanitary improvement in British India', *Report, Sanitary Measures in India, 1869–70*, p. 45.

107. For example, Dr J.L. Bryden, *A Report on Epidemic Cholera in the Bengal Presidency, 1866–68, with its relation to Cholera of Previous Epidemics*; Dr J. Murray, *A Report on the Treatment of Epidemic Cholera, 1869*; Dr S.C. Townsend, *A Report on the Cholera Epidemic in the Central Provinces and Berars, India, 1868*, referred to in *Report, Sanitary Measures, 1869–1870*, pp. 270–272.

108. *Report, Sanitary Measures, 1869–70*, p. 42.

109. Dr W.C. Maclean criticised Florence's remark in *The Lancet*, 29 October 1870, vol. 2, pp. 618–9, in a letter to the Editor, entitled 'Miss Nightingale on theories of disease'. In reply, Florence wrote: 'My object was, as I need scarcely say, purely practical. It was to deprecate a tendency complained by all of late years (this very complaint came to me from India) viz. the tendency to base sanitary proceedings on theory.' (FN (1870a), *The Lancet*, 19 November 1870, vol. 2, p. 725).

110. FN (1869–70), p. 40.

111. FN (1869–70), p. 43.

112. FN (1869–70), p. 44.

113. *Memorandum, Sanitary Measures*, 1867, p. 39.

114. FN (1869–70), p. 42.

115. *Memorandum, Sanitary Measures*, 1867, p. 47.

116. *Memorandum, Sanitary Measures*, 1867, p. 48.

117. Beverley (1876), p. 60.

118. 'Administrative Report of the Calcutta Municipality for 1869', submitted by Stuart Hogg, the Chairman of the Justices, in *Report, Sanitary Measures, 1869–70*, p. 20.

119. Beverley (1876), p. 60.

120. Lawrence to FN, 7 April 1865, BL Add. Mss 45777, fol. 64.

121. Lawrence to FN, 17 June 1866, BL Add. Mss 45777, fol. 79.

122. Lawrence to FN, 9 July 1867, BL Add. Mss 45777, fol. 102.

123. Dr E. Goodeve, 'Sketch of sanitary progress in the Bengal Presidency previous to 1864', in *Memorandum, Sanitary Measures*, 1867, pp. 18–31; Government of Bengal, Judicial Proceedings, Nos 37–38, October 1865;

Strachey to the Secretary, Government of India, Home Dept. No. 620, 5 September 1864, WBSA.
124. *Memorandum, Sanitary Measures*, 1867, p. 49.
125. FN (1869–70), p. 41.
126. FN to Lawrence, undated, 1868, BL Add. Mss 45777, fol. 172, draft.
127. FN (1869–70), p. 41.
128. FN (1869–70), p. 45.
129. Lawrence to FN, 25 October 1868, BL Add. Mss 45777, fol. 170.
130. Lawrence to FN, 31 October 1868, BL Add. Mss 45777, fol. 174.
131. Lawrence to FN, 28 February 1869, BL Add. Mss 45777, fol. 194.

CHAPTER FOUR

A Brief Encounter:
Florence Nightingale and the
Bengal Social Science Association

In 1870, Florence Nightingale was made an honorary member of the Bengal Social Science Association in Calcutta and she responded graciously:

May 25th, 1870

Gentlemen,

Pray accept my warmest thanks and tender them for me to the Bengal Social Science Association for the honor you have done me in electing me an honorary member.

Believe me it touches me the more deeply the less I am able to express it. For I am a poor woman, overwhelmed with business and illness.

For eleven years past, what little I could do for India, for the conditions on which the Eternal has made to depend the lives and health and social happiness of men, as well Native as European, has been the constant object of my thoughts by day and my thoughts by night.

These efforts on my part have been humble indeed, but if the Almighty has blessed them in some measure, and if they are recognised by you who have done so much more in the same cause – and we in England also recognise with admiration and shame that the native gentlemen of India have sometimes surpassed ourselves in progress in this matter – it is a source of the deepest thankfulness. May increasing success be granted!

The task before India is truly gigantic. But men have done greater things than these. What would you say, for instance, to draining and cultivating the great endemic area of cholera from the sea-board to the Himalaya where the waters of the Berhampootra, the Ganges, and the Mahunuddy flow out, and from which endemic district, the great epidemics of cholera rush forth to afflict the world! But a girdle has been put round the world by the electric cable, and the day may come when you will have brought the waters of this great area under some control, when you will have drained its marshes, cultivated its rich provinces, exchanged its desolating malaria for useful production, and possibly extinguished cholera as a scourge for mankind, as well as for India. If the work is a work for heroes, it is the more worthy of your ambition.[1]

It was not at all surprising that the Bengal Social Science Association elected Florence as an honorary member. Although she did not have direct contact with the Association prior to her nomination as a member, she was already well known in India among the educated class and the

British administrators for her work with the Royal Commission, and the sanitary changes she started to initiate through the Government for the army and the civilians. Besides, her paper, *How People May Live and Not Die in India*, presented at the Edinburgh Social Science Conference in 1863, was read by many. The founding members of the Association's Council, such as Dr T. Farquhar, A. Mackenzie and W. Clark, were well aware of Miss Nightingale's interest in sanitary reforms as in the past they had often been in her firing line. Most important of all, John Lawrence, the Viceroy, whose blessings the Association certainly received, was a personal friend of Florence, though by 1870 Lawrence had already left India.

The Bengal Social Science Association

The Bengal Social Science Association was the brainchild of Mary Carpenter and Rev. James Long. Mary Carpenter, the Unitarian philanthropist who made her name in the fields of reformatory schools, prison discipline, juvenile welfare and rehabilitation of young female prisoners in India, was associated with the British Social Science Association and knew Florence well, and so did Long. Mary Carpenter had been inspired by Raja Ram Mohun Roy, the social reformer and liberal thinker in India, and she wanted to go to India 'to benefit his country'.[2] Long was a more colourful person than Mary Carpenter and his contribution in founding the Bengal Social Science Association is often overlooked. Long, a Christian philanthropist with an egalitarian mind, was deeply interested in the structure and problems of Indian society and in its reformation.[3] As a missionary, he worked among the down and outcast of Bengali society and spread vernacular education in the rural areas of Bengal. Long was well versed in Sanskrit, Bengali proverbs and Russian history, but above all he was a social scientist. He regularly delivered thought-provoking lectures on a variety of subjects, which were published in various societies' journals and transactions in Calcutta.

As mentioned earlier, nineteenth-century Bengal was a breeding ground of societies, associations and organisations. They were the natural offspring of English education introduced in Bengal and the social awareness that was developing, partly because of such education and partly from the influence of people like Ram Mohun Roy, Iswarchandra Vidyasagar and Henry Louis Derozio. The societies and associations that grew in Bengal were the places where the English-educated elite of Bengali society, 'the enlightened Baboos', met liberal British administrators and missionary philanthropists for cultural exchanges. The Bengal Social Science Association was one such society. It had been preceded by quite a few other societies and associations which had performed more or less similar functions. James Long was involved with a number of them. He was often their president or vice-president, and a regular contributor. The proceedings of one such society, the Family Literary Club of Burrabazar in Calcutta, shows that on 27 April 1866, Long delivered a lecture on the British Social Science Association and the advantage of having a similar association in Bengal.[4] Pointing at the social discrepancies and depravity in India, Long told his audience:

> The great object of social science is to bridge over the chasm that divides the different classes of society.
> We believe that an association of this kind might have a very happy effect tending to harmonize some of the jarring elements which exist in this country.[5]

Long was always interested in the advancement of social science in India. When in England, he attended the British Social Science Conference and was appreciative of the contributions made by Florence and Mary Carpenter in this field. He wanted the elite of Bengal to understand the value of such voluntary associations, the changes they could bring and the pressure they could exert. Like Florence, Long was dissatisfied with the higher education system that existed in Bengal. As noted earlier, the system of education introduced by the British in India was totally alien to the masses of India. It remained confined within the urban upper class of society and hardly reached the rural population. The Indians welcomed such education, as it was modern, secular and more progressive than the indigenous system. Besides, it created job opportunities for them in the administration. But even for the urban Indians, the education system was foreign, both in its contents and in its medium of instruction. It was not easy for most of them to master the English language, and studying English literature, history or geography had no bearing on their social or private life. Inevitably, it led to a lot of cramming; swallowing a culture without digesting it. For Long, it was all 'book cram': 'It has been said, whether in jest or earnest, that educated natives are books in breeches, they have eyes but see not, ears but hear not, and their knowledge is acquired by book cram, it is lost when the book is shut.'[6]

Long felt that the study of social science, being essentially observational and data-based research, could remove this stigma of 'book cram' from Bengal's higher education system. It would also introduce positive and constructive thinking. It should be noted that Long was also a founding member of the Bethune Society, which was formed in 1851 to commemorate the work of John Drinkwater Bethune, an educationist, social reformer and founder of the Calcutta Female School for Girls, later renamed as Bethune School.[7] Long was in charge of the sociological section of the Bethune Society, which was already acting as a social science association in Bengal. Why Long felt the need for another society is not very clear, but the Bengal Social Science Association, which was formed in 1867, was very similar in structure, purpose and membership to that of the Bethune Society.

Long was not alone; some other enlightened Bengalis also felt the need for a forum where the social problems of Indian society could be discussed and debated in a secular and constructive way. Many of them came forward to help Long, among whom were people like Iswarchandra Vidyasagar, Keshab Chandra Sen and Peary Chund Mitra. Long, however, had a problem, or so it seemed. In order to found the Bengal Social Science Association, he needed the active co-operation and the membership of a group of influential people, both British and Indian, who would be willing to devote their time and energy to it. The initiative should actually be seen to have come from a person who would be above local politics of that time. But Long himself was not in a position to do so as he had already blotted his copybook by associating himself with the Indigo Revolt.[8]

Long had not actively been involved in the peasants' agitation against the Indigo planters, but he helped to publish the English translation of a Bengali play called *Nil Durpan*.[9] The play was written by a famous Bengal playwright, Dinobandhu Mitra, and was based on events of the Indigo Revolt in Bengal. Long was prosecuted for 'libel' and was fined and jailed for a month.[10] His fine was paid off by another famous Bengali writer, Kaliprasanna Sinha. Long's trial and subsequent fine and imprisonment made him unpopular among the European indigo planters and landholders, but, surprisingly, not so much among the British administrators. It certainly made him very popular in Bengal as a supporter of the peasants' cause against the planters. The Bengal Social Science Association came into being almost six years after this incident, but it is safe to assume that with such a stigma attached to his reputation, Long probably felt that he was in no position to secure the support of the influential British administrators, landholders and the elite of the Bengali society. Consequently, though the idea of a social science association in Bengal was Long's, Mary Carpenter stole the limelight.[11]

Before leaving England, Mary Carpenter was in touch with Florence asking for an introduction to John Lawrence and Florence agreed to give her such a reference:

> I am so overwhelmed with business – that – being also entirely a prisoner to my bed from incurable illness – I have not been able to answer your kind note of July 21 as yet.
>
> I thank you much for your generous offer of doing anything for me in India – but I will not trouble you – your time is already too well filled.
>
> I shall write to Sir John Lawrence (he is at Simlah, you know, till October or November) by this or next mail; and on your account. You have probably already introduction to him.
>
> But I enclose an envelope, which will serve as an additional one (to connect you with what I shall write).[12]

John Lawrence, then Viceroy, however, did not feel very elated about the prospect of Carpenter's arrival in India:

> If Miss Carpenter comes on my way [ ] I will look after her and take care of her. I much fear that she will [ ] find that, she cannot do much good. How anybody, in a brief visit, without any knowledge of the people or of their language can hope to gain any influence over their minds, passes my comprehension.[13]

Mary Carpenter was not a person to feel daunted by her lack of knowledge of the country, the people or their language. On her first visit to India, she arrived in Bombay on 5 September 1866 and reached Calcutta by 20 November 1866. She arrived by boat from Madras, but her friends did not turn up to receive her and she did not have their address. After spending the first night with an English couple who came to her rescue, she went to stay with 'Dr Chuckerbutty in Chowranghee'.[14] 'Dr Chuckerbutty' was Dr S. Goodeve Chuckerbutty, who later became an active member of the Bengal Social Science Association. Mary Carpenter had to wait to become the Viceroy's guest, as 'the court had not yet returned to Calcutta having been detained in the north by the great durbar'.[15] In the meantime, she met various famous Bengalis and Europeans such as Keshab Chandra Sen, Kissory Chund Mitra, Rev. Alexander Duff and the well-known Bengali reformer Iswarchandra Vidyasagar. The latter was at the time Secretary of the Bethune School and accompanied Carpenter on her visit to the school.[16] She also spent a day in the country with Long, who took her to see a village school, a *zemindar*'s house and a temple of Kali, which was to her 'all noise and confusion'.[17] Finally, she saw the Lawrences: 'On Saturday, December 1, the Governor General arrived. On the Monday following I was summoned to his presence. The interview was followed by a kind invitation from Lady Lawrence to take up my abode at Government House.'[18]

John Lawrence not only provided Carpenter with a luxurious residence for the remainder of her stay in Calcutta, he also gave her the opportunity to meet 'native' gentlemen in the Government House. In those days, it was a rare privilege. Lawrence also made it easy for her to visit institutions such as lunatic asylums, prisons and schools. Carpenter was so pleased with her achievements that she wrote an enthusiastic letter to Florence, telling her that she was well received by Lawrence and that women should now come and work in India:

> My own going out [as a] reformer [ ], and unconnected with any society, has produced a great effect on native gentlemen and ladies, and I have been received by them with the greatest kindness and gratitude. I shall henceforth do all in my power for India ... .[19]

Thus acclimatising herself and making full use of the opportunities presented to her, Mary Carpenter gave lectures, petitioned the Government for various reforms and finally lent a hand to Long in materialising his dream.

The birth of the Bengal Social Science Association was quite smooth, with the blessings of the Governor-General and the Lieutenant-Governor of Bengal. After an initial meeting, held at the Asiatic Society on 27 December 1866, a working committee was formed and later, on 22 January 1867, the Association's Council was established at a general meeting in Metcalfe Hall in Calcutta. W.S. Seaton Karr was the President, and H. Beverley and Peary Chund Mitra were joint Secretaries. The object of the Association was laid down as 'to promote the development of social progress in the presidency of Bengal by uniting European and natives of all classes in the collection, arrangement and classification of facts bearing on the social, intellectual and moral condition of the people'.[20] It was clear from the start that the Association was going to be a learned society, a forum for discussion and exchange of views. Many of the societies and associations formed a decade later in Bengal and elsewhere in India, took on a political colour, but the Bengal Social Science Association never did. It was not intended to be 'an agitating body'.[21]

After a somewhat shaky start, the Association continued to function for more than ten years. It organised various meetings where papers were read and debated, and the Association's transactions were published and distributed. The Indian members of the Association were mostly from the English-educated middle class whereas the British members were mainly the administrators of the Raj. The Association enjoyed not only the patronage of the successive viceroys and Lieutenant-Governors, but also of the Bishop of Calcutta and the Maharaja of Burdwan. In 1869, two years after its formation, three honorary members were elected in the Annual Meeting of the Association. They were Mary Carpenter, Justice J.B. Phear, the ex-president of the Association, and Florence Nightingale.[22]

One can easily assume that Florence was delighted with this recognition. For some time she had been trying to open a dialogue with leading members of the Indian community. Her friends and associates, such as Sir Bartle Frere and Mary Carpenter, were eager to introduce Florence to various renowned Indians. By the end of 1869, Florence was also feeling frustrated about her Indian work. Her mainstay John Lawrence had by then retired from the viceroyalty and returned to England. In the meantime, her influence in the War Office and the India Office had started to decline. The sanitary work in India as recommended by the Royal Commission was virtually at a standstill through general inertia and lack of funds, particularly in the public sector. At this time she almost lost her faith in governmental initiative and came to realise that she might not be able to make further progress through official channels. She started to despair that her Indian venture perhaps was a failure. Hope now only lay in bringing new converts into the fold. The honorary membership of the Bengal Social Science Association opened up that chance. She probably thought that her work would be easier if she could convert the educated Indians to her ways of thinking and encourage them to follow her guidance about health and sanitation.

Before accepting membership of the Association, Florence took time to deliberate and, as she always did, discussed the proposal with Sir Bartle Frere and Dr Sutherland:

> I have received the enclosed letter from Calcutta, I shall have to reply and [ ] the honour they have done me, but I want to do more than this, if you will be so kind as to tell what you think about the Association at Calcutta and whether from your knowledge any good would be likely to come of my [profound] letter to them.
>
>   It occurred to me that if they were people who were moving in the right direction, that I might use the opportunity for writing such a letter on the [ ] of the health question in India, especially with reference to what people might do for themselves ... .[23]

Florence's idea was that she would not only accept the honorary membership, but, as she said in her letter to Frere, she would also use the opportunity to pass on her ideas about sanitation to the members of the Association. The ideas of 'self-help', 'co-operation' and 'what could be done by the people themselves' were in the forefront of her mind, as official help was not forthcoming as expected. Florence at the time had just finished writing a sanitary memorandum for Lord Mayo, the successor to John Lawrence.[24] She wanted to incorporate some of the ideas mentioned in her memorandum in her suggestions to the members of the Association with the idea that her letter could be turned into a sanitary primer and translated into Indian languages. This idea had originally been suggested by her devoted friend, Benjamin Jowett. When Mary Carpenter was in India enjoying public adulation, Jowett wrote to Florence:

> ... I read today your pamphlet about India again. Did it ever occur to you that you might write a short pamphlet or tract somewhat similar to that for the natives in India and get it translated. That would be a curious & interesting thing to do. When I saw the other day the account of Miss Carpenter in India (a terrible woman but much to be respected), I felt half sorry that it was not you. They would have worshipped you like a divinity.[25]

In response to Florence's letter, Frere supplied the information she was looking for:

> The Bengal Social Science Association has been started since I left Calcutta – by Mr Justice Phear and other good men – and Miss

Carpenter and others have told me it is doing good work in the way of stimulating enquiry ... .

Mr Beverley, I believe is a young civilian – Registrar General of Bengal. Peary Chand Mittra is a very leading Baboo. The Association, from what I have seen of their Proceedings, seems a working body – and quite worthy the honour of having your letter addressed to them.[26]

Florence, however, had not waited for Frere's reply, but had accepted honorary membership of the Association on 25 May 1870. Acknowledging receipt of a copy of the Association's transactions at the same time, she added: 'I may perhaps be permitted to offer the Society a few books, and as my small contribution for a membership I do so much prize, shall beg to enclose Rs. 100 to your order.'[27]

After accepting the membership, Florence did not want to remain 'a sleeping partner'. She wanted to write to the members of the Association, to tell them how to cope with their own sanitary problems. She asked Dr Sutherland to prepare a draft of a letter containing her ideas and he readily obliged.[28] When the letter was ready she sent it first to Frere for his comments. Frere was ecstatic and described the letter as a 'cordial or tonic':

May I keep a copy to have it translated in Maharatti and Guzerratti. The Calcutta people will have it translated well in Bengali through which you may speak to 40 millions. The Maharatti speaking people are probably barely 20 millions and the Guzerratti perhaps 10 or 12, but they are most advanced in intelligence and most likely to profit of any nations in India – and many more will follow. There will, I am sure, be no expense in translating. It will be a labour of love to thousands.[29]

Frere confessed that he had already tried to translate it into Marathi and he would inform Dr Hewlett to look out for its appearance in Calcutta or to get it translated at Bombay into Western languages. The stage was thus set for a brief encounter.

Between May and June 1870, Florence wrote two letters to the Secretaries of the Bengal Social Science Association. The first was her letter of acceptance for the honorary membership. The second was a covering letter, accompanied by a long address to the members of the Association. In this address, she placed in front of them what she called 'the social aspect of the Indian public health problem'. She wanted ordinary Indians to appreciate it so that they would co-operate with the Government to protect their own health. She was also aware that her ideas written in English might not reach ordinary people of India for whom they were meant:

I must therefore trust to your good offices to make what I write known to those of your members who do not speak and read English in Calcutta and the North West Provinces. And I trust that I have your permission to do the same through other friends in other parts of India. I shall send a copy of my little paper enclosed, with your leave, to Lord Mayo who sometimes honours me with his commands on these subjects.

... P.S. I feel most unwilling that my ignorance of Indian languages should entail any expense on the funds of the Association. I should esteem it a favour if you would allow me to contribute further for the translation, if you do have it translated, of this humble little paper not only, but of other and better works which you translate for the peoples of India.[30]

Florence's address to the members of the Association was immediately published in the Association's transactions with the assurance from the President, Norman Chevers, that it would be translated into vernacular languages:

It is fortunate that the noble address to the people of India, upon the subject of sanitation, which we now print has been received from its distinguished author just in time for publication in this volume of the society's Transactions. Our Assistant Secretary, babu Nilmoney Dey has undertaken to translate it into Bengali, and it shall be the care of our council to provide that, before the end of the year, its wise and benevolent monitions shall have free means of access to every native homestead, at least in this Presidency of India.[31]

Florence's address to the members of the BSSA

Florence's address to the members in general was perhaps one of her best letters ever written to the Indians. It not only showed her skill in letter writing and mastery of language, but also her tact, which she applied to win the hearts of the 'Indian gentlemen'.

The best proof of my feeling of gratitude for the honour which you the Bengal Social Science Association, have offered me of membership is to show myself a member in spirit, however unworthy, and to send a few remarks, however imperfect, with reference to the health and habits of the great population inhabiting India which you know and understand so much better than I do. Yet still, I shall succeed, if in nothing else, in showing the great interest now felt by public opinion in England in the health, both physical and social, of those to whom we truly feel as to our beloved brother and sister subjects in India.[32]

Referring to the Royal Commission's inquiry, she pointed out that the sanitation problem in India was so 'immeasurable' and 'important' that it could only be compared with 'your own great Himalayas as you come nearer to them'. At that time, Florence was most concerned about two things: one, cholera epidemics in India and the possibility of their spreading beyond the boundaries of India; two, the habits of Indians, which perpetuated unhealthy conditions.

Like many others in the West, Florence also thought that cholera's natural home was in the marshy land of south-east Asia and that it spread in insanitary conditions. In 1867, the International Sanitary Congress had been held in Constantinople, which mentioned India as the birthplace of Asiatic cholera and blamed the British authorities in India for not doing enough to prevent its spread. There was also profound ignorance about the origin, cause and spread of the disease, and academic debate on cholera was rife in the Western world.[33] One contributor in this debate was Dr J.L. Bryden, who produced several reports on Asiatic cholera from his experience in India as a civil surgeon. Particularly relevant was his report on epidemic cholera in Bengal, published in 1869 in Calcutta, which had been included in the official sanitary reports.[34] He believed that cholera was an airborne disease and could spread like seeds in certain environmental conditions, with the climate of lower Bengal being a perfect place for this to happen. Referring to his report, Florence remarked:

> ... in all probability this pestilence is a product of the wet, drying-up sub-soil of Lower Bengal – that the whole country, including the deltas of Mahanuddy, the Hooghly, and the Brahmapootra, is the perennial home of cholera – and that this is mainly due to neglected subsoil and unused riches.[35]

Dr Bryden was not alone; as we have seen in the previous chapter, many British medical experts in India produced a number of reports on cholera at Government expense, which were included in the sanitary reports. They all had their own ideas about how cholera spread and more or less all believed in the non-contagion theory of cholera. They shared the view that cholera was endemic in lower Bengal and that the insanitary habits of Indians helped to spread the disease. It was still thirteen years before Robert Koch's arrival in Calcutta with the German Cholera Mission in 1883 and the subsequent discovery of the causal relationship between *Comma bacillus* and cholera.

Like the so-called 'endemic nature' of cholera in lower Bengal, the idea of Indians' 'insanitary habits' was also endemic in the minds of the British administrators and medical men. Indians were 'filthy' with 'unclean habits', they 'drank foul water' in the name of religion and they washed, bathed and drank from the same tank.[36] The administrators were afraid that one day, cholera would spread in Europe from India and destroy the Western world. Florence, however much she disapproved of theorising in sanitation, shared their fear:

> ... the Almighty has linked together the happiness and misery of all His creatures, that we in Europe can almost anticipate whether Indian cholera is to devastate the nations of the West by the number of people who are dying of it in Lower Bengal.

She put the fate of the people of the East and West together and asserted that the failure of one to act would mean failure and misery for the other:

> If we are not linked together in love and mutual help, as we ought to be, of our own free will, we shall be linked together by mutual injury, the injury inflicted by mutual ignorance and prejudice. ...

She saw the future advance of Indian social civilisation as being dependent on the eradication of cholera. If it could be done, 'the whole tone of Indian domestic and social habits will be raised in the process'. The task, in her opinion, was so enormous that both the Government and the people would have to work together

> Part of it is so great that it is quite beyond the power of private individuals to do it. But another part of it is so great that no Government can do it, and it *can* be done by the people acting for their own safety.[37]

The Government could possibly provide for public works such as drainage, clean water, better agriculture and regulation of rivers, but the people themselves would have to attend to their environmental cleanliness as well. For total sanitary improvements, it was as essential as public works. 'There is work enough to spare for both Government and people in the enormous field of usefulness.'[38] She asked the members to help shape public opinion about sanitary cleanliness, public and private, and to help to train 'tens of millions of Indians in improved domestic and social habits'.

As noted earlier, Florence was a staunch believer in the miasmic theory of disease. She retained this belief right up to the end of her life and refused to support wholeheartedly the contagion theory of disease. Consequently, environmental sanitation was important to her, which she emphasised to the members of the Bengal Social Science Association in no uncertain terms. In a very carefully worded passage, Florence drew the attention of the members of the Association to the so-called insanitary habits of Indians. She was quite aware that this was a sensitive area and should be handled carefully. She asked the members 'to look into the lowest habits of great people in order ... to awaken them to a sense of the injury they are doing themselves and the good they might do themselves'.[39]

One might ask here what were these 'habits' of the Indians? She made a list.[40] Accumulated household filth was left unremoved; private tanks were used for all purposes – drinking, bathing and washing clothes; religious ideas which favoured drinking foul water; in many houses the privy and the drinking well were too close; blood and offal of slaughtered animals were left within the dwelling places; many homes were overcrowded and the air poisonous; surface drains intended to carry off rain were deposits of every kind of filth. She was also critical about the defecation habits of Indians: 'One of the most filthy and injurious habits in India is fouling the ground, in compounds of houses by cesspits and the ground in the neighbourhood of villages for the purposes of nature. This foul habit is one of the principal causes of cholera and other epidemics.'[41] Her description of the situation was drawn from the information supplied to the Royal Commission by the army personnel from India.

Florence's letter to the members, like all her other works, was full of facts and figures. It was not a torrent of patronising advice but a reasoned argument full of evidence and examples cited from the Report of the Royal Commission. At the end of her letter, she suggested a few methods for improving the sanitary conditions in the villages such as draining away stagnant water, filling up holes, levelling the ground, improving roads, digging wells for clean drinking water, removing dung heaps and human excrement from the neighbourhood and using them as manure and, finally, building a few model dwellings with proper sanitary appliances. She also suggested health education for schools at primary level and asked the members to present themselves as role models:

> Example is the best teacher, and enlightened native gentlemen, especially landowners, who have influence among the working population in town and country, might work miracles. The munificence in charity of native men of rank in India is well known. ... Here is an equally noble and patriotic way of exercising charity.[42]

Florence's letter was not only published in the Association's transactions, it was also included in the official Blue Book.[43] Shortly after, in the Report of the Association for 1870, the following news was published:

> In June last, Miss Florence Nightingale favoured the association with an elaborate paper on the question of Indian sanitation, which has also been published in the above number of the Transactions. Agreeably to her wishes, the paper has been translated into Bengali and will shortly be ready for publication. The Council take the opportunity to tender their cordial acknowledgements to the distinguished author for her most practical suggestions on a vitally important subject. They are glad to announce that the paper has also been translated into the vernacular at Bombay for circulation in that Presidency.[44]

Florence would have been pleased at this outcome.

This was the last letter she wrote to the members of the Association, and there was no evidence in her private papers that she ever wrote again. Florence wrote the letter at a time when although almost 80 per cent of the Indian population was living in villages, there was a growing urban population in cities like Calcutta, Bombay and Madras. This population, a large section of which was English-educated middle class, started to become more vociferous against the poverty and deprivation that existed in the society, and that was what Florence was counting on. She was trying to make this educated group aware of some health hazards. She was trying to point out that diseases such as cholera, fever and dysentery, from which thousands of people perished every year in India, were preventable by adopting sanitary measures. She understood the magnitude of the problem. The task was so enormous that the Government could not tackle it alone unless the people came forward to help themselves. Florence, influenced by the nineteenth-century ideas of 'self-help' and 'co-operation', tried to pass on such ideas to a group of people who were enlightened and aware of their social need. But perhaps that was her mistake. Enlightened though the members of the Bengal Social Science Association were, their interest in the health and sanitation of the rural population was mostly academic.

It must also be said that in the third quarter of the nineteenth century it was not within the power of the Indian elite to implement changes or to improve public health conditions in India. That was the heyday of the Raj, when whether it was railways or irrigation, village sanitation or female nursing, all were the responsibility of a foreign Government ruling India. There were engineers, sanitary inspectors, army officers and town planners, all British and working for the Government. What should happen, and how much money should be spent in which public sector, was dependent on the Government's decision. This was all too evident in Lawrence's administration. The squalor, poverty and degradation of a vast number of people could not be eradicated unless there was a consolidated social and political policy to do so. Such eradication of poverty could be possible if proper education was bestowed upon them, agriculture was improved, trade and industries installed and revived, and basic health and sanitation were introduced. It was a Himalayan task, true, but it also needed the determination of an Everest climber. The British administration in India never had that determination. They either talked about the 'Indian cosmogony' or cited 'the caste system', but more often they appealed to the 'lack of funds'. Official memoranda and reports of 1860–70, and of the previous decade, continuously mentioned the 'problem of funding'.

Florence came to appreciate many of these facts in the next stage of her Indian work when she launched her campaign for famine-stricken Indian peasants. In 1870, after four years' experience with John Lawrence's administration, she started to place the problem of civil sanitation in India in its wider and more complex context. She began to understand that a 'poor people' is always 'an unhealthy and dirty people', unless their poverty is redressed.[45]

As for the members of the Bengal Social Science Association, they were not in a position to do much except writing, discussing and debating. The rules of the Association clearly said that it was not 'an agitating body' and would not try to change anything. Florence's attempt to bring some changes through the Association was futile from the start and, by March 1872, two of the Association's important patrons were assassinated. One was Chief Justice Norman, and the other was Viceroy Lord Mayo. After this, the Bengal Social Science Association continued for a few years, but gradually lost its efficacy, particularly after its founder Rev. James Long left India. It finally dissolved itself in 1878. Florence was more successful later with the Poona Sarvajanik Sabha and the Bombay elite of Indian society than she was with the Bengali *babus*.

This short-lived encounter between Florence Nightingale and the Bengal Social Science Association was significant on two counts. One, this was her first attempt to spread her ideas directly among the Indians by securing a different forum of publicity other than official. Two, her labour was not all lost: we shall see a few years later how deeply she became involved with the land tenure question in Bengal and in the plight of the *ryots*, and how some young professional Indians like Mr P.K. Sen, who obviously came to know her through the Bengal Social Science Association, got in touch with her to bring some changes in that field. As Bartle Frere aptly said to her, 'You have set a stone rolling in India which I do not think will stop in a hurry.'[46]

Notes

1.   FN (1870b), 'Letters to the Secretaries', *Transactions, Bengal Social Science Association*, IV, xiv–xv (letter dated 25 May 1870) and 1–8 (letter dated 24 June 1870). (Hereafter referred to as *Transactions, BSSA*.)
2.   Carpenter, M. (1868), *Six Months in India*, London: Longman, Green and Co., vol. 1, dedication.
3.   See Long, J. (1862), *Five Hundred Questions on Subjects Requiring Investigation in the Social Condition of Natives [of India]*, Calcutta; [Long, J.] (1865), *Russia, Central Asia and British India by a British Subject*, London: Trübner & Co.; Long, J. (1870), *Village Communities in India and Russia*. Reprinted from *Transactions, BSSA*, 1870, Calcutta.
4.   Long, J. (1866), 'Social science in England and social science for India', *The 8th and 9th Annual Reports of the Family Literary Club*, Calcutta, p. 15.
5.   Long, (1866), p. 28.
6.   Long, (1866), p. 28.
7.   *Proceedings of the Bethune Society*, Sessions of 1859–60, Calcutta, 1862.
8.   Kling, B.B. (1966), *The Blue Mutiny. The Indigo Disturbances in Bengal, 1859–1862*, Calcutta: Firma KLM Private Ltd., pp. 198–218.
9.   In Bengali 'Nil' stands for both 'indigo' and 'blue', and 'durpan' means mirror. Hence Nil Durpan – a blue mirror.
10. *The History of the Nil Durpan, with the State Trial of the Rev. J. Long of the Church Mission*, reprinted from *The Englishman*, Calcutta, July 30 1861. The libel case against Long was brought by the editor of *The Englishman*, the Landholders' Association of British India and the general body of the

indigo planters. In the Court, Long said that if the play *Nil Durpan* was as injurious as the Counsel for prosecution described, then he did a public service by making such a work known in English. The 'Nil Durpan' controversy and subsequent trial of Long gave him much publicity. His English pamphlet of *Nil Durpan* was distributed to various people under official frank for which W.S. Seaton Karr, Secretary to the Government of Bengal, was partly responsible, but Lieutenant-Governor Grant did not consider the matter as too serious. See Gopal, S. (1965), *The British Policy In India*, Cambridge: Cambridge University Press, pp. 22–29.

11. Mary Carpenter also admitted that the idea was Long's (Carpenter (1868), vol. 1, p. 218).
12. FN to Carpenter, 3 August 1866, BL OIOC, Mss Eur A 110.
13. Lawrence to FN, 1 August 1866, BL Add. Mss 45777, fol. 89.
14. Carpenter (1868), vol. 1, p. 164.
15. Carpenter (1868), vol. 1, p. 184.
16. Adhikari, S.K. (1990), *Vidyasagar and the new National Consciousness*, Calcutta: Vidyasagar Research Centre, pp. 37–8.
17. Carpenter (1868), p. 195.
18. Carpenter (1868), p. 198.
19. Carpenter to FN, 8 January 1867, BL Add. Mss 45790, fol. 100.
20. *Transactions, BSSA, Part 1, 1867*, vol. I, prospectus.
21. *Transactions, BSSA*, 1867, vol. I, Part 1, p. xv.
22. *Transactions, BSSA*, 1870, vol. IV, p. xiv.
23. FN to Frere, 24 March 1870, BL Add. Mss 45780, fol. 184, draft.
24. Frere to FN, 1 November 1868, BL Add. Mss 45780, fol. 141.
25. Jowett to FN, quoted in Quinn, V. and Prest, J. (1987), *Dear Miss Nightingale: A Selection of Benjamin Jowett's Letters to Florence Nightingale*, Oxford: Clarendon Press, p. 119, reprinted by permission of Oxford University Press.
26. Frere to FN, 1 June 1870, BL Add. Mss 45780, fol. 192.
27. FN (1870b), The BSSA's abstract of receipts and disbursements for the year 1870 shows receipt of a donation of Rs. 103 15 annas 6 pice (a considerable sum in 1870) from Miss Florence Nightingale.
28. Sutherland to FN, 8 June 1879, BL Add. Mss 45754, fol. 174.
29. Frere to FN, June 1870, BL Add. Mss 45780, fol. 199.
30. FN (1870b), pp. 1–2.
31. *Transactions, BSSA*, 1870, vol. IV, p. 1.
32. FN (1870b), p. 2.
33. Harrison, M. (1994), *Public Health in British India: Anglo-Indian Preventive Medicine 1859-1914*, Cambridge: Cambridge University Press pp. 99–115.
34. Dr J.L. Bryden, A report on epidemic cholera in the Bengal Presidency 1866–68, *Report, Sanitary Measures, 1869–70*, p. 11.
35. FN (1870b), p. 4.
36. Watts, S. (1997), *Epidemics and History – Disease, Power and Imperialism*, Boston: Yale University Press, pp. 200–212.
37. FN (1870b), p. 3.
38. FN (1870b), p. 4.
39. FN (1870b), p. 5.
40. FN (1870b), p. 5.
41. FN (1870b), p. 8.

42. FN (1870b), p. 8.
43. *Report, Sanitary Measures, 1869–70*, pp. 288–291.
44. *Transactions, BSSA*, 1871, vol. V, p. xi. Translated copies of her letter could not be traced in either the British Library, or the National Archives of India, New Delhi.
45. FN (1870b), p. 5.
46. Frere to FN, 22 August 1870, BL Add. Mss 45780, fol. 209.

CHAPTER FIVE

The Zemindar, the Sun and the Watering Pot

'With the sun in one hand and a watering pot in the other, we can produce everything, without nothing.'[1]

In the 1870s, Florence started a new campaign for India and a new phase in her career: she emerged as a spokesperson for India. The interest that started in 1857 with the mutiny had already passed through more than a decade. In the 1870s we find her writing and publicising less for the British Army and more for the Indians under British rule. This transition did not happen overnight. It took almost ten years of work experience for her to learn some plain truths regarding British India. Florence never dissociated army sanitation from civil sanitation, but working through the bureaucratic maze of the War Office, the India Office, and various Secretaries of State and Viceroys, she realised that very little could be done for civil sanitation through official channels. Either the money would run out or the inertia of the officials to tackle the problem at the root would be insurmountable. It was not only money that was needed; the correct political attitude was not there. Florence also realised that the problem of sanitation was not an isolated one. Sanitation was only the outer layer of a complexity of vast problems such as poverty and ignorance, famines and epidemics together with the British policy of land settlement, irrigation and investment. All these were combined in a package deal for the Indian peasant after more than a century of colonial exploitation and socio-political upheavals.[2] In her new appreciation of the problem, Florence often described it as a 'hundred-headed hydra'.[3]

With her foresight, Florence could see that the 'hundred-headed hydra' should be tackled at its source, the poverty of the Indians. One could not ask a person to keep clean when he or she was dying of hunger and disease: 'One must live in order to be a subject for sanitary consideration at all, and one must eat to live. If one is killed off by famine one certainly need not fear fever or cholera.'[4] In support of these poverty-stricken people of India, Florence emerged as a writer and reporter, a publicist and lobbyist.

From 1870 to 1896, Florence wrote untiringly about India, portraying the true picture of the country under British rule. She publicised the plight of the Indian peasants, the *ryots*, criticised the Government for failing to bring change and, finally, tried to mobilise public opinion in Britain. The articles, pamphlets, essays and letters she wrote during this period clearly showed the way her ideas were developing. Some of her articles were read in the meetings and conferences, some were published in journals and magazines. Others were so seditious that her well-wishers like Benjamin Jowett and John Lawrence advised her not to publish and they remained proof copies forever on the shelves of archives.[5]

Florence was extremely thorough and meticulous in collecting data and evidence for her articles and essays. She did not believe in theorising, but in facts. Having like-minded friends such as Sir Louis Mallet and Sir Bartle Frere, she had access to official materials and documents in the War Office and India Office, and made judicious use of them. Sir Bartle Frere as Chairman of the Sanitary Committee in the India Office would not take a step without consulting her first. He wrote a note to her almost every week and sent papers asking her opinion.[6] When she wrote a memorandum or an important letter she sent the draft to him for his comments. Often he would advise her what to write, where and to whom to write. As a member of the India Council, Frere was not always free to put certain questions himself but would advise Florence to raise them, and she would often incorporate what Frere had written to her in her articles and letters. Similarly, Charles Plowden, the Clerk of the India Office, always sent her official documents so that she could write her first draft of the sanitary reports and could study the memoranda and despatches sent from India.[7]

Florence also corresponded with Sir Stafford Northcote, the Secretary of State, asking him about the sanitary measures taken or sending him suggestions.[8] She also had a retinue of non-official people working in India, such as church missionaries, school inspectors and secretaries of various associations, who kept her informed about what was happening. It was often said that she had more facts at her fingertips than the War Office and the India Office put together. That caused a lot of irritation among the petty officials. Miss Nightingale always knew before them, always produced more authentic and factual reports than they could. No wonder at a later stage she was considered to be an outsider meddling in matters she had no right to: 'Her excursions into difficult problems of Indian policy and administration were regarded as unsafe and inexpedient, and this view was not confined to such officials as disagreed with her conclusions.'[9] The official brotherhood frowned upon her writing and publishing articles about the plight of the masses of India and thereby encouraging public opinion to develop in Britain. But they could not deny the facts of her articles. Almost all the books and documents found in her room after her death were Blue Books, proceedings, pamphlets and printed papers on India. They were also extensively annotated in the margins.[10]

From 1870, Florence started to make a great effort to establish a rapport with the Indians to convert them to her ways of thinking. Her liaison with the Bengal Social Science Association, as we saw in the previous chapter, might not have been quite as fruitful as she had expected, but it gave her the impetus to write to others, which she did with unfailing energy. Though Florence had now started to concentrate more on writing about India and establishing direct contact with Indians, she did not slacken her agitation for sanitation through official channels, which she kept up to the very end of her life. As an expert on army sanitary matters, she always exerted immense influence on people in power. They listened to her and paid heed to her suggestions, and made free use of her organisational efficiency and writing skill. But, as always happens with the passing of time, she found her friends among the high officials were gradually disappearing; they retired, moved away or died. The new blood that came in did not know her power and influence in the War Office as it had been in the days of Sidney Herbert. It was easy for them to ignore her enthusiasm and goodwill.

This was also a period when Florence suffered considerable stress and depression. Once, about this time, she wrote to her journalist friend Harriet Martineau, ' ... the absolute inefficiency and confusion of the War Office – especially of the "control" astonishes even me who have been in it for 17 years and who have watched its downward course ... for the last 5 years.'[11] But Florence was not one to give up. After Lawrence's retirement she promptly established contact with his successor, Lord Mayo. It was Frere who introduced her to Mayo. Both Florence and Frere were frustrated by the lack of sanitary progress in India during the last phase of Lawrence's viceroyalty. Frere, when he worked under Lawrence as the Governor of Bombay, did not get on well with him.[12] By 1868, Florence and Frere lost hope that sanitation-wise anything further would be done in Lawrence's time. Frere openly wrote to Florence:

> ... my hopes of getting anything done while Sir John Lawrence is Viceroy after ebbing for months and years have come to dead low water – and now I think it is almost to be desired that he should attempt to commence nothing, and that this, with so much in every other branch of the Administration should be left to his successor. Otherwise I much fear that the said successor will occupy his first year or two in undoing all that Sir John may have begun and left unfinished.[13]

Despite their disappointment with Lawrence, neither Florence nor Frere put their trust in Mayo. A known enemy is better than an unknown one; the unknown one was also Irish. Initially, both of them were sceptical about Lawrence's successor. ' ... you are quite right in thinking that his appointment would be a great blunder,'[14] Frere wrote to Florence, and advised her to write to Lawrence 'to get anything done which he can do before he leaves India'.[15] However, in spite of their English reservation about an Irish viceroy-elect, both Florence and Frere decided to play the sanitation card through Mayo. Frere arranged a meeting between Florence and Mayo:

> I think you will hear from Lord Mayo who I know is anxious to see you if you can grant him an interview next week. Could you, in the meantime, write down for him, as you did [when describing what the folk in India should now do] in a note to me a few weeks ago, the points to which he should first give attention? The sort of memorandum which will tell him what to do when he has mastered what Blue Books will tell of the question and presupposing a knowledge of the elements of the question.[16]

Mayo came to see Florence on 28 October 1868. He was co-operative and willing to abide by Florence's guidelines. She also wrote a memorandum for the new Viceroy,[17] setting out her thoughts about irrigation in India in the context of agricultural development. According to Florence's autobiographical note, Mayo 'corresponded' with her 'all the time'.[18] But once he reached Calcutta, he became as cautious as John Lawrence had been, and perhaps even more so. Mayo considered that Lawrence's administration had overspent in building palatial barracks for the army and on public works. He made drastic cuts in public works to bring expenditure down, but tried to alleviate the plight of ordinary Indians in a different way. He gave permission to build roads and canals and tried to tackle the sanitation problem in its proper context by emphasising the need for improved agriculture, irrigation and canal projects.[19] He also decided to have a census and survey of the country. However, the work Mayo started could not be finished. His untimely death in 1872 put a stop to Florence's renewed aspirations and dreams.[20]

The next Viceroy of India was Lord Northbrook. Although he was not hostile to the sanitation question, he was not as receptive as either Lawrence or Mayo had been. Before he left for India he did not come to see 'the Governess' and broke the rule as it was. Florence probably gave vent to her dissatisfaction about this to Benjamin Jowett, who consoled her in a letter:

> ... you have worked for eternity; why should you be troubled at the Gov. General not coming to see you [as he most certainly ought to have done]. Put not your trust in princes or in princesses, or in the War Office or in the India Office – all that sort of thing necessarily rests on a sandy foundation. I wonder that you have been able to carry on so long with them.[21]

Florence did not need any moral support. Her concern for India was stronger than her personal feelings. She wrote to Lord Northbrook without much delay, reminding him of the need for pure drinking water for the soldiers and the civilians. Northbrook answered her letter politely, saying that he fully understood the need for pure water for the soldiers and would welcome any suggestions from Florence, but he was also at present a little overwhelmed with his own work.[22] Northbrook also wrote to Lord Cranborne (later Lord Salisbury), the Secretary of State at the time, asking him to assure Miss Nightingale that he was not likely to forget his training under Sidney Herbert at the War Office, and that he would do what he could for the health of the soldiers: ' ... Miss Nightingale is evidently more anxious for the future than dissatisfied with the past. The best thing I can say to reassure her is that in the face of the financial difficulties of last year I left the expenditure upon military public works untouched.'[23]

After Northbrook, Lord Lytton became the Viceroy of India, and with him the focus of Indian administration changed completely. He engaged himself with frontier wars to pursue the forward policy of Disraeli's Government. Florence's sanitary efforts did not get a favourable wind until Lord Ripon took over the viceroyalty in 1880. As Florence's rapport with the Viceroys faded somewhat for the time being, she cultivated her friendship with administrators, who were perhaps less high ranking than Viceroys but were powerful within their own jurisdiction. These administrators worked as her emissaries and were willing to do her bidding. The 'Nightingale power' was still at work.

Life or death in India

In 1873, Florence wrote a paper called *Life or Death in India*, which was read at the Social Science Conference in Norwich. It was almost a sequel of what she had written ten years earlier and its aim, she said, was 'to reckon up our gains'.[24] Her verdict was that some sanitary progress had certainly been made in India, but not enough:

> We have made an impression on the sanitary state of that vast country; but 'impression', so far as this: only to show us the immense work that remains to be done; the immense success that can attend it – we cannot yet say the immense work that has been done.[25]

She gave credit to the Government of India for lowering the death rate of the European soldiers and making some progress in the areas of drainage and water supply, particularly in the three big cities of Calcutta, Bombay and Madras. 'Calcutta has its water supply complete; all classes, all castes use it; and find, indeed, the fabled virtues of the Ganges in the pure water tap.'[26] Now one could not blame the 'hopeless Indian climate' as the root of all evil, as problems could be solved in spite of the climate, and India was not necessarily 'fatal' to the Europeans. Wherever drainage, water supply and the surrounding areas were taken care of, epidemics did not appear; but this did not mean that the work of improvement was complete. 'Far from it. The general result only indicates progress towards realization; not realization.'[27]

In many ways, this article lacked the sharpness and anger of her first article, but a noticeable feature was that almost two thirds of it was devoted to the plight of Indian peasants. Her attention had already taken a major shift from the British soldiers to the people of India. In the appendix to this article she wrote at length on the desirability and viability of irrigation in India to counter famine and poverty. Since 1868, Florence had been considering the relevance of irrigation in India, and the frequency of famines brought her attention to the need for irrigation. She could see that most of the people of India lived in villages, and agriculture was their main occupation. Their economic conditions could be improved only through the development of agriculture, which eventually would lead to better sanitation and health. If famine killed the people of India in their millions, it was nonsense to talk about sanitation. To save them from the clutches of perpetual famine and starvation, the productivity of agricultural land had to be increased, and that could be done only by irrigation. The logic of her idea was indubitable, but to transform the idea into action was difficult. It was easier to erect 'palatial barracks' for the British soldiers than it was to give Indian peasants irrigation canals.

The lessons of Indian famines

Since Florence became involved with India, several major famines had occurred and killed several millions. During Lawrence's administration in India, in 1865–66, the catastrophic Orissa famine took place, which moved Florence deeply. The famine affected a large part of Orissa, Bihar and Bengal, extending as far south as Madras. The entire eastern coast of India was in the grip of famine. Rain failed to fall when it was needed and fell in plenty when it was not, causing widespread flooding and killing young rice plants. When the local officials drew the Government's attention to the impending calamity, it was ignored by the Lieutenant-Governor of Bengal, Sir Cecil Beadon. He failed to take relief measures in time and John Lawrence, in the name of non-interference into the affairs of the provincial government, turned a blind eye to the whole affair. When, finally, the Government was obliged to take some relief measures, they were insufficient, difficult to distribute and already too late. One million Indians died in that famine.[28] But this was not the only one. The Orissa famine led to the

Madras famine of 1866–67, and was shortly followed by the Bengal famine, which affected the northern United Provinces, north Bihar and north Bengal. Then in 1876–79 the infamous Mysore famine took place, affecting a vast tract of Deccan.[29] Florence was acutely aware of and well informed about all these famines. In 1873, she wrote:

> We must not suppose that famines in India are decreasing in extent and severity under our rule, on the contrary. The present famine in Bengal appears to be of more awful length, breadth, height and depth than any before known, except perhaps that of Bengal, a century ago, 1769–70, when one-third of the population of Bengal is believed to have been swept away, which seems to have nearly equalled it.[30]

A few years later, in 1878, she wrote again:

> A terrible famine not yet over – in Madras and Mysore out of 35 millions of people at least three millions dead of starvation, spite of all the Government and the 'Mansion House Fund' have done; in Northern India, looming upon us too, if not already here. For instance in Oude, Rohilcund and the North-West Provinces there is severe suffering if not actual famine.[31]

Famines were nothing new or unusual in a vast country like India, where the success of good crops depended on seasonal and timely rainfall. But famines occurred in British India with such frequency that, as historians have remarked, it would be difficult to find parallels in recent history. Throughout the nineteenth century and well into the twentieth, India was almost in a perpetual famine condition. Some famines were so catastrophic that they acquired their own names, such as the Orissa famine, the Bengal famine and the Deccan famine. Some were referred to by their year: 'By a moderate calculation, the famines of 1877–1878, of 1889 and 1892, of 1897 and 1900 have carried off fifteen millions of people. The population of a fair sized European country has been swept away from India within twenty five years.'[32] Even when in some years there was not a full-blown famine, there was a food crisis, which made the peasant population weak and vulnerable to the epidemics that invariably followed famines.

The British administrators in India at that time were baffled by the frequency and devastating consequences of famines. Throughout the nineteenth century and after, Famine Commissions were formed to investigate the causes of famines and hundreds of people gave evidence, which was meticulously recorded.[33] Famine codes and famine insurances were devised, and Relief Commissions organised, though often too late. In England, the British Parliament led debates on Indian famines and the press carried mournful stories of victims to stir up humanitarian generosity in the hearts of affluent occidentals. Even Florence herself contributed to famine relief funds. 'I have just received your magnificent donation to the Bengal Famine Relief fund,' wrote Frere to Florence in February 1874, 'which I will pay into the Lord Mayor's Comm'ee telling Lord Northbrook that I have done so.'[34] Funds were raised, relief was sent across the ocean, but nothing could avert the regular arrival of famine after each failure of the monsoon.

Causes of the famines

The official explanation of the causes of the famines in India was always either untimely rain or drought. But the fact which clearly emerges from all the reports and documents as to the real cause of famines was not the failure of the monsoon or the impact of an exceptionally dry season but the poverty of the Indian people, aggravated by the indifference, incompetence and exploitation of a colonial power. The disastrous economic conditions in which the vast majority of the Indian population found themselves explain quite clearly why when the rains failed and the earth dried up, the famine struck with such a devastating blow. 'We do not care for the people of India,' Florence wrote in 1878. 'This is a heavy indictment, but how else to account for the facts about to be given? Do we even care enough to know about their daily lives of lingering death from causes we could so well remove?'[35]

The class that suffered most in Indian famines was the agricultural class, the *ryots*. The confidential reports and famine proceedings of the Government of India showed that even in normal times these peasants lived well below the poverty line, maintaining a hand-to-mouth existence with very little savings to fall back on to meet bad seasons. Research showed that there was a steady increase in the number of people seeking famine relief between 1858 and 1900, which indicated the growing poverty of the nation.[36] 'In whole regions of the Deccan, of Madras, in some parts of Bengal, in other parts of India, a peasantry always in a chronic state of semi-starvation, always on the brink of famine fever, is to be found.'[37]

Whether British policy in India was responsible for the proverbial poverty of the Indian peasants and the stagnation of the Indian economy in the nineteenth century is still an open question, and the availability of documents, distance from the past and new approaches have started new debates on old issues.[38] Without undermining the importance of such academic debate, one could safely say that the policies followed by Britain in India were largely responsible for the situation that existed in India. While in Britain the utilitarian philosophy of free trade, industrialisation and freedom of action without hindrance created a climate of wealth, hope and benevolence, which made social and political reforms possible, in India it had almost the opposite effect. 'It was India which most clearly exposed the paradox in Utilitarianism between the principle of liberty and the principle of authority.'[39]

Traditional historians have often argued that India's industry, particularly textiles, was ruined by British policies. From a manufacturing country and supplier of finished products, India almost overnight became a supplier of raw materials and purchaser of manufactured goods from Manchester and the Lancashire cotton mills. Protective duties were imposed on Indian goods in Britain, which made them difficult to sell, whereas removal of tariffs on British goods made them cheaper to sell in the Indian market.[40] In addition, the Government did not have a definite industrial policy and there was very little investment in Indian industry. 'Among the many blessings which England has conferred on India, encouragement for Indian industry was not one.'[41] Questions such as whether such investment would have changed the Indian economy, or whether India was ready for an industrial revolution like Japan or Russia, fall outside the scope of this book. The fact remained, however, that the Indian economy faced widespread capital shortage in the quest for industrial development.[42] The stagnation in industry meant in reality the movement of the surplus labour from industry to the agricultural sector. In England, industrialisation caused the rural population to move to the urban sector, abandoning agriculture as their livelihood, whereas in India the trend was the reverse with more and more people depending on the land for a living. Florence was well aware of this fact: 'The consequence of the want of other employment is excessive competition for land, upon which follows rack renting. There is little competition in India except for land.'[43]

The agricultural class was further ruined by the land revenue system. Its demands were so excessive that often the landholders were unable to pay, and so were dispossessed.[44] How excessive these revenue claims were is well documented in the writings of traditional historians.[45] The British land policy in India also created immense hardship and poverty for ordinary peasants. In the Bengal Presidency, it created a class not directly involved in cultivating land but interested only in accruing benefit from it. Wherever the Permanent Settlement had been introduced, it gave the *zemindars* and the landlords a free hand in exploiting the peasants.[46] Where it was not introduced, the Government made a direct deal with the peasants, such as the *ryotwari* or *mahalbari* systems, where the revenue was assessed not only at a price beyond the means of the peasants, but also the deal was a short term contract. This enabled the Government to impose frequent price rises with each renewal of contract. As the price of land increased, it became a highly saleable commodity. 'A native said,' wrote Florence, 'the English law makes the sale of our land as easy as the sale of a bullock, or a turban.'[47]

Florence was fully aware of the exploitative elements in British policy in India and, with her anti-establishment critical attitude, was never hesitant in exposing the authorities. One such exploitative element was the systematic drain of India's national wealth.[48] Although some modern academics show uneasiness on this point, it cannot be denied that the British civil and military personnel sent all their savings and accumulated wealth home. In his evidence to an Inquiry Commission, Dadabhai Naoroji once said: 'With the exception of, perhaps meat, bread, butter, native servants, and so on, every farthing that the Europeans earn in India is naturally remitted to England in one shape or another.'[49] India paid their salaries, leave and pensions. The private British entrepreneurs did the same. They considered India as 'a vast estate or plantation, the profits of which to be withdrawn from India and deposited in Europe'.[50] To add to this, India had to pay for an expensive administrative establishment in London in the name of Home Charges.[51] Such an establishment in India was equally expensive and lavish, without any comparison in any recent colonial history. The British officials did not hesitate to throw expensive durbars when the country was in the grip of famine and Government funds ran low.[52] India also had to pay for the British forward policy on the frontiers. The Bhutan, Abyssinian, Burma and Afghan wars, and preparation for a possible Russian attack, were all paid for from Indian revenues, yet India had no interest in those wars.[53] India also inherited a vast amount of debt when, in 1858, the administration of the country changed hands from the Company to the Crown. The capital of the Company was paid off by loans; these loans became India's debt, and she paid the interest raised from her own taxes.[54]

In British India, the main source of foreign exchange was the export of food grains. During the Bengal and Orissa famines, export of food grains continued in the name of free trade.[55] The Government imported rice, while the private traders exported it. George Campbell, Lieutenant-Governor of Bengal, commented: 'The strange spectacle was seen of fleets of ships taking rice out from the Hooghly and passing other ships bringing rice in.'[56] Added to this was the indifference and incompetence of British officials. As mentioned earlier, extreme callousness was shown during the Orissa famine.[57] Lord Salisbury, who as Lord Cranborne was Secretary of State at the time, later regretted in a letter to Lord Northbrook that he had failed to take action:

> ... the monsoon had closed the parts of Orissa, help was impossible, and it is said a million people died. The Governments of India and Bengal had taken in effect no precautions ... I never could feel that I was free from all the blame for the result.[58]

During the Madras famine of 1875–77, Sir Richard Temple, the Finance Minister of the Government of India, urged the relief officers to be judicious and thrifty in doling out famine relief, which earned the nickname of the 'Temple ration'.[59] Relief operations during famines were invariably late and unprepared, and fraught with difficulties. Referring to this incompetence of the British officials Florence commented: 'If they were Germans, they would have known Trihoot like Berlin.'[60]

Florence and the people of India

Between 1870 and 1879, Florence published a number of papers and pamphlets drawing the attention of the British public to the miserable conditions of Indian peasants. They dealt with three main issues: the inability of the British administration to prevent famines in India, the evil of the moneylenders, and irrigation as a famine-preventive measure. Over ten years, she relentlessly put forward her arguments; she often repeated herself, but never deviated from her objective. Her voice became stronger as the years went by. Her pioneering work in this field was her unpublished book, *The Zemindar, the Sun and the Watering Pot as Affecting Life and Death in India*. The draft of the book was written between 1873 and 1874.[61] Although the book as such was never published, parts of it provided material for several articles published later. Apparently Florence regretted in later years that she was unable to finalise the book and left instructions in her will in 1896 that if anyone wanted to publish it, opportunity should be provided for that; in 1914 her friend William Wedderburn published a short article based on the book.[62]

Florence had used a great deal of information drawn from official documents and reports, as well as from the evidence given to the famine commission, to make the book as factual as possible. Her aim was to argue a case for irrigation in India as a famine-preventive measure and to show that what was preventable was not being acted on. She had her draft privately printed and sent to various interested people for their comments. One such person was Benjamin Jowett, her close friend and the Master of Balliol, who criticised her style of writing and gave her some practical advice:

> 11 August 1874
> ... The style is too jerky & impulsive, though I think it is logical & effective. You must avoid faults of taste & exaggeration. The more moderate any statement is, the stronger it is. Real strength lies in paragraphs, in pages, in the whole, not in single sentences. The force should appear to flow irresistibly from the facts and reasonings.
> 'What does the man mean by talking to me about style, when I am thinking only of the sufferings & oppression of 100,000,000 of *ryots*?' Yes, but if you want to make the English people think about the *ryots* you must be careful of the least indiscretion or exaggeration ... .[63]

Benjamin Jowett strongly advised her against publication, fearing that the book would start a political row that could not be handled:

25 December 1874

... I do not like your going on with the book on *ryots* at present, for you are not equal to it, and I think it must be rewritten to produce the right effect. You & I cannot be sure, either of our facts or of our remedies, from personal knowledge – the subject is a dangerous one ...

You have a great position at the India Office at present & can do much with Lord Salisbury & their friends, but if your book was deemed rash or inaccurate you would be discredited & your other books would be discredited & you would lose influence.

If the book is to be published & read in India, I should hang over every word with anxiety ... .[64]

As Jowett said, the book was highly critical of the performance of the Government in confronting famines in India. In it, Florence accused the authorities of being slow, callous and indifferent. She argued that the Government of India not only had failed to prevent famines, but also to understand that famine was expensive. She claimed that had the Government taken preventive measures in time it would have cost them less. The famine of 1866 cost the Government over £2 million, the Bengal famine would have cost nearly three times that amount: 'Would not twice these seven insure against future famines?' It would have also provided for irrigation, she claimed, at least in three vast districts of Punjab, in Bundelkhund, in the North-West Frontier Province and in parts of Bengal.[65] Florence tried to draw the Government's attention to the revenue losses in famines. In the famine of 1873, 'there was a loss of revenue in custom duty alone – of nearly 30,000 pounds'; 'Annual revenue in Agra division before famine £750,000, after famine £625,500.'[66] She also pointed out that famines caused disastrous migration of populations from one area to another in search of food, and that meant the total ruin of agriculture. It was not only the loss of capital; famines caused a staggering number of people to perish:

Five times number perished as in Franco-German war.

Half a million died in silence in Rajpootana. No one takes any notice. We say nothing of the famine in Orissa, when a third of its population were deliberately allowed to whiten the fields with their bones.

Florence commented that a single person's death from neglect in a Holborn workhouse would probably excite more attention in London than the death of millions in India.[67] Five years later, after the infamous Madras famine, Florence again tried to draw public attention to the decimation of the people of India:

In many parts [of Madras presidency] one-fourth have died. In Bellary, Kurnol Cuddaph and Nellore, the deaths from famine in one year have been from 21 to 27 percent.

> At the end of 1876, according to the estimated population Salem had 2,129,850 souls. On 14th March 1878, she had 1,559,876. More than one-quarter were lost.[68]

Previously, Florence's mind had been fully occupied with 'sanitation'; she did not quite see the issue in its broader context. From this time onwards, sanitation became somewhat inconsequential to her. The people of India gradually moved to the forefront of her mind with their poverty, hunger and famines, and the question of sanitation went out of focus for the time being. In her articles, *The People of India* and *The United Empire and the Indian Peasant*, both written in 1878 after the Madras famine, she wrote of the grinding poverty and hand-to-mouth existence of the peasants throughout the Indian sub-continent. She told their story in her eloquent and forceful style, with frequent jibes at the authorities. She wanted to convey her message with a pen sharper than a sword.

> What is the saddest sight to be seen in the East – nay, probably, in the world. The saddest sight to be seen is the peasant in our own Eastern Empire … .
>
> His dress is a coarse bit of rag and a scanty sheet. A tumble down hut of straw and mud, built by himself and not always thatched, a mat for a bed, one or two cooking utensils … and this is commonly shared by the beasts. As a rule he has no money whatever, but in some villages, the phenomenon may be seen of a ryot, possessing one or even two rupees.[69]

'In Burdwan, in 1876–77, the Lieutenant Governor's reports say that the country was prosperous,' she jibed: 'Does the prosperity there find its way into the pockets, or rather first into the stomachs, of the people?' It was not Bengal alone: such were the conditions of the agricultural labourers and peasants all over India. Year after year they became enfeebled, semi-starvation caused stunted growth, and then 'when a bad year comes these poor creatures are struck down in large numbers'.[70]

The British Government had a monopoly in salt and opium in India. Salt making was prohibited within the country and was punishable by law. Salt became an imported commodity from England with a fixed selling price.[71] This caused immense deprivation and hardship among ordinary people. As highly taxed salt was beyond their reach, they would go without salt or use earth substitutes. Florence openly deplored the situation.:

> The salt tax amounts now to 7 pounds a ton the salt itself being worth 12s 6d a ton in India. The people make 'earth salt' by washing the earth and boiling the food in the salt water, and for this miserable product they are punished.
>
> Manufactures are strangled by the tax on salt, such manufactures as bleaching, making of glass, glazing, extraction of metals from ores, salting of provisions, agriculture and the feeding of animals are hindered, and livestock die of disease from want of salt. Fish is ruined

by being cured with earth salt ... The smuggling of salt was enormous and necessitated a great increase of police.[72]

On top of all this was the indebtedness of the Indian peasants. Indian peasants, lacking capital to invest, always borrowed money from the moneylenders against their land and its produce as securities. With their increasing debt and continuous borrowing they found themselves in the clutches of the moneylenders, who would soon possess everything the peasant had, reducing him to the status of a bonded labourer. The legal system introduced by the British did not provide protection for them. It was comparatively easy for the *zemindars* and moneylenders to use the system effectively for their own interest. The illiterate peasants, on the other hand, had no idea how to use the system for their own protection. 'We are told that the ryot has the remedy of English justice ... he has not. A man has not that which he can't use.'[73]

Florence considered moneylending in India as an evil that overshadowed everything. Although in some districts there was some provision for getting cheap Government loans, the *ryots* did not utilise this opportunity, as they did not understand the rules and regulations:

> Our stamp laws meet and baffle him at every turn. He cannot possibly understand them, and for every step he has to pay and consult a vakeel [a lawyer] whose dishonesty and cheating is often second only to that of sowkars [money-lenders]. This in itself is almost certain to ruin him.[74]

If the poor peasant took the matter to the British court, he could not expect justice. Once the court discovered his signature on the money-lender's bond, whether he had signed it under duress or unwittingly out of ignorance, they could do nothing:

> The *ryots* cannot read or write, the money lenders forge what documents they please or enter in the bond the most extravagant terms. And these documents are allowed to pass by the courts as 'mutual' agreements. The borrower has no protection whatever.[75]

Florence complained about the general apathy that existed in Britain concerning India. When the Deccan riots took place, in 1874, in the Poona and Ahmednagar areas, and the agricultural labourers and peasants stood up against the exploitation of the moneylenders, the Government was forced to appoint an Inquiry Commission, which in due course issued a lengthy report. But the matter more or less ended ther;. ' ... none asked for the report. No one Englishman in Parliament or Press has asked the result. There is not a single member of parliament who has called for it. We do not care for the people of India.'[76]

Publicity for her cause

Florence's powerful article, *The People of India*, caused quite a stir. In the following issue of *The Nineteenth Century*, a number of comments and articles were published. The socialist journalist H.M. Hyndman observed that the causes of all the misery of Indian peasants that she had enlarged upon lie far deeper than the village usurer.[77] Hyndman's criticism was somewhat misplaced, as Florence did not fail to understand that the British trade and land revenue policy pushed the Indian peasants to the brink of extinction. This understanding eventually led her to get involved with land tenancy in Bengal, as we shall see later. In India, the article was reviewed in a Calcutta journal called *Brahmo Public Opinion*.[78] Florence, a believer in publicity, sent copies to several influential people in high places. But the officials of the War Office and India Office did not like the tone of her article, or the facts and figures presented in it. It created 'a wholesome shock to British complacency'.[79] Many thought that she had exaggerated the facts and figures of famine deaths and also the extent of the exploitation by the moneylenders. Her article was condemned as 'a shriek', but Florence had her answer ready:

> As to my paper being "a shriek", we cannot cry [loud enough to be heard] without crying anymore than we can fight without fighting. If a Town Crier as old and worn out and as cracked as I, his cry would be 'a shriek'. I do not at all quarrel with them for saying that; I am amazed at my own moderation in my paper.[80]

In her letter to Louis Mallet, she pointed out that the papers from the Government of India spoke only of 'registered deaths', but how many deaths were not registered? How to explain phrases like 'population unaccounted for' or 'population disappeared'?[81] The extent of famine devastation and exploitation by the moneylenders might have appeared as exaggeration when viewed from the cosy circle of the India Office, so to convince Lord Cranbrook, the Secretary of State, Florence sent him a copy of her article as well:

> 10 August 1878
> Very meekly I venture to send you a poor little article of mine on the people of India, in the Nineteenth Century. I hope if you read it, you will not call it a shriek (I am astonished in my own moderation) – I am not so troublesome as to expect that you can find time to read it, but the Indian Office has untold treasures (which it does not know itself) in Reports on these subjects which will engage your busy time, and especially the recent Deccan Riots Commission Report on the relation of the ryots and extortionate moneylenders in the Bombay Deccan, will, I am sure call for your attention.[82]

Cranbrook wrote back, saying that 'without underrating the grief of India', he thought that Florence had generalised too much from one locality.[83] Frustrated, Florence wrote again to her friend Louis Mallet:

> August 26, 1878
> I had a kind little note from Lord Cranbrook about my poor little paper in the XIX century.
> But he evidently thinks that the 'indebtedness' applies merely to the 'Poona and Ahmednuggar' Districts; and that I have exaggerated, if not the intensity of the evil there, [ ] the extent of it.
> Mr Stanhope in answering a question and [presenting] the Deccan Riot Report in the Ho. of C. said the same thing. Surely this can arise only from Lord Cranbrook not yet having had time to examine the case.
> Not only does the 'Deccan Riots' Report [Poona and Ahmednuggur] deal with nearly every part of Bombay Presidency, including Sind, but it also deals with the N.W.P., with the Central P. and in some measure with the Punjab and Oude.
> But I have also been amazed and as it were agonized with letters I have received directly or indirectly from Indian officials and ex-officials belonging to many other parts of India; saying, all this I have known in my district; or, I have had to condemn ryots [according to law] to be bond slaves; and have not been allowed [by law] to represent the case to higher authority.[84]

Although Lord Cranbrook did not quite agree with the facts and figures of Florence's article, it achieved at least one thing. Cranbrook wrote a letter to Lord Lytton, the Viceroy of India, almost immediately:

> August 13
> Miss Nightingale said that we, i.e. the English, do not care for the people of India, and her article in the 19th Century is a sensational commentary on that text. She sent it to me, and I have told her that she has generalized from one small unhappy area, to the whole. I shall be truly glad, however, if your legislation can afford a remedy to that limited locality referred to in the Deccan Commission report, and I am afraid that its application would be useful over a much extensive field, though not all our Indian Empire. Famine has outdone the usurer, and brought the peasantry to a more complete subservience to him than ever.[85]

Whether Cranbrook's letter had any effect on Lord Lytton is difficult to ascertain. But the Deccan Agriculturist Relief Act of 1879 was passed during his administration, and this brought the peasants some apparent relief from the oppression of the moneylenders. Under the new law, peasants could obtain receipts for payments, they could not be imprisoned for failing to pay, and in some cases the dispossessed land was restored to the cultivators; the law made the sale of land to some extent difficult.

Florence and Irrigation

In order to appreciate Florence's agitation for irrigation in India, we have to go back a few years in history when Lord Salisbury was the Secretary of State and irrigation was a political issue.

As mentioned earlier, Florence used the information and lessons of famines to argue a case for irrigation in India. She could see that the poverty of the *ryots* made them vulnerable to famine. Their poverty was aggravated by unscrupulous moneylenders and the indifference of the authorities. If their poverty could be lessened by irrigation and the money-lenders controlled, they would be better equipped to face famines: 'If we had given them water, should we not have to be giving them bread.'[86] Florence was perceptive enough to recognise symptoms that could undermine British supremacy in India. If nothing was done for the peasants, then, she anticipated, agrarian riots would become 'the normal state of things throughout India'.[87]

> What must it be to see and what must it be to be one of 'these patient, silent millions, toiling on day after day, enduring cold, heat, nakedness and hunger, with no hope before them but that of death.' But let us not be too sure that these patient silent millions will remain in silence and patience for ever![88]

Florence was not far wrong. Already, peasant unrest was evident in various parts of India – not so much against the British Raj as such, but against the moneylenders, planters and *zemindars*. As we have noted before, the famous indigo insurgence took place in 1859–60 when the peasantry stood up against the exploitation of the European indigo planters. In 1873, widespread peasant revolt took place in north and east Bengal – particularly in the Serajgunge and Pabna districts. The Deccan riot took place in 1874 when the peasantry revolted against the money-lenders. There were also sporadic uprisings in the western coast and in the Brahmaputra Valley in the east of India.

Florence was very much aware of these agitations. Referring to the Pabna disturbances, she said: 'Eastern Bengal is somewhat better off. The *ryots* have found their power.'[89] Referring to the Deccan riot, she remarked: 'Indebted Deccan does not wait for Secretary of State or Viceroy. Agrarian discontent is not impatient but sure.'[90] Florence always considered the peasants as friends of the British Empire: 'During the sepoy mutiny of 1857, the peasantry were our first friends and without them we could not have won.'[91] She felt that unless the sufferings of the peasants could be alleviated, they would not remain friendly towards the British and that would endanger the foundation of the Empire. Only improved agriculture through irrigation could change the situation. 'Has any effort been made, not to prevent deaths from famine but to prevent famine itself?'[92] Florence was not alone; many people at the time looked to irrigation as the panacea for India's troubles. Equally, there was a strong anti-irrigation lobby among Government officials.

One must not suppose that India did not have any irrigation works prior to the arrival of the British. Many famous irrigation canals such as the Eastern and Western Jamuna Canal and the Bari Doab canals existed in pre-British days, but many of them had fallen into disuse. During the Company Raj, some of these canals were restored and extended. Sir Arthur Cotton,[93] a friend and ally of Florence, restored the Grand Anicut Canal in south India and, since 1817, Arthur Cotton, Proby Cautley, Colonel Baird Smith and many other army engineers had carried on extending and restoring India's existing canals. Proby Cautley, who later became a member of Florence's Indian Sanitary Committee, was very much involved with the Ganges canals. However, their work often followed pre-existing patterns of work, and was restricted by insufficient funds.[94]

Expenditure for irrigation remained a questionable issue throughout the nineteenth century. Lord Dalhousie, the Governor-General of India (1848–56), saw the need for a specific fund for canal irrigation and a Public Works Department, but the revenue loss sustained by the Government during the mutiny of 1857 put a stop to most public works. When the Crown took over the administration of India in 1858, irrigation work slowed down considerably until Lord Curzon became Viceroy in 1899, and gave irrigation his official support.[95] The main irrigation issues that kept the Viceroys and Secretaries of State busy during this prolonged period of almost half a century were who should be entrusted with that work, the Government or the private companies, and how the money should be raised for such work, from revenue or loans. Deliberations on these issues went on throughout the viceroyalties of Lawrence, Mayo, Northbrook and Lytton.

Shortly before Lawrence became Viceroy in 1864, the Government tried to use the private sector to undertake irrigation work and, at Arthur Cotton's instigation, the Madras Irrigation Company, and the East India Irrigation and Canal Company, better known as the Orissa Company, took charge of digging some irrigation canals. These two companies started to work in 1863 on a state-guaranteed system, as was the case with the railways. But they failed to complete the work, and the Government had to buy their assets, suffering heavy losses.[96]

John Lawrence, during his viceroyalty, took some initiatives to start a fresh irrigation venture. He was keen to go ahead with his idea that the Government was capable of executing irrigation works without the help of the private sector, and the expense for such work could be met from surplus revenue and, if necessary, loans could be raised for further capital. Lawrence, with the help of Richard Strachey, then the Inspector-General of

Public Works, submitted his plans and estimates. But Charles Wood, the Secretary of State, in spite of his initial enthusiasm, rejected the proposals on the grounds that the estimates were not based on a proper survey of the areas concerned, and stressed that the irrigation work should be 'remunerative', an unfortunate word that was to dominate discussions about irrigation in India for the rest of the century. Wood was also afraid that the plans submitted were too large to get sufficient labour, which would lead to wage rises that would hurt British trade and industry based on low wages.[97] When Lord Salisbury became Secretary of State first in 1866 (as Lord Cranborne) and then later in 1874 and 1876, he also continued to emphasise the cost-benefit aspects of irrigation work in India.

At the time when Florence started her agitation for irrigation, 'railways versus canals' was a big issue in India. The primary concerns of the Government of India were quick communication, rapid movement of troops and the transport of exportable commodities from one part of the country to another, but, above all, a profitable return from the capital invested. The British manufacturers also put considerable pressure on the Government to extend railways in India.[98] It was easy to raise money for railways, although they did not always pay. As for irrigation canals, the British administration spent considerable time deliberating whether the canals would be cost-effective and whether loans could be raised for such work. Needless to say, in that competition, railways won: 'Annual outlays on irrigation works from borrowed funds fell steadily from the peak levels of £1.23 million in 1875 to around £600,000 in 1880. The total for the decade 1871–80 was £9.2 million as against £239 million spent on railways.'[99] It was also said that the Government wilfully neglected to recognise the remunerative aspect of irrigation and the fact that by 1870 the major irrigation works in India were no longer a burden on the budget.[100]

It was in this context that Florence launched her fight for irrigation in India, and found a true ally in Sir Arthur Cotton. Florence described him as 'the greatest living master of the water question'.[101] In 1864, Cotton came back to England and relentlessly agitated in favour of public works in India. Like Florence, he also wrote a number of articles on irrigation and famines in India, spoke in meetings and conferences, gave evidence before select committees on public works, and replied to anti-irrigation addresses such as Lord Salisbury's.[102] Florence and Cotton shared the same ideas, enthusiasm and dreams about India. She sent him the draft of *The Zemindar, the Sun and the Watering Pot* for his comments; Cotton sent her the irrigation map that he had prepared, and she made several copies to distribute. 'I have but few copies made,' she wrote optimistically to Cotton, 'because I hope that every year we shall have to make additions to this map; and that every year it will require correction.'[103] Cotton was delighted by Florence's involvement with the irrigation question:

If fifty years of hard work and contempt had produced no other return but a letter from you, it would be an honour beyond what I deserve. The plot is now rapidly thickening, and I have not the smallest doubt that your having taken up this great subject will turn the scale. It is impossible for any person not resident in India to conceive the strength of prejudice in the minds, not only of the civil officials, but of multitudes out of office on both the points of irrigation and navigation in India. I am assured that there is not a single person in high office now in India, who is not in his heart opposed to them both.[104]

Florence's arch-opponent on the question of irrigation was Lord Salisbury. It was unfortunate for India that during this vital period of history, Salisbury (Cranborne) was very much on the scene as Secretary of State for India. Salisbury believed in slow progress, economy and 'drift'. He did not think India needed any particular initiative or prompt action from her British rulers: 'We must be content to contribute our mite towards a gradual change.'[105] He maintained that India's problems would eventually but slowly find a permanent solution. He once remarked: 'The vast multitudes of India, I thoroughly believe are well contented with our rule. They have changed masters so often that there is nothing humiliating to them in having gained a new one.'[106] It was he who later, as Prime Minister, called Dadabhai Naoroji 'a blackman' when Naoroji was contesting from the Central Finsbury constituency as a Liberal candidate for the second time.[107]

Florence and Salisbury belonged to two opposite political camps, and never saw eye to eye on the question of irrigation. Addressing the members of the Chambers of Commerce in Manchester on 23 January 1875, Salisbury said: 'Irrigation is a very good thing indeed, but it won't prevent famine, for water will not flow uphill.' The only true remedy against occasional famine and scarcity, he contended, was the frugality of the people themselves in time of plenty, and when there were too many for the land, he advised, emigration must be resorted to.[108] ' ... though it is our intention to pursue a policy of irrigation,' said Salisbury, 'we shall press it with jealousy and more frugality than was our intention several years ago.'[109]

Salisbury's address was vehemently criticised by both Florence and Sir Arthur Cotton. Florence could not allow such a comment to pass unheeded. Referring to this later, she wrote:

It is said that thrift is what must save the Indian ryot. We have heard of the horse being made to live [or die] on a straw a day, but we don't know that ... the horse ought to exercise 'thrift' and save his own straw a day. Yet this is what it appears the country ryot has actually done. [He justified the Secretary of State and died.]

What thrift, what endurance have we Westerners compared to this. And we in the West preach thrift to them.[110]

Some of the points raised by Salisbury against irrigation in India had already been aired by the anti-irrigation lobby in the past, and some of their criticisms had already been answered by Florence as early as 1873 in the appendix to her article *Life and Death in India*. One such criticism was that irrigation was unhealthy; it encouraged malaria and fever. 'In irrigating a district you are apt to turn it into a marsh,' said Salisbury, 'however good a marsh may be for rice, it is not equally good for human beings and it has happened in some districts that having paid an enormous sum to bring the water in, you have to pay an equally enormous sum to take it out.'[111]

Some early irrigation works in India did cause swamps and marshy lands in some areas, as there was no adequate provision for drainage. Not only did a large portion of land become waterlogged near the Jamuna Canal, but also in some places saline efflorescence appeared on the soil, with malaria too becoming a problem. Lack of sufficient funds, however, made it impossible to introduce a proper drainage system.[112] Similar things also happened with the railways when sleepers were laid on embankments, causing waterlogging on both sides. Florence maintained that irrigation with proper drainage systems was not injurious to health. Drainage was absolutely essential in the low land of Bengal to carry away the excess of flood and monsoon waters. Besides, fever was not always a result of swampy areas, but a direct consequence of 'drinking foul water', and the peasants 'had no access to clean water in the rural areas'. Hence, the point at issue was not whether irrigation was necessary for India, but how to make irrigation healthy.[113]

Another problem, Salisbury argued in his speech, was that the *ryots* were unwilling to take water from the canals:

> One of the difficulties we ought to have foreseen, but did not, is that you may provide water, but the cultivators won't take it. The people are slow to believe in anything, slowest of all in what their rulers do. They can't be persuaded partly from natural torpor, partly from suspicion into taking water that is brought to their very doors.[114]

There was some truth in this. When there was plenty of rain the *ryots* were reluctant to pay for water from the irrigation canals. When they faced drought they waited for rain, hoping that it would soon arrive and then, at the last moment, they would rush for canal water; often that would be too late to save the crops. Then there were the *zemindars* and the petty officials, who would threaten the *ryots* or would ask for bribes or illegal taxes for using canal water. Florence claimed that the reason *ryots* refused to take water was administrative mismanagement. They were unwilling, because, as happened in Orissa, it put them in the power of the minor officials, who, Florence did not forget to mention, were 'all natives'. 'Bribery, oppression, corruption, bullying, are the rule, the universal rule, with these petty officials,' she wrote. 'They have unlimited power to make themselves disagreeable and must be bought off with a bribe.'[115] Florence's claim was based on evidence provided by various British officials working in India, who were her ears and eyes. Her draft letters and private papers show that she had at least four or five officers who regularly provided her with facts and figures from different parts of India.[116]

Arthur Cotton, another critic of Salisbury's speech in Manchester, also referred to 'the unaccountable mismanagement of the revenue authorities, because of which the *ryots* were placed in such circumstances that they could not avail themselves of water … '. He claimed that the refusal of water was not a common thing: 'It sounds amusing in my ears to hear a European saying, we are of course most anxious to give the natives water, we are so wise and energetic, but the poor creatures are so stupid and apathetic that they can't understand the value of it. I should like to see the picture painted by a native.'[117]

The most forceful criticism against irrigation stemmed, of course, from the financial perspective; it was not cost-effective, it would not pay. 'Where we began the projects of irrigation for ourselves,' said Salisbury, 'we have not yet reached, I believe, in any one instance, the desired result of a clean balance sheet.'[118] As mentioned before, the argument that irrigation was not financially viable had been afloat since Lawrence's time. Investors were not willing to invest and the revenue from India, being mainly land revenue, could not be increased, as the *ryots*, already overburdened with heavy taxation, would not be able to pay. This was used as an excuse by the British Government to cut down on public works and irrigation projects in India. 'We are constantly told that we cannot have "public works" in India,' wrote Florence, 'because we cannot raise the "revenue" to pay for them. So ingrained is the idea that taxes are to pay for works – not works to pay the taxes.'[119]

The beneficial consequences of irrigation in India, as Florence had pointed out as early as 1873, far outweighed the cost. Additionally, irrigation and navigation are inseparably connected. Once this was taken into account, irrigation would become a profitable enterprise. It was sheer short-sightedness on the part of the British Government not to borrow money and invest it in irrigation and canals. Irrigation would increase the quality and quantity of agricultural yield, and famine would be preventable. That would mean less expenditure on famine relief. If people were well fed, their good health would improve the quality of the workforce. Increased agricultural wealth would also mean increased revenue for the Government.

Florence's arguments for irrigation and water transport were written and partly published before Salisbury delivered his speech in Manchester.

Her book, *The Zemindar, the Sun, and the Watering Pot*, was a masterly compilation of facts and figures in spite of Jowett's reservations about it. She took India state by state, province by province, to show what sort of irrigation was needed. She took place by place, river by river, stating how they were approachable by metal or track road, what irrigation scheme already existed there, what was done by the British, and how famine was averted where it was done correctly, what was the result of irrigation on the population, both ordinary and tribal, and what were the socio-political effects of irrigation canals on local people: 'In the progress report of India, 1873, we are told that the people of Mairwara – once wild and unruly – became a thrifty, peaceful and industrious peasantry under the influence of improvements brought in by irrigation.'[120] She quoted Sir Montgomery's evidence to the Select Committee, saying that if a canal could be taken down past Amritsar and Lahore, and the vast wasteland irrigated, the Sikhs would forget swords and concentrate on agriculture. She claimed that the political and fiscal value of irrigation was immense. Irrigation canals would give a far greater command of the country: ' ... a canal is worth more than a regiment; for the one only represses disaffection, the other changes it to affection.' ' ... having half a dozen more canals ... would possibly enable us to dispense with at least half-a-dozen European regiments.'[121]

Florence was not opposed to railways. She agreed that India needed both railways and canals, but not at the cost of one or the other. 'What was wanted in India,' she quoted Lord Stanley's speech at the Manchester Cotton Society's meeting in 1857, 'was not costly lines for rapid travelling, laid down in a few parts, but a comparatively inexpensive though slow means of communication extending over the whole face of the country.'[122] Her argument was that canal transport was cheap with small running costs. It was also safer than river transport because the current was minimal and there was no fear of storms. Such transits could cover shorter distances and could be worked at night with a small crew to operate. Besides cheapness, there were other advantages too: any type of goods could be carried and the vessel could go at its own speed. Goods could be moved directly from where they grew to where they were wanted. The stations, unlike for railways, could be anywhere on the journey. The boats themselves could serve as warehouses. Lockage could be easily managed and one would not need State rolling stock or establishment. All these could be undertaken by private enterprise.[123]

Florence did not stop at just showing the advantage of canals and water transport, she also told the Government where to dig the canals, how to do it with British capital and engineers, and where the water transport could be introduced. The extent and depth of her knowledge of Indian topography was awesome: 'For Bengal [and part of Upper Province] where canals can be taken out of permanent rivers and can be worked into the immense existing system of navigable rivers, navigation and irrigation should be combined.'[124] For the Central Provinces, her recommendation was: 'A canal should carried down the Mahanuddy from above Sumbulpore, as the navigable portion near Cattack, giving an outlet for those districts to the sea via Orissa, and giving irrigation to Sumbulpore.'[125] For Sind she recommended connecting links: 'Indus should be connected with Kurachee harbour ... all future canals should be navigable. All traffic is now on camels – very costly. In Sindh the cost of transit is consequently high.'[126] She concluded that by doing all these, Britain would be doing her duty to 'one-fifth of the human race'. 'There is no time to spare in India. If only 14,000,000 were spent on irrigation and navigation, the returns will be vast; we should be saved from famine expenditure with no returns but the sad returns of loss of life.'[127]

Florence's ambitious and visionary projection was soon curtailed by Lord Salisbury, who was at the forefront of the anti-irrigation lobby, and as he was also the Secretary of State any decision about the future of irrigation in India very much depended on him. The correspondence between Salisbury and Florence had started in as early as 1866, when he was still Lord Cranborne and the Secretary of State for India. At that time, they corresponded mainly on sanitation and public health improvement.[128] In April 1874, Florence sent Salisbury her 'little pamphlet' with an explanatory note:

> I have now been engaged for 15 years in Indian sanitary administration; and that a great part of its official and private documents passes through my hands. The first part of my little book has grown out of this. The second out of this dreadful famine ... . With regard to the second part; the Irrigation facts – there is no one but yourself who could, if you believe in them, turn by their means death into life for India.[129]

Shortly afterwards, she wrote another letter to Salisbury, elaborating further on her suggestions about sanitation in India.[130] Replying on 4 November 1874, Salisbury reminded her of the financial situation and argued that sanitary improvement did not mean 'reckless finance':

> I assure you we are not blind to the importance of the objects which you advocate nor are we the least inclined to interpose any unnecessary delay in their prosecution. The difficulty, of course, is money ...
> You must always bear in mind that at this moment our expenditure treads very closely upon the heels of our revenue, and that we absolutely do not know where to turn in order to obtain any great increase of revenue. But if we borrowed very largely, a great increase of revenue would be absolutely necessary to meet the interest of the new debt. However great the value of the improvements, we cannot afford to be

bankrupt, and a new productive Indian tax seems as distant as the philosopher's stone.[131]

Although the question of irrigation was not raised in this letter, financial exigencies, as before, became his main argument against irrigation. He viewed it purely as a question of finance and non-availability of information. In May 1875 in a long letter to Florence, Salisbury once more put forward all his arguments against the viability of irrigation in India. He claimed that the Government could not act because there was not enough information, there was no balance sheet regarding unfinished irrigation works, irrigation works started by the Hindu or Muslim rulers had left no account of their expenditure, there were difficulties in assessing the revenue yield of the irrigated land, and there was the risk of epidemics because of irrigation. Finally, he asked a question, which only a Secretary of State like Salisbury could possibly ask: ' ... is irrigation the creation or merely the anticipation of fertility? Does it make vegetable wealth which but for it would never have existed – or does it crowd into a few years the enjoyment [ ] of the whole productive power of the soil?'[132]

When Florence asked for the financial returns of irrigation works in India, she was told that such returns were not available. He himself was looking for such returns and enumerated all the difficulties that lay in achieving satisfactory returns from irrigation. Although Salisbury gave Florence some assurance that on receipt of irrigation returns he would send them to her, he never did. Most likely he himself never received a full account of irrigation gains and losses from India.[133] We find Florence writing to him again, suggesting that in the absence of uniform irrigation returns, perhaps an Inquiry Commission for irrigation work in India should be set up:[134]

> Your willingness, some months ago to take steps for securing accurate irrigation statistics from India, and your just complaint that there were none, seem to show you as thinking that there is ample scope for asking for enquiry ... And if you are not satisfied with what you have obtained am I too daring in suggesting that now would be the time to give effect to your desire to make an enquiry such as shall secure results and returns which can be laid before Parliament and the public with confidence?[135]

Florence not only suggested an Inquiry Commission but also who should be in it, how it should be run, what was the shortest and best way of gathering authenticated facts through a printed questionnaire, and tables 'upon a uniform basis which can be compared and tabulated'. She also suggested that each local government and administration should collect replies to the questionnaire and return them to the Commissioner. The Commission would summarise the results, especially as regards the capital invested both by Government and by the cultivators. The information was to be obtained only from the regular cultivators, not from the hill tribes or forest tracts. Special information was to be obtained about irrigation works that affected more than one village, the extent and effects of incomplete irrigation works, and of old works that were repaired and extended. She even mentioned the headings under which the questions should be asked, such as area of the project, its description, cost of construction, maintenance and repair, interest paid and, finally, direct and indirect returns from such a project.

In case Salisbury took offence, Florence did not forget to placate him by saying that her notes were meant to help to show the direction the inquiry should take, if it was to have any real results and returns: 'But these notes can easily be set aside; the enquiry, I am sure you will not set aside; since evidence is necessary to show what is the duty of the Govt. in promising irrigation ... '.[136] With all her knowledge and experience she was desperate to help. She continuously, and sometimes almost tragically, referred to her years of experience and the work she had done in putting together facts and figures from India. But unfortunately, Salisbury was reluctant to act quickly or to raise the matter with the Government of India immediately.

In November 1875, Salisbury, in another long letter to Florence, presented all the difficulties of making quick progress in India, particularly in irrigation: 'I may as well make a comprehensive confession that Indian accounts are very bad.' The main difficulty, Salisbury pointed out, was the impossibility of separating irrigation receipts from land revenue. Undoubtedly the land revenue had increased, but how much of it was due to canals was difficult to ascertain; there were no old records to go by. Besides, not every peasant had used canal water; some did at first and then stopped. There were other factors that had contributed to revenue increase, such as waste ground reclamation, price rises, a better market for the peasants created by the railways, stability of the Government and introduction of remunerative crops. The effects of all these factors, Salisbury concluded, were not easily calculated, nor could they be credited to the canals. Salisbury maintained that although vast amounts were liberally spent by Parliament on canals, mistaken plans were adopted and imperfect work was done in the early years that had been necessary to repeat. Finally, he fell back on his famous 'drift' theory, and the need for economy:

> Now all these difficulties can, in part at least, be solved: but it requires time – the time of skilled Europeans, for which you pay about the money you give in England to an Under Secretary of State. With a Treasury fighting for its life to make two ends meet you must excuse us if we are chary of much time.

Florence's attempt to initiate an irrigation Inquiry Commission did not get very far. Salisbury was not willing to have that either:

As for a Commission – I doubt its efficacy, Commissions are very invaluable to collect and summarize opinion, and they are often able to decide well one or two distinct issues of fact. But they are too unwieldy for the collection and digestion of a great variety of facts and figures. With the best of intentions, their work is slow and routine and in their report they gloss over the weak places with generalities.[137]

Salisbury followed the official line that irrigation works in India would have to be remunerative, and loans for them would have to be raised in India. Otherwise, such public works must wait.[138]

As Florence waited for the Secretary of State to take action, the Governor-General in India changed. Lord Northbrook resigned and Lord Lytton took over. Each time there was a change of Governor-General or Secretary of State, Florence saw new hope to push forward her ideas. On 26 February 1876, she wrote to Salisbury again, reminding him of the unsatisfactory situation regarding irrigation works in India and the need for an official inquiry. 'Now that Lord Lytton is going out as Viceroy you might think it not inopportune to give him your instructions.'[139] No such instructions were forthcoming. However, during Lord Lytton's administration, a Famine Commission was appointed, which reported in 1880, pressing the need for irrigation work as a famine-preventive measure and repeating many of the arguments Florence had offered. Irrigation work in India did not get a favourable hearing until Lord Curzon took over the vice-royalty and appointed an Irrigation Commission. This Commission reported in 1904, almost 28 years after Florence had originally suggested it.

In the meantime, in 1876, when Florence wanted to conduct research on irrigational returns with the information available in the India Office, she was accused of meddling in a matter that was beyond her jurisdiction. The final rebuff was dealt in 1878, when she was sent a Minute paper from the Revenue Department:

> The Revenue Committee is of the opinion that an intimation should be made to Miss Nightingale to the following effect.
>
> The various subjects of high interest to which she refers are engaging the earnest attention of the Government of India and its most experienced officers. This may be accepted as a general fact, but in addition to this, a special inquiry is about to be made, by a carefully selected commission on the subject of famines, the investigations of which will embrace the many intricate questions to which Miss Nightingale refers. The instructions to the special commission will be of the widest and minutest character, and no exertion will be spared to render the enquiry complete.
>
> While then the Secretary of State would on public grounds, deprecate the researches which Miss Nightingale wishes to make, as possibly interfering with and embarrassing the comprehensive inquiry of a commission appointed by the Govt. of India under the order of H.M.'s Government, he would as a matter of official propriety, point out to

> Miss Nightingale, whose advice and intelligent philanthropy is univer-
> sally recognised, that to open the records of a public office to the free
> inspection of a private individual, however distinguished for character
> and ability, would constitute a very inconvenient precedent.[140]

As the official doors had closed to the 'private individual', the only way
that remained open to Florence was to write and publicise about India,
and that was when, in 1878, shortly after receiving the Revenue Department's Minute, she published her famous article, *The People of India*:
'We do not care for the people of India. This is a heavy indictment, but
how else to account for the facts about to be given?'[141]

Notes

1. FN (1873), 'The zemindar, the sun and the watering pot as affecting life or
    death in India: the zemindary system as affecting life or death in India'
    (proof copy), p. 1, BL Nightingale Papers, 1858–1894 (hereafter referred to
    as ZSW).
2. Dutt, R.C. (1874), *The Peasantry of Bengal*, Calcutta: Thacker, Spink &
    Co., pp. 151–170.
3. FN (1874a), *Life or Death in India, with an Appendix on Life or Death by
    Irrigation*, London: Spottiswoode and Co., p. 7. The opening page of this
    article also had another title, 'How some people have lived and not died in
    India'. The same with the Appendix (p. 27), 'Life or death by irrigation',
    subtitled 'How to make irrigation healthy'.
4. FN (1874a), p. 63.
5. Jowett to FN, 11 August 1874, as quoted in Quinn and Prest (1987), pp.
    261-266, reprinted by permission of Oxford University Press; Lawrence to
    FN, 21 December 1874, BL Add. Mss 45777, fol. 197.
6. See BL Add. Mss 45780. This volume contains most of Frere's letters written
    to Florence.
7. Plowden to FN, 22 July 1868, BL Add. Mss 45782, fols 165–167. The
    earlier sanitary reports were compiled and drafted by FN and still exist in
    her private papers in the British Library.
8. FN to Stafford Northcote, BL Add. Mss 45779, 25 July 1867, fols 93–99,
    and 28 September 1867, fols 114–119.
9. Cook (1913), vol. 2, p. 273.
10. BL Add. Mss 46385, fol. 101. This lists 71 books, official reports and Blue
    Books found in 10 South Street after her death. Except for two, all were on
    India such as the annual sanitary reports on Bengal, Assam, NWP, Oudh,
    Punjab; vital statistics reports; cholera reports; census reports, etc.
11. FN to Martineau, 20 September 1871, BL Add. Mss 45788, fol. 318.
12. Bosworth Smith (1883), vol. 2, pp. 435–438.
13. Frere to FN, 25 August 1868, BL Add. Mss 45780, fol. 117.
14. Frere to FN, 25 August 1868, BL Add. Mss 45780, fol. 118.
15. Frere to FN, 10 September 1868, BL Add. Mss 45780, fol. 124.
16. Frere to FN, 23 October 1868, BL Add. Mss 45780, fol. 135.
17. Frere to FN, 1 November 1868, BL Add. Mss 45780, fol. 141.
18. Cook (1913), vol. 2, p. 169.

19. Hunter, W.W. (1875), *The Life of Lord Mayo*, London: Smith Elder and Co., vol. 2, p. 272.
20. Mayo was assassinated in Port Blair, Andaman, by a Wahabi supporter in 1872.
21. Jowett to FN, 3 April 1872, as quoted in Quinn and Prest, 1987, p. 228, reprinted by permission of Oxford University Press.
22. Cook (1913), vol. 2, p. 214.
23. Northbrook to Cranborne (Salisbury), 11 March 1874, BL Add. Mss 45779, fols 16–24.
24. FN (1874a), p. 3.
25. FN (1874a), pp. 3–4.
26. FN (1874a), p. 13. Her enthusiasm about Calcutta being 'drained', and clean water supplied to all the households was based on somewhat incorrect data. Even three years later, in 1876, Beverley's Census Report (Beverley (1876)) showed that Calcutta was drained and clean water supplied largely within the boundaries of the white residential area.
27. FN (1874a), p. 12.
28. Bhatia, B.M. (1972), *Famines in India*, Delhi: Asia Publishing, pp. 65–69.
29. Dutt, R.C. (1901), *Indian Famines: their Causes and Prevention*, London: P.S. King & Son, pp. 1–2.
30. FN, ZSW, p. 141.
31. FN (1878a), 'The united Empire and the Indian peasant', *Journal of the National Indian Association*, June, no. 90, p. 232.
32. Dutt, R.C. (1902), *The Economic History of British India*, London: Kegan Paul, Trench & Trubner, p. vi.
33. See Baird-Smith, R. (1861), *Report on the Famine of 1860–61*, Calcutta: Government of India, Home Dept.; *Report of the Commissioners Appointed to Enquire into the Famine in Bengal and Orissa 1866*, Calcutta: Government of India, 1867; Dalyell, R.A. (1867), *Memorandum on the Madras Famine of 1866*, Madras; Government of India, Famine Commission Reports, 1880, 1898, 1901.
34. Frere to FN, 14 February 1874, BL Add. Mss 45780, fol. 229.
35. FN (1878b), 'The people of India', *The Nineteenth Century*, no. XVIII, August, p. 193.
36. Srivastava, H. (1968), *The History of Indian Famines and Development of Famine Policy, 1858–1918*, Agra, Sri Ram Mehra & Co., pp. 329–330.
37. FN (1878a), p. 232.
38. See Indian Economic and Social History Association (1969), *Indian Economy in the Nineteenth Century: a Symposium*, Delhi, Hindustan Publishing Corporation; Charlesworth, N. (1982), *British Rule and the Indian Economy, 1800–1914*, London: Macmillan; Ambirajan, S. (1978), *Classical Political Economy and British Policy in India*, Delhi: Vikas Publishing House.
39. Stokes, E. (1959), *The English Utilitarians and India*, Oxford: Clarendon Press, p. viii.
40. See Chatterjee, B. (1992), *Trade, Tariffs and Empire: Lancashire and British Policy in India*, Oxford: Oxford University Press.
41. Dutt (1897), p. 127.
42. Charlesworth (1982), p. 70.
43. FN (1883a), p. 48.
44. Charlesworth (1982), pp. 18–19.
45. Dutt (1902), pp. ix–x. 'In Bengal the land tax was fixed at over 90 percent of the rental, and in Northern India at over 80 percent of the rental, between

1793 and 1822. ... The last Mahomedan ruler of Bengal, in the last year of his administration (1764), realised a land revenue of £817,553; within thirty years the British rulers realised a land revenue of £2,680,000 in the same province ...'

46. The land revenue system introduced by Lord Cornwallis in the Bengal Presidency in 1793. See Chapter VI.

47. FN (1878b), p. 204.

48. Ganguli, B.N. (1965), *Dadabhai Naoroji and the Theory of Drain,* London: Asia Publishing House, pp. 1–36; Banerjee, A. (1995), *Finances of the Early Raj: Investments and the External Sector,* New Delhi: Sage, Appendix I, pp. 327–8; Dutt (1902), pp. 398–420.

49. Naoroji's evidence to the Finance Committee, as quoted in Seymour Keay, J. (1883), 'The spoliation of India', *The Nineteenth Century,* vol. LXXVII, July, p. 8.

50. Dutt (1902), p. xii.

51. Banerjee (1995), p. 59.

52. Lawrence threw a durbar during the Orissa Famine.

53. Lawrence to Stafford Northcote, quoted in Bosworth Smith (1883), vol. 2, p. 524.

54. Dutt (1902), p. xiii: 'The Indian debt which was £51,000,000 in 1837 rose to £97,000,000 in 1862. Within the forty years of peace which have succeeded, the Indian debt has increased continuously, and now (1901) amounts to £200,000,000.'

55. Bhatia (1972), p. 73.

56. Campbell, G. (1893), *Memoirs of my Indian Career,* Barnard C.E. (ed.), London, Macmillan & Co., vol. 2, p. 324.

57. Bhatia (1972), pp. 65–9.

58. Salisbury to Northcote, as quoted in Banerjee (1995), p. 78.

59. Bhatia (1972), p. 95.

60. FN, ZSW, p. 109.

61. The book has three sections and an appendix: 'Irrigation as affecting life or death in India'; 'Progress of irrigation in India – means of communication in India'; 'Famines in India'. The appendix consists of statistics on the financial effects of canals.

62. Wedderburn, W. (1914), 'Florence Nightingale on India', *The Contemporary Review,* April, vol. 105, no. 580, pp. 509–516.

63. Jowett to FN, 11 August 1874, as quoted in Quinn and Prest (1987), p. 261, reprinted by permission of Oxford University Press.

64. Jowett to FN, 25 December 1874, as quoted in Quinn and Prest (1987), p. 266, reprinted by permission of Oxford University Press.

65. FN, ZSW, p. 14. See also FN (1874b), 'Irrigation and means of transit', letter, 30 July 1874, *Illustrated London News,* August 1874, vol. 65, p. 99; also reprinted in *Journal of the National Indian Association,* September 1874, no. 45, pp. 215–219 (FN, 1874c).

66. FN, ZSW, p. 148.

67. FN, ZSW, p. 146.

68. FN (1878b), p. 194.

69. FN (1878b), p. 193, 200.

70. FN (1878b), p. 198.

71. Dutt, R.C. (1904), *The Economic History of India in the Victorian Age,* London: Kegan Paul, Trench & Trubner, pp. 144–153.

72. FN (1878b), p. 199.
73. FN (1878b), p. 218.
74. FN (1878b), p. 208.
75. FN (1878b), p. 210.
76. FN (1878b), p. 212.
77. Hyndman, H. (1878), 'The bankruptcy of India', *The Nineteenth Century*, no. XX, October, p. 588.
78. Sen, P.R. (ed.) (1937), *Florence Nightingale's Indian letters*, Calcutta: M.K. Sen, p. 49.
79. Cook (1913), vol. 2, p. 290.
80. FN to Louis Mallet, 10 August 1878, BL Add. Mss 45779, fol. 170, draft.
81. FN to Louis Mallet, 10 August 1878, BL Add. Mss 45779, fols. 170–176, draft.
82. Garthorne-Hardy, A.E. (ed.) (1910), *Garthorne-Hardy, First Earl of Cranbrook. A Memoir*, London: Longman, vol. 2, p. 79.
83. Cook (1913), vol. 2, pp. 290–291.
84. FN to Louis Mallet, 26 August 1878, BL Add. Mss 45779, fol. 175.
85. Cranbrook to Lytton, 13 August 1878, Garthorne-Hardy (1910), vol. 2, p. 80.
86. FN (1878b), p. 200.
87. FN (1879b), p. 566.
88. FN, ZSW, p. 115.
89. FN (1878b), p. 198.
90. FN (1879b), p. 638.
91. FN (1879b), p. 568.
92. FN (1878b), p. 195.
93. See Cotton, A. (1854), *Public Works in India: Their Importance with Suggestion for their Extension and Improvement*, London: Wm. H. Allen & Co.
94. Stone, I. (1984), *Canal Irrigation in British India: Perspectives of Technological Change in a Peasant Economy*, Cambridge: Cambridge University Press, p. 16.
95. Banerji (1995), pp. 73–121.
96. Bhatia (1972), p. 125.
97. Banerji (1995), p. 78.
98. Dutt (1904), p. 174.
99. Stone (1984), p. 25.
100. Banerji (1995), p. 23.
101. Cook (1913), vol. 2, p. 284.
102. See Cotton, A. (1880), *Reply to the Report of the Committee of the House of Commons on Indian Public Works*, Dorking: R.J. Clark; Cotton, A. (1875), *Irrigation in India: an Address in Reply to the Marquis of Salisbury, 26 February 1875*, Manchester: Guardian Letter Press.
103. Hope, E.R. (1900), *General Sir Arthur Cotton – his Life and Work*, London: Hodder & Stoughton, vol. 2, p. 504.
104. Cotton to FN, Cook (1913), vol. 2, pp. 284–5.
105. Cook (1913), vol. 2, pp. 298–99.
106. Pulling, F.S. (1885), *Life and Speeches of the Marquis of Salisbury*, London: Sampson Low & Co., vol. 1, p. 222.
107. Anon (1889), *Lord Salisbury's 'Black man'*, Lucknow: G.P. Verma & Brothers Press, p. 1. Lord Salisbury, speaking of the Holborn election, said in 1888: 'Mr. Gainsford Bruce's is undoubtedly a small majority than [sic]

Colonel Duncan won last time; but then Colonel Duncan was opposed to a black man, and however great the progress of mankind has been, and however far we have advanced in overcoming prejudices, I doubt if we have yet got to the point when a British constituency will take a black man to represent them. Of course you must understand that I am speaking roughly and using language in its ordinary colloquial sense, because I imagine the colour is not exactly black, but at all events he was a man of another race who was very unlikely to represent an English community.'

108. Pulling (1885), vol. 1. pp. 254–55.
109. Cotton (1875), p. 19.
110. FN (1878b), p. 205.
111. Cotton (1875), p. 18.
112. See Harris, D.G. (1923), *Irrigation in India*, London: Oxford University Press; Whitcombe, E. (1972), *Agrarian Condition in Northern India*, Berkeley, CA: University of California Press.
113. FN (1874a), Appendix, p. 27.
114. Cotton (1875), p. 14.
115. FN (1878a), p. 237.
116. BL Add. Mss 45827, fol. 121. Her contacts were: 1) Mr Auckland Colvin for N.W. Provinces; 2) Mr Morris for Central Provinces; 3) Mr Pedder for Bombay; 4) Mr Dalyall for Madras; 5) Mr Princep for Punjab.
117. Cotton (1875), pp. 14-16.
118. Cotton (1875), p. 13.
119. FN, ZSW, p. 91.
120. FN, ZSW, p. 94.
121. FN, ZSW, p. 99.
122. FN, ZSW, p. 136.
123. FN, ZSW, p. 135.
124. FN, ZSW, p. 116.
125. FN, ZSW, p. 126.
126. FN, ZSW, p. 128.
127. FN, ZSW, p. 141.
128. FN to Cranborne (Salisbury), 18 August 1866, and 4 February 1867, BL Add. Mss 45779, fol. 5 and fol. 7, drafts.
129. FN to Salisbury, 25 April 1874, BL Add. Mss 45779, fol. 8, draft. It is not clear which 'little pamphlet' she sent. It seems from the date that it must have been her *Life or Death in India*, (FN, 1874a) which contained 'Irrigation' in the appendix.
130. FN to Salisbury, 28 October 1874, Cook (1913), vol. 2, p. 277.
131. Salisbury to FN, 4 November 1874, BL Add. Mss 45779, fol. 10.
132. Salisbury to FN, 10 May 1875, BL Add. Mss 45779, fols 32–35.
133. Banerji (1995), p 89.
134. Banerji (1995), Preface, p. 15.
135. FN to Salisbury, 5 October 1875, Add. Mss 45779, fol. 38, draft.
136. FN to Salisbury, 5 October 1875, Add. Mss 45779, fol. 38 draft.
137. Salisbury to FN, 1 November 1875, BL Add. Mss 45779, fols 50–54.
138. Banerji (1995), p. 120.
139. FN to Salisbury, 26 February 1876, BL Add. Mss 47779, fol. 56.
140. Minute Paper, Revenue Department, 7 February 1878, BL Add. Mss 47779, fol. 77. See also Cook (1913), vol. 2, pp. 287–88.
141. FN (1878b), p. 193.

CHAPTER SIX

The Ryot's Faithful Servant

In April 1878, a young Bengali lawyer from Calcutta, called Prasanna Kumar Sen, wrote a letter to Florence Nightingale, which she answered. This was not the only letter Prasanna Kumar Sen, or P.K. Sen, wrote to Florence; they carried on a regular correspondence for almost four years. The subject of their correspondence was the land tenure system and the conditions of the *ryots* that existed at the time in Bengal. It is not clear how many letters Florence wrote to P.K. Sen, as her private papers show no evidence that either P.K. Sen's letters to her or the draft copies of her replies were saved. However, a collection of Florence's letters to P.K. Sen was published in Calcutta in 1937, which showed that between April 1878 and March 1882 she wrote at least 14 letters to him.[1] P.K. Sen was 28 years old and Florence 58 at the time.

P.K. Sen wrote to Florence at a time when she herself was involved with the land questions and the conditions of the *ryots*. It was not surprising that Florence should get involved in matters such as land tenancy, rent laws and the occupancy rights of the *ryots*. For her, it was almost a logical step to take. Just as she had arrived at the conclusion that the talk of sanitation for the Indian masses was meaningless if they did not stay alive to enjoy the benefits of good health, pure water and drainage, in the same logical way she arrived at the conclusion that it was futile to increase the productivity of the land by irrigation to prevent famine if the *ryots* did not benefit from it, but it only lined the pockets of the *zemindars* and the moneylenders. She often asked who would benefit from the increased productivity of land by means of irrigation, who would make the gain. The Government certainly would, as they would collect increased revenue. The *zemindars* and the landowners would also profit, as they would collect more rent. But would the *ryots*, the poor peasants, also benefit from increased productivity of the land by irrigation? 'If there is irrigation the ryot says ... the *Zemindar* takes the whole profits of the water.'[2] Florence could see that unless the land tenure system and the occupancy right of the *ryots* were changed there was no hope for achieving real benefit for them. From irrigation and navigation, she thus took a logical step forward towards the most crucial and fundamental problem of agrarian relations in India, and moved closer to the 'hundred-headed hydra'. Considering the colonial context of nineteenth-century India, her decision to get involved in the land tenancy issue of Bengal was a remarkably bold move to make. Ignoring the advice of her well-wishers, she landed herself in a controversy that lasted almost seven years.

The land situation in India was a new territory for Florence, but the conditions of the *ryots* were nothing new. She was already well informed about their miserable conditions, their poverty, disease and death. Florence was not alone. Just as there was growing discontent about the situation in India, a number of British liberal thinkers and administrators were also deeply concerned about the conditions of the Indian peasantry and so too were the church missionaries. Over the years, several attempts were made to draw the attention of the authorities to the conditions of the Bengal *ryots*. The Protestant missionaries in Calcutta gave great importance to the question, and drew it to the attention of the Lieutenant-Governor of Bengal. Long and his fellow missionaries tried to persuade the Government to pass legislation to this effect. They even sent a signed petition to a Member of Parliament in 1852, asking for reform in the land system of Bengal. The petition was, however, ignored by the House of Lords.[3]

In October 1867, the Bengal Social Science Association prepared and circulated a questionnaire relating to the state of agriculture in Bengal and the conditions of the agricultural classes. H. Beverley, the Secretary of the Association at the time, prepared a statistical report from the information gathered by the Association's questionnaire.[4] The people who took part in answering the questionnaire were both Indian and British officials working in various parts of the presidency. The clerks working in the judge's courts also helped to compile the statistics. The list of names provided in the appendix of the report showed many well-known Bengali names. Among them was P.K. Sen from Narail. P.K. Sen and his uncle Parvoti Churn Roy were both involved with the question of land tenancy in Bengal and later, when it became a socio-political issue, Sen appealed to Florence for help.

Beverley's report, read in the meeting of the Bengal Social Science Association on 31 March 1868, was one of the earliest statistical reports on the Bengal *ryots*. The report took into consideration all aspects of peasant life, including the size of land holdings, capital, the role of the money-lender, hired hands, regulation of rent, disposal of crops, and social life and education. The report described the cultivation in Bengal as 'a system of la petite culture, or minute farming', where the actual cultivator, the *ryot*, was a mere tenant, not a proprietor. The owners of the land, the *zemindars*, were often absentee landlords. They either hired labourers to cultivate the land or sub-let it to small cultivators such as *patnidars* and *ijaradars*, who again sub-let it to the *ryots*. In some cases, the *ryots* had a right of occupancy; in others, they were tenants at will with no occupancy right. The rent of the land was often ill defined and arbitrary. Apart from fixed rates of rent, the landlords frequently demanded illegal payments such as 'salamis' or 'abwabs'. Whenever land changed hands, the rent was increased, and was 'payable as often in kind as in money and liable to be as frequently enhanced by illegal extortion as by the ordinary agency of the courts'. The result was constant antagonism and litigation between the *ryots* and the *zemindars*. Besides, a Bengal *ryot* was so poor that he could not carry on cultivating without the support of a moneylender: ' ... he has rarely the capital necessary for the seasons operations and in consequence has to borrow at usurious rates of interest, which absorb all the profits of cultivation.'[5] Such were the conditions of the Bengal *ryots* in the middle of the nineteenth century. But Bengal was not alone; similar situations existed all over India. To understand why, one has to look at the British land revenue policy.

Permanent Settlement of 1793

The big blot on the land revenue system in Bengal and some other parts of northern and eastern India was the Land Regulations of 1793, or Permanent Settlement as it is commonly known. Lord Cornwallis, the Governor-General, introduced it to facilitate the collection of land revenue and to secure the maximisation of revenue collected. Before 1793, the collection of land revenue was in disarray. The old Indian system had broken down and the new systems had not got a foothold. Different systems of rent collection existed in different parts of India, and without sufficient manpower or knowledge of the customs and languages of the country, the British found the land revenue system in India not only a mare's nest, but also not collectable to their satisfaction. Some attempt was made by Warren Hastings to introduce some regularity into the system, but the revenue he assessed was so excessive and arbitrary that people often failed to pay, so their properties were sold at auction.[6] There was also another drawback. The British, accustomed to their own land system where a landlord was proprietor of the land and the cultivator cultivated his land, found Indian land systems totally incomprehensible, particularly in Bengal. Here, between the State and the cultivator, there was no third party claiming a right over the land. The cultivators enjoyed their customary rights on the land and paid revenue to the Government. The Government officials, the so-called *zemindars*, were in fact revenue collectors.[7] The British also wanted to use the *zemindars* as revenue collectors, and at the same time to create a landed gentry in the same fashion that existed in Britain. The idea was that if these *zemindars* could be recognised as the proprietors of the soil, they would not only ease the burden of revenue collection, but would also invest in the productivity of the land out of their own interest and, above all, would remain faithful and friendly to the foreign Government because of the benefit and power they were given.

The Permanent Settlement of 1793 was a deal made between the Government and the *zemindars*. The Government recognised the *zemindars* as the proprietors of the land and it was agreed that they would be able to hold their land on the basis of paying a fixed amount of revenue to the Government. The revenue was assessed at a very high rate, on the grounds that it was going to be fixed for ever. What was settled here was the revenue payable to the Government by the *zemindars*, but the rent of the cultivators, the *ryots*, payable to the *zemindars*, was left unsettled. As long as the *zemindar* paid the fixed revenue, he was free to assess his own rent collectable from the ryot who cultivated his land. This unlimited and, in practice, uncontrolled power given to the *zemindars* in Bengal, and the non-interference of the Government for a prolonged period in history, were the two most important factors that caused so much suffering among the peasants. The unscrupulous *zemindars* were left free to exact as much rent as possible, legally or illegally, from the *ryots*. If his land was sub-let to middlemen like the *patnidars* or the *ijaradars*, they equally squeezed out more and more rent from the *ryots* and any extra profit they could make in cash or in kind. No one was interested in investing in the productivity of the land. The profitable present was more alluring to them than the distant productive future. Where the *ryots* were unable to pay, they lost their occupancy right or tenure.

By another act in 1799, Regulation VII, the *zemindars* were given power of distraint and imprisonment. The *ryots* could be evicted from their land for failing to pay rent, and all their possessions such as cattle, household goods, agricultural crops and implements could be taken away and the *ryots* could be imprisoned by the *zemindars* without going to the Court of Law. The Government also retained such powers where it was directly involved in managing land through the cultivators. These were all in the name of recovering the rent arrears. In 1812, another regulation was introduced, making the sale of land and the granting of leases easier for the *zemindars* and the Government.

It would be wrong to say that the Permanent Settlement did not make any provision for the *ryots*. There were some clauses in the agreement protecting the interests of the *ryots* and retaining the power of further legislation by the Government.[8] But this power was seldom used. For instance, the 1793 regulation made provision for written agreement between the *zemindar* and the *ryot* as to their mutual rights and duties, and rent assessed. Both parties were to have written documents of the contract, called the *kabuliyat* and *patta*. The *zemindar* would keep the former and the *ryot* would have the latter. What was not entered on these documents would be considered as illegal. To supervise and authenticate such documents, Government officials, the *kanungoes*, were appointed. But such measures were ineffective from the start since, as Florence had pointed out, the illiterate *ryots* did not know what they were signing for and the Government on the whole followed a policy of non-interference, as long as there was a smooth collection of revenue.

By the second half of the nineteenth century the agrarian situation in Bengal gradually reached such an intolerable and appalling state that the Government could not ignore it anymore. In India, as well as in Britain, public opinion started to turn against the Government's inertia. The power of the *zemindars*, and the extra profit they made by imposing illegal taxes while the Government's revenue remained the same, also started to cause concern. In 1859, the Government passed a law, the Bengal Rent Act of 1859, to protect the interests of the *ryots*. This was the first attempt by the Government to put into practice some of the safeguards for the *ryots* originally mentioned in the act of 1793. This new act gave the *ryots* 'occupancy' rights if they had been cultivating the same piece of land for 12 years continuously. This made it somewhat difficult for the *zemindars* to evict the *ryots* from their land, but the powerful *zemindars* tried to prevent the *ryots* occupying a piece of land continuously for 12 years and thus avoided creating 'occupancy rights'. However, only a small proportion of *ryots* could claim occupancy rights; the conditions of those who were tenants-at-will remained unchanged. The new act also curtailed some of the *zemindar*'s power, such as forcing the *ryot* to attend his court and, in some cases, his power of distraint. The enhancement of rent was also made subject to certain conditions. Needless to say, the *zemindars* did not feel happy about these changes, as they considered them as interfering with their ability to collect rents. They demanded a change of the law, and the European planters, who were also landowners, closed ranks with them.

Although the act of 1859 provided some protection for the *ryots*, it was difficult to supervise its application in distant villages. Besides, the law had so many loopholes that it was subject to legal interpretation, which the *zemindars* took full advantage of. In litigation, the illiterate *ryot* had no effective protection, as the law was often interpreted in favour of the *zemindars*. Where the unscrupulous *zemindars* could not achieve their goal through legal means, they continued their illegal oppression of the *ryots*, which knew no bounds. Their illegal demand for enhanced rent worsened the situation so much that, while the Government was busy deliberating with tenancy reform, there was a widespread peasants' revolt in 1873 in the Pabna district in north Bengal, which gradually spread to east Bengal. The *ryots* there refused to pay illegally enhanced rents, and organised themselves into solidarity groups and land leagues to resist the *zemindars*' oppression. This was inevitably followed by the breakdown of law and order, looting, arson and violence.[9]

As agrarian tension heightened in Bengal, the Government was under pressure to take action. After much hesitation, a new law was passed, the Agrarian Disputes Act of 1876, which proposed to fix rent on the basis of competition. The law was considered a failure from the start in sorting out the relation between the *zemindars* and the *ryots*. In the meantime, the clamour for change in the rent law from the *zemindars* and the planters continued. They claimed that the existing law did not allow them a speedy collection of rent arrears. In 1878, the Government brought out a new bill to facilitate the collection of rent arrears for the *zemindars*. But this new bill, the Arrears of Rent Realization Bill of 1878, caused widespread protests in various quarters, particularly among the *ryots* and their sympathisers. There were *ryots'* meetings in various parts of Bengal and in Calcutta. The *ryots* submitted a petition against the bill to the Lieutenant-Governor of Bengal,[10] a copy of which also reached Florence in England, which she used to write an article later.

The tension regarding the Arrears of Rent Realization Bill of 1878 reached such a height in the Bengal Presidency that the Government decided not to proceed further with the bill, but instead to appoint a Rent Law Commission to inquire into the entire rent question. This Commission reported in June 1880, and shortly afterwards produced a draft tenancy bill that contained various progressive measures for the benefit of the *ryots*.[11] The bill received support from the *ryots* but strong opposition from the *zemindars* and the landholders. In the face of such opposition, the bill was drafted and redrafted and later amended considerably. It was submitted to the Bengal Legislative Council by Sir Courtney Ilbert on 2 March 1883, during Lord Ripon's viceroyalty. The bill was finally passed on 1 November 1885, during Lord Dufferin's administration, and came to be known as the Bengal Tenancy Act of 1885.

It was during this period of 1878–82, when protests and agitation were taking place all over Bengal over rent realisation and land tenancy reform, that Florence and P.K. Sen exchanged correspondence; her letters reflect some of the events that took place at that time. Sen wrote to Florence at a very appropriate time, when she herself was deeply concerned about the well-being of the *ryots*. She was also frustrated at the inefficiency of the British officials in handling famine situations effectively and the insufficiency of the British justice system to save the *ryots* from the clutches of the moneylenders. Her own failure to rally the authorities to uphold the importance of irrigation in India also annoyed her. Yet she fully understood that the improvement of irrigation or the justice system was not enough to eradicate the misery of the *ryots* without a new system of land tenure that would secure their legal rights on their holdings. She considered the health and sanitation problems of the *ryots* as the direct result of the existing agrarian system, which had kept them in a perpetual poverty-stricken condition.

Sen's first letter to Florence was written on 21 February 1878, when the Arrears of Rent Realization Bill was the topic of the day. He sent her a book and sought her support for the cause of the *ryots*. She responded in her usual manner in a long letter, referring to the contents of the bill, and the peasant disturbances in the Pabna district:

> April 4 – [18]78
>
> I am extremely obliged to you for your letter of Feb. 21, and for your marked copy of the 'Arrears of Rent Realization Bill' and the discussion upon it in the Bengal Council. I have made what use of this I could ...
>
> ... you would be doing an enormous good, if you were to collect and give facts – individual and personal histories of ryots – as to this his zeal.
>
> ... Many of the provisions of the Bill which you notice do certainly seem far too severe and one-sided.
>
> Neither the Backergunge nor any other ryots are nearly so bad as they are painted. On the contrary, it is a good sign that they learn to stand up for their rights. Only let them do so by lawful means. And remembering that, besides, the wickedness of murder and robbery, such evil deeds do the greatest possible harm to their own cause and their country's.
>
> I thank you again and again for your extremely interesting letter. I shall have much to say to it some day, but there is no time this mail ...
>
> ... and pray believe me, wishing you success.
>
> ever your and the Ryot's faithful servant
>
> Florence Nightingale.[12]

As mentioned earlier, this letter started correspondence that lasted almost four years. Sen sent her a number of books and pamphlets on the question at issue, including his own, and Florence circulated them among her friends 'who care for India and who have influence'. In another letter, she told P.K. Sen that she was already collecting information that could not be challenged on the questions of land tenures, *zemindar–ryot* relations and illegal taxes imposed by the *zemindars*:

> 20 December 1878
>
> ... you will not wish me, I know, to take up time and paper with idle tho' well deserved compliments, when the object for both of us is one of such pressing, such vital importance.
>
> I would earnestly request you to put down narratives of individual ryots (with time, name and place) in this connection. English people will not read Reports in general, nor generalities, abstractions, statistics, or *opinions*, such as most Reports are full of. They want *facts*; individual facts concerning particular instances, real lives and effects.[13]

In spite of her sympathy with the *ryots*, Florence never approved of violence. She knew such action would only alienate the British administrators from the *ryots'* cause. She wanted to proceed through more acceptable means, such as publicising the *ryots*' conditions in British newspapers and journals, and mobilising public opinion in Britain. She had already started to do that. As mentioned earlier, between 1873 and 1879, she had published a number of articles and letters on Indian famine, the poverty of the *ryots* and the need for irrigation. Now, the tenancy issue in Bengal, and P.K. Sen's letters, gave her another opportunity to write. Florence urged P.K. Sen to send her facts:

> Give us detailed facts. We want to rouse the interest of the public: for behind the Cabinet in England, always stands the House of Commons and behind the House of Commons, always stands the British Public. And these are they we want to interest; and these can only be interested by narratives of real lives.[14]

Florence sought information from Sen about the *ryots*, their daily food and habits, their land assessment and land tenures; whether they had irrigation facilities, markets, water communication and roads. She wanted to know their agricultural methods, their names and biographies, and their villages by name. 'It is true that villages are "mere dots" let them cease to be "mere dots" to us in England thro' Mr P.K. Sen's pen.'[15] Florence wanted to use the materials sent to write an article similar to those she had published before:

> It seems like a Providence that you should have written on this subject and kindly sent it to me at the very time that we were seeking for information on the above points.
>
> *As you request it*, I feel bound to promise, God willing, that, if you will have the great kindness, as you have the power, of writing and sending us the accounts and facts which I venture to suggest to you, I will write a paper upon a subject which I may almost say interests me as much as it does you according to your desire.[16]

In fact, Florence had been preparing herself to write such an article for quite some time. As early as 1874, she had asked John Lawrence for information and advice on Bengal land tenancy. Lawrence had admitted that he was not an expert, but, ' ... if you like to entrust me the proof sheets of your work on the Ryot in Bengal, I will do my best to correct them ... At present I would be disposed to dissuade you from publishing anything.'[17] But Florence was the least likely person to listen to others, particularly when she could see the real point at issue was not so much a question of famine or of irrigation, it was primarily a question of land policy and the cultivator's right on his holding, and it was by British law that this right had been taken away in 1793.

Florence kept her promise to P.K. Sen and, in June 1883, she published her famous article, *The Dumb Shall Speak and the Deaf Shall Hear, or the Ryot, the Zemindar and the Government*. Like her previous articles, this one also was based on facts, which, as she had said in her letter to P.K. Sen, 'could not be successfully challenged'.[18] She gathered information from all sources to make the article as objective and impartial as possible. She used official documents, legal and judicial reports, select committee reports, newspaper editorials and materials from the 1793 Land Regulations. She also quoted from books, pamphlets and newspaper cuttings sent by P.K. Sen. She was certainly well versed in the intricacies of Bengal land tenancy, just as she was in sanitation, nursing or irrigation:

> It seems almost an impertinence to lay my facts before any who have been in India – which I have not – and who may even have seen great service in India; but what I have to try to state on these vast questions rest upon a mass of documentary evidence which few in India, and very few in England have seen. India has been familiar to me for more than twenty years from documents, the plain unvarnished evidence of plain witnesses.[19]

The land tenancy dispute of Bengal

To understand the full implication of Florence's article, it is necessary to put it in the context of the extent of the dispute over the Tenancy Bill. As mentioned earlier, the bill that was submitted by the Rent Commission in 1880 went through several years' gestation before it became an act. It bore the marks of at least two Lieutenant-Governors of Bengal, three Viceroys and two Secretaries of State. There were various socio-political and cultural forces at work as well. It polarised Bengali society, with the *ryots* and their friends on one side and, on the other, the *zemindars*, the landholders and their friends. The bill as first proposed had a number of safeguards for the *ryot*'s interests. It immediately created uproar among the *zemindars* and European planters, who were also landholders. They threatened to join together in a solidarity group in their protest, and were supported by powerful associations such as the British Indian Association and newspapers like the *Hindoo Patriot*.

In England, it was also a time when the Irish land reform was very much a topic of the day, and there was dark suspicion in some people's minds that such a pro-ryot Bill in Bengal could only be the work of the 'Irish factor' in the Rent Commission.[20] There was even disagreement among the members of the Rent Commission that drafted the bill. Two of the Indian members signed the report subject to separate minutes recorded by them, in which they expressed their strong disapproval of many of the proposed changes and said that some of them would virtually amount to a confiscation of private property.[21] The fear of the 'Irish factor' in the Tenancy Bill was so strong that Sir Courtney Ilbert, the Law

Member of the Governor-General's Council, had to dispel it in the final presentation of the Bill in 1883. He went so far as to say that the Bengal Tenancy Bill was not fashioned after the Irish law. It was based on the recommendations of the Bengal Rent Commission, and it endeavoured 'to redeem a pledge which was given at the time of the Permanent Settlement, and which has never been adequately redeemed'.[22]

The irony of the situation was that in this rent and tenancy question the British administrators were far more favourable towards the *ryots* than the Bengali *zemindars* and landowners. 'These are hundred times more anti-people, anti-own people,' wrote Florence to Toynbee in 1882, 'than the straightest English officials are.'[23] However, it must be acknowledged that not all Bengali *zemindars* were against the *ryots*; some *zemindars* actually agitated for them. But the wrath of those who opposed the bill knew no bounds. Jatindra Mohon Tagore, an ex-member of the Governor-General's Council, described the Bengal Tenancy Bill as singularly 'one-sided'. It was all for the *ryots* and nothing for the *zemindars*. In a meeting of the British Indian Association on 5 April 1883, he said:

> I think that this bill if passed into law, will effect a redistribution of property on communistic principles, for the ryots are to be raised to the status of co-partners, and the zemindars relegated to the position of only one fifth share holders in the estate though their responsibilities as owners will perhaps remain the same.

He was vehemently opposed to any concessions given to the *ryots*, and thought that such ideas were 'evidently imported from the New Irish Land Law which has justly raised so much dissatisfaction among the landowners of England and Ireland'.[24] Similarly, Kristo Das Pal, a member of the Legislative Council and the editor of the *Hindoo Patriot*, though keen to see 'that justice was done', took the side of the *zemindars* on points of law. He described the Permanent Settlement of 1793 as the 'Magna Carta' of the rights of *zemindars* and *ryots*, which should be respected. He argued that the Permanent Settlement accepted the *zemindars* as the proprietors of the land and they should have all the rights as enjoyed by the British landlords under British law.[25]

Just as the *zemindars* considered the new Tenancy Bill as the curtailment of their rights and privileges and a confiscation of their properties, the *ryots* and their friends, some of whom were also progressive *zemindars*, maintained that the bill did not go far enough to secure the *ryots*' interest and that some of the provisions in the draft bill were 'ill-calculated to better their condition, and may lead to quite unexpected results'.[26] In between these two poles were the Lieutenant-Governors of Bengal, the Viceroys and the Secretaries of State. It is interesting to see that there were interactions of political leanings among the administrators as well. Most of them felt the need for a change in the tenancy law in Bengal for one reason or another. Many of them were on the side of the *ryots* and wanted to give them back their customary rights. Many others did not want a complete reversal of policy that would curtail some of the *zemindars'* privileges.

George Campbell, the Lieutenant-Governor of Bengal from 1872 to 1874, was sympathetic towards the *ryots*, but did not want to upset the *zemindars*. Campbell was replaced by Richard Temple in 1874, who was unquestionably in favour of the *zemindars* and planters. He wanted to help them with quick recovery of arrears of rent, and during his time the Agrarian Disputes Act V was passed to deal with rent disputes quickly. He also proposed to fix the rent payable by the *ryots* on the basis of competition, but his terms of office ended before he could put his proposal into practice. Temple was replaced by Ashley Eden in 1877. Eden to a certain extent acknowledged the *ryots'* customary rights on land, but he also favoured the *zemindars'* need for the recovery of rent arrears. However sympathetic some of these administrators might have been towards the *ryots'* cause, one thing was certain: they did not want to rock the boat and abandon the *zemindars*, who were loyal friends. After all, they had not taken part in the mutiny. As Kristo Das Pal said in the Legislative Assembly: ' ... in times of difficulty the *zemindars* have loyally, willingly and cheerfully placed their services at the disposal of the Government.'[27]

The dumb shall speak and the deaf shall hear

Although more than a hundred years have passed since Florence wrote the article at the height of the Tenancy Bill controversy, with land tenancy in Bengal undergoing radical transformation with the abolition of the *zemindari* system after independence in 1947, it is still worthwhile looking at her suggestions and criticisms of the bill to appreciate how well ahead of her time this extraordinary woman was.

The aim of Florence's article was twofold. She wanted to make the British public aware of the need for a pro-*ryot* tenancy act in Bengal and to also draw their attention to Ripon's good work in India, particularly to the changes he was trying to introduce in the bill (to which we will return in the next chapter). Florence's argument was that the Government reports had conclusively shown that the *zemindars* had not fulfilled their part of the bargain made in the Permanent Settlement. They had failed to honour their obligations and duties as laid down in the regulations of 1793, and had imposed illegal taxes on the *ryots*. The time had arrived for restoring the rights of the *ryots*. She also argued that the Government should have intervened wherever and whenever the rights of the *ryots* were infringed, but they had not done so.[28] On the one hand, she tried to establish the illegality of the *zemindars'* action and, on the other, she tried to shame the Government for its incompetence. She maintained that the Tenancy Bill did not confiscate the *zemindars'* rights as was alleged and was only wanted to restore the rights of the *ryots*. What had really been 'confiscated' so far, she added sarcastically, was the *zemindars'* duties towards the *ryots*.

> We seem to have 'confiscated' the Zemindar's <u>duties</u>, while confirming and enlarging his [so-called] <u>rights</u>; we seem to have allowed these fictions of rights – at first only winked at by Governments' sleepy eyes – to become settled rights and ownership; to have allowed the duties which we forgot, or neglected to require from him to become <u>nil</u>, though he held the land on these sole conditions; to have conferred new rights without conditions or corresponding duties.[29]

Referring to Regulation VII of the 1793 act, which asked the proprietors of the land 'to conduct themselves in good faith and moderation towards their dependent Talookdars and *ryots*' and not to demand rent increase or levy arbitrary taxes, Florence asked: 'Have they done this? ... What is the fact?'[30] The facts showed, she gibed, quoting the Bengal Government records, 'The ryot seems always to pay and not often be paid.'

> He pays on his own marriage, he pays on his son's marriage, he pays on his daughter's marriage ... he pays on Zemindar's marriage, he pays on Zemindar's son's marriage, he pays on the Gomastah's [agent's] son's or Gomastah's daughter's marriage, he pays on the Zemindar's son's birth, he pays on the Zemindar's son's first taking rice, he pays on the Zemindar's funeral, he pays on his own 'ploughing of the land', he pays to the Zemindar 'making a tour' through his estate [when the Zemindar goes to his estate, the ryot has to pay for everything, and also to pay the servants], he pays for being 'permitted to perform puja, or any festival', himself, he pays equally for the Zemindar performing puja, he pays a tax for 'presents to fakirs', the very drum pays for being beat 'at processions, marriages, and feasts ... The ryot pays a fee for everything he does himself, and for everything the Zemindar does not do for himself or the ryot, and makes the ryot do for him.[31]

There was no doubt that a large portion of the blame did lie with the Government, as it took an ambivalent attitude towards the *zemindar–ryot* relationship. Its policy of non-interference, from 1793 up to 1859, allowed the insufferable situation of the Bengal peasantry to be perpetuated. The laws were passed only as a piecemeal effort to rectify the situation, and most of the legislation favoured the *zemindars*.

It is also interesting to note that just as one day the British Government did not hesitate to vest unlimited de facto power in the hands of the *zemindars* to facilitate and maximise their land revenue collection, almost a century later they wanted to curtail such powers, primarily for their own pecuniary interest. Over the years, the Permanent Settlement caused a massive revenue loss for the Government. The amount payable by the *zemindars* to the Government was fixed. As the value of land increased due to the introduction of railways, irrigation canals and other public works, it brought extra income for the *zemindars* but the land revenue for the Government remained the same. The *zemindars* were able to extract more rent and profit from the land, but the income of the state remained unchanged. The Government was unable to share in the zemindari profits. Florence did not underestimate this, but she looked at it from the *ryots*' point of view:

> In three-quarters of a century the Government revenue has increased from about 3 millions to three and half millions, whilst the Zemindar's rental has grown from about a third of a million gross to more than thirteen millions. But this rental of thirteen millions is only an official return for road cess purposes. The real amount, including illegal exactions, paid annually by the occupants of the soil, is said to be between twenty-five and thirty millions. But taking it at thirteen millions only, the ryots now pay an excessive exaction of £8,273,000 yearly. If this be valued at twenty years purchase, we have deprived the cultivators of this enormous sum of £165,000,000 and given it to the zemindars who still cry for more.[32]

The financial interest did help to modify the attitude of some of the British administrators towards the *ryots*. But there were other interests too. One such interest was to defuse any possibility of a peasant uprising in India, as had happened in various parts of Europe and in Ireland. Florence herself was very much aware of this. As we have seen in the previous chapter, she continuously pointed out that the masses of India would not remain quiet for long if their conditions did not improve. Florence knew that both in England and Europe there was a growing consciousness among the peasants and working class about their political rights. She was well informed about the working class movements in Britain and the liberal social policies that were adopted to cope with such agitations. Similarly, she knew that in India, peasant uprisings or revolts were no more unheard of. There had been the Deccan riot of 1874 against the moneylenders; a few years earlier the Indigo Revolt had taken place in Bengal against the exploitation of the European planters, and then there was the Pabna disturbance against zemindar oppression in 1873. As previously noted, in the Pabna disturbances, the peasants had organised themselves to form land leagues to stand up against the *zemindars*. Although the British Raj was politically and militarily established at the time and there was no threat to their power, such peasant organisations caused concerns among the administrators as the possibility of another large-scale uprising was never ruled out from their mind after 1857.

Florence shared this concern and expressed the fear that unless the new Tenancy Bill laid a foundation for a better state of things, the general discontent would continue. She urged the Government to consider her paper as a timely warning and to undo the harm they had done:

> If not, what a future of trouble, ending we know not how, not only for Bengal, but for India. ... And there is not an hour to be lost. It has been truly said that it is not despair, not utter want and misery which leads to revolution; it is the gradual awakening from this state to know our higher wants.

She pointed out that the present events and reports from India showed which way the tide was turning: 'The ignorant ryot is learning his rights.'[33]

It did not escape Florence's notice that some of these disturbances, particularly in Pabna, had an apparent religious colour.[34] She blamed the British Government for leaving everything to chance. 'In the end, the reformed Puritan Mahommedan doctrines have made their democratic way among the Mahommedan cultivators, chiefly in Eastern Bengal, and these have formed powerful land leagues against the *zemindars* and have successfully rebelled against the indigo planters.'[35] Florence appealed to the British Government and the British public about the urgency of the situation. She implored them to take notice, if not for any other reason but to 'avert political danger of the sg more embittered and threatening every day'.[36]

What Florence was trying to do in her article was not only to review the redrafted Tenancy Bill from all possible perspectives but also to give a voice to the plea of the *ryots* as expressed in their petition.[37] Florence could see that in this confrontation between the *zemindars* and the *ryots* the former were occupying a stronger position:

> The landed and wealthy classes of Bengal have powerful organs in the press and powerful friends, both here and at home. They are, many of them, very amiable persons, of great intelligence, and great benevolence. Officials are glad to do them favours and find it pleasant to be on friendly relations with them. Every prejudice arising out of the Western notions of property, and the relations of landlord and tenant in Great Britain is entirely on their side.[38]

She feared, with the other well-wishers of the *ryots*, that in all probability the *zemindars* would get the proposed Rent Bill amended in their favour whereas the illiterate *ryots*, with no access to legal protection, would lose out on even the slightest concession that was given to them in the bill. She could also see that the so-called 'native' members of the Legislative Council were more likely to serve the *zemindars*' interests. There was no one to represent the interests of the *ryots* in the Council. 'The difficulty is that,' she wrote to P.K. Sen, 'in all these cases the zemindars are strongly represented in the Bengal Council, while the *ryots* are not at all, except in so far as the official men protect them.'[39] '[W]here are the native members of the Council ?' Florence asked, 'Do these members help or do they join against their own flesh and blood, like Satan devouring their own children?'[40]

It was mentioned earlier that the British Indian Association, a powerful and influential organisation, came forward to support the *zemindars*. The Association, founded in 1851, was an all-India-based organisation, but the members of the Bengal branch were mostly *zemindars*. The membership subscription was so high that ordinary people could not afford to join. It was an exclusive political forum for the upper class, and its members were also leading personalities of Bengali society. It was not therefore surprising that the British Indian Association would support the *zemindars* in the land tenancy debate. With the help of the British Indian Association, the *zemindars* organised themselves through meetings, lectures and publicity in the press. They even sent a petition to the British Parliament on 3 October 1883.[41] They were out en masse to protect their own interests. But who should be protecting the *ryots*' interest, Florence asked:

> ... there should be lawyers – noble native gentlemen – who despising worldly advantage, and gain, should be at the service of the ryots, the weaker interest: that there should be newspapers, fearlessly but with the utmost attention to accuracy of facts, to advocate his cause. And we may hope that the day will come when the native members of Council will not be only in the interest of the Zemindar.[42]

Such a group of educated middle class Bengalis, who were mostly lawyers, barristers, teachers and journalists, did come forward to support the *ryots* and started agitation on their behalf. Most of them were educated young men who were involved with the Indian Association. This organisation was formed in July 1876 under the leadership of Surendranath Banerjee and Ananda Mohon Bose, who came back from England with the intention to start an all-India-based organisation that would represent everybody, from the oppressed coolies and the *ryots* to the most affluent members of society.[43] They were inspired by the Italian leader Mazzini, and their aim was to create strong public opinion by unifying the people of India for their political interests. They also wanted to promote better understanding among different communities, and mobilise the masses for a common purpose.[44] Once formed, the Indian Association opened branches all over India. Its membership list included renowned people such as Shibnath Shastri, Raj Narain Bose, Gurudas Banerjee, and Manmohun Ghose, a Bengali barrister and an acquaintance of Florence. He was also the Chairman of the Executive Committee.[45]

The Indian Association was involved with the rent and tenancy question from the beginning. In 1876, when Richard Temple, the Lieutenant-Governor of Bengal, tried to propose changes in the Rent Determination Law, the

Indian Association appointed a sub-committee to consider the proposal. They also prepared and distributed a questionnaire asking the members' opinions. In July 1880, the Government asked the Indian Association to express their views on the draft Tenancy Bill. In response, the Indian Association set up another committee to consider it. The activists and organisers of the Association went round the interior of the rural districts of Bengal and helped to form *ryots*' unions to express the *ryots*' opinions on tenancy questions.[46] They organised meetings on behalf of the *ryots* in the towns and villages of Bengal, which were attended by tens of thousands of people. It was a massive undertaking, but the leaders of the Indian Association did as they promised – to mobilise the masses for a common purpose. Almost one year later, on 27 June 1881, the Indian Association provided a detailed reply to the Government of Bengal, setting out the *ryots*' sentiments about the Tenancy Bill.[47] This not only received good press reviews in Bengal, but also a compliment from Florence:

> It is the only Association in Bengal which may justly be called the people's Association. It begins by noticing the ryot's public meetings, which enable us 'to form a tolerably correct' idea of the views of the ryots themselves and by showing the importance that Government should know what the views of the ryots are.[48]

Florence had been interested in what the Indian Association was trying to do for the *ryots* for quite some time. In the past, she had received information about their activities from P.K. Sen:

> I feel I have never half-thanked you for your kindness in sending me Mr Reynold's Draft Rent Bill and the ryots' Memorial to Sir Ashley Eden and 4 copies of the 'Indian Association' address of June to Mr Mackenzie.
>   Would you kindly tell me more particularly the character of the 'Indian Association' & its constitution, especially as regards the ryots?[49]

Sen obliged Florence by sending reports and the proceedings of the Association's meetings, particularly on the Vernacular Press Act.[50] Florence never directly addressed the members of the Indian Association as she had done with Bengal Social Science Association or would do with the Poona Sarvajanik Sabha and Bombay Presidency Association. But she made considerable use of the materials sent by P.K. Sen as to the agitation led by the Indian Association.

As the controversy with the Tenancy Bill went on, the Government became totally embroiled in the debate. Lieutenant-Governors came and went. In order to reach a solution acceptable to all parties, what one administration proposed was often discarded or changed by another, and then further amended by the next. Like Lieutenant-Governors, Viceroys and Secretaries of State also changed. Viceroys like Lytton, Ripon, and

Dufferin tried to put their mark on the bill, so did the Secretaries of State, Cranbrook and Salisbury. In their midst, the fate of the *ryots* perpetually swung like a pendulum. The original version of the Tenancy Bill was formulated with the *ryots'* interests in mind. The second draft, under the pressure of the *zemindars*, had left out some of the positive steps regarding the *ryots*. Florence, as expected, criticised the new version of the bill for its shortcomings. In her criticism she was well prepared as always, and her suggestions were relevant, logical and cogently argued. She supported occupancy right for all *ryots* on their holdings, a proposal Ripon, as Viceroy, was advocating at the time.

Florence's first criticism of the Tenancy Bill was that it offered fixity of tenure only to the limited number of *ryots* who had occupied their land continuously for 12 years. She saw this as a major defect of the bill. She suggested that the occupancy right or fixity of tenure should be extended to all *ryots*, whether resident or non-resident. She also criticised the bill for giving the *zemindars* the right to enhance rent through a Collector, but did not make similar provision for *ryots* to get rid of illegal taxes imposed on them:

> ... the object should be not only to prevent undue enhancement, but to allow existing unfair rents to be reduced. And for this due provision should be made. It however hardly appears to have been made ...
>
> If improved means of enhancing the rent are to be given to the Zemindar, at the option of the Zemindar, then the ryots should be enti-tled to come in and demand that a public record should be made for their protection. The Zemindar should not have sole option to this.[51]

Florence argued for fair rent and fixity of tenure for the *ryots*, but not free sale as proposed in the bill:

> To give power of free sale to a people unaccustomed to such rights seems to be giving them the power of killing the goose which laid the golden eggs.
>
> ... What is wanted is: To take away from the ryot the power of contracting out of his rights and so protect him in the privileges granted to him.[52]

She once pointed out the danger of free sale in her letter to P.K. Sen: 'Whether the right of sale, and consequently of running into debt and pledging their properties might not be as fatal a gift to the Ryots as it has been to the small proprietors of the Deccan.'[53] She suggested that if there was going to be free sale then the sale must be to another cultivator and not to a non-cultivator, who might keep the old *ryot* on without any rights at all. She held that Indian peasants had no inclination to emigrate, as had happened in Ireland. They did not 'urgently desire the right of free sale. On the other hand it is liked by the landlords on account of the facility for realizing rent which it gives them'.[54] She was also against forced sales: 'Forced sales are an almost unmitigated evil, owing to the presence on the soil of an expropriated people, deeming themselves unjustly deprived of their immortal rights, as in the North West provinces in the time of mutiny; and as in Deccan so lately.'[55] Florence was not indifferent to the *zemindars'* difficulties in collecting rent arrears. In 1878, she wrote to P.K. Sen, agreeing that ' ... there is need of an easier and less expensive process for realizing undisputed rents, in the interest of the tenants who have to pay costs.'[56] Facilities for collecting rent arrears should, she suggested, be made through summary courts, but at the same time a survey, a complete record, of the *ryots'* holdings should be kept. Furthermore, she argued: 'If the more summary procedures for rent suits is to be given to the Zemindars then sufficient protection against illegal execution must be given to the ryots.'[57]

Florence made a plea to her listeners to act promptly to maintain the safeguards originally given to the *ryots* in the first draft of the Tenancy Bill proposed by the Rent Commission. She forwarded two more ideas that would help the *ryots* indirectly. These were the revival of old village communities, the *panchayats*, and increase in trade and industry:

> There is an increasing feeling in favour of reviving as far as possible the ancient village communities, of paying greater attention to the village system indigenous to the soil of India, but much destroyed in Bengal, of making the immemorial headmen of the village act more as organs of the cultivators ... .[58]

Florence pointed out that Ripon as a Viceroy was trying to do just that by Indianising the administration at the local level: 'It would appear as if Lord Ripon's local representation scheme were to begin, as it ought, by village representation which is almost identical with India.'[59] As she followed the logic of her interests, she found herself agitating for the rights of the *ryots*, the village *panchayat* and, finally, for industrial development in India.

Florence's article was read at a meeting of the East India Association in London. Sir Bartle Frere took the chair, and the paper was read by Florence's nephew Frederick Verney.[60] 'There was a full attendance of distinguished Anglo-Indians, and a lively discussion followed. The discussion showed much difference of opinion, but every speaker paid a tribute to her knowledge and devotion.'[61] Her friends and well-wishers such as Sir William Wedderburn, Rev. James Long and Sir Arthur Cotton were present in the meeting and Florence did not fail to note that Cotton did not take part in the debate that followed: 'I only wish that you had spoken.'[62] Florence's article was printed in the East India Association's journal and also as a pamphlet, which was widely distributed. It was reviewed in many journals and newspapers in India and the editors passed their own judgements. The *Indian Spectator* of Bombay wrote:

The present miserable condition of the Bengal ryots has deeply moved
Miss Nightingale. It speaks volumes in favour of her unselfish
humanity that she has imposed on herself, a task at once laborious and
painful ... we have hope that this pamphlet coupled with the Rent Bill,
for sometime past before the Supreme Legislative Council, will lead to
some good. The time is approaching when the Dumb will speak out
and the Deaf shall hear.

The *Lahore Tribune* was not so congratulatory as The *Indian Spectator*.
It thanked Miss Nightingale for drawing British public attention to the
plight of the *ryots* but warned her of the 'grave injustice she might be
doing to a respectable class of men, some of whom regarded the welfare of
their tenants with as much anxiety as that of children of their own. The
Tribune did not think the picture of the *ryots* as painted by Miss Nightingale was a 'faithful representation of the state of things as it exists ... '.
However, favourable comments were published in the *Bengalee* and the
Brahmo Public Opinion, two Calcutta-based journals. The strongest criticism of course came from the *Hindoo Patriot*, the journal that allied with
the *zemindars* in the tenancy dispute. In three articles, the paper covertly
criticised Florence for ignoring the rights of the *zemindars* and upholding
the rights of the *ryots*.[63]

Florence's article thus reached a far greater audience than she could
have ever hoped for. Her aim of mobilising public opinion at home in
Britain and abroad in India was, to a certain extent, successful. Soon after,
in October 1883, she published another article on the Bengal tenancy
issue, a shorter version of the previous one, emphasising once again the
need for safeguarding the *ryots*' interest before it became a law.[64] In this
article as well, she emphasised the need for active administration in India,
effective survey and record keeping to ensure settlement of rights, and
employment of a paid agent to investigate complaints and disputes. 'And
let us not think the "dumb *ryots*" have been silent. The dumb will speak,
and the dumb have spoken for such a crisis as this.'[65]

The handicap Florence had in her Indian work was that she could put
pressure on the Government by publicising a cause, but she did not have
the power to implement a change. That depended on the Viceroys and the
Secretaries of State. And there the machinery moved slowly. As mentioned
earlier, she wrote the articles also to support the Indian policy of Ripon,
who proposed some relevant changes in the Tenancy Bill very similar to
Florence's ideas. In Ripon, Florence saw a new hope for the realisation of
her ideas. Ripon was not only an old acquaintance but also of the same
political persuasion. In the next stage of her Indian work we thus find her
joining hands with Ripon in common pursuit of doing good for the
Indians. 'India says: we want all the help you can give us from home (in
the way of support)'[66] and support she gave, as we will see next.

Notes

1. Sen (1937).
2. FN (1883a), p. 21.
3. Oddie, G.A. (1979), *Social Protest in India: British Protestant Missionaries and Social Reforms 1850–1893*, Delhi: Manohar, pp. 113–123.
4. Beverley, H. (1868), 'Statistics of agriculture in Bengal', *Transactions, BSSA*, July, vol. 2, part 2, pp. 143–166.
5. Beverley (1868), p. 162.
6. Dutt (1902), p. 44.
7. Gopal, S. (1949), *The Permanent Settlement in Bengal and its Results*, London: Allen and Unwin, p. 9.
8. Such as Regulation VIII of 1793, Land Regulation Act, Sec. 48–51. See Roy, P.C. (1883), *The Rent Question in Bengal*, Calcutta: M.M. Rakhit, p. 88 (reprinted from *Bengal Public Opinion*).
9. See Sen Gupta, K.K. (1974), *Pabna Disturbances and the Politics of Rent. 1873–1885*. New Delhi: People's Publishing House.
10. Sen Gupta (1974), p. 137.
11. Buckland (1901), vol. 2, p. 706.
12. Sen (1937), pp. 1–4.
13. Sen (1937), p. 5.
14. Sen (1937), p. 6.
15. Sen (1937), p. 7.
16. Sen (1937), p. 8.
17. Lawrence to FN, 21 December 1874, BL Add. Mss 45777, fol. 197.
18. Sen (1937), p. 5.
19. FN (1883a), p. 7.
20. This apparently refers to C.D. Field, the Secretary of the Commission, who was Irish. The idea of an Irish contribution in the Bengal Tenancy Bill was also developed in Cook, S.B. (1993), *The Imperial Affinities*, London: Sage, pp. 84–86.
21. Mukherjea, A. (1880), *The Proposed New Rent Law for Bengal and Behar*, Calcutta, p. 1, (reprinted from *The Calcutta Review*, October 1880).
22. *Bengal Tenancy Bill: a Speech into the Legislative Council of the Governor General by Courtney Peregrine Ilbert*, 2 March 1883, Simla: Government Central Branch Press, pp. 1–2.
23. FN to Toynbee, 30 May 1882, BL Add. Mss 45806, fols 258–261.
24. *Report of the Debate on the Bengal Tenancy Bill at the Annual Meeting of the British Indian Association*, 5 April 1883, p. 2 (printed at the Hindoo Patriot Press, Calcutta).
25. *The Speeches of the Native Members in the Governor Generals' Legislative Council on the Bengal Tenancy Bill*, Calcutta 1883, p. 32 (reprinted from the *Gazette of India*, 1883).
26. Mukherjea (1880), p. 2.
27. *The Speeches of the Native Members*, p. 13.
28. FN (1883a), pp. 13–15. 'It being the duty of the ruling power to protect all classes of people and more particularly those who from their situation are most helpless, the Governor General in Council will, whenever he may deem it proper, enact such regulations as he may think necessary for the protection and welfare of the dependent Talookdars, *ryots* or other cultivators of the soil; and no Zemindar, independent Talookdar or other actual proprietor

of land shall be entitled on this account to make any objection to the discharge of the fixed assessment, which they have respectively agreed to pay.' Reg. VIII Article VII, Land Regulation Act, 1793.

29. FN (1883a), p. 19.
30. FN (1883a), p. 11.
31. FN (1883a), p. 18.
32. FN (1883a), Introduction, p. 1.
33. FN (1883a), pp. 6–7.
34. Most of the peasants involved in the Pabna disturbances were Muslims and the *zemindars* were Hindus. But Florence was wrong in assuming total Fairazi influence and advance of Islam in the movement. The movement itself was secular, comprising Hindu and Muslim peasants, though there was some Fairazi influence. See Sen Gupta (1974), p. 51.
35. FN (1883a), p. 20.
36. FN (1883a), p. 29.
37. FN (1883a), p. 43.
38. FN (1883a), pp. 31–32.
39. Sen (1937), p. 1.
40. FN (1883a), p. 26.
41. Sen Gupta (1974), p. 14.
42. Sen (1937), p. 15.
43. Mehrotra (1971), pp. 165–6.
44. Bagal, J.C. (1953), *History of the Indian Association*, Calcutta: Indian Association, p. 13.
45. Bagal (1953), p. 16.
46. Bagal (1953), pp. 53–4.
47. A.M. Bose, Hon. Secretary, Indian Association to A. Mackenzie, Secretary to the Government of Bengal, 27 June 1881, Calcutta, as quoted in Bagal (1953), Appendix A, p. I.
48. FN (1883a), p. 46.
49. Sen (1937), p. 30.
50. Sen (1937), p. 33.
51. FN (1883a), p. 35.
52. FN (1883a), p. 36.
53. Sen (1937), p. 2.
54. FN (1883a), p. 36.
55. FN (1883a), p. 36.
56. Sen (1937), p. 2.
57. FN (1883a), p. 35.
58. FN (1883a), p. 47.
59. FN (1883a), p. 48.
60. FN to Long, 14 May 1883, BL Add. Mss 45807, fols 63–64.
61. Cook (1913), vol. 2, p. 334. Also see *Journal of the East India Association*, 1883, vol. xv, pp. 163–210.
62. FN to Cotton, 23 June 1883, BL Add. Mss 45807, fols 78–80.
63. *Indian Spectator*, 1 July 1883 (Bombay); *Lahore Tribune*, 30 June 1883, (Lahore); *Bengalee*, 30 June 1883 (Calcutta); *Brahmo Public Opinion*, 5 and 12 July (Calcutta); *Hindoo Patriot*, 18 June, 9 and 16 July 1883 (Calcutta), all as quoted in *Voice of India*, July 1883 vol. I, no. 7, pp. 223–224.

64. FN (1883c), 'The Bengal Tenancy Bill, October 1883', *The Contemporary Review*, vol. 44, pp. 599–602.
65. FN (1883c), p. 602.
66. FN to Wedderburn, 15 August 1883, BL Add. Mss 45807, fol. 95.

CHAPTER SEVEN

Florence and Ripon: Two Old Comrades

'Dear Lord Ripon, May I venture to recall to your kind remembrance one Florence Nightingale, & to ask you a favour for 'auld lang syne' at the War Office?'[1] wrote Florence to Ripon[2] shortly after he went to India as Viceroy.

Ripon was no stranger to Florence. She had known him since the days of the Royal Commission's inquiry into the sanitary state of the British Army in India, when he was Lord de Grey and Secretary of State for War. As a matter of fact, it was Florence who secured his appointment to that position. At the time, Florence was deeply involved with sanitary reforms in the army and she wanted a sympathetic minister in the War Office to work with. When Sir George Lewis died in 1863, she put pressure on the 'powers that be' to appoint Lord de Grey to the vacant post. In order to create an air of public approval for de Grey, she used the effective technique of leaking information to the press. The famous and much quoted telegram, 'Agitate, agitate for Lord de Grey', which she sent to her journalist friend Harriet Martineau, is still preserved in her private papers.[3] She also sent her brother-in-law, Sir Harry Verney, to impress on the Prime Minister Lord Palmerston, and through him the Queen, the wisdom of appointing Lord de Grey.[4]

Lord de Grey, at the time, probably was not aware that Florence was pulling strings for his appointment, but he was certainly aware of 'Nightingale power' as he asked for her help on another occasion. When Matthew Higgins, an Irish journalist, was about to publish an article regarding a scandal in the British Army in India that could be damaging for the War Office, de Grey asked for Florence's help to suppress it, which she tried to do without complete success.[5] Florence was also involved with de Grey in the War Office reorganisation, the lack of speed of which annoyed her immensely.[6] When, during Lawrence's viceroyalty, de Grey became the Secretary of State for India for a short time, Florence corresponded with him regularly on army sanitary matters, and on more than one occasion she let him know her opinions on the lack of progress of sanitary reforms in India: 'Of course want of money, as well as of energy is at the bottom of the difficulty. But none but Sir John Lawrence are enlightened enough to see that a single epidemic costs the country more than all the works necessary to prevent epidemics.'[7]

Ripon's appointment as a Viceroy in 1880 raised hope in Florence's mind after a period of lull during Lord Lytton's administration. Just as she regarded John Lawrence as a co-thinker and believer in sanitation and health, similarly she looked upon Ripon as someone who, sharing the same political ideas, would turn her dreams into reality. Florence's expectation was not unfounded. Just like Lawrence, Ripon was interested in India, and well informed. He was a Liberal Viceroy, an emissary of Gladstone. He also had a positive attitude towards Indians, which was rather rare at the time. With the sole exception of a few administrators and some missionaries, the general opinion of the British administrators in India was that Indians were lazy, corrupt and unreliable. They were incapable of decision-making, always needed to be told and, finally, were not suitable for responsible jobs with high salaries.[8] The English viewed the Indians with more or less the same contempt that they viewed the Irish. In the middle of this, Ripon brought a breath of fresh air. He was keen to give Indians a chance in the administration of the country, and was determined to do something beneficial for the masses in India. Florence could not have asked for a better worker in India.

Unfortunately, a considerable part of Ripon's viceroyalty was spent in undoing the retrograde steps taken by the previous Viceroy, Lord Lytton. The rest was spent in trying to introduce liberal measures in the face of various odds and mounting criticisms. As Gopal puts it, his 'immediate achievements were minor, but the impact on the minds of Indians was far reaching'.[9] Indians worshipped him as the embodiment of British political liberalism, whereas the Tories at home, and most of the Anglo-Indians in India, regarded him as an Empire wrecker.

Ripon went to India at a time when the forward policy of Disraeli and Lord Lytton were instrumental in causing India to embark on a futile war with Afghanistan. It was Ripon's legacy from Lytton, and the first year of his administration was occupied with this extravagant war with the Afghans and to counter a possible imaginary threat from the Russians. Like Lawrence, Ripon did not believe in pushing the frontiers of India beyond its traditional and natural boundaries. It was not surprising that he wanted to bring the Afghan war to 'an honourable conclusion'.[10] His intention was that as soon as the war was over he would concentrate on the internal problems of India. In the meantime, Ripon had a serious illness, and the first year of his viceroyalty went by with war and illness before he could turn his attention to other matters. On 26 May 1881, he wrote to his friend W.E. Forster:

> ... Now that I have, thank God, got clear of the war, I have more time to turn my attention to internal matters, and am hard at work at famine prevention, primary education, the extension of the elective system in municipalities, the relaxation of the existing regulations on

the subject of the possession and carrying of arms, etc., besides large measures of Army reform and organization; and there are, in addition, questions connected with the relations between landlord and tenant very similar to, and scarcely less difficult than, those with which you have to deal in Ireland, which are pressing for early and careful consideration. ... Of course, the chance of succeeding in any of the objects at which I am now working depends upon the amount of support which I receive from Hartington ... .[11]

The list of jobs to be done as enumerated in Ripon's letter were all measures that he subsequently tried to introduce in India, but, as he feared, the lack of support from his Secretaries of State in Council, and from his own Council, did not allow many of these measures to be effective during his administration.

Ripon arrived in India at a time when the controversy over the Tenancy Bill in Bengal was in full swing. But there was another political storm blowing over the country at the time that needed urgent attention, which was the infamous Vernacular Press Act passed by Lord Lytton in 1878. The aim of the act was to gag the newspapers and journals published in Bengali and other Indian languages on the grounds that they were publishing seditious material and creating disaffection against the Government. The act applied only to the vernacular press and not the English press, though a number of English newspapers were owned by the Indians. The act demanded security from the vernacular newspapers and journals that they would not publish seditious material or misrepresent the Government's views. Failure to do so would forfeit the security, and failure to pay would entitle the Government to confiscate their press. The most undemocratic aspect of the act was that there was no provision for making an appeal to the judiciary. There was, however, provision for making an appeal to the Government within a time limit.

A Press Commission was also appointed to feed the press with official versions of news and the Government's aims and objectives. It was believed that this Commission was financed by the Secret Service in Britain. Ripon wrote to Hartington:

> At the present moment, the Press Commissioner has little or nothing to do with the Vernacular Press. I look upon him as the embodiment of a scheme of Lytton's for *managing* the Press by secret means of which no record remains, and with secret service money, of which no account is rendered, and as such I want to root him up.[12]

The racially discriminatory tone of the Vernacular Press Act caused tremendous resentment, not only in Bengal, but all over India and united the vociferous elite of the country in a way that had never happened before. It also caused uproar among the Liberals in Britain. Gladstone openly denounced the act in his election campaign, and as soon as the Liberals came to power he repealed it in 1882. Although the credit for repealing the act was Gladstone's, Ripon basked in borrowed glory as he won instant fame and admiration, and Indians took him to their heart.

Land Tenancy Bill

Once the Vernacular Press Act and the Afghan War were more or less out of his way, Ripon had time to take up the question of land tenure in Bengal. By the time he arrived in India the Rent Commission appointed by Sir Ashley Eden had already submitted its report and produced the draft Tenancy Bill. As noted before, the bill provoked public outcry from all quarters, particularly from the *zemindars* and the European planters. Ripon arrived in the middle of all those petitions, protests, public meetings and agitation in Bengal. His scope for contribution to the bill was, however, limited. It was not his brainchild, and by the time the bill was passed in 1885 he had already left India.

The prolonged deliberations with the bill continued throughout Ripon's administration, during which time Ashley Eden left his Lieutenant-Governorship of Bengal and joined the India Council in London, and seemed only to oppose Ripon in his progressive measures. Eden was replaced by Sir Augustus Rivers Thompson as Lieutenant-Governor of Bengal, and Ripon's relations with him were not particularly amicable either. Back at home, Ripon had to deal with at least two Secretaries of State, Lord Hartington and Lord Kimberley, who could not always ignore their Council. As was seen again and again, although the Governor-Generals in India were the supreme decision makers, they sometimes worked with handicaps. They had to please two gods – one, their own Council, and two, their Secretary of State. However liberal the Viceroy might be, and Ripon certainly was, his efforts could not take shape unless he had the goodwill of the members of his Council and of his Secretary of State. This was unfortunately too true about Ripon's administration. His four years in India failed to be a success for lack of co-operation from officialdom.

The same happened with the Bengal Tenancy Bill. Ripon was unable to pay attention to the bill before June 1882. The controversy with the bill had been going on far too long, and he wanted to hasten the matter. The Rent Commission's draft bill had already laid down the details and direction of tenancy reform. Ripon wanted to separate occupancy rights from the status of the individual. He wanted all land, except private land, to be considered *ryotwari* land, and any individual cultivating such land was to have occupancy rights; occupancy status was to be attached to the land. This change would mean most of the *ryots* would get occupancy rights, whether they were resident or non-resident. The fear of eviction and enhancement of rent could then be minimised.[13]

The Secretary of State Lord Hartington, however, did not agree with Ripon. He considered this as a departure from 'customs and existing laws of Bengal'. In spite of his disagreement he asked Ripon to prepare an amended bill and submit it to the Legislative Council. He wrote: 'I will not refuse sanction to introduction of measures in form you prefer.' But Ripon did not want to do that, as in the absence of support from the Secretary of State he faced the possibility of defeat in the Council. In the meantime, Hartington left and Kimberley took over. He asked Ripon to submit the bill. Ripon replied: 'We must decline to introduce a bill which the Secretary of State expressed disapproval on material ground. We shall, therefore, prepare a bill in accordance with general views expressed in Lord Hartington's, 17 August, and shall introduce it in the Viceroy's Council as soon as it is ready.'[14]

The amended bill was finally presented to the Legislative Council in March 1883 by Sir Courtney Ilbert. Even after the presentation of the bill, it went to the Select Committee for consideration and almost another two years passed before it became an act. It was about this time that Florence wrote her article, *The Dumb Shall Speak and the Deaf Shall Hear, or the Ryot, the Zemindar and the Government*, in support of the interests of the *ryots* and to provide a boost to Ripon's morale. 'This is a humble earnest contribution to our understanding of part at least of Indian legislative work,' she wrote, 'which is now so actively undertaken by the Viceroy and the Government of India.'[15]

Ripon's proposal, had it been accepted, would certainly have benefited the majority of the *ryots*. Some of the earlier proposals mentioned originally in the Rent Commission's draft bill, and supported by Florence and other well-wishers of the *ryots*, were dropped from the bill's final version. The Tenancy Act, passed in 1885 during Lord Dufferin's administration, helped the resident *ryots* to some extent, but the general conditions of the *ryots* in Bengal, particularly of those who were tenants at will, did not change very much. In land tenancy, the final round was won by the *zemindars* and the planters.

Though Ripon failed to pass the Tenancy Bill in his time, some other measures he adopted must have gratified Florence. His arrival in India coincided with the submission of the Famine Commission's report of 1880. Most of the recommendations of the Famine Commission were what Florence wanted to see happening in India, and Ripon followed the guidelines laid down by the report. These were for the establishment of a famine insurance fund, creation of agricultural departments, extension of railways and irrigation as famine-preventive measures, maintaining statistical records, opening up small-scale industries, and forest preservation.

Florence had been agitating for most of these measures for a long time. Where Ripon differed from Florence was that he gave more importance to the extension of railways than to irrigation. It was said that there was never a total shortage of food in the whole sub-continent. When one area suffered from drought and famine, another area of India had a food surplus. Only a railway could carry food grains from one part of India to another quickly and efficiently.[16]

However, Ripon was not altogether indifferent towards the need for irrigation. But, as we have seen earlier, irrigation was never a favourite subject with the authorities, and the emphasis on the cost-effectiveness of irrigation canals remained alive throughout the nineteenth century, including during Ripon's administration. Nevertheless, some irrigation projects that were already under way were completed during his time, of which the Buckingham Canal in Madras was of much importance. His administration also saw the start of some new projects in the Mahanadi area in Orissa and in Bellary, and the construction of some other main and branch canals.[17] But these were all 'auxiliary developments', as Gopal put it; the primary emphasis was on railway extension.[18]

Agricultural education and the loan bank

The aspect of Ripon's administration that interested Florence immensely was his attempt to bring forth some agricultural reforms, particularly in education and agricultural banking. Florence herself was very keen on agricultural training and introducing improved agricultural methods in India. She was still very much concerned about the plight of the *ryots*. The Bengal Tenancy Bill was still in limbo. Similarly in the Deccan, even after the submission of the Deccan Riot Commission's voluminous reports, not much was achieved for the peasants. Florence felt that a pro-*ryot* tenancy act would certainly help them, but the introduction of improved agricultural practices was also necessary, and that would require agricultural training, not only for the Indian civil servants who would work with the *ryots*, but also for the young British officers who would go to India as administrators.

In collaboration with Benjamin Jowett, Florence was already trying to introduce agricultural studies in Oxford for aspiring young Britons wanting to join the Indian Civil Service.[19] She felt that these young would-be administrators of India should not just be time-servers, but should contribute something worthwhile for the masses in India. Before going to India they were to receive some proper agricultural training and be made aware of their responsibilities. She wrote to Arnold Toynbee, a lecturer in economics in Balliol at that time, that the future administrators of India must be awakened here to the intense interest and importance of their position in India. ... Balliol sends forth new missionaries. And in four years from the time he was a Balliol undergraduate, see what Mr Wilson has done. I know nothing that tells so soon, so widely and so vigorously as Indian Civil Service education, because nowhere is there such a field.[20]

When Florence was told that making provision for agricultural education for the young civil servants might be possible, she wanted to make sure that the subjects taught to them would be relevant for India:

I hope that lectures on Land Tenure, Provincial Administration etc. will form part of your future course as you desire. And more – if your 2 years can be made into 3, that something of instruction on Agricultural and technical science, including Forestry, may direct your students' attention at least to what are the peculiar wants of India – a knowledge often absent in her rulers. ... The future of India depends, more than on anything else, on the rulers we bring up ... .[21]

Florence was practical and to the point. She wanted the Indian Civil Service candidates to learn about agricultural chemistry, botany as regards plants and wood, geology as regards soil and water supply, and animal physiology as regards animal breeds, fodder and disease of cattle. She was well aware that manure in India was used as domestic fuel, and every year a vast number of cattle died due to starvation and malnutrition. There was much ignorance in India.[22]

Florence wanted similar educational opportunities for Indians in India as well as for the aspiring Indian Civil Service candidates in Britain. In 1879, one year before Ripon went to India, she established contact with W.R. Robertson, the Principal of the Madras Agricultural College and Superintendent of the Government Agricultural Farm. Robertson, interested in farming and modern agriculture in India, wrote occasional papers and reports on the subject and sent them to Florence. This led to a correspondence between the two, lasting almost 20 years. The main subjects of Florence's letters to Robertson were what sort of students received agricultural training in the Madras Agricultural College and how could they be used to improve agriculture in India. This was after the Deccan riot, and Florence was aware that a lot of land had passed from the poor peasants to the moneylenders in the Deccan. Her worry was whether these new masters would do anything to improve the productivity and techniques of agriculture. The long letter she wrote to Robertson in March 1879 shows how concerned she was:

Might I ask if any of the Moneylenders, particularly those from Bombay (I see a proportion of Bombay men in your College) who have acquired large properties in land, have sent sons or relations to your Farm and

Agricultural College in Madras to learn how to improve these lands? ...
One would feel encouraged if one heard that the sons of these new
proprietors were learning to manage the acquired lands from you.

It is an encouragement to see the Parsees – whose energy has been I
suppose in commerce – carrying that energy into 'land' and sending
their young men to your agricultural College, as well as the Brahmins.

If this process of agricultural education extends, if there could be
model farms and native teachers and managers in every province – and
these be widely imitated, much of the desperate condition of India
might disappear.

It was not only the nature of the students that interested her; she also
wanted to know whether the syllabus was relevant to India and what sort
of work was going on.

Might I ask further – are there in the village schools of the Madras
Pres^y any manuals of agriculture to give simple information, in an
interesting way, on common agricultural subjects? Are there model
Farms not only for the culture of valuable produce, but carried on in
such a way as to instruct poor men with small or moderate means how
to improve their agriculture & make the best of what they have, e.g.
with regard to the rotation of crops, and the chemical laws on which
these are founded, to manures – fodder crops for cattle – the introduction of new plants, deeper ploughing with English plough, irrigation
with relation to manuring? How are these taught?[23]

Florence was always ready to appreciate and praise the good work done
in India by people like Robertson. She was also quick to use her contacts
to find out more about India. The year 1879 was a time of agitation in
Bengal over the Rent Realization Bill and tenancy reform. Just as she
asked P.K. Sen to supply her with facts about the *ryots* of Bengal, she also
wrote to Robertson to send her more information:

Facts, personal narratives of individual natives with name and place, how
I wish these could be brought into the popular literature of England –
then England would discover India – instead of being, as now, certainly
more ignorant of our own vast dependency than of Turkey.[24]

If there is anything that England wants to know about and knows
nothing about is: agriculture in India. And when one thinks that we take
20 millions Land Revenue out of India's agriculture & give nothing back,
one almost wonders that there is not an universal agrarian mutiny. But
the day cannot be far distant if we shall continue doing nothing.[25]

The method of work Florence followed all her life was of extensive fact-
gathering and intensive lobbying. She never allowed a matter to rest until
the work was done. Quite often it paid dividends. Just as she lobbied
Jowett and Toynbee to introduce agricultural training for the Indian Civil
Service candidates, she lobbied Robertson to introduce relevant agricultural training for Indians and modern implements for farming. When an

Indian contact of Robertson's arrived in England, she wanted to utilise the opportunity to send new implements to India:

> Could anything be done now Mr. Benson is in England about improved agricultural implements for India? For instance he might go round to the agricultural implement manufacturers at Ipswich, Bedford and Leeds, and say <u>what they</u> <u>could do for</u> <u>you</u> in the way of ploughs – what articles would suit you etc. etc. These manufacturers would send out specimens to try out in India. And of some things Mr. Benson might obtain models, such as the steam plough.
>
> Have you or would you recommend, at least for Bengal, steam threshing machine, for threshing rice? (like wheat?) One threshes as much in a day as 60 men.[26]

The appointment of the new Viceroy, Lord Ripon, and his known interest in agriculture, also made Florence enthusiastic but not too trusting. She wanted to keep a track of how things were developing. 'How is your new Governor entering upon office with regard to agriculture?' she asked Robertson, 'And what are your financial prospects? ... Is agriculture getting its proper share?' 'You know, I dare say, that Sir Ashley Eden, urged by the Supreme Govt. has sent home 2 very good men, one a Bengalee Baboo and one a Mahomedan to Cirencester for 2 years. Will they be able to instruct when they return without further experience in India?'[27] This refers to four Indian civil servants sent by Ripon in December 1881 to receive agricultural training in England. Two went from Punjab and one each from Bengal and Bombay. Ripon also asked for an agricultural chemist from England.[28]

During his administration, Ripon wanted to set up agricultural departments both in the centre and in the provinces. The aim and purpose of the Agricultural Department was to deal with agricultural questions and to maintain regular statistical information regarding all issues concerning famine and agriculture. But setting up provincial agricultural departments proved difficult for Ripon. He faced much opposition, particularly from Ashley Eden in the India Council where he opposed Ripon's agricultural reforms. It was Eden who, as the Lieutenant-Governor of Bengal, had once proudly said: 'The Government of Bengal has no agricultural department and does not attempt to teach the Bengal cultivator his business.'[29] Ripon was afraid that the Secretary of State would veto his ideas under the influence of Ashley Eden. Such was the Viceroy's trust and faith in the ability of his old friend that Ripon asked for Florence's help as he sent her information about agricultural reforms in Bengal:

> ... My special reason for asking your attention to this pamphlet at the present moment is that I have too good reason to believe that the establishment of an Agricultural Department in Bengal, though thoroughly recommended by the Local Govt., and by the Govt. of India is likely to be refused by the Sec. of State in consequence of the opposition

of Sir Ashley Eden, who is as you know, a member of the India Council
at home.

If you can do anything to avert this misfortune, for such it would
really be, you will confer a real benefit upon the Bengal *ryots* and will
much oblige.[30]

The 'Governess of the Governors' must have pulled some strings, as
Ripon was soon able to confirm that the Secretary of State had sanctioned
the Agricultural Department experimentally for two years only, although
he was confident that it would not be abolished.[31]

Indian agricultural bank

One aspect of Ripon's agricultural measure that interested Florence immensely
was the idea of an Indian agricultural bank that would provide cheap loans
to the *ryots* on a co-operative basis. It was first suggested by Lord Elphinstone's
government in Bombay in as early as 1860, when a resolution was passed for
a loan bank for the *ryots*. The idea was again revived during Ripon's administration in 1882 by Sir William Wedderburn.[32] William Wedderburn,
following the path of his father and elder brother, went to India in 1860 as a
young civil servant and worked in various administrative and judicial capaci-
ties. He was a good friend of Ripon and also a correspondent of Florence.
During Ripon's administration, he was a District Judge in Poona and later
one of the founders of the Indian National Congress. Like Florence, Wedderburn was deeply interested in the poverty of the *ryots* and their indebtedness
to the moneylenders.

As we know, from the 1870s, Florence continuously wrote about the
evil of moneylending and usury in India and the need for the *ryots* to get
cheap loans from a reliable source. At that time, the *ryots* did not always
go to the Government for loans because the rules and regulations of
borrowing money baffled them. They understood the system of the village
moneylenders and the *sowkars*, but that was sure to ruin them. The
existing British judicial system was not geared towards helping the *ryots*.
'The mistakes which our lawgivers have made,' Florence commented, 'has
been to oblige our civil courts to aid and abet the practices of usury.' She
wanted to see the *ryots* themselves turn into mini-capitalists and start a
loan system based on the principle of co-operation. 'Make the *ryots*
moneylenders themselves and a more prosperous peasantry would not
exist in the world.'[33]

About this time, in 1879, Florence was emphasising the need for co-
operative organisations in India where the *ryots* would be able to help
themselves. She asked Gladstone:

Do you think that Co-operation could be introduced in India among
the measures to cope with the terrible poverty and indebtedness? ...

> Do you think that a National Bank could be formed – a private Joint Stock Institution but under the supervision of the Government – starting with a paid up capital ... a bank to make small advances of capital to the *ryots* for seeds, tools, wells and tanks?[34]

She even suggested how branches of such a co-operative bank could be formed in every district, the District Collector being its ex-officio chairman.

Florence's attention was drawn to a little pamphlet suggesting this very idea. The author of the pamphlet wrote that in the context of the impending bankruptcy of the Indian peasant and soil, a national agricultural bank could be of some help. The bank could make

> small cash advances for purchase of agricultural implements, seeds, manures and the construction of wells and tanks ... offering them good interest for money, to stimulate them to save and deposit. The rich landowners would also be encouraged to bring his bullions and cash – his dormant hoards into a wage or mobilised fund.[35]

The idea caught Florence's imagination and, without wasting any time, she again wrote to Gladstone, drawing his attention to the business acumen of an Indian community from the south of India called 'the Chetties', and suggesting that the efficiency and the skill of the Chetties could be used to open up a national agricultural bank in India:

> 7 July 1879
>
> I venture to send you the sketch of the National Bank of India – proposed by a Mr Fox, [ ] at Bristol – which you were so good as to discuss with me.
>
> It has been submitted to Lord Northbrook who 'thought that [Govt.] would hesitate to interfere with the native Bankers' and to Mr Pedder, one of the able collectors of India, the new Revenue Secretary at the India Off. who has only just returned from the Deccan. He recommends that English 'capitalists should enlist the co-operation of some of the best native Bankers who he thinks would be more qualified to manage the details of the business than Englishmen', and to manage the *ryots*.
>
> I remember that you did not discourage such an institution and I fancied you might perhaps allow me to submit to you some details I have received, about a new association of native traders and ask how they strike you in connection with Mr Pedder's suggestion.
>
> ... Now these people are samples of the pure oriental trader, money lender and usurer. With external peace, order and contentment, their trading instincts reach a high development. Up to this time they have not felt the wants of an English education, but, with the extension of their commerce beyond Indian limits, they will find it to their advantage to avail themselves of our schools. Having established a reputation for keeping to their engagements they can make use of the facilities the Banks give to traders, and in this respect they have not been backward.

> These people are essentially the monied classes of Tanjore and Madura. Their wealth and importance have received a new development from the grain trade of the Famine year and they bid fair to become a power in the state – for good or evil, who shall say.
>
> Now could these people but be enlisted in a National Bank scheme, of what benefit might that be ...
>
> ... Indian races have such extraordinarily strong instincts – both of co-operation and combination and of trading and business – what a pity it is that we never know how to utilize these for the good of the people.[36]

Florence's letter to Gladstone raised the issue of starting an agricultural bank almost a year before Ripon went to India and Wedderburn initiated his proposal. Like Florence, Wedderburn saw the necessity of providing cheap capital to the *ryots* to check the overwhelming oppression of the moneylenders in the Deccan area. He had been there when the Deccan riot took place and he was one of the witnesses to the Deccan Riot Commission. He published his ideas for an agricultural bank in the *Bombay Gazette* for general discussion. In his article he referred to co-operative agricultural banks existing almost everywhere in Europe, even in Turkey with 'marked benefit to the rural population'. But no such system existed in India, despite legislation to provide advances for the improvement of land by irrigation, drainage and reclamation. He noted that the Indian system, which relied entirely on official agency and ignored private enterprise, had proved a failure.[37]

Wedderburn started to work on the plan for an agricultural bank in 1881. He made enquiries, organised local meetings and negotiated with all the interested parties. The idea of using native capitalists received support in the Indian press. Journals like *The Indian Spectator* and *Indu Prakash* of Bombay, and the *Indian Mirror* and *Brahmo Public Opinion* of Calcutta, congratulated Wedderburn for such an endeavour.[38] As a result, a scheme was more or less agreed upon and accepted by 'the *ryots*, money-lenders, native capitalists and the promoters of the enterprise'.[39]

In July 1883, when Wedderburn was in England, he gave a paper on *The Poona Raiyat's Bank* in a meeting of the East India Association. This lecture caused a considerable stir in the press and it was shortly followed by his paper given in the Manchester Chamber of Commerce, entitled *The Government Concessions to Agricultural Banks*, and then, in December, another paper, entitled *The Indian Raiyat*, before the London Institution.[40] In the meantime, Ripon and his Finance Minister supported the scheme and gave the idea the go-ahead on condition that it would be on an experimental basis within a limited area. In May 1884, the Government of India sent a memorandum to the Secretary of State to this effect, asking for his sanction:

'We are anxious to give effect to a scheme which we believe to be advocated on purely disinterested grounds, which can, under the experimental conditions proposed be carefully watched, and which is likely, if successful, to be productive of much benefit to the country.'[41]

Unfortunately, this request for sanction never arrived. Negotiations over the project continued throughout 1884. In the meantime Ripon left; even Wedderburn retired in 1887. Kimberley was replaced by Lord Randolph Churchill, then by Lord Cross, who finally refused to recommend the proposal altogether. Years later, on 18 March 1898, in a lecture on agricultural banks for India in a meeting of the East India Association, Wedderburn gave vent to his disappointment:

> In India, the authorities were desirous of giving this remedy a trial in a cautious experimental way; all public opinion in India and in England had declared itself in favour of the movement. Only a formal sanction of the India Office at Westminster was required; but this, unfortunately, was just what we could not obtain, the India Office revising a fruitless controversy regarding hypothetical difficulties and eventually, in 1887, refusing absolutely to allow the experiment to be made.[42]

In his language, it 'was stabbed to death in the dark when it entered the portals of the India Office'.[43]

The native army hospital corps

As soon as the Afghan war came to a conclusion, Ripon turned his attention to army reorganisation. Measures were taken relating to army health, contagious diseases and retrenchment in the native army. He also started to think of a native army hospital corps. This stirred Florence into action. She probably felt that the time had arrived once again to have a go at army sanitation. Ripon had been her colleague and confidante in the War Office. Now she wanted to revive the old comradeship and get things going again:

> With joy I have heard your measure, so much needed; viz., the creation of a Native Army Hospital Corps.
>   The wants of the present system or no system of Hospital attendance in the Indian Army were so enormous the name even of nursing was such a farce.[44]

The favour she asked for in her very first letter to Ripon in India was about this native army hospital corps. The training and creation of a native army hospital corps had first been suggested by Sidney Herbert, and later by Lord Stanley, to the Royal Commission. Among the various recommendations of the Royal Commission made at the time was the training of Indian hospital attendants in the basics of nursing. The nursing in the army hospitals was mainly done by these Indian attendants, and only when a patient was seriously ill was a regimental comrade sent to nurse him. But generally speaking, these untrained Indian attendants, or 'ward coolies' as they were commonly known, nursed the sick soldiers without any supervision or organisation. They usually came from the lowest strata of society and were often very badly treated:

> These Ward Coolies or Nurses may be children of 10, old men of 80, cripples, blind, – anyone, in short, who will come for 4 rupees a month. No other inducement is given: no promotion: no reward: no good conduct pay: no increase of pay for long service: no camp equipage. The Nurses' Shelter is to lie in the bitterest nights under the Hospital tent walls to be either roasted or drowned in a Cholera Camp in the monsoon: having no uniform & not enough pay to feed them, to be perhaps seized for entering their own lines.[45]

Since the days of John Lawrence, Florence had been trying to achieve some standard of nursing in the army hospitals in India: 'The British Army in India is the worst nursed of any army in the world if indeed it can be said to be nursed at all.' Yet the ward coolies were 'excellent stuff' for nurses, 'if only trained, supervised and organized'. 'The ward coolies seem to be there merely to be "kicked" by the European soldier who, if rebuked, says and says truly, "he didn't know who the native was"'. Florence was pleased that Ripon had decided to take up the Royal Commission's recommendation: 'No one has taken it up but you,' wrote Florence to Ripon, 'You have come to India, it has been left to you to save them from all this misery. All this will now be altered by your truly wise and beneficent measure.' Florence's main concern was how these 'ward coolies' would be trained, where, and by whom. She asked Ripon to send her the particulars. ' ... Perhaps a copy of the Regulations, but especially, if possible, what is the proposed system of ward training. What the organization, what the supervision. If I may be so venturesome as thus to trouble you.'[46]

Ripon obliged her by sending a copy of the Government order for a native army hospital corps, and wrote:

> You gave me a very undue amount of credit in respect to the creation of a Native Army Hospital Corps. The proposal was under consideration before I came out here, and it is only my good fortune that it was brought to practical completion under my administration, and will, therefore, be, to some extent, connected with my name. A scheme so recently inaugurated is, of course, only in a tentative state at present, and your letter has, therefore arrived most opportunely to indicate to me the direction in which improvement is needed, and the points which will specially require watching. I will give my careful attention

to these matters, and I shall rejoice if with your assistance, I am able to effect any good in regard to them.[47]

In return, Florence sent him suggestions for a structured training scheme. Her suggestion was that the trainers should be a nucleus of 'trained European men', 'volunteers from the regimental ranks to the Garrison Hospitals'. The medical officer should pick the best men – good character and sobriety was essential. Perhaps a colloquial vernacular examination should be arranged for them. Learning the language would obviously help in communicating with the coolies. These volunteers should be trained for one year before being sent to train the native ward coolies. Florence had various suggestions for where these training schools could be, perhaps in Bombay or Madras, but 'not alas Calcutta, for in a town like that, the men lose as much in conduct as they gain in learning'.[48]

Florence did not stop just with the trainers, the trainees were very much her focal point. She had great faith in the capabilities of the low-caste people of India, particularly those who came from the community of the 'Mehtars' and 'Chumars': 'They are physically strong ... often do devoted but ignorant service in time of cholera. The material is good; but unorganized, untrained material is like bricks unbuilt, or bricks unburnt.' Florence recommended that these ward coolies should be uniformed, and there should be provision for promotion and reward for good service:

> Would it not be useful to have it laid down that the Hospital Servants, just like the Sepoys, are eligible for medals, clasps & for the various Indian local decorations for good services? Also, for carriage for their baggage on the line of march, & for shelter in tents while marching, (or in cholera camps), in fact for everything that the Sepoy has?[49]

The attention to the detail, the practicality of planning and shrewd knowledge of human character that prospects of promotion and reward produce good service were always the hallmark of Florence's advice, and Ripon got plenty of that. Florence kept on reminding him: 'What has been done about an organized system of training these men at some central hospital, or hospitals, and might I see the regulations?'[50]

By February 1883, Ripon had become totally embroiled with a number of political issues such as the Ilbert Bill and Indianisation of administration at local government level. As a result, although the training of ward coolies had started, it did not quite take off. This becomes apparent from the letter that Catherine Loch, the first lady superintendent of the female nurses in army hospitals in India, wrote to Florence five years later, in June 1888:

> ... I was very wrong if I gave you to understand that there is no native hospital orderly corps. I think that I did not realize at first that the tribes of coolies, ward servants, sweepers etc. about the hospital do

belong to a regular organized Corps and are enlisted as part of the
Bengal Army – but they are quite hopeless as nurses – according to the
Army Regulations they are supposed to receive training and they are
supposed to be able to pass an exam – in simple dressings, poultices, &
bandages etc. before they can be promoted to higher grade. This looks
very well on paper but practically it is of very little use.[51]

It was Catherine Loch who, finally, in 1894, initiated proper training
facilities for the ward coolies in the army hospital and helped to establish
a proper native army hospital corps.[52] Thus Florence's proposals came to
fruition twelve years after they had been initiated.

Village sanitation

Ripon's measures of decentralisation and the introduction of an elective
indigenous element at the municipality level created an opportunity for
Florence to lobby for another subject close to her heart:

> Your immense kindness to me encourages me to submit to you
> another, an immense subject, which it is scarcely presumptuous to
> hope will interest you, because it is yours. It is the great sanitary
> subject in India … .
> … It is particularly on behalf of the Village Sanitation that I am now
> trusting to enlist your imperial power, & that you will put a crowning
> stone to your edifice.[53]

Florence always believed that unless the sanitation of the towns and
villages in India could be achieved, army sanitation would be meaningless. She also understood from her experience that the task of community
sanitation was riddled with difficulties and without some sort of village
organisation to take initiative, sanitary reforms at village level would be
almost impossible. From now on, village sanitation would occupy much
of Florence's immediate attention, and as we shall see in the following
chapter, for the remaining part of her working life she dedicated herself to
the cause of village sanitation and education in India.

It could be asked why she became interested in sanitation again at this
time. The fact was that she never lost sight of her goal. Sanitation, to her,
was still the most valuable asset of progress, and hygiene was still the hand-
maiden of civilisation. It remained a recurring theme in all her efforts for
India. Ripon's progressive measures also encouraged her to send practical
suggestions for village sanitation. In her letter, she admitted that considerable progress in sanitation was made in the army barracks and in the big
towns. 'The great blot however in the sanitary history of India is: the condition of my poor clients, the villages. They are now known to be the foci of
Indian Epidemics & the most unhealthy spots in the whole country.'[54]

Florence was convinced that, 'Under proper care even an Indian village may be made quite healthy.' Just as she had done in the case of female nursing, or the native army hospital corps, she sent suggestions to Ripon that were thorough and practical, and she paid attention to infrastructure, cost and administration. She referred to the already existing village system, which could be used for introducing sanitary measures. There were the *patels* in Bombay, village chiefs in Madras and *zemindars* in Bengal. She suggested to Ripon that these people could be used for implementing sanitary measures in the villages. She also pointed out existing acts and regulations that could be utilised for this purpose. She prepared the groundwork for Ripon for all the presidencies:

> Might I venture to ask: How far should you think it possible to impose on the Zemindar some of the duties – either actually intended or in a corresponding form to the duties which it was intended that he should perform by the Permanent Settlement? May it then be said that the case stands thus:-
> In Madras it is the statutory duty of the Village Headman to carry on village sanitation.
> In Bombay the machinery exists by which it could be made the duty of the village Headman [see the Bombay Village Police Act of 1869 & the Government Resolution of January 1878].
> In the Punjab the village organization is very complete – could therefore the duties be enforced by the existing machinery?
> In the N.W.P. it appears that in certain districts rules have been framed, & the Lumberdars & 'Zemindars' are held personally responsible for the cleansing of their villages – & that cases of persistent neglect are punished under the Indian Penal Code.[55]

Florence felt that sanitation should be made obligatory for every person throughout the village, men or women, and that there must be some legislation to keep the village machinery in operation. She was convinced that a large part of village sanitation 'could be done by every household with little or no expense'. For some projects such as wells or tanks, financial aid would be necessary, but, she pointed out, in many cases it had been observed that the villagers themselves were willing to supplement the Government grant for such work by subscription. She was fully aware of the difficulties that existed. But her argument was that any reform work would face such difficulties; they were not insurmountable. She cited how sanitary work was done efficiently and successfully at big fairs and religious gatherings in India, which were once centres of epidemics:

> Is not all that is wanted simply to set existing methods in motion <u>by law</u> & then the local authorities to keep the machine going.
> ... Is not what we want simply that what is done for the fairs periodically should be done for the villages under legal sanction continuously?
> ... Could an enabling Act be passed by the Government of India, or by the Local legislative councils – with suitable clauses empowering

Local Governments to frame <u>sanitary rules</u> for giving effect to the purposes of this Act? and to apply them on their own responsibility?[56]

Florence felt that what was needed in India was 'a much required spur to the work', and how to do that only 'the Governor General could answer'.

It must be said that Ripon's reform measures were that 'much required spur to the work' in an atmosphere of bureaucratic opposition, where, as he himself had expressed it:

> A set of old gentlemen, whose energies are relaxed by age, and who, having excellent salaries, and no responsibility, amuse themselves by criticizing the proposals and obstructing the plans of those who have the most recent knowledge of the real state of India and who have on their shoulder the whole responsibility for the good government of that country.[57]

One major contribution of Ripon was his reform at the local self-government level. Florence wrote to Ripon in 1881, and Ripon's Local Self Government and Municipality Bill was passed in May 1884, a few months before he left India. Some form of local self-government already existed in India before his time. Previous Viceroys like Lawrence and Mayo had tried to introduce some decentralisation at the municipal level. Organisations like local boards already existed in the three main presidencies, Bombay, Madras and Bengal. Ripon's credit was that he wanted to introduce elective elements into the system, so that the local people could look after their own interests at local level. Local public works and its finance would thus be the responsibility of local boards with elected members. Ripon's idea was that this would help develop civic awareness and 'training in the exercise of power'. The educated Indians, who were often criticised as unworthy of responsibility and apathetic towards self-government, would get a chance to exercise their talents and abilities.

Ripon also reorganised the Sanitary Department throughout India and made it a separate department. The vaccination and registration of vital statistics were brought under its control. Better job opportunities and prospects for promotion were created to make sanitary work more lucrative, and stir up the sanitary officers from their 'vis inertiae'. The Sanitary Commissioners were allowed extra staff to bring to their notice defects in village and town sanitation. A memorandum was also sent to the Lieutenant-Governor of Bengal, asking him to create an efficient village police force. Probably Ripon would have done all this on his own, but Florence was there in the background, ticking and reminding him of the good works that had to be done, and providing him with ideas, information and guidance.[58]

When Ripon was in India, Florence and Ripon corresponded frequently, if not as prolifically as she had done with John Lawrence. Ripon sent her official papers and documents; she sent her advice and know-how. Ripon kept her informed about all the liberal measures he was trying to introduce in India, and she in return did her best to help him and his policies. Above all, she continuously cheered him, praised him and acted as his big morale-booster. Long after Ripon left India, she carried on corresponding with him, almost up to 1902. During Dufferin's and Lansdowne's administration she continuously asked Ripon's advice on measures undertaken by these later Viceroys.

The Ilbert Bill

The debacle that finally made Ripon resign before his term of office ended was known as the Ilbert Bill controversy. The Ilbert Bill, named after the Law Member of the Council, Sir Courtney Ilbert, was presented in the Council on 2 February 1883, and it was about giving power to Indian magistrates belonging to the Indian Civil Service to try Indians and Europeans alike in criminal courts in India. In January 1882, an Indian covenanted civil servant, Behari Lal Gupta, asked the Government to give such powers to Indian magistrates in order to remove the anomaly that existed in the criminal procedure code. Without anticipating the commotion that it might cause, Ripon gave the go-ahead to the bill, to remove restrictions based on racial grounds and to give Indian and European magistrates equal legal power.[59]

The racial prejudice that the bill evoked among the British and European community had no parallel in Indian history. For Ripon, it was only a matter of procedure, a part of his liberal policy in India. He had not anticipated the strength and depth of the fury that he caused among the Anglo-Indians. Everyone who had a grievance against Ripon's administration jumped on to the bandwagon. From ordinary British planters and traders to the high court judges, lawyers and barristers, even the leader of the opposition in the British Parliament – all became thoroughly horrified at the thought of a native Indian magistrate trying a Briton in the Court of Law. In Birmingham, Lord Salisbury, in a speech on the subject, asked his audience: 'What would your feelings be if you were in some distant and thinly populated land, far from all English succour and your life or honour were exposed to the decision of some tribunal consisting of a coloured man.'[60]

Ripon had already earned the displeasure of the Anglo-Indian community in India by repealing the Vernacular Press Act. They were not keen to understand that he had only carried out Gladstone's instruction. At this time, the Bengal Land Tenancy Bill was also causing quite a furore among the Bengal *zemindars*. Attempts to give occupancy rights to the *ryots* made the planters and *zemindars* equally unhappy. There was a rumour that the Anglo-Indians approached the Bengali *zemindars* to support them. 'The Anglo-Indians are making efforts to get up a cross with the Zemindar party in Bengal,' wrote Ripon to Kimberley, 'with a view to induce the latter to go against the Ilbert Bill on the understanding that the Anglo Indians will as a body throw themselves warmly into the opposition to the Bengal Rent Bill.'[61] Similarly, Ripon's proposals to share administrative power with the Indians, even though that was only at the municipal level, was not something that the Anglo-Indians aimed for. Finally, that Ripon was admired and liked by the Indians roused dark suspicion in their minds. They viewed Ripon as a possible Empire wrecker. Their fear and fury erupted, centring around the Ilbert Bill, and they organised themselves to oppose. They presented all sorts of excuses; some were rationalisations, some were openly racist. P.G. Melitus, an assistant magistrate from Kushtea, argued:

> The principal classes of Europeans outside Cantonment likely to be affected by the Bill are, 1) planters, 2) steamer captains, railway servants etc. 3) loafers. Leaving out of consideration the last class, with whom a native magistrate would probably be far more lenient than a European, we find that planters and railway servants have unanimously expressed their disapproval of the Bill. And I agree with them in thinking that a Native magistrate would be an unsafe judge of their actions. Native feeling is strong against the planters, who have generally some sort of dispute with the neighbouring zemindars and ryots, and I think there is a danger of a Native Magistrate with the very best intentions, but ignorant of the ways and habits of Europeans being misled by the prevailing prejudice against them. As to railway servants, etc., they are a class with whom the educated natives can have no possible community of feelings. A Native Magistrate with native habits and ideas, would, I think, be hard put to fathom the thoughts and ways of the British guard or driver or skipper.[62]

Not everyone was as restrained as the author of the above letter. At a meeting in Calcutta Town Hall, the Anglo-Indians accused Ripon and Courtney Ilbert of placating the 'blatant Bengali babus' by removing 'only a sentimental grievance'. Unbelievable anxieties were displayed that Ripon and Ilbert's action would place the European women at the mercy of unsympathetic Indian magistrates. The leaders of the Anglo-Indian community urged that, unlike Indian women, their women were not used to the 'foul multitudes of the Court'. M. Townsend, the ex-editor of the *Friend of India*, expressed his incredulity at the possibility of European women being tried by 'a copper coloured magistrate who probably worshipped the Linga, and certainly exalts in any opportunity of showing that he can insult white persons with impunity'.[63] The European women residing in Calcutta also made an appeal to the Queen.[64] The crux of the matter was that a large part of the Anglo-Indian community, racially motivated as they were, did not consider Indians fit to try Europeans. There were others who did not think that everything would be lost if Indian magistrates were given equal judicial power. But they were few in number. Ripon himself, as said before, did not anticipate the far-reaching impact of the Ilbert Bill. The storm that was raised reached the shores of England as well. The bill was discussed in Parliament, questions were asked, articles were written, and meetings were called. In the middle of this volatile climate, Florence did her best to cheer Ripon up:

> 29 June 1883
> ... Do not think that we are all gone mad: tho' I confess that I have never yet seen, in my long & busy life, such an instance of mania as seems to have seized London against the so-called 'Ilbert Bill'. But there was a remnant of good man left. And London is now resuming her sanity, & will soon again appear 'Clothed, and in her right mind'.[65]

In her long letter to Ripon, Florence praised him profusely for his reform work in India, particularly for his encouragement of local industries, allowing promotion for native officials, for local self-government and decentralisation schemes, education, the Bengal Land Tenancy Bill and proposed agricultural banks: ' ... I cannot speak for I should say too much – but to wish them God Speed. ... All these measures and many others may be called the "Saviours of India" without exaggeration.' Florence claimed that anti-Ripon Anglo-Indians had ignored what had been done by Ripon's government and policy: 'They ignore all acknowledgement of the fact that we cannot educate the Baboos so highly - and then leave things just as they were ... .' She urged Ripon not to give in to the demands of the anti-Ilbert Bill Lobby:

> And the echoes of your own mind in the old country urge, of course, that there should be no yielding, no appearance even of yielding to clamour – no resigning or withdrawing.
> 'Ease it off' they say, that is the Ilbert Bill 'As the Government of India has begun it must not leave "off" and as regards the policy in general.' Explain it as much as possible, but do not yield any essential point.
> They urge the fatal consequences of yielding to clamour; they urge the effect upon the natives which would be produced by anything like the idea that the Viceroy, who has so honourably and wisely carried out the promises of Crown, Cabinet and Commons to them, had been compelled to withdraw; God forbid![66]

In no time, a grateful Ripon replied:

> I have been much gratified by the receipt of your letter of 29th June. I have a stiff battle to fight here and it is a great help to receive such proofs as your letter affords of the interest which is felt in my work by

my friends in England and of the approval with which my policy meets from persons so well qualified to judge of it as you are.

In your letter you have touched upon many points of importance and have shown that you understand such and all of them – I only wish that there was even a modicum of your intelligent sympathy to be found in the India Council.

It is not easy to tell you how pleasant it is in the midst of much obstruction and misconception to learn that one, whose opinion I value so highly, understands so thoroughly the spirit in which I am labouring and the aims which I have set before me.

You ask me not to yield to the storm which rages round me. I have no inclination to do so. Reasonable amendments I am prepared to admit but to the principles of my measures I adhere.

I shall however need all the support that there in England who agrees with me can give me, for, my adversaries will leave no stone unturned to secure the overthrow of my plans.

Again thanking you very heartily I remain always yours most sincerely.

Ripon.[67]

The chance to support Ripon arrived soon. In July 1883, J. Seymour Keay wrote an article called *The Spoliation of India*, published in *The Nineteenth Century*, where he criticised British rule in India as rule by bureaucracy. It was a 'Government by officials united to the people by no ties of blood or property and practically unsupervised even by their own countrymen at home ... ' . These officials were eager 'to extend the area of their own patronage and power' but not 'the interests of the native races'. Seymour Keay's main criticism was that the institutions through which administration was carried out in India were unsuitable and expensive, and now to avoid such expenses drastic retrenchment was going on.[68]

Florence was afraid that this article might be considered as an attack on Ripon's administration. Already Edward Stanhope, a Member of Parliament, had highly criticised Ripon's administration as extravagant.[69] His liberal policies were viewed as suspect and his public works were regarded as draining the Imperial fund. Florence felt that the public should be made aware of Ripon's policies in India. She used Seymour Keay's article as a springboard to publicise Ripon's good work. Florence's article, *Our Indian Stewardship*, was published in the December issue of the same journal and her starting point was the comment made by Seymour Keay about the way India was governed. She claimed that the allegations brought in by Seymour Keay were just what Ripon was trying to get rid of in India: 'Lord Ripon had struck at the very root of both these evils by his measures of decentralization and by the steps he has taken for the employment of natives.'[70]

Florence argued that under Ripon's Local Government scheme, highly paid foreigners would be replaced by local people, the villagers, and there would be a great reduction of salaries. She considered the Ilbert Bill as an integral part of Ripon's policy of 'employment of natives in official positions'. 'Offices of responsibility cannot be conferred upon natives unless they are at the same time granted the powers required to perform the duties of those offices.'[71] In case anyone was under the impression that Ripon was introducing his own policies in India, Florence pointed out that he was actually following the guidelines and decisions of 'the Crown, Cabinet and Commons at home'. 'The Viceroy is the Cabinet's agent. If any man has a quarrel with his policy, the quarrel is with the Cabinet. The policy is theirs.'[72] What Ripon was doing in India was fulfilling the pledge given by the Queen to the people of India, ' … that there to be no race distinctions, that where there is fitness the employment of natives and Europeans is to be alike; that race is not to be a qualification or disqualification.'[73] This was certainly a bold statement in the context of the political climate that existed at the time. It needed a lot of conviction, courage and political foresight to express such a view. But Florence had that conviction and courage.

The Queen's Proclamation was also of immense value to Florence. She used it to justify Ripon's measures such as the decentralisation of administration and the Ilbert Bill. She pointed out that both Lawrence and Mayo saw the need for decentralisation and municipal extension:

> But it was reserved for Lord Ripon to deal effectually with the ever more pressing danger, both political and financial, and to do so in a way eminently satisfactory to the conservative instincts of the Hindoo race. By his cautious yet comprehensive scheme of Local Self Government he has gone to the root of the whole matter, restoring life to the ancient village and municipal institutions under which, with due guidance, the real needs of the people can be supplied, cheaply and without oppression, by and through the people themselves.
>   The object is not to import a foreign exotic, but to revive and strengthen a plant of home growth.[74]

Florence was determined to uphold Ripon's measures in India. She could see that at last India was being 'conquered by civilisation' by the liberal policies of Ripon and not by force. In order to help India and Ripon, she did not leave any stone unturned. There was an unfinished draft letter in her private papers, which suggests that about this time she also wrote to the Queen referring to the petition made by the Anglo-Indian women of Calcutta against the Ilbert Bill. In carefully-chosen words, she reminded the Queen of her pledge given to the Indians:

> … This refers particularly to the two measures long promised now being carried out (coming at least into execution) of local self government and of the due employment of natives in official positions together with the encouragement of local industries.

It is known that a largely signed petition to the European ladies of Calcutta and elsewhere in India against the so-called Ilbert Bill – an integral but by no means the most important part of the present just and generous policy, so wisely carrying out Your Majesty's proclamation – is to be presented to Your Majesty.

May I be permitted to add my deep regrets to those of many worthies than I – that such a movement should be possible in which the Queen can have no sympathy and which would find a sufficient answer were the movers referred to the Queen's own words in her gracious proclamation.[75]

By 1883, it was clear to Florence that Ripon needed more of her support in England than he could offer her in India. In the meantime, Ripon received another encouraging letter from her:

Great is the Anglo-Indian mutiny. But we do not apologize. On the contrary. It is the grandest triumph perhaps this time has seen. 250 millions for the first time satisfied with our rule – perfectly content in hope and in confidence. We might disband our army. The Governor General is in himself an army.[76]

Ripon realised that people like Florence would not have liked him to make any concessions regarding the Ilbert Bill, for to have done so would be considered a defeat. But he had no option in the face of the reactionary storm that was blowing at the time. The Ilbert Bill was passed with some compromising amendments on 25 January 1884.[77] On 4 March 1884, Ripon wrote to Florence:

Since your letter was written the I. Bill has been passed with modifications which have been [seriously] judged both here and in England. I do not know how you may have regarded them; but I think that if you knew all the circumstances of the case you would be of opinion that as much as was practically possible was accomplished. I enclose a copy of a speech which I made in the Legislative Council here on the subject and which explains their real nature and given the general and public reasons for the so-called 'compromise', but you will readily understand with your experience of affairs that in a composite and complicated government like this other considerations besides these which can be openly declared may have influenced the conclusions arrived at.[78]

Ripon consoled Florence that the Ilbert Bill was important, but his other measures were much more valuable, and now he had more freedom to push on with them. In the meantime, Ripon had already decided to leave India, which caused concern for Florence. She wanted to know whether Ripon's measures would be safe in the hands of the next viceroy. 'You ask me,' Ripon wrote back, 'whether my various measures are sufficiently advanced not to suffer under a new viceroy. To this inquiry, I answer that I think they are, provided the new Viceroy is likely to sympathize with the general principle of my policy.'[79] Ripon further assured her that the reason for his early retirement was to make sure that the 'completion of his work should not fall into hostile hands'. Ripon did not want the liberal reforms he had initiated further delayed. But in 1884–85, the political uncertainty in Britain was such that there was every possibility of that happening. All that it needed was the appointment of an unsympathetic Tory Viceroy for India. As a matter of fact, Ripon pleaded with Gladstone to ensure that his chosen successor was of liberal persuasion:

> Let me earnestly beg you to give me as a successor a man of really liberal opinions. In the present condition of this country, a truly and broadly liberal policy is essential not only to the discharge of our duty as a nation, but to the security of our power as a government.[80]

In London, Florence too made a plea for Ripon to Gladstone. She wanted Gladstone to put his weight behind Ripon's measures. Only a Prime Minister could ensure that Ripon's liberal measures would not be abandoned. When Gladstone called in to see her on 3 December 1884, Florence did not see him. Apparently she was in bed with an eye inflammation.[81] Florence knew a letter to Gladstone would speak more strongly about Ripon's achievements and Gladstone would have more time to think than a face to face discussion would achieve. A shrewd politician as she was, she wrote to Gladstone the next day:

> Dec. 4, 1884
> I have no words to tell my regret that when you were so very good as to call and offer me a moment of your most precious time I was unable to avail myself of it. To hear a word from you upon India & Lord Ripon's policy would have been priceless to me.[82]

In her long letter she mentioned each measure taken by Ripon and made a case for it. From land tenure to local self-government acts, from elementary education to the Covenanted Civil Service, from the encouragement of native arts and industries to the employment and promotion of the natives – she covered them all:

> How much more I could say and ask, has not Lord Ripon shown your liberal policy on the most colossal scale in the world with the result that 200 millions and more of this vast empire have for the first time confidence in our rule? No other Governor General has yet been able to conciliate them as he has.[83]

Florence's main concern was that Ripon's policies should not be abandoned but implemented. She suggested to Gladstone that if he wanted, she could write down for him 'the briefest of notes' as to the way Ripon had carried out Gladstone's liberal policy. She hoped they would still be carried out:

> Lord Ripon is obliged to leave while as yet his measures are scarcely
> launched; or indeed have even been negotiated. But let Lord Dufferin
> continue his policy. And shall you not see the triumph of your princi-
> ples in tranquillizing and developing your vast Asiatic Empire?[84]

Florence's plea, however, fell on deaf ears. Gladstone passed her letter to
Lord Kimberley, the Secretary of State, and the matter rested there.

Ripon, a liberal Viceroy, started too many reforms all at once, most of
which he could not finalise within the limited period of viceregal tenure.
He was able to pass the Factory Act in March 1881 limiting the age and
working hours of child labourers. But the act was inadequate for the
purpose. He wanted to modify the Arms Act as it existed and drafted a bill
in 1881, but could not get the support of his Secretary of State. He also
wanted to make it easy for the Indians to enter the Covenanted Civil
Service, but could not secure this during his viceroyalty. In education, he
wanted to introduce primary education all over India, and appointed the
Hunter Commission, which reported in March 1883, favouring Ripon's
idea in education, but by the time he accepted their recommendations in
October 1884 it was too late for him to see it implemented. The same
thing happened with the Tenancy Bill; it became an act after he left India.

Ripon's viceroyalty in India ended with a tumultuous farewell. It was
an overwhelmingly sincere thanksgiving by the people of India to a
Viceroy who wanted to give them a fair deal.[85] Ripon himself had not
expected it. He wrote to Lord Kimberly:

> Dec 6, 1884
>
> We arrived in Calcutta on Tuesday last, and had a most cordial recep-
> tion from the Native population. ... The streets from the Station to
> Government House were crowded to the utmost, the lowest estimate
> of those present being 100,000, while the Police Superintendent (a
> European) puts them at a much higher figure. The enthusiasm was
> such that I hardly like writing about it, but I may say that I am assured
> by most competent judges that it was quite genuine. ... You must take
> all this for what you consider it to be worth, and judge how far it
> makes in favour of the policy which has elicited such strong feelings. It
> at least shows that it is possible for an English ruler to obtain a
> powerful hold upon the hearts of the people of this country.[86]

In the meantime, Florence tried to arrange an impressive welcome for
Ripon's homecoming, but there was a general lack of enthusiasm. She
approached various newspapers to publish articles praising Ripon's
policy in India. She herself was prepared to write anonymously, but most
of the newspaper editors were unwilling to publish for the fall guy.[87]

When Ripon came back to England, not just Florence, but most of his
well-wishers as well as the Indians wanted to see him reappointed, if not
as Viceroy, at least as a Secretary of State for India. The Indians went as

far as to appeal for the extension of his viceroyalty period.[88] But after the debacle in the election of 1885, Gladstone wanted to play it safe in the existing political climate, and Ripon was sent to the Admiralty. Florence wrote to Wedderburn:

> Lord Randolph – the 'Boy with the drum', is doing untold harm – literally untold ... by attacking Ld Ripon and Sir Evelyn Baring at the I.O. Council [this is strictly between you and me].
> I am afraid we have lost all chance of having Ld Ripon at the I.O. at least at present. It would have been a difficult matter to manage at the best. Now it looks as if it were impossible. That would have been the best way to heal all our woes. But I trust in God and the Right – tho' I may not live to see it.[89]

As said before, Florence kept in touch with Ripon almost until 1902. In a way, Florence and Ripon were more close in ideas than Florence was to Lawrence. For Lawrence, she had a romantic appreciation, but Ripon was her true comrade. What she wrote in the postscript of one of her letters to Ripon was probably the most apt appraisal of this whole episode of Ripon in India: 'Lord Ripon's grand title to honour would be that he had acted on the principles of the equal treatment of the English and the natives, and of trusting those natives who had proved themselves worthy of it.'[90]

Ripon's policy won him 'the glory of unpopularity in a good cause' and Florence stood by her comrade all along.

Notes

1. FN to Ripon, 14 April 1881, BL Add. Mss 43546, fols 158–165.
2. Ripon in his long political career had many titles. He was in his youth Viscount Goderich, then during his War Office days, Lord de Grey and Ripon, and finally, the Marquis of Ripon or Lord Ripon.
3. FN to Martineau, telegraph, 15 April 1863, BL Add. Mss 45788, fol. 174. ('Agitate agitate for Lord de Grey to succeed Sir George Lewis.')
4. Cook (1913), vol. 2, pp. 29–31.
5. FN to de Grey, 23 October 1863, BL Add. Mss 43546, fols 76–79; 24 October 1863, fols 80–81. See also Wolf, L. (1921), *The Life of the First Marquis of Ripon*, London: John Murray, vol. 1, pp. 194–197.
6. FN to de Grey, 16 May 1862, BL Add. Mss 43546, fols 19–20.
7. FN to de Grey, 10 June 1865, BL Add. Mss 43546, fols 105–108; see also FN to de Grey, 7 May 1866, BL Add. Mss 45778, fols 36–37.
8. The general European view that native officers were all corrupt, was sometimes, if not always, shared by Florence. See FN to de Grey, 10 June 1865, BL Add. Mss 43546, fols 105–108. Also see Gopal (1965), pp. 36–37, 56–57, 95.
9. Gopal (1965), p. 129.
10. *Speeches and Published Resolutions of Lord Ripon, Viceroy in India*, Palit, R.C. (ed.) (1882), Calcutta: J.W. Thomas, vol. 1, p. 3.
11. Ripon to Forster, 26 May 1881, as quoted in Wolf (1921), vol. 2, p. 67.

12. Ripon to Hartington, 9 August 1880, The Marquis of Ripon's Correspondence with the Secretary of the State for India, 1880, BL B.P.7(3), no. 17, pp. 66–67.
13. Despatch, Govt. of India, 17 October 1882, Selection of letters, etc. relating to the Bengal Tenancy Bill, p. 36.
14. Despatch, Govt. of India, 17 October 1882, Selection of letters etc. relating to the Bengal Tenancy Bill. p. 41.
15. FN (1883a), p. 32.
16. Gopal (1953), p. 179.
17. Mathur, L.P. (1972), *Lord Ripon's Administration in India*, New Delhi: Chand & Co., pp. 152–153.
18. Gopal (1953), p. 185.
19. Jowett to FN, June 28, 1883, as quoted in Quinn and Prest (1987), p. 287, reprinted by permission of Oxford University Press. The Chair of Agriculture was established at Oxford in 1884 and the Board of Studies included agriculture as a subject in 1886 (Quinn and Prest (1987), p. 297).
20. FN to Toynbee, 30 May 1882, BL Add. Mss 45806, fols 258–261; Cook (1913), vol. 2, p. 333 gives a somewhat different rendering of this letter.
21. FN to Toynbee, 20 October 1882, BL Add. Mss 45807, fol. 14.
22. FN to Toynbee, 30 May 1882, BL Add. Mss 45806, fols 258–261.
23. FN to Robertson, 7 March 1879. BL OIOC, Mss Eur B 263.
24. FN to Robertson, 7 March 1879, BL OIOC, Mss Eur B 263.
25. FN to Robertson, 5 May 1880, BL OIOC, Mss Eur B 263.
26. FN to Robertson, 9 December 1881, BL OIOC, Mss Eur B 263.
27. FN to Robertson, 9 December 1881, BL OIOC, Mss Eur B 263.
28. Government of India, Resolution 8, December 1881, BL Add. Mss 43634, fol. 47.
29. Buckland (1901), vol. 2, p. 707.
30. Ripon to FN, 21 April 1884, BL Add. Mss 45778, fols 94–95.
31. Ripon to FN, 2 May 1884, BL Add. Mss 45778, fols 96–97.
32. *Speeches and Writings of Sir W. Wedderburn*, Natesan, G.A. (ed.) (1918), Madras: Natesan & Co., p. 185.
33. FN (1879c), 'Co-operation in India', *Journal of the National Indian Association*, no. 101, May 1879, p. 220.
34. FN to Gladstone, 12 May 1879, BL Add. Mss 44460, fols 35–38.
35. Fox, F.W. (1879), *On Reform in the Administration of India* (no publisher detail), p. 2.
36. FN to Gladstone, 7 July 1879, BL Add. Mss 44460, fols 242–246.
37. Wedderburn, W. (1880), Agricultural Banks for India, Bombay. Reprinted from *Bombay Gazette*, p. 27. Also see Wedderburn, W. (1883), 'The Poona Raiyat's Bank: A practical experiment', *Journal of the East India Association*, vol. XV, July, pp. 325–345.
38. *Voice of India*, January 1883, vol. 1, no. 1, p. 11.
39. Natesan (1918), p. 185.
40. Ratcliffe, S.K. (1923), *Sir William Wedderburn and the Indian Reform Movement*, London: Allen and Unwin, p. 40.
41. Natesan (1918), p. 187.
42. Natesan (1918), pp. 187–8.
43. Wedderburn, W. (1913), *Allan Octavian Hume: Father of the Indian National Congress, 1829–1912*, London: Fisher Unwin, p. 32. The plan for an agricultural bank was implemented almost 20 years later during Lord Curzon's viceroyalty.

44. FN to Ripon, 14 April 1881, BL Add. Mss 43546, fol. 158.
45. FN to Ripon, 14 April 1881, BL Add. Mss 43546, fol. 162.
46. FN to Ripon, 14 April 1881, BL Add. Mss 43546, fols 162–164.
47. Ripon to FN, 12 May 1881, The Marquis of Ripon's Correspondence with Persons in England, 1881, BL B.P.7(5), no. 49, pp. 57–58.
48. FN to Ripon, 28 July 1881, BL Add. Mss 43546, fols 166–175.
49. FN to Ripon, 28 July 1881, BL Add. Mss 43546, fol. 173.
50. FN to Ripon, 14 April 1882, BL Add. Mss 43546, fols 194–196.
51. Loch to FN, 12 June 1888, BL Add. Mss 45808, fol. 114.
52. 'In 1893, Miss Locke [sic] stressed the great need to establish the training of hospital orderlies on a regular basis, and in the following year a regular system of training men for hospital work was inaugurated.' Wilkinson (1958), p. 10.
53. FN to Ripon, 12 August 1881, BL Add. Mss 43546, fols 178–193. This author has separately referred to the various sections of this long letter.
54. FN to Ripon, 12 August 1881, BL Add. Mss 43546, fol. 182.
55. FN to Ripon, 12 August 1881, BL Add. Mss 43546, fols 183-184.
56. FN to Ripon, 12 August 1881, BL Add. Mss 43546, fols 189–190.
57. Ripon to Hartington, 14 September 1882, as quoted in Wolf (1921), vol. 2, p. 53.
58. Principal Measures of Administration ... during the Viceroyalty of Marquis of Ripon, BL B.P.7(15), pp. 94, 439.
59. For full analysis of the Ilbert Bill controversy and its background history, see Gopal (1953), pp. 113–166; Mathur (1972), pp. 206–230.
60. As quoted in Hobhouse, A. (1883), 'Native Indian judges; Mr Ilbert's Bill', The Contemporary Review, vol. 43, June, p. 796.
61. Ripon to Kimberley, 14 September 1881, The Marquis of Ripon's Correspondence with the Secretary of State for India, 1883, BL B.P.7(3), no. 66, pp. 260–265.
62. The Local Opinions on the Criminal Procedure Code Amendment Bill 1883, [Calcutta], p. 34, reprinted from The Englishman.
63. Wolf (1921), vol. 2, p. 131.
64. Florence made a reference to that in her letter to the Queen. Also see Sinha, M. (1992), '"Chathams, Pitts, and Gladstones in Petticoats" – The politics of gender and race in the Ilbert Bill controversy, 1883–1884', in Chaudhuri, N. and Strobel, M. (eds), Western Women and Imperialism – Complicity and Resistance, Bloomington and Indianapolis: Indiana University Press, pp. 98–116.
65. FN to Ripon, 29 June 1883, BL Add. Mss 43546, fols 197–198.
66. FN to Ripon, 29 June 1883, BL Add. Mss 43546, fols 200–202.
67. Ripon to FN, 20 July 1883, BL Add. Mss 45778, fol. 88–89.
68. Seymour Keay (1883), p. 2.
69. Wolf (1921), p. 82.
70. FN (1883d), 'Our Indian Stewardship', The Nineteenth Century, vol. XIV, December, p. 337.
71. FN (1883d), p. 337.
72. FN (1883d), p. 335.
73. FN (1883d), p. 332.
74. FN (1883d), p. 338.
75. FN to Queen Victoria, 1882 [undated], BL Add. Mss 45750, fols 10–11, draft. Cook also mentioned that she wrote to the Queen about the Ilbert Bill,

but the content of the letter Cook cited is somewhat different from this letter. See Cook (1913), vol. 2, p. 339–341.

76. FN to Ripon, 14 December 1883, BL Add. Mss 43546, fols 203–207.
77. Gopal (1953), p. 161.
78. Ripon to FN, 4 March 1884, BL Add. Mss 45778, fols 90–91.
79. Ripon to FN, 10 October 1884, BL Add. Mss 45778, fol. 98.
80. Ripon to Gladstone, 25 June 1884, the Marquis of Ripon Correspondence with Persons in England, BL B.P.7(5), no. 55.
81. FN to Gladstone, 3 December 1884, BL Add. Mss 44488, fol. 196.
82. FN to Gladstone, 4 December 1884, BL Add. Mss 44488, fols 204–13.
83. FN to Gladstone, 4 December 1884, BL Add. Mss 44488, fol. 208.
84. FN to Gladstone, 4 December 1884, BL Add. Mss 44488, fol. 209.
85. Mehrotra (1971), pp. 372–75.
86. Ripon to Kimberly, 6 December 1884, The Marquis of Ripon's Correspondence with the Secretary of State for India, BL B.P.7(3), no. 63, pp. 183–184.
87. Cook (1913), vol. 2, p. 346. (According to Cook, the only article published was written by Florence's nephew, Frederick Verney, in the *Pall Mall Gazette*, January 22, 1885.)
88. Mehrotra (1971), p. 371.
89. FN to Wedderburn, 17 November 1885, BL OIOC, Mss Eur B 151.
90. FN to Ripon, 14 December 1883, BL Add. Mss 43546, fol. 207.

CHAPTER 8

The Health Missioners for Rural India

> I have for many years been interested in questions affecting the health of the people of India. At first my attention was chiefly directed to the cities, and I watched with great interest what was being done by the municipalities, not only in the presidency towns of Calcutta, Bombay and Madras, but also in important local centres such as Ahmedabad … But the number of large towns in India is very small. India is mainly a country of peasant cultivators. And I came to understand that 90 per cent of the 240 millions of Indians dwell in small rural villages … . It thus became impressed upon me that the sanitation affecting the great bulk of the Indian population was village sanitation, and, in order to benefit the people of India, we must try to learn the actual conditions under which they live in these village communities.[1]

Florence's interest in village sanitation started as early as 1862 with her work with the Royal Commission and remained, as she said, an ongoing theme in all her reform proposals for India. Since her young days in Leahurst, where she gathered some experience and insight into working with socially disadvantaged people in her father's estate[2], she maintained an interest in the health and sanitation of small rural communities.[3] Both in her *Observations* and *Suggestions*, she drew the attention of the Government to the wretched conditions in the Indian villages. She emphasised repeatedly that India was a cluster of villages and any attempt to improve the health and sanitary matters of the army should also include the sanitation of the towns and villages.

Florence had by now been involved with her Indian work for almost three decades. There was a period in her career when she turned her attention from sanitation for a while and concentrated on larger problems such as famine, irrigation and land tenancy. By the mid-1880s, after the departure of Ripon, she probably realised how difficult it was, even for a determined Viceroy, to change the status quo in India and how strong the racist and reactionary forces could be, as was evident in the cases of the Vernacular Press Act, Ilbert Bill and the Bengal Land Tenancy Bill. When Florence tried to draw the attention of the British authorities to the real causes of India's distress and poverty, she only caused irritation, antagonism and annoyance and, in later years, she received little co-operation from the India Office although a lot of verbal respect was paid to her. She was already in her mid-sixties, which must be considered as 'old age' in the context of nineteenth-century British society, and was, in her own words, 'a prisoner in her own bedroom' suffering from ill health. The days when she could easily draw the attention of Viceroys and Secretaries of State to her ideas were long gone. The new Viceroys were far too distant for comradeship, though they still came to her for advice and goodwill before leaving for India.

When Lord Dufferin was chosen as the Viceroy of India, he came to see Florence and she, as the Governess of the Governors, once again initiated him in her sanitation doctrines. In the postscript of her long letter to Gladstone, she wrote:

> Lord Dufferin most kindly gave me the opportunity not only of seeing him and talking over these things with him but also of writing notes of our conversation for him. He spoke so highly of the clearness and statesmanship of Lord Ripon's letters and measures as to lead one to hope that tho' an anti-tenant right man in Ireland, he might carry them out in India.[4]

Florence did not forget that the Bengal Land Tenancy Bill had still not been enacted and that Dufferin did not support Gladstone's Irish land policy. She did not want to leave anything to chance. She wanted to make sure that Dufferin should have first-hand knowledge of Ripon's measures in India, and would not be brainwashed by the 'Governor-General's Council', most members of which were against Ripon's measures. It was not just sanitation; all the progressive measures Ripon undertook were at stake. As noted before, both Florence and Ripon wanted to ensure that Ripon's policies were not undone by the next Viceroy. After consultation with Ripon and Florence, Dufferin left for India well equipped with reading materials on sanitation and other reforms. On 13 November 1884 while en route to India, Dufferin wrote:

> My Dear Miss Nightingale,
>   I duly received the papers you were good enough to send me, and you may be quite sure of my studying them with the attention they deserve. I well know, how well entitled you are to speak with authority in reference to Indian questions, and I can well believe that you have thought out many conclusions which it would be of the greatest benefit to me to ponder over.[5]

The same thing happened when Dufferin was succeeded by Lansdowne in 1888. The added advantage with Lansdowne was that he was a pupil of Benjamin Jowett. It was Jowett who insisted that Florence must see Lansdowne before his departure for India and educate him in her ideas. 'Could you write me down, in simple words only,' Jowett urged Florence on March 22 1888, 'the principal questions which a Governor-General

should consider & perhaps the titles of some books which he should read
e.g. irrigation, Instruction in Agriculture.'[6] Although more than four
years had passed since Ripon's departure from India, Florence was still
committed to Ripon's progressive policies. She wanted Lansdowne to
become aware of what Ripon had been trying to do in India. So she
responded to Jowett's letter by seeking Ripon's advice:

> It is of immeasurably more importance that 'he' (you will infer for
> whom this is) should consider what you have done and what remains
> to be done to carry out your views as to local self government in
> municipalities, districts, villages; it is in the rural districts of India ...
> that least has been done and most wants doing.[7]

After consulting with Ripon, Florence carefully prepared a list of questions which the new Governor-General should look into and try to
resolve, as well as a list of books, memos and reports that he should read
to acquaint himself with the Indian situation.[8] Florence was impressed
when Lansdowne came to see her. 'He was most favourably disposed to
these objects we have at heart,' she confided to Ripon, 'but specially well-
disposed to village native agencies, to Panchayats and the like – to Local
Self-Government, & which I attributed to his having had the advantage of
seeing and hearing you.'[9]

Florence thus started the last phase of her Indian work with the goodwill
of two successive Viceroys. This time, she wholeheartedly concentrated
on village sanitation and education. She probably thought that the time
had come to pay attention to less controversial but more practical problems. In as early as 1881, she wrote to Ripon that though a lot had been
done for the big towns and cities, the villages were still 'a blot' in the sanitary history of India.[10] She increasingly felt the need for proper education
in the Indian villages and for introducing sanitation through education. It
is needless to say that she was also involved with many other issues that
will unfold as we proceed.

There might be another reason why Florence felt that she could now
concentrate once again on sanitation. We have seen before how she
argued that sanitation was meaningless if there was no one alive to enjoy
the benefit of it, and that realisation led to her involvement with famine,
irrigation and land reforms in India. But now, in 1885, after Ripon's
administration, she could see some changes in the offing. Although
Ripon's viceroyalty raised a storm of reactionary forces in Britain and
India, some of his liberal measures were later implemented. The decentralisation of the Government gradually took place at local level; the
Tenancy Act of 1885, however inadequate, introduced some improvement for the *ryots*; the railways flourished and some irrigation works
were extended; the age limit for Indians to compete for places in the

Covenanted Civil Service was later raised; and India stepped into a relatively slow but stable path of political progress.

Between 1885 and 1894, the period of Dufferin's and Lansdowne's viceroyalties, Florence's efforts to bring about sanitary changes in India as usual went through two channels. One was through her official contacts, which included the Viceroys and the Secretaries of State, and the other through her non-official sources, where she tried to involve Indians in village sanitation and education. In addition, she did not cease to publish articles on issues vital for India. During this last phase of her work, the foci of her attention were Lord Dufferin's proposal for Sanitary Boards in India, the Bombay Village Sanitation Bill and, finally, sanitary education for the rural population, especially for women.

Lobbying the Viceroys

Florence's relationship with viceregal sources was quite amicable to start with. Lord Dufferin's administration introduced several army reforms that must have pleased her, such as the employment of female nurses in regimental hospitals and ward servants in the hospitals of native troops. In addition, as mentioned earlier, under Miss Loch's supervision and initiative, the training of native hospital corps was properly introduced. The barrack canteens where the soldiers could indulge in alcohol were now replaced with coffee shops and recreation centres. This was a change Florence had been fighting for since the days of John Lawrence. However, when it came to the question of civil sanitation, the viceregal approaches were not fully satisfactory to Florence, and in this matter she was a difficult mistress to please.

Both Dufferin and Lansdowne supported Florence's ideas on sanitary matters, but once they reached India, other administrative priorities took over. The matters that concerned most Indians like health, sanitation and education got lost in competition with more imperialistic issues such as the annexation of Burma, reorganisation of the army and countering the imaginary threat from Russia. On top of all these, the rising tide of Indian nationalism was another factor to cope with. 'Lord Dufferin is not obstructive, he has allowed every one of my reforms to go on, but he has not forwarded them – he is a diplomat, not an administrator. And his hands have been full of Russia and Burmah. And he has done diplomatic work by preference.'[11]

In 1885–86, the political situation in Britain changed considerably. Lord Salisbury's second Tory government came into power, and Lord Randolph Churchill was the Secretary of State for India. India was no longer a favourite topic among British politicians. Ripon consoled Florence:

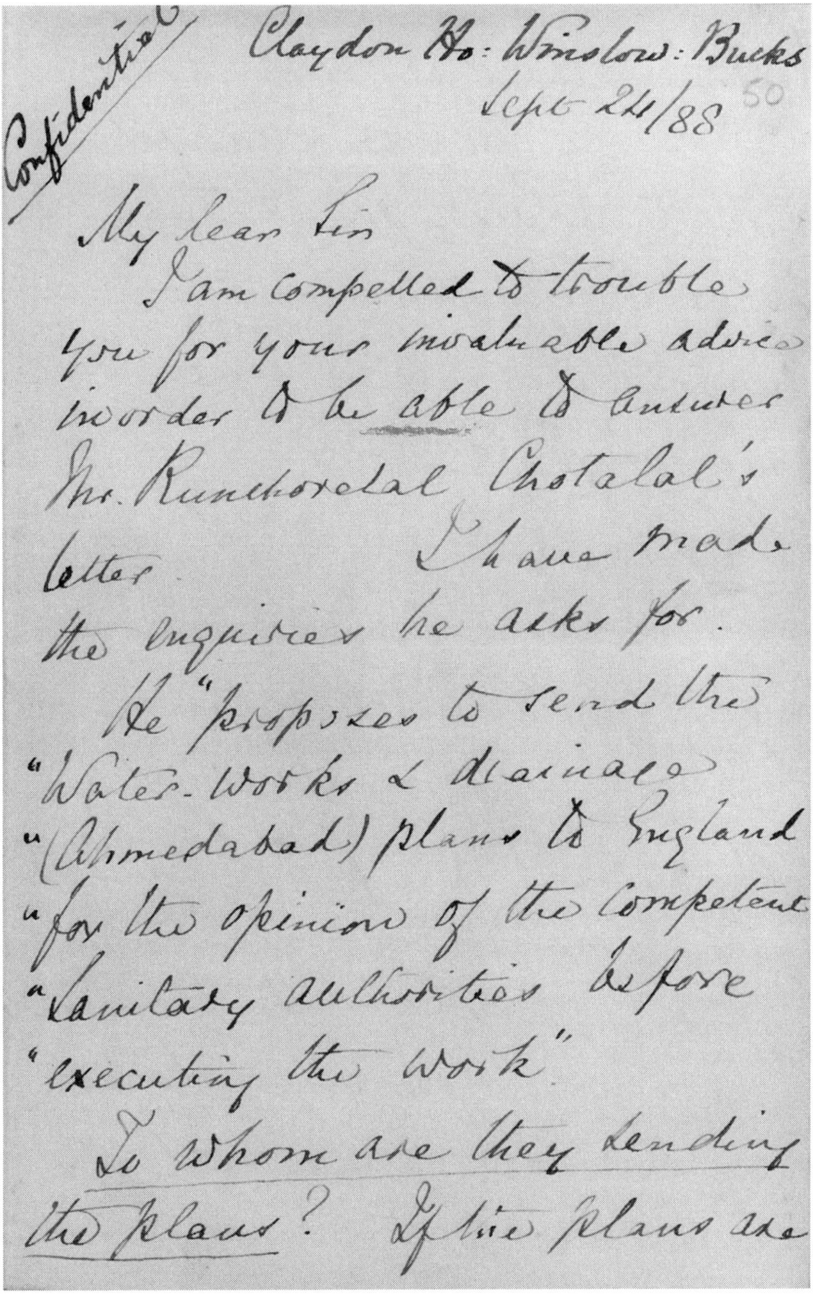

Confidential

Claydon Ho: Winslow: Bucks
Sept 24/88

My dear Sir
    I am compelled to trouble
you for your invaluable advice
in order to be able to answer
Mr. Runchorelal Chotalal's
letter.   I have made
the enquiries he asks for.

    He "proposes to send the
"Water-Works & drainage
"(Ahmedabad) plans to England
"for the opinion of the competent
"sanitary authorities before
"executing the work".

    To whom are they sending
the plans? If the plans are

Plate 5   Florence Nightingale's letter to Dr Hewlett, Sanitary Officer, Bombay
regarding sanitation of Ahmedabad. (The British Library)

Plate 6   Florence Nightingale, *c.* 1890. (The Wellcome Library)

> There are waves, the thing is to come in upon waves. You would have
> done nothing for the Army Medical and Sanitary Service if it had not
> the crash in Crimea. Now the wave is against interest in India. Every
> effort would be wasted. Now, no interest in the Parliament. This
> Parliament not good for the Native Indians to sit in. Let us wait till
> spring – see what Randolph's Commission comes to. Next spring the
> wave may be in our favour.
>
> If there comes another Russian scare all eyes will be directed on
> India. Then will be the time.[12]

Once in the position of Secretary of State, Randolph Churchill bitterly
criticised Ripon for failing to see the Russian threat in India and to
prepare against it.[13] The Finance Committee, headed by him, suggested
economies everywhere, and as sanitary reforms were expensive, the
Indian sanitary service was in line for drastic cuts.[14] This was a real
setback for Florence, as she could see that her thirty-odd years of hard
work was about to be destroyed. There were, however, good reasons for
the Finance Committee to take a harsh attitude towards the sanitary
service in India. It had not produced the expected results. The Sanitary
Commissioners suffered from a lack of enthusiasm and initiative. The
local authorities had been unable to provide the necessary funding. A
number of sanitary projects had been started, but not quite finished.

Lord Dufferin, Ripon's successor in India, was not happy about the
way the Sanitary Commission was functioning, and Florence was in
agreement with him. The sanitary officers were 'time-servers'. 'Perhaps
the thing most against us,' she later wrote to Ripon, 'is the present low
stamp of sanitary commissioners in India, – the no stamp of sanitary engineer there … '.[15] Yet abolishing the posts of the Sanitary Commissioners
would be a great loss, as, to Florence, these were the 'health missionaries'
in India, 'to educate people to know and practise the first elements of
living a sound and healthy life; to indoctrinate the people with a new
moral sense.'[16] Such an action of abolition would be a 'good bye to all
hopes of sanitary reforms in India'. In order to stop such a measure being
taken, Florence wrote a long letter to Dufferin, expressing her anxiety and
anger.[17] Dufferin replied that she need not worry. The recommendations
of the Finance Committee in London did not mean that the Government
of India would act automatically. 'On the contrary, I will go most carefully into the question in which you naturally take so deep an interest and
will be careful to have it thoroughly discussed in Council by my colleagues
with the advantage of having had your views placed before them.'[18] The
idea of abolishing the Sanitary Commissioners was finally given up, but
Dufferin wanted to revamp the service:

> We are now however taking the question up, and the result of the
> attack upon your protégés will be, not their disappearance, but their

> being compelled to give us the worth of money we spend upon them. I
> am also inviting all the local governments to put the whole subject of
> sanitation upon a more satisfactory footing, and to establish a system
> of concerted action and a well worked out programme in accordance
> with which from year to year their operations are to be conducted.[19]

Dufferin's solution to the problem of sanitary reform in India was to create
Sanitary Boards. In July 1888, the Government of India passed a resolution
to introduce Sanitary Boards into every province under the control and
supervision of the Supreme Government. These Sanitary Boards would be
'entrusted with the control and supervision over sanitary works' in rural
and urban areas. They would not only be consultative, but also executive.
Through these boards, the Government would act if necessary and pass
laws. Upon Florence's persuasion, special emphasis was to be given to rural
sanitation. It was also decided that a Sanitary Commissioner and a Sanitary
Engineer, as Florence was insisting upon for a long time, would be
appointed to inspect and advise local bodies on sanitary work. Provision
for Government loans for this purpose would also be made.

Before the resolution was passed, Dufferin sent the papers privately to
Florence for her consideration. 'The G.G. of India has sent me the "resolution" he has issued to the local Govt. and a memorandum,' Florence
wrote to her old friend Sir Douglas Galton. '[N]either have yet reached
the I.O. He has written me twice and I have answered pointing out that
the "Resolution" will not do without a Sanitary executive administration
in India.'[20] The Governor-General of India also wanted to know the
response of the Secretary of State to their proposals. Lord Cross, the
Secretary of State, turned to Florence for her advice and asked her to write
'anything we had to say for his consideration'.[21] Florence, the effective
arbiter of policy in this matter, as both parties sought and valued her
opinion, helped the Secretary of State to draft a despatch.[22]

Florence was not altogether happy about Dufferin's scheme for Sanitary Boards. She considered the resolution as only sketching the outline of
some of the work to be done.[23] In a more elaborate memorandum to the
India Office, she criticised Dufferin's idea of Sanitary Boards on the
grounds that the success of his measures would depend on the willingness
of the local governments to act, and proper funding: 'It provides a central
board for the consideration and control of sanitary action in each province. But it neither indicates the way the orders of the board are to be
carried out, nor the sources from which funds for the necessary establish-
ments are to be provided.'[24] She asked how the Government envisaged
tackling the funding question: 'Will it allot a certain portion of the
revenue derived from each village or will it impose additional taxation to
meet these expenses?' In a private letter to Ripon she also expressed her
candid opinion about Dufferin's ideas:

It is no doubt a great step forward that the Govt. of India would adopt the two most important principles we have fought for: viz. efficient central control & executive agency, provision by Govt. of the necessary loans. The degree in which these reforms are likely to produce useful practical results must depend of course, on the way in which the Govt. of India regards the question, & is willing to turn the new machinery to good account. But, if the higher authorities in India are too busy or too little serious to care, the I.O. Council too being so formidable an instrument of delay & obstruction, then these reforms are likely to be coldly received and feebly worked.[25]

Florence was always a great believer in peoples' initiatives and power. She wanted the executive power to rest in the hands of the people, that is, with the village *panchayat*, and that villages should have access to the money raised. The people should be allowed 'to choose their own way of doing this' and 'it must be done to the satisfaction of the officers Government will appoint to supervise the work ... '. She wanted the re-establishment of village *panchayats* and granting of authority to the village headman to punish those who disobeyed the order of the *panchayat*, and finally to give the village sweepers or scavengers land in exchange for sanitary work.[26] Florence cited the unique example of the town of Ahmedabad, where local people on their own initiative raised money and sorted out the sanitary situation of the town:

> Ahmedabad is working splendidly at water supply and sewerage ... under its native president Mr Runchorelal Chotalall, who is worthy of you – they are now about to lay on a water supply, inexhaustible, obtained from a well built in the river bed [a 5 percent loan for this was taken up locally – the whole of it – immediately – above per value – we hope the good example will be followed by other cities for their cash-hoard savings]. Ahmedabad will be the first Mofussil town to be sewered. Its death rate was enormous.
>
> This Mr Runchorelal Chotalall (who is a correspondent of mine) is by no means anglicized. He does his pilgrimages properly to the Himalayas. I think it must be satisfactory to you when a native of the natives takes this enlightened and vigorous line overcoming opposition from within and without.[27]

Runchorelal Chotalall, the President of the Ahmedabad municipality, often sought Florence's advice on sanitary matters. He came from a Nagar-Brahmin community, the members of which had mostly worked as Dewans or Government officials during the reign of the Muslims and the Marathas. Chotalall himself rose from a relatively humble position and became a prominent figure in Ahmedabad in the 1870s and 1880s. A self-taught man in English, he was the first to start the Ahmedabad textile industry under Indian ownership in spite of repeated setbacks. A considerable amount of sanitary work involving drainage and filtered water was executed in Ahmedabad because of Chotalall's initiative and enthusiasm.[28] Over the years, Florence mentioned the praiseworthy work Chotalall had done in Ahmedabad as the President of the local municipality. Florence never shared the British officials' view that Indians were apathetic towards sanitation. She always felt that proper education and sympathetic communication could change the deplorable sanitary situation of the Indian towns and villages and, for any Indian who was willing to be helped, she was there to help. When Chotalall wanted a sanitary engineer for Ahmedabad, Florence sent copies of his letter to her friend Sir Douglas Galton, asking him to look for a good sanitary engineer: 'We cannot abandon the Ahmedabad people after they have done everything we have asked them to do about the city.'[29] In 1891, when the International Congress of Hygiene and Demography was held in London, Florence took the initiative to include Chotalall's much acclaimed paper, *The Sanitation of the City of Ahmedabad in the Bombay Presidency*, in the Congress's transactions.[30]

It is worth noting that even in as late as 1888 Florence was going through all the sanitary papers and memoranda sent to her unofficially or privately, often by the Viceroy or the Secretary of State himself. They taxed her brain, sought her advice and used her skill and ability to produce a quick report on the question at issue. But when it came to the question of implementation, inertia and apathy took over. Dufferin passed the Sanitary Board Resolution in July 1888, and left India in December that year. He was satisfied with the idea that his administration

> ... has given sanitation a local habitation and a name in every great division of the Empire, and it has arranged for the establishment of responsible central agencies from one end of the country to the other, who will be in close communication with all the local authorities within their respective jurisdictions.[31]

Florence, however, knew that Dufferin's proposal was only an outline of 'the work to be done' and not 'work done'. She could not rest until she saw that it was done. She criticised the speech Dufferin gave in Calcutta on St. Andrew's day. She pointed out that the speech was given to an audience mainly comprised of planters, entrepreneurs and speculators, who were always rather uneducated and in opposition to every form of liberal government. Florence did not forget that it was this section of British expatriates in India that had vehemently opposed Ripon's progressive measures.[32]

When Dufferin was replaced by Lansdowne, she repeatedly wrote to him to find out whether such Sanitary Boards were in existence, and whether Dufferin's proposal actually came to fruition. She was worried that 'their existence was cited to justify abolishing the Army Sanitary Commission ... ' so they had better be there.[33] As soon as Lansdowne informed his Governess that the provincial sanitary boards did exist, she promptly asked him about their structure and efficacy, emphasising at the same time the importance of having a proper sanitary engineer on these boards: ' ... if they can only have Engineers who give their whole time to the work! The knowledge of sanitation is a very special branch.'[34]

When, in 1892, the India Office sent Florence the reports of the provincial sanitary executive boards, she in no uncertain terms expressed her dissatisfaction to Lansdowne: ' ... in looking the papers through I regret to see that in several of the Reports, no notice is taken of Village sanitation. And in Bengal, the Local Govt. seems to have restricted the operation of Sanitary Boards to municipal areas.'[35] One year later, in 1893, she asked Lansdowne once again to send her detailed reports from each presidency and province on the workings of the sanitary executive boards of the local governments as well as of the working of the village sanitary acts, together with the copies of the remarks and orders of the Government of India on that. Her letter shows how deeply involved she was in the question of village sanitation, and how determined she was to put pressure on the Governor-Generals to achieve some tangible results. Florence wanted to know everything: how the principle of selecting particular villages for sanitation was working, whether 'each village should be legally authorized to reserve and spend a part of its own cess paid by itself till the minimum of sanitation required by this particular village is attained', and whether health lectures were arranged for the villages. 'Health in the Home has not been carried home to the millions of villagers upon whom the health of Indian people so much depends.' She also questioned the total power of the District Officers on whom everything depended. She pointed out that if the District Officer had no sanitary education or inclination, 'the roads by which the District Officer are to go may be cleansed, but the by-lanes and houses and compounds of the poor be left in a horrible state'.[36]

In time, Lansdowne sent Florence a detailed but cautious reply to all her queries and, like his predecessors, advocated slow progress. He told her that in some parts of India such as in Madras, Bombay and the Central Provinces, the village Sanitary Boards or committees were to some extent established. In the North-Western Provinces and Oudh, an act to that effect was passed and the Supreme Government was in correspondence with the Bengal Government as to the formation of village union committees.

> You will therefore see that we are making good progress with the villages, although it must be gradual, as the villagers have to be educated up to the idea. I am convinced that there is an appreciable risk of rendering sanitary reform unpopular by pushing it on too fast.
> ... An Indian village is so very unlike anything to which we are used to at home that until one has been in this country, he does not realise how misleading are any analogies drawn from British experience.[37]

Echoing Salisbury, Lansdowne also fell back on the two familiar excuses of inaction, India was difficult to change and there was no money in the kitty.

Knowledgeable and far-sighted as she was, Florence must have realised by this time that official initiative in sanitary matters would always be limited. Other political and financial matters would receive priority. She obviously felt the need for cultivating non-official sources in India more than ever. She could see that if anything was to be done, the idea of 'self-help' needed to be engendered among the people. To appreciate the extent of this extraordinary woman's attempt to help the people of India we have to deviate a little from village sanitation and go back a few years to pick up the thread of this story.

Florence and the Indian National Congress

The period between 1885–94 was not only the most active period of Florence's Indian work but also a remarkable period in the history of India. Florence could see that things were at last changing for India, within India. The politicisation of the Indians was almost complete as the 'multitudes' were finally finding their voice. This period saw the manifestations of strong political aspirations of the Indians and the birth of the Indian National Congress. Florence, who initially never thought of relinquishing the Empire, but always maintained that it should be kept, not by force, but by exporting civilisation, now in her old age wholeheartedly supported the efforts of Allan Octavian Hume and William Wedderburn, the two Britons who were associated with the founding of the Indian National Congress.

Both Hume and Wedderburn had worked in India as civilians and were interested in India's social and political reforms. William Wedderburn, as mentioned in an earlier chapter, went to India in 1860 as a civil servant and in 1882 he was a District Judge in Poona. He was also a good friend of Ripon, Dadabhai Naoroji, M.G. Ranade and Gopal Krishna Gokhale. Both Hume and Wedderburn knew Florence, and Wedderburn in particular had worked closely with her. Hume joined the Bengal Civil Service in 1849 and, like Florence and Wedderburn, was also interested in agricultural reform. During Lord Mayo's viceroyalty, he proposed to organise the Agricultural Department of the Government of India as an independent bureau.[38] But Mayo was not able to carry out his scheme. Hume became the Secretary to the Government of India in due course, but because of his independent spirit he was removed from his office for 'insubordination' in 1879, during Lord Lytton's administration. Hume finally resigned from the Service in 1882.[39] The reason that led Hume to become involved in the founding of an organisation like the Indian

National Congress has been a subject of in-depth historical research.[40] Hume was a close friend of Ripon and certainly Ripon's ideas and visions inspired him. What Hume wanted was to build a bridge of communication between the British ruling class and the Indians. He warned the Government that unless such scope was given to educated Indians, there would be widespread disaffection, and perhaps a revolt. He looked on the Indian National Congress as a 'safety valve', a forum for self-expression for Indians. Florence understood the need for this very well. In her long letter to Gladstone in 1884, she drew his attention to what was happening in India:

> India is not standing still. We have talked much about giving her 'Western civilization'. Western Civilization has given her, whether we will or no, western powers ... with western power must we not give them gradually western responsibilities? If we did not would they not take them?[41]

It must, however, be said that though the initiative of people like Hume and Wedderburn no doubt contributed to the founding of a national association like Congress, it would have happened in any case, as Indians were already aware of the strength of 'combination' on an all-India basis and had derived their political lesson from the Ilbert Bill episode. According to Seal: 'By the early 1880s the idea of a national representative body was being discussed in every presidency of India, and there had already been a number of attempts to bring it into being.'[42] The Indian National Conference was held in Calcutta on 28 December 1883 under the leadership of the Indian Association, where delegates from different parts of India participated in discussing various national issues. People such as Surendranath Banerjee, M.G. Ranade, Pherozshah Mehta, Dadabhai Naoroji, K.T. Telang, B.Tyabji, B.M. Malabari, together with various political organisations from Poona, Bombay, Madras and Calcutta, were already working towards an all-India organisation. Hume and Wedderburn's initiative only hastened the process of the birth of the Indian National Congress. The credit which Hume could certainly claim was that he played the vital role of a negotiator, a liaison officer. As an ex-civilian, it was easy for him to liaise with the Government on the one hand and the Indians on the other. 'If the founder of the Congress had not been a great Englishman and a distinguished ex-official,' as Gokhale said in Hume's memorial meeting in London, 'such was the official distrust of political agitation in those days that the authorities would have at once found some way or other to suppress the movement.'[43]

In July 1885, Hume went to London to organise publicity for the forthcoming first session of the Indian National Union, as the Congress was initially called. His objective was to gather Liberal support for the Indian

National Union and, among the Liberals, Florence Nightingale's name certainly carried weight. 'Mr Hume, who brought me a letter from Mr Ilbert,' Florence wrote to Wedderburn on 27 November 1885,

> was so good as to give me a good deal of his time. This 'National Liberal' Union, if it keeps straight, seems altogether the matter of greatest interest that has happened in India, if it makes progress, perhaps for a century. We are watching the birth of a new nationality in the oldest civilization in the world. How critical will be its first meeting at Poona. I bid it God speed with all my heart.

Florence also wrote that she wished that this new organisation 'would lay down principles and not try to throw down men'.[44] Her fear was that the first session of the Congress might end in personal attacks and bickering. Florence's letters to Wedderburn during this period were particularly significant, because they referred to all the events and matters with which she was associated at the time.

As mentioned earlier, 1885 was a time of change in Britain. Gladstone's Liberal government lost the general election and the Conservatives formed a minority caretaker government with Lord Salisbury as Prime Minister and Lord Randolph Churchill, who Florence called 'the boy with the drum',[45] as the Secretary of State for India. Another election was imminent in the autumn, and Hume and other well-wishers of India wanted to use the uncertain pre-election climate of Britain for their purpose. Hume not only saw Florence, but other influential people too such as Lord Ripon, Lord Dalhousie, John Bright, James Caird, Mr Baxton, Mr Reid and Mr Slagg.[46] Hume and his friends tried their best to publicise in Britain the forthcoming session of the Indian National Union in Poona in December 1885 by holding meetings, conferences and by lobbying.[47] They tried to persuade Members of Parliament and other election candidates to commit themselves to a pledge that, if elected, they would pay attention to Indian affairs.

Immediately before the 1885 election, William Digby, the Secretary of the National Liberal Club, wrote to the Bombay Presidency Association about the importance of the election for India and 'offered to act as a member for India in the British Parliament' if the Indians would guarantee his election expenses together with £1000 per annum and office expenses.[48] Digby was sympathetic to Indian interests and was encouraged by Ripon. The Bombay Presidency Association and the Poona Sarvajanik Sabha came forward to help Digby, and they also sent the lawyer and journalist N.G. Chandavarkar to England to lobby and lecture on behalf of India. Similarly, the Madras Mahajan Sabha sent Salem Ramaswamy Mudaliar to represent the south, and Manmohun Ghose was sent by the Calcutta Indian Union.[49] The Indian delegates went round Britain addressing public meetings and lobbying people sympathetic to the cause of India. It was clear from Florence's letters that Hume and Wedderburn encouraged her to see them, particularly Mr Chandavarkar, and Mr Mudaliar. This she did more than once, and was highly impressed by both of them:

> Thanks for your introduction to Mr Chandavarkar, whom I had a long talk with. I believe their meeting had been very successful throughout the country in attracting attention. We rather regretted that they had fallen so entirely into the hands of Mr Digby, who has lost his election – and is no great loss to our cause – and who used them merely as his Electioneering agents ... .[50]
>
> Mr Chandavarkar, the second time I saw him, was so full of interest. How much he has done and is doing in Bombay that we English know nothing of. I should like to have heard more of this religious Theistic Association and of their schools for Millhands and women. ... Likewise Mr Mudaliar, the Madras delegate, was most interesting.[51]

Soon after his return from England, Chandavarkar published an account of his meeting with Miss Nightingale:

> I had the pleasure of calling on her at her house in Oxford Street twice. Though now old and obliged to confine herself to her bed on account of illness, the capacity for work is still in her. She is always doing something – writing for the papers or reviews on some subject or other. Earnestness is still discernible in her expression. Nothing interests her so much as the well being of the poor and helpless. We talked more than an hour on a number of things relating to India but it was the condition of the lower classes in this country that seemed to interest her most. Speaking about our workmen and agriculturists particularly, she enquired: 'How do they live?' 'What sort of education do they receive?' What sort of dress do they wear? Can they read or write?' With the delegation movement she expressed herself strongly in sympathy and warmly commended the step adopted by the Indian Associations in sending a deputation to arouse English interest in Indian affairs. 'We English people', she said to me, 'will not learn to take interest in India unless you seriously press Indian questions on our attention.' She regretted that almost all the friends of India had been defeated at the Election, but her advice for us was that we should not lose heart on that account. 'We are passing through a crisis. No one can say what will come out of it. The Irish question is itself a source of great anxiety and trouble. And I do not wonder that the elections have been to India a great disappointment. But your friends must not despair. Work on and it will be all right.'[52]

Among the other delegates Florence met were Mr and Mrs Manmohun Ghose, and Lalmohun Ghose. She was impressed by Mrs Ghose, who 'might vie with a well-educated English lady',[53] and invited her to her house in South Street:

You were kind enough when I had the pleasure of seeing you to give
me hopes that Mrs Ghose would do me favour of coming to see me
some day. Might I hope that she would fix some afternoon this week
that would be convenient to her at 5 or at 6 o'clock to give me the great
pleasure of making her acquaintance?[54]

However, 1885 was not a good year for the Liberals in Britain, nor for the
Indian parliamentary candidates such as Lalmohun Ghose, who stood as
a Liberal candidate for Deptford and lost. Lalmohun Ghose, a Bengali
barrister and brother of Manmohun Ghose, had previously been sent to
Britain to plead against the lowering of the age limit in the Indian Covenanted Civil Service. Florence's letter to Wedderburn referred to these
people and the Liberal candidates losing the election in her characteristi-
cally sarcastic manner:

We have lost, as to Indians, 'all along the line'; excepting dear old Mr
Bright who is India. But he will not work alone. Mr Slagg's gone, ...
    ... About Mr Lalmohun Ghose's defeat, it is deeply to be regretted as
being that of the first educated Hindoo we have had as a candidate. But
not otherwise. It was well known, I believe & to Mr Bright himself,
that, as soon as he was safely elected, he would play the game of the
zemindars. When I saw him he appeared ignorant, with claptrap
phrases, and nothing sound about him. He knew nothing, tho' he
pretended to know, of what had been done in Bombay, and could have
been convicted of ignorance even by me. But I carefully kept his secret.[55]

Florence was eager to emphasise to Wedderburn that despite the election
debacle, the visit of the Indian delegates to England had not been in vain.

... you must not think that your delegates have made a failure. Far
from it. They have fought a good fight; they have kept the faith; they
have made a great impression in favour of India, or what is better in
favour of looking into & learning the case of India. ... I am sure a great
interest has been aroused for India. And associations will be formed in
different towns, besides London.[56]

Florence felt the lack of interest shown by the British public in Indian
affairs was due to ignorance. She was keen to see leaflets published with
facts and figures regarding India and about 'the measures to which they in
India attached most importance' so that the politicians in Britain could
know what India wanted.

One important thing that Hume, Wedderburn and many other British
and Indian enthusiasts were trying to achieve at the time was to persuade the
British press to publish the Indian side of the story. The British newspapers
always published what was called the 'official version' of an event. It was not
easy for the British public to know, or even to read about, what was really
happening in India. Projecting Indian news fairly and accurately was also of
vital importance in the summer of 1885, with a view to the forthcoming first

session of the Indian National Union in Poona. Before leaving India, Hume had toured its various parts to discuss the possibility of establishing an Indian telegraphic agency, which would sent prompt telegrams to the British newspapers, so that there could be an alternative source of information from India other than the official one. He was also raising funds for it. While in Calcutta, Hume met the Secretary of the Indian Association, Mr Ananda Mohon Bose, who wrote in his diary on 22 March 1885:

> ... Had talk with him [Hume] principally about the National Tele-graphing Agency matter. He has already raised more than Rs. 400 a month at Bombay, Rs. 200 a month in two or three other Bombay centres [Poona, Ahmedabad and Surat], nearly Rs. 350 a month from Calcutta to complete the amount of Rs. 1,250 a month necessary to give effect to their plan.[57]

Hume's venture, of course, secured whole-hearted support from Florence, who always felt the need for an independent voice for India, preferably from India. With her natural shrewdness and sense of strategy she advised Wedderburn which day and time would be most suitable to send such telegrams from India, and which day people in Britain were most likely to read them:

> Also might I say that the enormous harm which the 'Times' has done us by its Telegrams – has been done by publishing them on <u>Monday</u>, because it was enabled to have long telegrams by *[mid] [the]* Sunday wire – and during the Parl'y Session people will only read these long telegrams on India on Monday, because there is no Ho. of Commons report on that day. I could wish that the 'D. News' might publish your telegrams on <u>Monday</u> too.[58]

The working relationship between Florence and William Wedderburn lasted for years, and they corresponded regularly on vital matters regarding India. Like Florence, Wedderburn was very much in favour of Ripon's policy in India, particularly that of decentralisation and of reviving the village *panchayat* system.[59] Wedderburn and Florence shared many ideas about policies, administration, education, and particularly about village sanitation. It was at the initiative of William Wedderburn that the Florence Nightingale Fund for Village Sanitation was started in Bombay after her death in 1910.[60]

Rapport with Indians: the Poona Sarvajanik Sabha and the Bombay Presidency Association

During this phase of her life, Florence's rapport with Indians increased immensely. We find her corresponding with prominent Indian leaders such as Dadabhai Naoroji, Behramji Malabari, Rustomji Cursetji and Manmohun Ghose. Another interesting development was her liaison with the Poona Sarvajanik Sabha and the Bombay Presidency Association. It was William Wedderburn who introduced Florence to these organisations. Referring to them, Florence wrote in 1894 that these two associations, ' ... occupy themselves with the social and physical condition of the people. And I have the advantage of corresponding both with these associations and also with several educated Indian gentlemen interested in the condition and customs of the people.'[61]

The Bombay Presidency Association, formed in 1885, was an urban organisation and a large number of its members came from the wealthy Parsi community of Bombay. The activities of the Association were confined to urban politics.[62] In 1885, the Bombay Presidency Association joined hands with other Indian associations to form the Indian National Congress. In contrast to the gentlemanly character of the Bombay Presidency Association, the Poona Sarvajanik Sabha was more catholic and involved with the interests of both the rural and urban communities of Deccan. Under the leadership of M.G. Ranade, the Sabha, since its inception in 1870, had launched a concerted fight for the rights of peasants and artisans. There was continuous exchange of letters between the Secretary of the Sabha and the Government, which were duly published in the proceedings of the Sabha. On several occasions the Sabha incurred the displeasure of the Government. In 1878–79 when Wasudeo Balwant Phadke declared himself as an anti-British activist and his followers carried out organised robberies in the villages of Deccan, Government suspicion fell on members of the Sabha as Phadke's sympathisers. The Sabha, however, dissociated itself from Phadke by writing at least three letters to the Chief Secretary of the Government of Bombay, and publicising them in the proceedings.[63] By 1885, the Poona Sarvajanik Sabha had emerged as a powerful voice whose political influence in the western part of India could not be ignored. It was working hand in hand with other Indian associations to set up the Indian National Congress, a process with which William Wedderburn was very much involved. It was not, therefore, surprising that he would recommend the Sabha to Florence.

Florence wrote several letters to the Joint Secretaries of the Poona Sarvajanik Sabha and the Bombay Presidency Association. These letters were later published in the Sabha's quarterly journal and in the annual reports of the Bombay Presidency Association.[64] The occasion of her initial letter was the Bombay Village Sanitation Bill of 1885, which the Government of Bombay was trying to enact. The Village Sanitation Bill had been conceived when Dufferin was Viceroy and Lord Reay was the Governor of Bombay. It was passed in 1890 when Lansdowne replaced Dufferin. During these five years of gestation, the bill was drafted and redrafted several times. Each time, the papers were sent to Florence both by the Governor-General and the Secretary of the State for her consideration and comments.

In 1887 the bill came up for consideration again. Though the villages in the Bombay Presidency were in dire need of sanitation and conservancy, the Village Sanitation Bill had been formulated with limited application in mind. The villages would have to have at least 500 inhabitants to qualify for the benefit of the act. The bill, as it stood, would exclude a large portion of the rural population. Out of some 24 600 villages of the Bombay Presidency, only about 9000 villages would qualify. This meant that almost two thirds of the rural population of the Bombay Presidency would not have the benefit of these sanitary reforms.[65]

Florence seized this opportunity to introduce her ideas about village sanitation to the members of the Poona Sarvajanik Sabha and the Bombay Presidency Association to impress upon them the need to keep a watchful eye on the Government. She could see that powerful Indian associations like these could influence the measures taken by the Government. She asked the members of the Sabha to remain vigilant in this matter:

> ... I feel confident that the Poona Sarvajanik Sabha, as leaders of public opinion in the Dekkan, will carefully watch this Bill; that they will take the best means to bring it into a form well suited to local conditions; and, when it is passed into law, that they will use all their influence to make its working effective and beneficial. And I shall esteem it a great favour if, with the permission of the council, you will inform me how far the provisions of the Bill as it now stands will be effective for the end proposed; and in what respects modifications are required? I shall also be glad to be informed what other practical steps can, in the opinion of the Sabha, be best taken in this most important matter of Village Sanitation?
>
> Pray believe me, Gentlemen – or in all true phrase may I not say that I have the honour to be the faithful servant of yourselves and, if it be not too presumptuous, of India?[66]

It is worth noting that twenty-odd years previously, Florence had immense faith in the Government to introduce sanitary civilisation to India. Now she felt she could not trust officials any more, and asked Indians to keep a vigilant eye on the bill. In her letter she also indicated how the villagers exercising 'self-help' could organise themselves for sanitary purposes; how in their spare time of the year they could work towards cleansing their environment and in providing pure drinking water for their families.[67] Florence never stopped at just writing a letter. Publicity of her ideas was another tool she often used. In the postscript, she mentioned that she had taken the liberty of forwarding a few printed copies of it for distribution among the members of the Sabha, and that she had also written to the Bombay Presidency Association on the same subject in similar terms.

There is no evidence in Florence's private papers of whether the members of the Poona Sarvajanik Sabha or of the Bombay Presidency Association were in touch with her at this stage. However, on receipt of her first letter on sanitation addressed to the members of the two associations, there was immediate publicity and reaction in the Indian press. Her letter was fully published as a supplement in the April 1887 issue of the *Voice of India*.[68] The Editor of the *Indian Spectator* wrote:

> Her position with regard to questions of Indian reform has always been characterized by a spirit of sympathetic enquiry, of shrewd insight and sturdy independence. ... it goes without saying that Miss Nightingale's letter is already receiving careful attention. Copies of it are to be sent to mofussil Associations and it is hoped that the letter will be translated into the Vernaculars and brought within easy reach of every villager who can read or understand it. This time Miss Nightingale may be assured that she has the opportunity of addressing the rural population directly. And her words are not likely to fall on deaf ears.

Not everyone was as enthusiastic as the editor of the *Indian Spectator*. *Indu Prakash*, an Anglo-Marathi weekly in Bombay, admitted that the duty of the social reformers was limited and the actual responsibility for village sanitation should be with the municipalities and the local boards. These boards should exert themselves more actively. *The Hindu*, a paper from Madras, cautioned everyone against the excessive zeal of the theorists and the philanthropists who might do more harm than good by forcing their ideas upon the simple and ignorant villagers. *The Native Opinion*, Bombay, suggested that such reform efforts would give a new scope for the subordinate official tyranny on the villagers. Finally, *Kaiser-i-Hind* held that the aim of Miss Nightingale's letter was good, but was not suited to the requirements of life in Indian villages.[69]

In the meantime, the Bombay Village Sanitation Bill was amended and redrafted to include all the villages, and was again sent to Florence for her comments. Her behind-the-scenes work in London continued, as was evident from her letter to Ripon:

> ... The latest Draft [1888] 'Bombay Village Sanitation Bill' was put into my hand and I was asked to make my criticisms and suggestions, and send them to Bombay, which I have done.
>
> The Bill is of such vast importance to the Bombay Presidency; for it embraces the whole of its [more than] 24,000 villages, without reference to numbers of inhabitants being less or more.
>
> The Bill has these two great merits, I. All the moneys raised in the village, are to be spent in the village. II. The village menial servants [Mhars and Mangs] are to have Government lands and their dues are to be recoverable as part of the Land Revenue.
>
> Its defects are – that it is a distinct return to stringent absolutism; that it leaves no initiative in the hands of the villagers – but its

machinery is active interference by Government Officers – that it gives great opportunities for being dishonestly worked ... .

Florence was annoyed because the amended bill did not give enough power to the villagers or to the village *panchayat* to decide for themselves, which Ripon, Wedderburn and Florence were strongly in favour of. Instead, the power rested in the hands of the District Collector, and Florence was afraid of malpractice:

> ... By this Bill we have [instead of the Panchayat] the Collector and a 'Sanitary Committee' appointed by the Collector himself – to do the work. The Collector is to assess the rate for Sanitary purposes 'in conference' with his 'Sanitary Committee'. The Sanitary Committee-man is to summon the offending neighbours, perhaps out of private spite, before themselves [not the Police Patel].
> ... The Sanitary Commissioner and Department are entirely ignored, though the Collector does not know where to look for filth and disease-causes – with some brilliant exceptions, and the Mamlutdar [magistrate] – who also comes on the stage – knows nothing about Sanitation except to clear the road the Collector is to pass through ... .[70]

Florence was afraid that the redrafted Bombay Village Sanitation Bill was only an empty gesture to transfer local self-government to the Indians. In practice, the power would be retained in the hands of the Collector, who would always be a 'sahib'. She sent an indignant note to Lord Lansdowne who, by that time, had replaced Lord Dufferin as Viceroy: ' ... the Bill rather makes a show of granting local self govt. to the Native public [which is shrewd enough to see that it does not] whereas I believe you will think it a Bill actively interfering by Govt. Officers and giving opportunities for being dishonestly worked.'[71]

In 1889, Florence once more got in touch with the Poona Sarvajanik Sabha and the Bombay Presidency Association and drew their attention to the contents of the amended bill:

> Since I had the honour of addressing you just two years ago on the subject of village sanitation, there has been published in the 'Bombay Government Gazette' of January 24, 1889, a new Draft Bill entitled the Bombay Village Sanitation Bill, 1889, which in many respects, makes an important advance upon previous projects of legislation. Especially it is a cause for satisfaction that the new Bill proposes to extend the benefits of sanitary legislation to all Bombay's 24,600 villages, without excluding any ... and I am again advised by Sir William Wedderburn to submit for your consideration some points with regard to this amended measure, and to ask the favour of your opinion and advice.[72]

Self-help and collective cleanliness

The letters Florence wrote to the Poona Sarvajanik Sabha and the Bombay Presidency Association over a five-year period had two clear themes: self-help and collective cleanliness. On the one hand, she alerted the members to the impact of the forthcoming sanitation act; on the other hand, she told them in no uncertain terms their own responsibility in this matter. She urged the members to consider sanitary work in rural India as missionary work, the work of a preacher. One would have to do it with devotion, dedication and zeal, and who else could do it except educated Indians:

> The educated native gentlemen who know the people will show a prac-tical example. They will first, as has been well said, 'observe sanitary rules themselves'. Then, must they not give their invaluable, their indispensable influence to help Government in village sanitation by creating a public opinion in its favour among their countrymen, and showing them the benefits?[73]

Florence always made it clear that no one was questioning the high stan-dard of 'personal cleanliness' of the Indians, rich or poor. It was the communal cleanliness that was in question: ' ... all that we want is collec-tive cleanliness carried out collectively with the least possible annoyance and the greatest possible advantage to the individual.' She also insisted that the aim of sanitary legislation should be to encourage people to organise themselves to do the work. The villagers were to do the work with the necessary advice and stimulus from outside, when and if neces-sary. She never succumbed to the official theory of Indian apathy towards sanitation. 'In advocating a measure of this kind for India,' she wrote, ' I am anxious that India should have the benefit of a system which I have seen working with so much advantage in England. Fifty years ago the state of England was much what the state of India now is.' Her principle was: 'The community itself is the engine that does the work.'[74]

The main problems of the Indian villages, as Florence saw it, were overcrowding, removal of sewage and better water supply. In her fourth letter to the Poona Sarvajanik Sabha, in December 1891, she asked the members to look into these issues. She pointed out that to achieve simple measures of health hardly any money was required, but the villagers needed to be taught that their suffering and diseases were preventable. It is ' ... not so much the want of money as the want of knowledge that produces bad sanitary conditions.'[75]

She urged the members of the Sabha to arrange for sanitary education and lectures in the village schools with the help of magic lantern shows. But lectures were only the first step towards real education. The lecturer should go and show the villagers how to keep their environment clean, how to get clean drinkable water. Books, being sanitary primers, were of course needed, but 'what is read in the book, stays in the book'. 'The Officer of health is too often only a book and a pen. So is the school master. He must be a voice – a voice as it were, among the villages. Books often do no good and so few can read.'[76] So far as financing such sanitary operations was concerned, she was happy with the bill's proviso that all money collected in the villages through cess, subscriptions and fines should be spent in the villages. But initially, the villages would have to show what they could do on their own by using their own resources.[77]

The main issue, however, was how to set up an infrastructure to introduce a rudimentary health scheme at the village level, as that needed funding. It was clear from the beginning that the aim of the Bombay Village Sanitation Bill, 1889, was not to introduce any extra expenses for the Government or to levy taxes on the villagers: 'There was the risk that the villagers would be encouraged to ask Government for assistance, which Government could not grant.'[78] Hence the onus of sanitary responsibility was passed on to the villagers. They would be responsible for keeping their villages clean. Only when they failed to do so would a sanitary committee, consisting of local headmen, be empowered at the discretion of the District Collector to make regulations and impose fines. Bigger villages would have Sanitary Boards, composed of local residents and Government officials. But so far as the small villages were concerned, 'self-help' was the measure recommended.

The Bombay Village Sanitation Act of 1890 was criticised for its total lack of understanding and knowledge of the village community as existed in India at the time. Indian peasants who lived in villages always lived a hand-to-mouth existence, without any spare cash to invest in communal sanitation of their villages. If they had spare cash they would rather buy food for their family. Besides, they were already heavily taxed. Any extra tax or cess or fines for sanitation would only break the camel's back. Yet, without proper funding, village sanitation was an impossible task. This was the thought expressed by Vishnu Moreshwar Bhide, the Chairman of the Poona Sarvajanik Sabha, in a letter to Florence as he asked for her help:

9th June 1891

Madam,
    ... With respect to village sanitation the Local Government has passed an Act, but as it has not provided for any special funds for the purposes of village sanitation the Act remains virtually a dead letter. While the Bill was under consideration, the Native members of the legislative Council strongly insisted upon the necessity of making a statutory provision of funds for village sanitation by appropriating a portion of the Local Funds which as originally intended both for improving communications and sanitation. Latterly nearly the whole

of the money is absorbed by the Public Works and repairs. ... the suggestion of the Native members was overruled, and as the people are too poor to pay additional taxes or to raise voluntary subscriptions and as Government themselves are not prepared to make any sensible allotment out of provincial revenue, matters remain as a standstill. If you move the Hygiene Congress to invite the attention of the Indian Authorities to this subject, there is every reason to hope that the present inactivity will be remedied.[79]

Indian Committee in the International Congress of Hygiene and Demography

Bhide's letter was in answer to an invitation sent to the members of the Poona Sarvajanik Sabha and the Bombay Presidency Association for the forthcoming session of the 7th International Congress of Hygiene and Demography, which was to be held in London in August 1891. Florence managed to introduce an Indian Committee within the Congress where papers on India's sanitary state could be read and discussed. She wanted a substantial Indian representation from India to make sure that the real condition of the sanitary state of India should not be whitewashed by the official delegates, who invariably would be all British. The Indians should tell their own stories in their own words. 'You will observe,' she wrote to the Joint Secretaries of the Poona Sarvajanik Sabha,

> that this is the first time that the meeting has been held in England; and as a special feature of this Congress it is hoped that there will be a full representation from India and the Colonies. It is also very desirable that this representation should be not only official but also non-official. I am therefore anxious to urge upon Indian friends interested in the cause of sanitation the importance of the present occasion, so that the representatives from India may include as large a number as possible of those possessing detailed and accurate knowledge of the condition and wants of the Indian people.[80]

In spite of Florence's urgency Indians were not given much time to choose their delegates carefully, nor were they given any funding to go abroad. Dinsha E. Wacha of the Bombay Presidency Association wrote to Dadabhai Naoroji:

> The Government of Bombay inquired of us ... to name two most prominent members of the Association for the Hygiene Congress. The letter was of an emergent character and they wanted to reply within twenty four hours ... I took upon myself saying that you were the only prominent member who had a prolonged stay in London and was likely to do so yet; and therefore the Association would propose you.[81]

The Joint Secretaries of the Poona Sarvajanik Sabha, G.K. Gokhale and K.P. Godbole, also faced a similar problem. They wrote to the Government that due to the consideration of time, distance and expense, the Sabha would ask the Government to send official delegates from the presidency. They also made further request that Indian gentlemen residing in England as well as retired Anglo-Indians who had taken interest in the Sabha's work, such as Sir William Wedderburn, should represent them.[82]

As a result of Florence's initiative and enthusiasm, the Conference was well attended, not only by the 'sahibs' but also by the 'natives'. There were official representatives from all the presidencies and provinces as well as delegates from the Indian universities, Chambers of Commerce, leading municipalities and associations.[83] In the Indian Committee, one finds names like Dadabhai Naoroji, B.M. Malabari, Mancherjee Bhownaggree, Badruddin Tyabji, together with John Strachey, Dr Sutherland, W. Hunter, G. Yule, E. Ollivant, S. Digby, Douglas Galton, Dr Cunningham, Lord Reay, and many others. Florence brought her new Indian contacts and the old Anglo-Indians on to the same platform. William Wedderburn was there too, on behalf of the Poona Sarvajanik Sabha, and presented papers written at the special request of the Sabha.[84] In his opening speech, the Chairman, Sir Mountstuart Grant Duff, told the audience: 'I have here a letter from a lady for whom all English men and English women have the most profound respect and affection, I mean Miss Florence Nightingale, in which she urges that prominence should be given on this occasion to village sanitation in India.'[85]

During the session, Florence made sure that the Indian delegates were well looked after. In a letter to Douglas Galton she wrote:

> Sir Harry Verney renews his invitations to Claydon to the Native Indian delegates, three or four at a time. I have seen Mr Bhownaggree, who seems to be acting for the other native gentlemen, not yet come, and asked him to manage this, as is most suitable to these gentlemen. I may hope to see them one by one, if I am able to be there.[86]

A number of Indian leaders went to see Miss Nightingale and Sir Harry Verney at Claydon. One such guest was Dadabhai Naoroji. Naoroji, a leading member of the Indian National Congress at the time and a delegate to the Conference, received a cordial invitation from Florence's brother-in-law, Sir Harry Verney, which he readily accepted:

> Mr Bhownaggree has communicated to me your kind invitation to Claydon House. I accept it with pleasure. I propose to leave on Friday by the 3 o'clock train from Euston for Claydon and to return by 10.29 train on Monday. Kindly let me know whether Claydon or Winslow station will be the right one.[87]

Florence and Naoroji had been in correspondence since 1867. They regularly sent each other books and pamphlets and shared news and information about India.[88] In July 1888, Florence wrote to Naoroji:

> How can I thank you for your great kindness in sending me 10 copies of the Report, so interesting, of yours (& our, may I not say?) third National Congress – may its affairs and recommendations prosper, urged as they are in so moderate & wise a spirit! Approved even by lawyers here.
>
> And for the volume of your own valuable Essays, speeches & writings, accept my sincere thanks which would have been offered before but for an unusual pressure of illness & work.
>
> I trust, you think that progress has been made. God speed in the constant progress of yours & India's.[89]

During the sessions of the International Congress of Hygiene and Demography, Florence did not forget the plea made to her by V.M. Bhide, the Chairman of the Poona Sarvajanik Sabha. She wanted to have a motion moved for adequate funding for village sanitation in India. She passed the contents of Bhide's letter to Sir William Moore, a surgeon and delegate from Bombay, to publicise its contents in the Conference. In this matter she also received support from other delegates from India. Lionel Ashburne, an ex-member of the Bombay Government's Council, criticised the Bombay Village Sanitation Act as a complete failure for lack of adequate funding and for ignorance of the conditions of social life in an Indian agricultural community. He claimed that the act 'has even intensified the evil it was intended to remove'.[90] William Moore also took up the points and said that this act would probably become a dead letter for lack of funds, and certain regulations it provided were impracticable.[91] After successfully publicising the fact that the Bombay Village Sanitation Act was a non-starter without sufficient funding in front of an international gathering, Florence's next move was to secure a memorandum signed by the members of the Indian Committee and to send it to Lord Cross, the Secretary of State. This was evident from her letter to Naoroji:

> March 15 / 92
>
> Dear Mr Dadabhai Naoroji
> I hope your election affairs are going on prosperously.
>
> I venture to enclose a copy of a memorandum, & to ask if you approve it and if you do whether you think well to give us your signature? & to return it to me as soon as possible.
>
> It has already been signed by
> Sir Douglas Galton
> Dr Cornish
> Sir W. Wedderburn
> Sir William Moore
> Sir George Birdwood
> Dr. Poore

Sir Guy Hunter
Professor Corfield (of the Permanent Comms.)
The Memo with its Signature is to go in to Lord Cross enclosed in a
letter from me.[92]

The Indian leader was also eager to push the matter through, and replied
immediately: 'I return the memorandum signed. I have not attended to
Indian matters lately, but I feel sure that any facts and figures put forward
by you will be alright ... '.[93] Naoroji at the time was trying to get elected as
a Liberal candidate and asked for Florence's help in his letter, but she
politely refused:

> I am entirely a prisoner to my rooms from illness & overwhelmed with
> work. It is therefore impossible for me to do as you wish.
>   I rejoice beyond measure that you are now the only Liberal Candi-
> date for Central Finsbury.
>   With all my heart and soul I wish you success. <u>Now</u> subjects seri-
> ously affecting the welfare of great India – subjects too so near my
> heart – will receive increased attention, being urged by a man like
> yourself – and we eagerly need such members in the House of
> Commons.[94]

Once Florence had gathered the signatures of the members of the Indian
Committee, she sent the memorandum to Lord Cross with a covering
letter.[95] The message of her letter to Cross was that nothing could be done
to improve rural health without proper funding and that any new taxation would only defeat the purpose. On top of that there were prejudices
and ignorance to overcome. She politely reminded the Secretary of State
that if the aim of the act was 'to constitute a good village organization for
the purpose of sanitation', then it should also have the power to administer the fund raised by village cesses. The villagers did not have to ask
back a portion of the amount paid by them. However, in 1891, the British
administrators in India were more keen to make roads and railways than
to spend on rural sanitation. But Florence reminded them of their priority:
'We must live in order to work. We must live in order to drive the cart or
cross the bridge. Is not the life more than meat and the body than raiment.
A village free from choleraic and typhoidal poisons is more important to
the village population than the best means of communication.'[96]

The response of the Secretary of State to Florence's argument for
funding was as expected. Lord Cross himself did not answer, but one of
his officials, Horace Walpole, wrote on 8 April 1892: ' ... while thanking
you for your remarks, Viscount Cross desires me to say that a copy of
your letter and enclosures will be forwarded for the consideration of the
Governments of India and Bombay.'[97] Apparently Florence's letter was
circulated in India by Lord Lansdowne, and many reports were collected
under the heading 'Reporting on the proposals made by Miss Nightingale,

relative to the better application of the proceeds of village cesses to the purposes of sanitation'.[98] But the official attitude towards village sanitation remained as implacable as ever; they wanted roads and bridges, not drains or pure water.

A year later, we find Florence writing to the Secretary of State again, who by that time was no longer Lord Cross, but Lord Kimberley, enquiring about her previous letter of 21 March 1892 on sanitary reforms in Indian villages. On 19 December 1893, she received an answer from one of Kimberley's men, Arthur Godley:

> Your letter of last year with its enclosure was forwarded by Viscount Cross to the Governments of India and Bombay for consideration. A recent intimation has been received from the Government of India that they are still consulting the various Local Governments on this important subject. The Government of Bombay have however made a report showing that they appreciate the need for sanitary improvement in villages, and that they sympathize with your suggestion that educated Indians should be induced to lead their rural fellow countrymen towards the adoption of simple hygienic regulations. A copy of the Bombay letter is forwarded to you for your perusal (Letter No. 22, 2nd September 1892, with all enclosures). When he receives the expected report from the Government of India, Lord Kimberley will be in a position to consider the subject again.[99]

While the British administrators, Secretary of State and the Government of India showed bureaucratic inertia to act on Florence's advice, she continued her sanitary *jihad* through her writing. Shortly after she sent the memorandum of the Indian Committee to Lord Cross, the editor of the journal *India* announced: 'We have much pleasure in publishing the correspondence which has taken place between Miss Florence Nightingale and the Secretary of State for India.' The journal published Florence's letter and the memorandum in unabridged form and added a leader on it.[100]

Publicity in *India*

The journal *India* had been inaugurated in 1890 as the mouthpiece of the Indian National Congress in Britain. It was the brainchild of A.O. Hume and a few other British liberals who wanted the British public to know what was really happening in India and to promote India's political interests in Britain. Hume and Wedderburn's attempts to establish an independent Indian news agency in 1885 did not succeed. Through the publication of *India*, that need was partially fulfilled. The journal was held in high esteem by Indian leaders. In 1893, at the 9th Session of the Indian National Congress in Lahore, Dadabhai Naoroji commented that without *India*, 'our work will not be half as efficient as with it', and 'every possible effort must be made to give it the widest circulation possible both here and in the United Kingdom.'[101]

The publication of Florence's letter to Lord Cross in *India* must have drawn the attention of Indians and British alike. Florence made further use of the opportunity the journal provided to make contact with Indians and convey her message to them. In October 1893, she published *Health Lectures for Indian Villages*, which was followed in December 1896 by *Health Missioners for Rural India*, the second article being a sequel to the first, both aiming for the same goal, sanitation in rural India. The main purpose of her articles was to allay the fear of taxation for village sanitation and to emphasise the importance of health education in the rural areas:

> I observe that some Native journals express a fear that if Government undertakes village sanitation the result will be increased taxation in some form. They also fear that the work of sanitation will be promoted 'in accordance with European ideas', thereby weakening the sense of Indian nationality. I do not presume to say that these fears are without any foundation. But I desire to suggest the direction in which our Indian reformers might work ...

In this first article, Florence again emphasised the need for self-help and communal cleanliness, and asked: 'Does it not appear that a great part of the evil can be removed by the people themselves, without expense, if they can be persuaded to adopt a few simple precautions which will ward off suffering and loss from themselves and their children?'[102] Florence was aware of the gulf that existed between the 'sahibs' and Indians. The British officials were so far removed from Indian villagers that their advice would not be as effective as that of the Indians. In order to persuade the villagers to act, one needed practical demonstrations by enlightened Indians: ' ... the villagers would listen more readily if addressed by those ... who exercise no authority as servants of the Government ... .'[103]

Florence with her natural caution suggested that health lectures with demonstrations of a popular kind should first be tried in a few selected villages in different parts of India on an experimental basis. She was convinced that a little effort and determination could change the situation in rural India: 'The watchword is, small beginning under favourable circumstances.'[104] Almost 30 years earlier she had given the same advice about female nursing. Her aim was always small beginnings, a humble start. She suggested that a system of lectures should be organised by local associations showing the villagers the need for a better water supply, removing sewage and reducing overcrowding: 'These lectures being given from village to village by men, 1) well versed themselves in the principles of sanitation, and 2) knowing the habits of the people and able to sympathize with and help them without offending their prejudices.'[105]

When it came to the cost of the operation, Florence had her own plan to submit. Bearing in mind that Government funds were not easily available, she suggested that a special fund could be raised for this purpose:

> I know how from ancient times up to the present day, large sums have always been forthcoming in India from charitable men and women for wells, tanks, hospitals, dispensaries and other institutions for the public good. Would not the comparatively small sum required for the present experiment be forthcoming if the case were urgently represented to those having the means?

Florence assured the readers: 'If such a fund is started I will, with the help of a few English friends, gladly send a small contribution as token of my earnest good will.'[106]

Before publishing her article in *India*, Florence was in touch with Wedderburn. Their correspondence shows how they were colluding and collaborating to induce Lord Lansdowne to facilitate village sanitation schemes. Florence felt that if an Indian association like the Poona Sarvajanik Sabha could submit a good plan of action for this purpose, the Government would probably provide a moderate grant without hesitation:

> Would it be possible to suggest to him [Lord Lansdowne] to give a very small grant to a native association, to initiate the lectures to villages? (This is a thing he could easily do, if he would before December.)
> ... How would it do to give the Poona Sarvajanik Sabha very small grant to start such a system of lectures among the villagers? Lord Lansdowne says that the native associations would not go to the expense of organizing a system of lectures. How would it do to induce one Native association to initiate the thing by a very small grant? If you could let one native society to do this would not others follow?[107]

Florence's article in *India*, as expected, drew attention at home and abroad. In India, her old friend B.M. Malabari wrote in response that though Miss Nightingale's paper was 'wisely written', it was ineffective because of want of 'effective machinery'. By 'want of effective machinery' Malabari meant lack of funds, difficulties in diverting the energy of a few overworked associations and, finally, the lack of interest among the English-educated Indians. According to him, they were not interested in village sanitation, only in 'big games'.[108] Malabari, a close friend of Hume, Ripon, Naoroji and Florence, and a social reformer himself, also had an axe to grind. On social issues, he differed from the other Congress leaders. Since the inception of the Congress in 1885, Malabari tried hard to introduce social reform into the Congress agenda, but failed. Hume, Naoroji and many others were reluctant to do so. In its initial stage, the aim of the Congress was to unite Indians for political purposes only. The Congress leaders of the time did not want to include anything in the agenda that could divide Indians from each other, like the Hindus from the Muslims or the South from the North: 'The decision to keep social reform out of Congress was carefully calculated, since this was above all the type of issue likely to divide Indians.'[109] Naoroji, in his Presidential Address to the 2nd Session of the Indian National Congress in Calcutta in 1886, stated quite clearly that social reform was a subject that did not fall within the legitimate sphere of Congress's deliberation. He held that the Congress was a political body to represent political aspirations, not to discuss social reforms. It was an aggregate of people from all over India with different castes, creeds, culture, religion and social values: 'How can this gathering of all classes discuss the social reforms needed in each individual class?'[110]

Malabari was more or less alone in his crusade for social reforms, and there is no doubt that he assessed the situation correctly when he said that the middle class elite of India were not interested in social reforms. They were highly politicised, and the associations they led had higher political goals. Removal of social evils, health and sanitation were low in their list of priorities. In his article in *India,* Malabari presented a rough scheme for health missions for rural India for consideration, which pleased Florence very much:

As regards the Bombay Presidency I have been so fortunate as to obtain the powerful aid of Mr. B.M. Malabari, who has recently paid his periodical visit to England, and with whom I have had the opportunity of full consultation. And I do not think I shall be betraying confidence if I say that he is turning his special attention to Guzarat and Sind, and will probably make his first attempt by establishing small committees at Rajkot, Ahmedabad, Surat, and Haidarabad in Sind.[111]

There was one idea in Malabari's rough scheme that fired Florence's imagination, an idea which she herself had been cultivating for quite some time. It was the idea of appointing female health workers in the villages. 'Village sanitation must begin with villagers,' said Malabari in his article, 'with women even more than with men, and chiefly within the village limits.'[112] Florence took up the idea of female health workers in her plan for rural health education:

Mr Malabari would have them married men whose wives would accompany them and preach health and cleanliness amongst the village women. In this proposal I would most heartily concur. Indeed from my point of view, to enlist the sympathy and gain the approval of the good mother who rules the home, is the keystone of the whole position. If her authority is on our side, I feel little fear for the result.[113]

Needless to say, to secure that authority this extraordinary woman had already cast her eyes to the possibility of utilising zenana power in India and in her indomitable and practical way went about to achieve that.

Notes

1. FN (1894a), 'Village Sanitation in India', in *8th International Congress of Hygiene and Demography*, Gerlöczy, Z. (ed.), Budapest, Tom. 2, pp. 580–583.
2. Woodham Smith (1950), p. 44.
3. See FN (1894b), *Health Teaching in Towns and Villages: Rural Hygiene*, London: Spottiswoode & Co.
4. FN to Gladstone, 4 December 1884, BL Add. Mss 44488, fol. 213. By 'these things' she meant sanitary matters and Ripon's policies.
5. Dufferin to FN, 13 November 1884, Cook (1913), vol. 2, p. 344.
6. Jowett to FN, 22 March 1888, as quoted in Quinn and Prest (1987), p. 309, reprinted by permission of Oxford University Press.
7. FN to Ripon, 24 March 1888, BL Add. Mss 43546, fols 208–211.
8. FN, private notes, 18 July 1888, BL Add. Mss 45778, fols 171–180, draft.
9. FN to Ripon, 13 November 1888, BL Add. Mss 45778, fol. 150.
10. FN to Ripon, 12 August 1881, BL Add. Mss 43546, fol. 182.
11. FN, private notes, 30 July 1886, BL Add. Mss 45778, fol. 107, draft. It seems this is what Ripon told Florence and she made a note of that.
12. FN, private notes, 30 July 1886, BL Add. Mss 45778, fols 104–107, draft.
13. *Voice of India*, September 1885, pp. 431–433.
14. Cook (1913), vol. 2, p. 372.
15. FN to Ripon, 24 October 1888, BL Add. Mss 43546, fol. 214.
16. FN (1879b), September, p. 635.
17. FN to Dufferin, 4 November 1886, BL OIOC, Dufferin Papers, Mss Eur fol. 130-24B, No. 228.
18. Dufferin to FN, 18 January 1887, Cook (1913), vol. 2, pp. 372–3.
19. Dufferin to FN, 20 August 1887, BL OIOC, Dufferin Papers, Mss Eur fol. 130-2bc.
20. FN to Galton, 28 November 1887, BL Add. Mss 45766, fol. 55, draft.
21. FN to Galton, 13 September 1887, BL Add. Mss 45766, fols 48–9, draft.
22. FN to Galton, 19 June 1888, BL Add. Mss 45766, fols 96–7, draft.
23. FN to Dufferin, 6 September 1888, BL Add. Mss 45808, fols 206–211, draft.
24. FN, Report to the India Office on the Sanitary Resolution of the Government of India, September 1888, BL Add. Mss 45808, fols 247–52, draft.
25. FN to Ripon, 24 October 1888, BL Add. Mss 43546, fols 214–215.
26. FN, Report to the India Office on the Sanitary Resolution of the Government of India, September 1888, BL Add. Mss 45808, fols 247–52; FN to Dufferin, 3 August 1888, BL Add. Mss 45808, fols 183–4.
27. FN to Ripon, 24 October 1888, BL Add. Mss 45778, fol. 139.
28. Tripathi, D. and Mehta, M. (1990), *Business Houses in Western India*, New Delhi: Manohar, pp. 37–54; Gillion, K.L. (1968), *Ahmedabad – a Study in Indian Urban History*, California: University of California Press, pp. 81–84.
29. FN to Galton, 13 December 1888, BL Add. Mss 45766, fol. 197.
30. Chotalall, R. (1892), 'Sanitation of the City of Ahmedabad in the Bombay Presidency', in Shelley, C.E (ed.), *Transactions, 7th International Congress of Hygiene and Demography*, London: Eyre & Spottiswood, vol. XI, pp. 166–169.
31. *Speeches Delivered in India by the Marquis of Dufferin and Ava, 1884–1888*, Calcutta and London: J. Murray, 1890, p. 243.

32. FN to Ripon, 2 February 1889, BL Add. Mss 45778, fols 160–161.
33. FN to Lansdowne, 21 June 1889, BL Add. Miss 45778, fols 200–201, draft.
34. FN to Lansdowne, August 1889, BL Add. Mss 45778, fols 209–212.
35. FN to Lansdowne, May 1892, BL Add. Mss 45778, fols 217–219.
36. FN to Lansdowne, 16 June 1893, BL Add. Mss 45778, fols 225–226.
37. Lansdowne to FN, 1 August 1893, BL Add. Mss 45778, fols 229–230.
38. Wedderburn (1913), p. 27.
39. Wedderburn (1913), p. 32.
40. See Mehrotra (1971), pp. 378–420; Seal (1968), pp. 245–297.
41. FN to Gladstone, 4 December 1884, BL Add. Mss 44488, fol. 212.
42. Seal (1968), p. 272.
43. Wedderburn (1913), p. 64.
44. FN to Wedderburn, 2 November 1885, BL OIOC, Mss Eur B 151.
45. FN to Wedderburn, 2 November 1885, BL OIOC, Mss Eur B 151.
46. Wedderburn (1913), p. 54.
47. The first session of the Indian National Union was finally held in Bombay
     because there was a cholera epidemic scare in Poona. See Mehrotra (1971),
     p. 410.
48. Wacha to Naoroji, 13 May 1885, in Patwardhan, R.P. (ed.) (1977),
     Dadabhai Naoroji Correspondence, Bombay: Allied Publishers, vol. 2, p. 9.
49. Mehrotra (1971), p. 404.
50. FN to Wedderburn, 27 November 1885, BL OIOC, Mss Eur B 151.
51. FN to Wedderburn, 11 December 1885, BL Add. Mss 45807, fol. 195.
52. Chandavarkar, N.G. (1887), *English Impressions gathered in Connection
     with the Indian Delegation to England during the General Election of
     1885*, Bombay: Radhabai Atmaran Sangoon, pp. 40–41. The interview
     was also republished in an obituary notice written by Chandavarkar after
     Florence Nightingale's death in 1910. See Chandavarkar, N.G. (1910), 'Flor-
     ence Nightingale: the heroine of the 19th century', *Subodh Patrika*, 21
     August 1910 (Bombay), Servants of India Press Clippings, NMML, New
     Delhi.
53. FN to Wedderburn, 27 November 1885, BL Add. Mss 45807, fols 189–93.
54. FN to Ghose, 10 November 1885, BL Add. Mss 45807, fols 181–2.
55. FN to Wedderburn, 27 November 1885, BL OIOC, Mss Eur B 151.
56. FN to Wedderburn, 4 December 1885, BL Add. Mss 45807, fols 193–4.
57. Sarkar, H.C. (1910), *The Life of Ananda Mohun Bose*, Calcutta: A.C.
     Sarkar, p. 85.
58. FN to Wedderburn, 27 November 1885, BL OIOC, Mss Eur B 151.
59. Wedderburn, W. (1878), *The Village Panchayet – a Remedy for Agrarian
     Disorders in India*, London: East India Association. March 1878.
60. Ratcliffe (1923), pp. 125–126.
61. FN (1894a), p. 580.
62. 'The Bombay Presidency Association kept carefully aloof from the people.
     Its public meetings were infrequent, and they were of a different nature from
     those in Calcutta ... Most of the Association's members lived in the city, and
     there were no branches in the mofussil.' In Seal (1968), p. 233.
63. *The Quarterly Journal of the Poona Sarvajanik Sabha* (hereafter referred to
     as *Quarterly Journal, PSS*), July 1879, vol. 2, no. 1, *Proceedings*, pp. 68–76
     (the *Proceedings* were bound in with, but numbered separately from the
     Quarterly Journal, PSS); *Quarterly Journal, PSS*, April 1880, vol. II, no. 4,
     Proceedings, p. 120.

64. Bombay Presidency Association, 3rd and 4th *Annual Reports* 1887 and 1888, Bombay 1889, pp. 69–73, 152–156; FN (1892a), 'Letters to the Joint Secretaries', *Quarterly Journal, PSS*, July 1892, vol. XV, no. 1, *Proceedings*, pp. 1–21. These letters were published under the title *Village Sanitation in India*.

65. FN to the Joint Secretaries, 22 February 1887, *Quarterly Journal, PSS*, July 1892, vol. XV, no.1, *Proceedings*, p. 4.

66. FN to the Joint Secretaries, 22 February 1887, *Quarterly Journal, PSS*, July 1892, vol. XV, no. 1, *Proceedings*, p. 1.

67. FN to the Joint Secretaries, 22 February 1887, *Quarterly Journal, PSS*, July 1892, vol. XV, no. 1, *Proceedings*, p. 3.

68. *Voice of India*, April 1887, vol. V, No. 4, p. 183. The *Voice of India* was a monthly journal publishing the opinions of the native press. It was started in 1883 at the initiative of William Wedderburn and B.M. Malabari. 'It has been a complaint in England,' wrote Wedderburn, 'that the opinions given by official experts are contradictory while the masses are inarticulate and cannot give expression to their needs. To rectify this situation the *Voice of India* was launched. It was hoped that by reproducing the views of the Indian press from all over the country the journal would be able to express Indian public opinion, it will make known the true wishes and the feelings of the people.' In Wedderburn, W. (1883), *Voice of India*, Poona, January, vol. I, no 1., p. 1.

69. *Indian Spectator*, 20 March 1887 (Bombay); *Indu Prakash*, 21 March 1887 (Bombay); *The Hindu*, 23 March 1887 (Madras); *The Native Opinion*, 27 March, 1887; *Kaiser-i-Hind*, 27 March, 1887 (Bombay), all as quoted in *Voice of India*, April 1887, vol. V, no. 4, pp. 183–188.

70. FN to Ripon, 13 November 1888, BL Add. Mss 45778, fol. 150.

71. FN to Lansdowne, 6 November 1888, BL Add. Mss 45778, fol. 192.

72. FN to the Joint Secretaries, 20 February 1889, *Quarterly Journal, PSS*, July 1892, vol. XV, no. 1, *Proceedings*, p. 5; Also published in the *Annual Reports*, Bombay Presidency Association, 1889, pp. 152-156.

73. FN to the Joint Secretaries, 16 February 1891, *Quarterly Journal, PSS*, July 1892, vol. XV, no. 1, *Proceedings*, p. 11.

74. FN to the Joint Secretaries 22 February 1887, *Quarterly Journal, PSS*, July 1892, vol. XV, no. 1, *Proceedings*, p. 3.

75. FN to Bhide, (no date) December 1891, *Quarterly Journal, PSS*, July 1892, vol. XV, no. 1, *Proceedings*, p. 14.

76. FN to Bhide, December 1891, *Quarterly Journal, PSS*, July 1892, vol. XV, no. 1, *Proceedings*, p. 16.

77. FN to the Joint Secretaries, 20 February, 1889, *Quarterly Journal, PSS*, July 1892, vol. XV, no.1, *Proceedings*, p. 7.

78. Hunter, W.W. (1892), *A Study in Indian Administration: Bombay 1885-1890*, London: H. Frowde, p. 321.

79. Bhide to FN, 9 June 1891, *Quarterly Journal, PSS*, July 1892, vol. XV, no 1, *Proceedings*, pp. 12-13.

80. FN to the Joint Secretaries, 16 February 1891, *Quarterly Journal, PSS*, July 1892, vol. XV, no 1, *Proceedings*, p. 10.

81. Wacha to Naoroji, 12 June 1891, as quoted in Patwardhan, 1977, vol. 2, p. 247.

82. *Quarterly Journal, PSS*, 1891–1892, vol. XIV, pp. 8-9.

83. Shelley (1892), p. 3.

84. The three papers presented by Wedderburn were: 1. Dr K.R. Kirtikar: 'Our sanitary wants in the Bombay Presidency' (in Shelley (1892), pp. 113–128); 2. V.R. Ghole: 'Notes on hygiene and demographic condition of India' (in Shelley (1892), pp. 128–136); 3. K.V. Dhurandhar: 'The sanitary condition of the towns and villages in Bombay Presidency' (in Shelley (1892), pp. 136–145). Apart from these three specially requested papers there were a few other papers written by Indians, including Chotalall (1892) on the sanitation of the city of Ahmedabad in the Bombay Presidency.

85. Shelley (1892), p. 15.

86. FN to Galton, 1 August 1891, Cook (1913), vol. 2, p. 378.

87. Naoroji to Verney, 24 August 1891, Naoroji Papers, N-1 (1961), NAI, New Delhi.

88. FN to Naoroji, 1 July 1888, Naoroji Papers, N-107(2), NAI, New Delhi. See also Naoroji to FN, 29 July 1888, Naoroji Papers, N-1 (1089), NAI, New Delhi; Naoroji to FN, 27 April 1888, Naoroji Papers, N-1 (536), NAI, New Delhi.

89. FN to Naoroji, 28 July 1888, Naoroji Papers, No 14, File No. 193, NMML, New Delhi.

90. Shelley (1892), p. 145.

91. Shelley (1892), p. 29.

92. FN to Naoroji, 15 March 1892, Naoroji Papers, N-107, NAI, New Delhi.

93. Naoroji to FN, 15 March 1892, Naoroji Papers, N-1 (2250), NAI, New Delhi.

94. FN to Naoroji, 24 June 1892, Naoroji Papers, N-107(1), NAI, New Delhi.

95. Memorandum to Lord Cross, 21 March, 1892, *Quarterly Journal, PSS*, July 1892, vol. XV, no 1, *Proceedings*, pp. 17-19.

96. Memorandum to Lord Cross, 21 March 1892, *Quarterly Journal, PSS*, July 1892, vol. XV, No. 1, *Proceedings*, p. 19.

97. Walpole to FN, 8 April 1892, *Quarterly Journal, PSS*, July 1892, vol. XV, No. 1. *Proceedings*, p. 20.

98. Cook (1913), vol. 2, p. 379.

99. Godley to FN, 9 December 1893, BL Add. Mss 45812, fol. 64.

100. *India*, July 15, 1892, vol. 3, No. 39, pp. 200–201.

101. Zaidi (1985), vol. 1, p. 63.

102. FN (1893), 'Health lectures for Indian villages', *India*, 1 October, p. 305.

103. FN (1893), p. 305.

104. FN (1896), 'Health missioners for rural India', *India*, December, p. 359.

105. FN (1893), p. 305.

106. FN (1893), p. 306.

107. FN to Wedderburn, 1 September 1893, BL Add. Mss 45812, fols 12–18, draft.

108. Malabari, B.M. (1896), 'Health missioners for rural India; a rough scheme for consideration', *India*, September, p. 1.

109. Seal (1968), p. 295.

110. Zaidi (1985), vol. 1, p. 7.

111. FN (1896), p. 359.

112. Malabari (1896), p. 1.

113. FN (1896), pp. 359–360.

CHAPTER NINE

Florence and the Zenana Force

'Ye gentlemen of India, that sit at home at ease'.[1]

The idea that was gaining momentum in Florence's writings on rural sanitation apart from 'self-help' and 'collective cleanliness' was the need for education, particularly sanitary education for village women.

Florence had been interested in the conditions of Indian women for quite some time. She was interested in infant marriage, widow problems and Hindu religious laws. When her friend B.M. Malabari was trying to bring social changes in India through the Age of Consent Bill,[2] she sought Ripon's advice on the matter. She once wrote to Ripon, asking how to deal with such questions from a legal rather than a social point of view.[3] She understood that a large number of Hindu women, like their men, were against change, and any laws passed would legalise a bill but would not make it socially acceptable. The women needed to be made aware of their circumstances, for which education was essential. With her total dedication to the cause of sanitation, she wanted such education to be health education and to be spread among the rural population. This should start at home 'with the working hands of an Indian mother'. 'The mother's influence in India is so great,' wrote Florence in the introduction of the biographical sketch of B.M. Malabari in 1892, 'that in truth, it moulds the character of the nation.'[4]

It must be made clear that Florence was never a feminist in the modern sense of the term, and during her long life she never quite identified herself with the nineteenth-century feminist movement, either in the political arena or in the medical profession. In her early career of hospital improvement and nurses' training, she showed some reservations about women being trained as doctors. She was well acquainted with Dr Elizabeth Blackwell and Dr Elizabeth Garrett Anderson, the two pioneers in the medical profession and the movement they led. But Florence considered nursing and midwifery as natural aptitudes of women. In her opinion, they should rather do that well instead of competing with male doctors: ' ... instead of wishing to see more doctors made by women joining what there are,' she wrote to John Stuart Mill in as early as 1860, 'I wish to see as few doctors, either male or female, as possible. ... the women have made no improvement – they have only tried to be "men", and they have only succeeded in being third rate men. They will not fail in getting their own livelihood, but they fail in doing good and improving Therapeutics.'[5]

Later, in a similar letter to her brother-in-law, Sir Harry Verney, she reiterated her feelings about women becoming doctors:

> Let women begin by that branch of the profession (Midwifery) which is undoubtedly theirs. Let them do it as well as possible – let them conquer their place in it – instead of, as it seems to me, lady Doctors affecting to despise it. All the rest will follow.
>
> But none of the rest will follow, if their only aim is to be to extort from men a man's place.[6]

In the context of nineteenth-century social attitudes towards women's professions, it was not surprising that even Florence, in spite of her political liberalism, sometimes succumbed to such stereotypical ideas, but it is not difficult to understand why she did. She obviously wanted to see that nursing as a profession should get a strong and respectable foothold in society and the issue should not get lost in the wider political question of women's place in the medical profession, for which Blackwell and Garrett Anderson were agitating.

Likewise, Florence was not too concerned about women's right to vote. Though she agreed with the general idea that women should have the vote, as it was important for a women to be a person, she felt that there were more pressing problems for them that should be tackled first before obtaining voting rights. When John Stuart Mill asked her to join the National Society for Women's Suffrage, she wrote:

> That women should have the suffrage, I think no one can be more deeply convinced than I. It is so important for a woman, especially a married woman, especially a clever married woman to be a 'person'. But it will probably be years before you obtain the suffrage for women. And in the mean time are there not evils which press much more hardly on women than not having a vote?

She politely refused Mill's offer on the ground that she had no time to do so:

> I could not give my name without my work. This is only personal. (I am an incurable invalid). I entirely agree that women's 'political power' should be 'direct and open'. But I have thought that I could work better for others, even for other women, off the stage than on it.[7]

Even in her later years, Florence was not totally convinced about women's right to vote. 'You said there are two things in which the women's vote could help,' she wrote to William Wedderburn in 1896,

> 1. Temperance: not to be beat up by drinking husbands. 2. What? ... Please tell me what the other thing is that a woman's vote is to do? I am afraid I have been too enraged by vociferous ladies lecturing upon things they knew nothing at all about – & have not thought of the rank and file.[8]

There was always an ambiguity, a dilemma, in Florence's attitude towards women. On the one hand, she was not too enthusiastic about women's political rights, on the other, she wanted them to be strong-minded and professional. She could not see that to achieve that, women needed political rights as well. To Florence, most women lacked the power of concentration, sympathy and motivation. The threshold of her patience was extremely low for women who did not display the same strong will and determination as herself. On her return from Crimea in 1856 she wrote to Lady Charlotte Canning: 'One is sick of the cant about Women's Rights. If women will but shew what their duties are first, public opinion will acknowledge these fast enough.'[9] In a similar letter to Madame Mohl, Florence categorically expressed her antipathy towards women who showed no interest or enthusiasm to do things, change their circumstances, or follow a career:

> ... my doctrines have taken no hold among women. Not one of my Crimean following learnt anything from me, or gave herself for one moment after she came home to carry out the lesson of that war or of those hospitals. [10]

Later on, she expressed similar views to her journalist friend Harriet Martineau:

> I am brutally indifferent to the wrongs or the rights of my sex. And I should have been equally so to any controversy as to whether women ought or ought not to do what I have done for the Army; though a woman having the opportunity and not doing it ought I think, to be burnt alive.[11]

In spite of her impatience with women's lack of motivation, Florence was not altogether indifferent to the socio-cultural and economic restrictions that were often imposed on women, whether that was in nineteenth-century England or India. She herself had undergone many agonising years of indecision and torment to ignore the taboos of an upper middle class family in order to pursue her path of self-fulfilment.[12] She knew how difficult it was to break the mould. In 1857, after she had come back from Crimea in the midst of national fame and popularity, she wrote in a private note how things had changed because of her fame. She recalled how her mother and sister, who had once been vehemently opposed to her choosing a nursing career, were now basking in her glory. 'I was the same person who went to Harley St. and who went to Crimea. There was nothing different except my popularity. Yet the person who went to Harley St. was to be cursed and the other was to be blessed.'[13]

Florence's book, *The Suggestions for Thought*, written in the relatively early years of her life, spoke in no uncertain terms of the conditions of

women in nineteenth-century England, and how every scope and opportunity for self-fulfilment was denied to them: 'Why have women passion,
intellect and moral activity – these three and a place in the society where
no one of the three can be exercised.'[14] Florence knew very well from her
own experience that women's fate often rested on the decisions made by
social oligarchs. And in spite of her occasional impatience with her own
species, her own life was an epitome of women's struggle for equal rights,
particularly the right to make a choice.

This was typically exemplified in the introduction of the so-called
Contagious Diseases Acts in England and in India in the 1860s.[15] Here
was certainly one case where Florence did not hesitate to lend her name to
the fight against it. In England, the Contagious Diseases Act of 1864 was
introduced as a public health measure to prevent the spread of venereal
diseases in the army. Later, the act was extended to some towns and cities
as well. It required that all prostitutes working near military cantonment
or port areas needed to be registered for medical inspection. The act was
clearly discriminatory and anti-women, as it only applied to them and not
to the men.

Florence was very much against what she described as 'the State Regulation of Vice'. She rejected it primarily on moral grounds, but also on the
grounds of the non-availability of convincing statistical data. She maintained that there was not sufficient reason to believe that such state regulation could actually improve soldiers' sexual health. Apparently she even
sent a paper to Lord de Grey and Gladstone to persuade the politicians
against such an act but without much effect. Throughout the 1860s and
1870s, Florence continued to lobby against the act and gave her full
support to the women's agitation that was building up against it. When
Harriet Martineau wrote articles on the subject in the *Daily News*, Florence as always, supplied her with facts and figures.[16]

In England, the National Association for the Repeal of the Contagious
Diseases Act was formed in 1870, and Josephine Butler, then only a
housewife, led the agitation against it. When Harriet Martineau drafted a
protest letter, pointing out that not only was the act discriminatory but
was also singling out a particular group of helpless women for degrading
treatment, the letter was published in the *Daily News* with the signatures
of more than 150 distinguished women of that period, including Florence.[17]

In India, the Contagious Diseases Act was passed in 1868 during
Lawrence's viceroyalty, though a similar act aimed at regulating prostitution in the cantonment areas (Act XXII of 1864) was already in existence.
The new act required compulsory registration, medical examination and
treatment of Indian prostitutes working in the cantonment areas.[18] Florence's attitude to this act in India was somewhat ambivalent. Earlier, in

her *Observations*, she was extremely critical of the Lock Hospital system in India where prostitutes were compulsorily treated for venereal disease. She considered army prostitution and army drunkenness as parts of the same vice and both had the same causes:

> India has its licensed 'lal bazaars', and its licensed spirit selling. And both are encouraged to the utmost by leaving the men utterly without rational employment for their time. The 'lal bazaars' and the canteen both send men into hospital in abundance. While, instead of confronting both evils with the strong arm, and providing men with useful occupations and manly amusements, Government sets up lock hospitals under its authority, and makes ineffectual attempts to stop drunkenness by keeping the supply of drink, as far as it can, in its own hands, and so encouraging the evil by its own authority. The authority of Government is avouched for both evils.[19]

Florence maintained that if the soldiers were allowed to marry and were provided with better recreation facilities, the need for sanitised prostitutes in the cantonment area would automatically decrease. She advocated marriage and healthy living quarters for the soldiers by pointing out that among the British soldiers the 'diseases engendered by vice' were five times as much as existed among the native troops. Her other concern was for the British soldiers' wives who were in India. She claimed that the soldiers' wives were sometimes in a worse situation than the barrack prostitutes. The Government would take care of the Barrack prostitutes and pay for their treatment but would give no such help to the soldiers' wives.[20] Lawrence, however, was very much against married soldiers bringing their wives to India. His reasoning was that there were not enough married quarters and also that a considerable number of British children died in India every year.

In the 1860s, Florence was not so much concerned about the sexual harassment of the Indian prostitutes who worked for the soldiers as she was about soldiers' health, and she viewed the application of the Contagious Diseases Act in India from that angle. Much later, in 1897, she supported the act with some reservations when its repeal was considered in India.[21] However, the question of the sanitary education of Indian women was a completely different issue than that of the Indian 'Admiralty wives', and there she showed no hesitation in offering her organisational and lobbying skills for a good cause.

Sanitary education for Indian women

Florence focused on Indian women's sanitary education at a relatively late stage of her Indian work, but she was extremely knowledgeable about the situation. The health education of Indian women, like their general education, was neglected until the second decade of the nineteenth century. The early years of the Company Raj in India saw no official encouragement for women's education as such. The English education system that was gaining ground in Bengal, and later in other presidencies, only benefited upper and middle class Indian men. Women's education was considered unimportant and not viable, as there was no demand for it. The Government also thought it safe not to get involved in this particular controversial area, which was a stronghold of traditional values and profound prejudices. The education of women was mainly left in the hands of Christian missionaries, British philanthropists and Indian social reformers.[22]

The initial attempt came from the missionaries when the Baptist mission started a school for Calcutta girls in 1819. Under the supervision of the Church Missionary Society, one Miss Mary Ann Cooke arrived in Calcutta in 1821 and helped to open at least eight schools for girls gathered from the lower strata of Calcutta society. She received generous financial help from Bengali philanthropists such as Raja Vaidyanath Roy, Nilmoni Das and Kashinath Ghosal. In 1824, Miss Cooke also helped to found the Ladies Society for Female Native Education, which received patronage from Lady Amherst, wife of the Governor-General.[23] In 1849, John Drinkwater Bethune started his Calcutta Female School for middle class Bengali girls and by 1854 the importance of female education in India was also recognised by the Board of Directors of the East India Company in their famous educational despatch: 'The importance of female education in India cannot be overrated. ... Our Governor General in Council has declared in a communication to the Government of Bengal that the Government ought to give to Native female education in India its frank and cordial support; in this we heartily concur.'[24] In spite of the recommendation of the Directors, women's education remained as neglected as vernacular primary education for the Indian masses. After the mutiny of 1857, the Government of India became even more reluctant to interfere in an area that could raise the question of religion and customs.

The demand for modern secular education for Indian women did not, however, die out. The English-educated Indian elite came forward and, like other social reforms, the need for women's education also caught their attention. In this respect, the contributions made by Ram Mohun Roy, Iswarchandra Vidyasagar, Pandit Madan Mohan Tarkalankar, Keshab Chandra Sen and Shibnath Shastri in Bengal helped to change male attitudes towards women's education, and that eventually led to the establishment of a number of girls' schools in the presidency. In a meeting of the Bengal Social Science Association, Keshab Chandra Sen asked for secular teaching for the girls, regular school inspection, provision for adult classes and educational visits for the students.[25] Bengal was not the only presidency where education among women started to make an impact. In other parts of India, particularly in Bombay, Poona and Ahmedabad, women's education started to spread due to the initiative of the enlightened leaders of the region.

When Mary Carpenter visited India, she also encouraged the establishment of native female normal schools, but the Government of India's response was lukewarm. By 1869–70, however, there were 2000 girls' schools in British India, and almost 50 000 girls were receiving education. There were even *Zenana* Schools for women who observed strict *purdah* and would not come out in public to attend schools. The *zenana* teachers would visit private houses to teach these women, and in Bengal they were supported by the missionary societies and Government grants.[26] Praiseworthy though these efforts were, they were almost insignificant gestures in the context of the vastness of illiteracy and ignorance that existed among the women of India, particularly in rural areas.

As mentioned earlier, the attitude of the Government towards female health or sanitary education in India was no better than the attitude shown towards their general education. There was no funding and no infrastructure for women's health education. The little knowledge of health care that was spread among the rural population was mostly due to the philanthropic work of the medical missionaries in India, both British and American. The Church of England Zenana Missionary Society and the Women's Medical College of Pennsylvania played a significant role in sending women doctors and nurses to help Indian women. They were responsible for spreading the rudiments of health awareness among village women.[27] But that was also a drop in the ocean compared to the need that existed.

Florence could visualise the immense impact that health and sanitary education could have on the rural community of India. In a country like India where most of the people lived in villages, in poverty and ignorance, Government action could only impose rules and regulations from the top. But the changes would have to come from within: 'If villagers are not taught to do simple things that they could do for themselves to promote health at home, law cannot enforce them, nor can funds help them.'[28] Self-help became the axiom of her venture.

This was not the first time that Florence focused on the education of the rural population. In as early as 1879, she published a series of articles on education in the *Journal of the National Indian Association*.[29] At the time, she was deeply involved with the land tenancy issue in Bengal and was publishing articles in favour of the *ryots*. Like many others, she also felt that the *ryots* could not exercise their legal rights because of their illiteracy and ignorance. Where the *ryots* were slightly educated and aware of their circumstances, they were able to stand up and fight for their rights. The main theme of her articles on education published during the Bengal land tenancy issue was the irrelevance of Government education for the *ryots*' children. There, she raised a number of unpalatable questions for the Government, and criticised the school education system in India on two counts: one, education was not reaching the children of the *ryots*, male or female, and two, the little education they received was not relevant to their life. It did not teach them how to cope with injustice and social prejudice: 'It is not enough to read Locke and Stuart Mill, excellent as such reading is. We must carry it out in life through life.'[30]

A pioneer of statistics and believer in facts as she was, Florence had her educational data always scrupulously collected by her acquaintances in India.[31] She had the Government annual education reports handy. She pointed out that between 1876–78, out of 638 510 pupils of all the colleges and schools of Bengal, only 269 940 were from rural backgrounds, from the families of cultivators, gardeners or *ryots*, and the majority of these were in primary schools. Even these children could hardly be called children of the tillers of the land. 'What proportion of the boys in our Government schools are the children of the *ryots*, and what other classes?' she asked; 'What proportion do boy-ryots bear at school to the actual numbers of boy-ryots who ought to be at school?' When it came to the question of gender, they were all boys. 'From the annual reports on Education for 1876–7 and 1877–8 will be seen how small is the number of girls at school, so that for practical purposes, we must call the scholars all boys.' Quoting the 1872 Census, Florence showed that out of the 17 million cultivators (men and boys) in India, at least one fifth of them would be of school age, whereas in actual practice only one per 12 or 13 who ought to be in school was at school: 'What classes of people take so little advantage of the Government education, and the answer is, as might be expected, the poorest, the most money-lender ridden, the most Zemindar ridden, those in fact who want it most to show them how to live.'[32]

Florence was not oblivious to the social conditions that existed in India. She knew that the children from the upper caste and class had the best chance for education; the untouchables hardly went to school, and the poor who needed education the most lived a hand-to-mouth existence: 'They have no time, no energy for anything that does not directly bear on how to keep alive; and the labour of their children is too valuable to be spared to go to school.' But she believed that education was the only key that 'would unlock their minds', though such education had to be relevant to their life and purpose.

Florence then arrived at a radical conclusion. It was essential for the children of the *ryots* to learn their rights, the ways to defend themselves from the tyranny of the moneylenders and *zemindars*, and to be sufficiently literate to detect false documents and deeds:

... what instruction do we give in our schools, so as to enable the future ryot to know what he is putting his signature to? To know what legal arms he has to use ... ; as regards leases and illegal cesses, and any kinds of illegal exactions, and as regards documents which bind him hand and foot to the sowcar? ... What do our Government schools teach the boy-ryots as to these things? It would seem really as if nothing but education could guarantee the cultivator against exactions by his own countrymen.[33]

Quoting from the Report on Public Instruction in Bengal 1877–78, she showed that the village primary schools or 'pathshalas' did not teach a boy to read a printed paper. He could not write out a *patta* or *kabuliyat*: 'The schools do not even supply a standard of instruction sufficient for the very moderate requirements of the peasants' daily life.'[34]

In 1879, when these articles were written, it was a difficult time in Bengal as well as in other presidencies. The *ryots* everywhere were decimated by famines. Those who survived were exploited by moneylenders and *zemindars*, while the British legal system was incapable of saving them. It was also a turbulent time, especially in Bengal, where the heat generated by the Pabna *ryots'* agitation still had not died down, and the reactionary forces against land tenancy reform in Bengal were gaining momentum. In that confusion of agitation and combination, Florence's sympathy understandably went to the *ryots*. Florence pointed out how a little education helped the *ryots* of Bihar to refuse to pay more than the amount written in their rent receipts, and stopped illegal exactions by the landlords. Similarly, she believed that the spread of education in the eastern districts of Bengal helped the Pabna *ryots* to combine and achieve what they wanted:

> ... the rent leagues of Eastern Bengal are leagues of all ryots, whether educated or not, ... primary education has made remarkable strides in that quarter, and very many of the ryots, compared with those of the other districts, have been to school.
> ... It is a satisfaction to know that instead of the ryots being always at the mercy of their landlords, it is possible now for unjust landlords to be at the mercy of their ryots.[35]

In spite of her sympathy, Florence did not approve of the violence that occurred during the agitation led by the Pabna *ryots*. Yet she understood the inevitability of such violence in the face of the unlimited oppression of the *zemindars* and the moneylenders: 'When these illegalities and excesses are carried to extremes, the ryots can only resist the Zemindar by combining. A small combination may defeat a small zemindar. It requires a large combination to defeat a big Zemindar; but such large combinations do exist and not unfrequently do defeat the big zemindars in Bengal.'[36]

In 1878–79, Florence was writing to portray the situation that existed in India to British readers. She probably did not realise that, by her prescription for education and combination, she was also endorsing a class struggle. She was, however, aware that such struggles of the poorer people in India might end up in anarchy. She concluded: 'The *ryots* must fight for their rights by lawful means.' 'Lawful means' to her meant non-violent agitation. 'You must educate education to do real good, to teach the Ryot his best course, to teach him to be a man.'[37] She asked the Indians to work against the corruption of petty officials: 'Is it impossible for the Native gentlemen to speak and work against corruption?' She appealed to the higher castes to raise the lower. She referred to the piety of the Hindus and the Muslims: 'Will you shut out the child from education because he is not of the same caste as your own?' Florence also asked them to respect manual labour, to go back to their own social classes after being educated and to improve their own conditions. But the educated Indians did not do that: 'Everyone in India wishes to be educated. But he does not wish to go back to his own life and improve that life by his education. He wishes to be educated that he may become a government clerk.'[38]

Although Florence concentrated mainly on the primary education of the peasants' children, the lack of education that existed among village women did not escape her attention. She claimed that the intolerable health and sanitary situation that existed in rural India was, to a great extent, due to the ignorance of the women. In her words, 'The graceful, timid, affectionate, self-sacrificing Hindu women' were against any changes. Even where men were educated and progressive they could not introduce changes at home, because their women would not have them: ' ... elementary ignorance stands, the mightiest engine of oppression of all, to stop good work at every turn.' Florence knew that in some parts of India education had entered the *zenana* and the husbands did help their wives to write examination papers. But 'Where is the help in giving these women the most elementary notion of what constitutes the life of a race, of what makes a healthy home, of home happiness and domestic economy?' Florence claimed that most of them had no conception of the connection between health and cleanliness, and they needed to be educated. But there were not enough schools for girls. The primary schools for the *ryots'* children were certainly needed, 'But far and above all in importance in this health matter are girls' schools.' Without education in sanitation and health they would not be able to run a healthy home and raise healthy children. Florence cited the cases in England where the women of the working class who once would not wash their children, except their hands and faces, changed their attitude after receiving some education and experience in health matters. Similarly, she felt, health education would bring immense change in India, and education was also needed to emancipate the women of rural India:

The British Government has justly forbidden the widow to be a suttee;
but it has left her a slave.
    We want something more than merely making murder and suicide
by fire illegal. We want education to prevent family and custom from
making the lot of the poor little widow intolerable.[39]

A few years later, in 1885–87, Florence returned to the theme of women's
health education with renewed enthusiasm. By this time, she had mellowed
considerably and talked no more about 'combination' or 'agitation'. Instead,
she appealed to educated Indians, especially Indian women, to redress the
situation. Like her friend, B.M. Malabari, she wanted to focus on the utilisa-
tion of women power in India. Florence fully appreciated the gap that existed
between European and Indian women, not only in their circumstances, but
also in their understanding of each other. But she knew that in spite of the
zenana system and their seclusion from the outside world, Indian women,
particularly older women, wielded immense power within the household,
and male family members often respected their wishes.:

> We English women understand as little the lives and circumstances, the
> ideas and feelings, of these hundred millions of women of India as if
> they lived in another planet. They are not reached by us, not even by
> those of us who have lived in powerful positions in India. Yet the
> women of India possess influence the most unbounded. In their own
> households, be it in hut or palace, even though never seen, they hold the
> most important moral strongholds of any women on earth. Did not a
> well known Indian gentleman declare that it was easier to defy the
> Secretary of State than to defy one's own mother-in-law? Supported by
> ancient custom, Indian women are absolute within their sphere.
>   How may we hope to reach this great influence and utilize it for the
> cause of social progress? The answer seems to be that the women of
> Indian can only be reached by educated ladies of their own country –
> ladies of pure life and enlightened enthusiasm in doing good. They
> have ready access to their poorer sisters – they understand their
> circumstances and feelings. It is to them, therefore, that we must
> appeal to convince their country women.[40]

Florence wrote this in appreciation of Malabari's effort to change social
attitudes in India towards early marriage and the age of consent, but the
possibility of using women power to introduce health education had
occurred to her long before that. She considered the middle class women
of India as an 'overground' source of power, and the *ryots'* wives, daugh-
ters and mothers as the 'underground' one. She now wanted to tap this
hidden resource of *zenana* power. 'There is such a vast underground
structure of Hindoo women whom we never reach,' she wrote to Ripon,
'yet in whose hands the practical problem really lies … The only way to
work upon this underground seat of power (as it is now) is, I suppose by
cultivated irreproachable Hindoo ladies.'[41] Florence did not want to stop
just with the women. She also approached Indian men to educate their

womenfolk in sanitation. In her letters to the members of the Poona Sarvajanik Sabha, she advised them about their duties:

> ... may I as a woman venture to whisper that one of their first duties at home will be to influence their ladies? There is perhaps no country in the world where women's influence is so high as in India; nor where ladies have sometimes manifested such capacity of governing and administration ... And perhaps there is no civilized country in the world where there is such ignorance among women of the first and simplest rules of health for themselves and their children.[42]

Florence told the members that domestic health depends on women, who should be instructed by their husbands and fathers in hygiene matters. Then these women could instruct other women: ' ... for women can only be taught by other women in these matters. Least of all they can be taught by legislation. A private public opinion must, so to speak, be created among them how to save their own and their children's health.' She knew the importance of an appreciation or reward to elicit good work. In the past, she had mentioned a turban for the village sweepers, or a clasp for native orderlies. Now she talked about the possibility of Royal patronage for the Indian ladies' sanitary associations!

> In India let the time be near when there will be Indian Ladies Sanitary Associations of which our Empress, who is deeply interested in the welfare of her beloved daughters of India, might no doubt become the gracious Patroness. Let them begin during her life on earth.[43]

A common purpose

From 1885 onwards, Florence involved herself in a project for the promotion of female health care and education in India. This was a project started by Lady Dufferin, the Vicereine, which later became popularly known as the Dufferin Fund. Lady Hariot Dufferin was interested in the welfare and medical care of Indian women. As mentioned earlier, modern medical care and health education for Indian women was practically non-existent in the nineteenth century. The main problem was to bring women out of their *zenana* to the hospitals and to receive treatment from a male doctor. Women doctors, mostly Europeans, were few in number and often did not have access to the *zenana* due to religious or cultural prejudices. The Zenana Mission, organised by the Baptist Missionary Society, tried to send medical help to the 'Purdah Nashin' Indian women, but they had limited access.[44] Most Indian women, rich or poor, found it difficult to get medical care, either because of social barriers, or the non-availability of such facilities. Even the Government of the time realised this was a problem:

> If medical aid is to be brought near to Indian women, that result, it is
> evident, cannot be attained by means of lady doctors brought from
> England; a much cheaper agency must be provided by educating, to
> different degrees of skill, women whose home is in this country,
> whether they are an Indian or of European extraction.[45]

The suffering of Indian women, rich or poor, was such that in England it
received the attention of Queen Victoria, who apparently asked Lady Dufferin
to pay special attention to the situation.[46] Shortly after arriving in India, Lady
Dufferin started a special project for health care and health education of Indian
women. The fund she started was officially known as *the Association for
Supplying Medical Aid to the Women of India*. It received an official blessing
from the Queen, and successive Viceroys and Vicereines were its patrons and
presidents. It also gathered support and donations from wealthy Indians such
as the Nizam of Hyderabad and the Maharaja of Jaipore. With such high-
ranking support, the Dufferin Fund soon became an all-India organisation
with branches in Calcutta, Bombay, Lahore, Bhagalpore, and many other
places. The Fund had three primary objectives: to provide medical care to
women and children; to offer medical training to women; and, to supply
trained nurses and midwives to hospitals and private homes.[47]

The Fund opened dispensaries and cottage hospitals, female wards in
large hospitals and exclusive *zenana* hospitals, all under the administrative control of women doctors. However, the women doctors had to
endure 'superior male supervision', as they did not always hold a full
medical degree. The most important aspect of the Dufferin Fund was its
endeavour to train Indian women as doctors, nurses and midwives. The
money raised was invested to provide grants-in-aid to pay the salaries of
doctors and nurses and to give scholarships to women students and
probationary nurses. The educational side of the Fund and the job opportunities it created opened up a new horizon for health care and education
for Indian women, and that interested Florence immensely. 'We hear with
hope and admiration of your intended meeting on "Female medical aid"
this month', wrote Florence to Lady Dufferin in January 1886, 'May it
prosper as it deserves. May God speed follow all you do for India: May
what you allow us to do be not quite in vain. For you is the warmest wish
of your Excellency's devoted servant Florence Nightingale.'[48]

Although the main purpose of the Dufferin Fund was to provide
medical care for the women in *purdah*, for its educational effort it needed
books and sanitary primers to train women in various aspects of medical
work and health care. There, Lady Dufferin needed Florence's expertise,
and asked her to organise the preparation of materials for simple sanitary
tracts that could be used for teaching.[49] Nothing could have suited Florence more, and with her indomitable energy at the age of 65 she immediately launched herself in the task.

Florence knew from the start that simply translating English health primers into Indian languages would not serve the purpose. They would have to be written by people who were familiar with Indian situations and knowledgeable about the special health requirements of Indian women. Besides, there was the question of copyright to consider. In pursuit of suitable health primers, Florence established contact with people both inside and outside her known circle. First, she turned to her old friend and co-worker Dr Sutherland:

27 November 1885

Sanitary Tracts for India
   ... I should be very much obliged for a List marked by yourself & Mrs. Sutherland of those which you think might possibly do, adapted, for India. I am also grateful for the caution conveyed in Miss Adams' letter about translation or adaptation, which I will carefully transmit to Lady Dufferin.
   But I could very much have wished that nothing had been said to Miss Adams or Jarrold about leave to translate or adapt till we had decided whether we should have even one book or tract to recommend to Ly D. for translation or adaptation. At present I have not one. And I had made up my mind to tell her so. Now, if she puts that 'Cleanliness is necessary to health', Jarrold will say it is 'adapted' from him. I have other books to send to Lady Dufferin which I have just ordered from my Bookseller, but without any intention of asking for leave to translate or adapt till we know whether we want it.
   I have got together such a mass of information & advice for Lady Dufferin that I hardly know how to arrange it for her – from Dr. Hewlett, from Mr. & Mrs. Man Mohun Ghose ... from Mrs. Hume Lothers.
   ... Dr. Hewlett recommends that in each province should be selected an Indian native to write, under the superintend'e of the Sanitary Commissioner of the province, a Sanitary home manual for women & girls.
   But what Sanitary Commissioner is there besides himself & Dr. Bellew, of the Punjab, who is fit for the task?
   No one knows so well as you. Please tell me.
   ... Could you kindly send me a List of the present Sanitary Commissioners whom you would consider fit for supervising the writing a home Manual for women – each for his own Province?
   I shall take care to include in my letter to Lady Dufferin (when it gets written) your excellent suggestion for teaching home Sanitary practice in any proposed Ladies Med'l college, that the Lady Doctors may lecture to the women – one of the principal suggestions of Mr. Man Mohun Ghose, ...
   ... Every one of my advisors has considered adaptation or retranslation from any English books as useless, except that, as you say, hygienic principles are the same everywhere; but we need not ask Jarrold for these.
   According to Dr. Hewlett, it is also useless to send these kinds of things to 'Parsees' whose women's habits & superstitions are unknown to English people.[50]

Another person whom Florence utilised for her purpose was John Murdoch, a teacher, writer and distributor of English and vernacular evangelical tracts and educational literature in India and Ceylon. John Murdoch, born in Glasgow in 1819, went to Ceylon in 1844 as a head teacher of a Government school. But he soon became interested in evangelical work, particularly in promoting Christian literature among converts, and felt that it would be unsuitable for him to work in a secular Government institution. So he resigned in 1849, and dedicated the rest of his life to producing tracts for native Christians. In 1858, Murdoch became the Secretary of the Christian Vernacular Education Society in India. 'My sphere of labour will thus be extended from the Himalayas to Cape Comorin,' he joyfully wrote in a letter, 'and from the borders of Afganistan to the frontier of Burma.'[51]

Murdoch never missed an opportunity to write long letters to people in power, narrating in great detail the educational need of the people of India. He himself produced a number of educational books, some in vernacular languages. In 1881, he wrote a long pamphlet on education in India and sent it as a letter addressed to Ripon.[52] In the same year he wrote another long letter to Lord Hartington, the Secretary of State for India, narrating England's duty to India, and prescribing that India should be governed wisely and justly, emphasising the need for the development of industries, food supply and free trade.[53]

Florence came to know about Murdoch's educational ventures from Ripon. At the same time, Murdoch also sent her some of the educational materials he had produced. Florence took interest in what he wrote about health and sanitation in India. She immediately established contact:

> July 6/86
>
> I consider it a privilege to enter into correspondence with you whose good work in India which interests me so much it would be impertinent in me to praise. [Your letter to Lord Ripon on Education I have read again and again, and I asked a number of copies to be sent to me from Madras].
>
> I thank you for 'The Way to Health' which seems to me exceedingly good & for your 'India's Needs' which I was [ ] going to procure.
>
> The request to give a list of 'suitable easy English (Sanitary) Tracts' etc. to be adapted for use in India has been made to me twice in the last twelve months from India. And I have sent over all I could recommend to India, but with the special warning that they could not be adapted to native or Indian circumstances – for reasons I would like to submit to you who know India so thoroughly and at the same time I ventured to suggest means by which suitable tracts could be written in India 'for use in India' which also I should like to submit to you. But I will delay no longer answering your note.
>
> Could you let me know how long you are likely to remain in England, as I should much like to be allowed to seek information from

you, who are so well qualified to give it, upon Educational matters in India, if you would be so kind.

I am a great invalid & always overworked so that I must have your indulgence.[54]

At Florence's request Murdoch went to see her, and later wrote in his diary:

On Friday evening (July 16th, 1886), had a long interview with Miss Nightingale. She was very pleasant. Was pleased to hear that she had circulated thirty copies of my letter to Lord Ripon, and given copies to Lords Dufferin and Reay. But was chiefly delighted to hear that she and Dr. Sutherland, Secretary of the Army Sanitary Commission, thought that the *Way to Health* was the very book they could send to Lady Dufferin, who wished to get out a series of simple sanitary tracts. Miss Nightingale had applied for a list of books used in school on Hygiene, and promised to let me have a copy. Went away greatly pleased. Hope good may come out of my visit. Anyhow, Lady Dufferin's proposal is excellent.[55]

With Florence's weighty support, Murdoch returned to Calcutta and found no difficulty in making Lady Dufferin interested in his books. He was also invited to dine with the Viceroy, where he was seated next to Lady Dufferin and was able to have a long conversation about her project.[56] Although at that time Murdoch felt that the meeting would not have much effect, something did come out of it. *The Way to Health* certainly made an impact among the ruling authorities in India as a sanitary primer for school education. The provincial Government of Bombay passed a resolution that a copy of the book should be sent to the Director of Public Instruction and that he be asked to get it printed in a 'convenient form' so that it could be sold at the Book Depot. The Bombay Government also wanted to have it translated into the vernacular languages with 'appropriate additions or alterations' so that it could be used in the vernacular schools of the presidency. The educational departments of Berar and the Central Provinces also expressed their intention to use the book as a sanitary primer. By 1887, the Government of India also started to see the relevance of health education in rural India and put their support behind such publications.[57]

Murdoch's enthusiasm for sanitary education must have impressed Florence, as years later she wrote to Wedderburn praising his enthusiasm: 'I never knew a man of his age taken up the sanitary problem so quickly and so well. His little books for natives are far superior to anything our Anglo-Indian medical officers have done.'[58] Florence also sent a similar letter to Murdoch: 'Your little books are a great deal better than anything we have done.'[59]

John Murdoch was not the only one to be blessed by Miss Nightingale's letters. Florence's quest for suitable sanitary primers made her get in touch with many others. She asked her contact Mr Pedder to send her a report by Dr Bellow of the Punjab so that she could answer one of Lady Dufferin's queries: 'I am ashamed to ask it, but Lady Dufferin has given me rather a hard task.'[60] She also wrote to Dr Mary Scharlieb, one of the pioneering British women who practised medicine in Madras for the benefit of Indian women.[61] Scharlieb first went to India in 1866 with her husband. The unnecessary sufferings of Indian women due to lack of medical care drew her attention and she decided to qualify herself, first in midwifery and then as a doctor. Once qualified, she returned to Madras and devoted herself to building up medical facilities and hospital care for Indian women. It was she who enlightened Queen Victoria on the suffering of Indian women.[62] She came back to England in 1887, which was when Florence got in touch with her. Florence corresponded with Scharlieb on various subjects such as the *purdah* system among Muslim women, job possibilities for Indian lady doctors outside the Government sector and, most importantly of all, about the suitability of a simple sanitary primer:

> Herewith comes Lady Grant Duff's book the 'Sick Nurse' in Tamil which you were so good as to say you would take to a gentleman at Oxford tomorrow, the Rev. Dr. Pope I think who would be able to read it, and give us some idea whether it was to be recommended as a sanitary book, with the object of mentioning it to Lady Dufferin.[63]

Later, Scharlieb paid homage to Florence in her memoirs:

> At the time I first visited her she was a chronic invalid. She was never seen except on her bed, but she was always fully dressed in a black silk gown and dainty cap, and she sat upright, not deigning to rest on the pillows.
> Miss Nightingale was deeply interested in the circumstances of women in Eastern lands, especially in Hindu and Mahomeddan women. She was never tired of hearing my stories of their lives, their manners and customs, and sufferings.
> … Miss Nightingale threw herself enthusiastically into my work, she shared my hopes and fears, and by her great sympathy and powerful interest she helped materially in the completion of the task I had set before me.[64]

Thus the last few active years of Florence's Indian work were spent in educating the *zenana* force by arranging suitable sanitary primers for them. In the course of time, a number of suitable books were written and distributed. There were translations of such books into various Indian languages. Eventually, hygiene and domestic science were introduced at school level, and girls in particular were encouraged to study them in school-leaving examinations.

It must be mentioned that Lady Dufferin's venture to provide medical aid to the women of India, and Florence's attempt to provide suitable books for their sanitary education did trickle down to some extent from the upper crust of Indian ladies to the 'underground' hidden resource of woman power. It benefited the working class city dweller women more than their village counterparts. The Dufferin Fund 'met a want long acknowledged and severely felt'. How grateful the women were could be seen from their presence in the farewell they gave to Lady Dufferin on 4 December 1888 in Calcutta. They called her venture 'a memorable attempt to alleviate the fearful amount of female suffering' that prevailed in India. The farewell party was arranged in Government House in Calcutta: 'The greatest privacy was observed in receiving the ladies, all male visitors being excluded. There were nearly seven hundred native ladies present, there being barely standing room in the Throne Room where the address was presented and the reception took place.'[65]

By the end of the nineteenth century a number of medical schools and universities opened their doors to the women of India, and in the course of time produced a large number of female doctors and nurses, totally indigenous, and well suited to the needs of the country. By 1895, at least 300 Indian women were preparing themselves for medical degrees.[66]

One significant trait in Florence's character was that if she thought someone was good for a particular job, she never hesitated to exercise her 'Nightingale power' to pull strings and lobby for that person. This often earned her the reputation of being a manipulator. But she wanted the work done and done in the best possible way by the best possible person. In the past, she had lobbied for Lord Ripon when he was Lord de Grey, for Dr Sutherland, Sir Douglas Galton, Dr Farr and Dr Hewlett, and for many others, particularly in the nursing world. Now, in the last phase of her Indian work, we find her recommending Mrs Kadombini Ganguli, a relation of her friends Mr and Mrs Manmohun Ghose for 'any post about the female wards in Calcutta'. She wrote to Mary Scharlieb: 'Mrs Gangooly is, I believe, a woman of high caste and cultivation – and it would be a great encouragement to Hindoo ladies to embrace medicine if she was appointed.' In the postscript of her letter, Florence added a few more lines to show how determined and strong willed Kadombini Ganguli was:

> … Mrs Gangooly still studying in the medical college at Calcutta – has already passed what is called the First Licentiate of Medicine and Surgery examination and is to go up for the final examination in March next.
> This young lady, Mrs Gangooly, married! after she had made up her mind to become a Doctor! and has had one if not two children since. But she was only absent 13 days for her lying in!! and did not miss, I believe, a single lecture.[67]

Kadombini Ganguli, more commonly known as Kadombini Bose, did not disappoint Florence's expectations. She earned her fame as the first

Bengali woman doctor, and paved the way for the next generation of women doctors in India. But Kadombini probably never knew that it was no one but the 'Lady with the Lamp' who lobbied for her and had done much to remove the darkness of social prejudice that was lying on her way to success.

The remaining years (1896–1910)

After the publication of *The Health Missioners in Rural India* in 1896, Florence did not publish any more articles on India. She was by that time 76 years old, and as the years progressed she gradually lost her eyesight. The active busy days of keeping contact with the outside world through writing letters were slowly coming to an end. She found it difficult to read and needed secretarial help to write. 'Oh, how I wish you could give us a better print, or an "Edition de Luxe",' she wrote to William Wedderburn, referring to the small print of *India*. 'Don't you see, we are all blind!'[68]

Her physical incapacity, however, could not diminish her interest in India. She remained enthusiastic about Indian politics and social changes and totally committed to the sanitary reforms of the country. Particularly, the well-being of the *ryots* remained a focal point right up to the very end of her life. She kept in regular touch with events in India and the progress or regress that was taking place there. She was so interested in Indian affairs that she even asked Malabari to put a resolution on her behalf in the annual session of the Indian National Congress in 1896.[69] She never failed to see any Indian leader or old Indian acquaintance who came over to London. When they met, she would ask them the most pertinent questions about the country; for example, whether sanitary education was finding a foothold, whether the *ryots*' children were getting relevant education and whether hygiene could be made a compulsory subject in the school syllabus, and also would share her experience and expertise with them. Indians of different political persuasions such as M. Bhownaggree, G.K. Gokhale, the Aga Khan and Dinsha Wacha went to see this formidable legendary woman. Those who did not come in later years were still writing letters to her, asking her advice on various matters, and she was never hesitant to act on that.

In 1896, when she received some distressing news about 'the evils and abuses of the Government General Hospital at Calcutta', she immediately made some enquiries and in her usual fashion wrote a rough remedial scheme to improve the situation.[70] When her old friend Manmohun Ghose from Calcutta asked her help in publishing an article in *The Nineteenth Century*, she replied tactfully referring to the lack of interest in Britain regarding India and advised him how to go about it:

It is true that editors are not greedy for Indian subjects but you have made a speciality of 'failure of justice' arising from the combination of judicial & executive powers in one person; and we think that if in illustrating the evils of the system you were to give one or two interesting cases in your telling way from your own experience, this would form an article which an editor might be glad to accept.

I would therefore suggest that if you would be glad to send such an article, I might then try it with Mr. Knowles. The topic is one which has already been brought to the front, as you will have seen.[71]

It was not Indians alone who wrote. English nurses who went to work in the military or other hospitals in India also maintained regular correspondence with her, and furnished her with up-to-date information about Indian states of affairs. Florence in turn advised them on how to run an efficient nursing service by incorporating indigenous nurses: ' ... I live in hopes that the English nurses will have native male nurses under them for the men-patients, & native women nurses in Hospitals, them for the women. There are excellent native nurses in Hospitals.'[72]

Florence continued to keep contact with the British administrators as well. The private secretaries of the Governor-General or of the Secretary of State were still sending Indian sanitary papers for her to look at and that was done until 1906, when her secretary asked the India Office not to do so any more.[73] In spite of her old age, Florence remained well informed about Indian matters and carried on exerting pressure on the administrators to ensure sanitary reforms. 'I have never thanked the Viceroy as I ought for so kindly sending me the papers regarding 'Village Sanitary Inspection Book' – invaluable, if carried out,' she wrote to H. Babbington Smith, private secretary to Lord Elgin, the Viceroy, in November 1896:

> May I venture to ask what is the 'progress and maintenance' of this Village Sanitary Record in the Bombay Presidency – and if it is not too much to ask: in the Madras Presidency, in Bengal, the Punjab, N.W. Provinces etc., etc. especially as regards the sort of persons who 'furnish the information' & if any pains are taken by native 'literates' to insense them with the value of 'points'?

Florence was not a person to remain satisfied with just receiving sanitary papers. She always raised a multitude of queries and expressed her doubts about keeping the village inspection records, which Lord Lansdowne introduced before he left India. Florence was always apprehensive about the effectiveness of such records. She knew very well that reports and facts were not the same thing, and 'the district officer only sees the main street prepared for him – not the dirty small alleys'.[74]

In the successive years of 1897 and 1898, Florence met two Indian leaders, Gopal Krishna Gokhale and the Aga Khan. Gokhale was at the time a young moderate leader of the Indian National Congress. He arrived in England on 20 March 1897 to give evidence before the Royal Commission on Indian Expenditure, commonly known as the Welby Commission. The Welby Commission was appointed to inquire into the question of Indian finances and the fairness or unfairness of them, as there were continuous complaints from Indian national leaders about the drain of wealth and over-expenditure of the establishment at the cost of the well-being of the ordinary people of India. Well-known people like Dadabhai Naoroji, William Wedderburn and W.S. Caine were on the Committee of the Commission, together with other veteran Anglo-Indians.

Gokhale was not the only one to give evidence to the Commission. Dinsha E. Wacha and Badruddin Tyabji were already in London to represent the Bombay Presidency Association. G. Subramania Ayer was there to represent the Madras Mahajan Sabha, and Surendranath Banerjee from Calcutta represented the Indian Association. Gokhale went to England to represent the newly-formed Deccan Sabha. Gokhale's evidence before the Commission went well. In his own words, ' ... everything passed off first-class – far better than I had ever ventured to hope.'[75] While basking in the glory of achievement as a worthy disciple of Ranade, whose place he took before the Welby Commission, Gokhale met various important people in England, and gave lectures in meetings of various associations under the watchful eye of William Wedderburn. Apparently Wedderburn was specifically asked by Ranade to provide such opportunities for Gokhale.[76]

It was not surprising that Gokhale should meet Florence. As an ex-editor and secretary of the *Quarterly Journal of the Poona Sarvajanik Sabha*, Gokhale was well aware of Florence's correspondence with the Sabha. William Wedderburn also wanted him to meet her. 'I saw Miss Nightingale yesterday and she will be pleased to have a visit from you. You might write her a note saying that I had told you this and offering to call at the time she may appoint.'[77]

Florence did not waste time in inviting Gokhale:

> Dear Sir, I hope you received a note from me asking you to make an appointment to come and see me some afternoon at 5.30 P.M. as Sir Wm. Wedderburn led me to hope.
>   He also led me to hope that you would give me your valuable information in answer to some questions of mine as: could hygiene be taught by school books in Elementary Schools – could it be made a compulsory subject even in the matriculation Examination of Universities?
>   I was sorry to hear of the Plague Camps at Poona – one of our nurses is there and I hope & believe doing good work with others.[78]

The nurse Florence referred to was Georgina Franklin, who went to Poona to work in the Plague Camp. Florence actually wrote to Franklin about her forthcoming meeting with Gokhale: ' ... We have several

Indians of mark in England, sent for over here to give their evidence before the "Indian Expenditure Royal Commission". The one from Bombay I have seen already and I am to see the one from Poona soon.'[79]

The summer of 1897, however, was not an auspicious time for Gokhale. In March 1897 when he left India for England, parts of Deccan and the west coast of India were in the grip of plague and famine. To cope with the plague, a committee was formed by the Government, with W.C. Rand as Chairman. The committee imposed stringent rules. House-to-house searches were carried out to look for plague suspects and British soldiers were employed to do the inspection and disinfecting. This caused a tremendous public outcry, as the soldiers were neither reverent to the customs and culture of the Indians, nor did they observe any decorum in doing this unpleasant job. As Chairman of the Plague Committee, Rand became particularly unpopular.

In May 1897 the people of Poona, irrespective of their religion or culture, submitted a protest memorial to the Governor of Bombay, Lord Sandhurst, complaining about the misbehaviour of the soldiers, including public stripping, destruction of property, disregard of religious customs and, in some cases, indecent treatment of women. Such news reached Gokhale in London through letters and newspapers, and he was deeply distressed. In the meantime, the situation in Poona took another serious turn. On 22 June 1897, W.C. Rand and Lieutenant Ayerst were shot on their way back home after a celebration party, held for the 60th anniversary of Queen Victoria's reign. Ayerst died on the spot, and Rand later in hospital.[80] The incident immediately let loose all the anxieties and fears in British minds; perhaps another 1857 was about to occur. In the middle of the condemnation of the British press and public, a meeting of the Indian Parliamentary Committee was held in London at the initiative of William Wedderburn. Gokhale was asked to provide information on what was happening in Poona. Gokhale, in his own words, 'placed everything unreservedly before the Indian Parliamentary Committee and also communicated it to a representative of the Manchester Guardian'.[81]

The *Manchester Guardian* duly published what Gokhale said, and that immediately brought protests from Lord Sandhurst, the Governor of Bombay, who claimed that Gokhale's allegations were without foundation. When asked to substantiate his claims, Gokhale could not divulge the names of his informants, nor were they willing to come forward. Gokhale was thus immediately labelled as a slanderer. On his return to Bombay, Gokhale 'withdrew all his allegations and tendered unqualified apology to the Government',[82] which made him equally unpopular both in Britain as well as in India, and considerably damaged his political reputation for a while. Gokhale left England in the middle of July 1897 and probably met Florence shortly before that.

Florence was well aware of what was going on in the political arena, and the letter Gokhale later wrote from India in his depressed and demoralised state of mind suggests that Florence did discuss the situation in India with him, and Gokhale supplied her with news and shared his feelings about Indian politics. However, this led to a misunderstanding about what Gokhale actually said to Florence and what she understood him to have said. A letter in Gokhale's private papers, unfortunately without an addressee, narrates from Gokhale's perspective what had happened in that meeting:

> As regards what you were kind enough to tell me about Miss Nightingale's remarks to Mr Birdwood, let me repeat that there has been some grave misunderstanding. My respect for the lady is so great that I should myself mistrust my own version of anything if it conflicted with hers. But in this matter I am positive I never said anything of the kind attributed to me. I certainly did tell her that as far as I could judge, I perceived that during the last five or six years, British rule had been losing ground in the Deccan, that sullen discontent was growing especially on the Konkar side owing to forest and other grievances and that men like myself felt ourselves helpless as we had the confidence neither of Govt. nor of the masses. But I never said that I expected a rebellion in four years. Such a mad idea had never occurred to me till you mentioned it the other day.
>
> If you will allow me, I would write to Miss Nightingale and get the things cleared up. Of course I cannot take such a step without your permission, but I feel the humiliation of my present position so keenly that the thought of this misunderstanding has become positively oppressive. I may mention that I did not go to pay respect to Miss Nightingale till I got a very kind and pressing letter from her asking to see me.[83]

Gokhale's encounter with Florence in 1897 was a short one with an unhappy ending for him. However, more than a decade later, Gokhale and other prominent citizens of Bombay raised a considerable sum of money to give a farewell present to William Wedderburn and his wife in appreciation of his work in the Bombay Presidency, and for India. Both Wedderburn and his wife wished that part of the money should go to the Florence Nightingale Fund for Village Sanitation. 'Sir William has told me of a kind proposal with regard to the fund received for his Bombay entertainment,' Mrs Wedderburn wrote to Gokhale on 6 February 1911, 'I should of course like a small memento of his visit but hope that the bulk of the fund may be employed for the Florence Nightingale Scheme. I may mention that from my conversation with her, I know she had India's village sanitation very much at heart.'[84]

The 'small memento' for Mrs Wedderburn was 'a beautiful necklace of Indian work, set in diamonds and pearls, with a pendant of enamelled lotus leaves surrounded by precious stones', and it was presented to her by

Gokhale himself at a London party on 4 July 1912. The remaining sum of about Rs. 1000 went to the Nightingale Fund.[85] The Nightingale Fund for Village Sanitation in India was started by William Wedderburn after Florence's death in 1910. She left a legacy of £250 to him 'for some Indian object' to which Wedderburn himself and many others made generous contribution. With the help of the fund, experimental work was carried on in two villages near Bombay and Poona in the way Florence dreamt of. The work continued for a few years until the First World War broke out. Later, after Gokhale's death, The Nightingale Fund was renamed the Gokhale Fund and scholarships were given to Indian girls to study sanitation.[86]

In July 1898, soon after Florence met Gokhale, she also met the Aga Khan, the spiritual leader of the Ismaili sect in India, and one of the richest men in the world. As a politician, he was influenced by Pherozeshah Mehta and Badruddin Tyabji of the Bombay Presidency Association and from 1892 onwards, in his own words, 'took the standpoint of moderate Indian nationalism of that time'.[87] When in Britain in 1898, the Aga Khan mixed with the high and mighty of British society, including people like Queen Victoria and the Prince of Wales (later Edward VII). He also called on Miss Florence Nightingale, as she was 'one of the most eminent women of the time'. Referring to the meeting, the Aga Khan later wrote in his memoirs:

> Though now advanced in years and a complete invalid, confined to a sofa in her drawing room in her Park Lane home, Miss Nightingale retained a formidable interest in affairs. One of the topics on which she kept herself most closely and fully informed was the British Administration in India – especially so far it concerned matters of health and hygiene.[88]

It is evident from her papers that Florence prepared herself well to meet this young man from the East and ask him questions about village sanitation, *panchayats* and British centralisation.[89] After meeting the Aga Khan, Florence wrote a memorandum of her conversation with him. It was evident that while Florence was eager to ask questions about sanitation, the Aga Khan wanted to talk about spirituality and religion: 'To him sanitation is unreal and superstitious and religion and spirituality is the only real thing.' The Aga Khan unwittingly asked her: 'Do you think that sanitation can make much difference in life?' and Florence, the high priestess of sanitation, commented ruefully in her memorandum:

> A very touching man, but you never could teach him sanitation. ... I never understood before how really impossible it is for an Eastern to care for material causes. Sanitation is the superstition and religion is the reality.[90]

The meeting was innocuous enough, but somehow later it attained a prominence in the writings about Florence Nightingale to substantiate the claim about Indian apathy for hygiene and sanitation. The encounter between Florence and the Aga Khan was mentioned by biographers of Florence Nightingale, such as Edward Cook, Lytton Strachey and F.B. Smith, to suggest opaquely that sanitary reforms for the Indians were impossible as they themselves were indifferent to the issue. The legacy of the imperial belief that Indians did not care for mundane comforts does not die easily. But Florence had always disassociated herself from such an excuse and considered it as a political ploy for official inaction. She spent almost four decades of her life in fighting for sanitary reforms and public health in India. But in her remaining years she was frustrated about the slowness of the result. Why that was so, why progress in public health and civil sanitation moved at a snail's pace in nineteenth-century India, we will return to that in the next chapter. But so far as Florence was concerned, she felt that she had not achieved anything:

> I am painfully aware how difficult, how almost impossible, it is for anyone at a great distance to do anything to help forward a movement requiring unremitting labour and supervision on the spot. But it is my privilege to meet in England from time to time Indian friends who are heartily desirous of obtaining for their poorer fellow countrymen the benefits which, through sanitary science, are gradually being extended to the masses here, both in town and country, and which are doing so much to promote their health and happiness; so I never lose an opportunity of urging a practical beginning, however small, for it is wonderful how often in such matters the mustard seed germinates and roots itself ... .[91]

The seeds of reforms, sanitary or others, which Florence tried to introduce in India, did eventually take root, but a long time had to pass before that.

Notes

1. FN (1879d), 'Can we educate education in India to educate men and women?', *Journal of the National Indian Association*, no. 106, October, p. 540.
2. Malabari, B.M. (1887), *Infant Marriage and Enforced Widowhood in India: a Collection of Opinions and Letters received by B.M. Malabari*, Bombay: Voice of India; Gidumal, D. (1888), *The Life and Life work of Behramji M. Malabari*, Bombay: Education Society of Bombay.
3. FN to Ripon, 29 October 1890, BL Add. Mss 43546, fol. 249.
4. Nightingale, F. (1892b), 'Introduction', in Gidumal, D. (1892), *Behramji M. Malabari: a Biographical Sketch*, London: Fisher and Unwin, pp. v–vi.
5. FN to Mill, 12 September 1860, BL Add. Mss 45787, fol. 11.
6. FN to Verney, 16 April 1867, as quoted in Vicinus and Nergaard (1989), pp. 281–282.
7. FN to Mill, 11 August 1867, BL Add. Mss. 45787, fols 38–42.

8. FN to Wedderburn, 13 August 1896, BL Add. Mss 45813, fols 227–228.
9. FN to Canning, 23 November 1856, as quoted in Vicinus and Nergaard, (1989), p. 166.
10. FN to Mohl, 13 December 1861, Cook (1913), vol. 2, p. 14.
11. FN to Martineau, Cook (1913), vol. 1, p. 385.
12. FN (1991), *Cassandra and Other Selections from Suggestions for Thought*, Poovey, M. (ed.), London: Pickering and Chatto, pp. 180–191.
13. FN, private note, 1857, BL Add. Mss 43402, fols 178–179.
14. FN (1991), pp. 205–208.
15. See Walkowitz, J.R. (1980), *Prostitution and Victorian Society: Women, Class and the State*, Cambridge University Press: Cambridge.
16. Cook (1913), vol. 2, pp. 74–75.
17. Shiman (1992), pp. 138–142.
18. For detailed analysis of the Contagious Diseases Act in India and its implication see Ballhatchet, K. (1980), *Race, Sex, and Class under the Raj*, London: Weidenfeld and Nicolson, pp. 40–67; Levine, P. (1994), 'Venereal disease, prostitution, and the policies of Empire: the case of British India', *Journal of the History of Sexuality*, no. 4, pp. 579–602.
19. FN (1863a), p. 90.
20. FN (1863a), p. 86.
21. Cook (1913), vol. 2, p. 408; Ballhatchet (1980), p. 92.
22. Richey (1920), p. 32.
23. Cowan, M.G. (1912), *The Education of Women in India*, Edinburgh & London: Oliphant, Anderson & Ferrier, p. 106.
24. Richey (1920), p. 388.
25. Sen, K.C. (1871), 'The improvement of Indian Women', *Transactions, BSSA*, vol. V, pp. 8–12.
26. Bureau of Education, India (1888), *Review of Education in India in 1886 with Special Reference to the Report of the Education Commission etc.*, Calcutta, p. 293.
27. MacPhail, J.M. (1905), *A General Survey of Medical Missionary Work in India*, Calcutta: The Indian Medical Missionary Association; Balfour, M.I. and Young, R. (1929), *The Work of Medical Women in India*, London: Oxford University Press; Gourlay, J. (2001), 'Medical women and female medical education in nineteenth century India', in Bagchi, J. et al. (eds), *Education and Empowerment: Women in South Asia*, Calcutta: Bethune School Praktani Samiti, pp. 117–138; Fitzgerald, R. (2001),'Clinical Christianity: the emergence of medical work as a missionary strategy in Colonial India', in Pati, B. and Harrison, M. (eds), *Health, Medicine and Empire: Perspectives on Colonial India*, New Delhi: Orient and Longman, pp. 88–136.
28. FN to the Secretaries, *Quarterly Journal, PSS*, vol. XV, no. 1, July 1892, *Proceedings*, p. 14.
29. FN (1879e), 'Can we educate education in India to educate men?', *Journal of the National Indian Association*, August, no. 104, p. 417; FN (1879a), p. 478; FN (1879d), p. 527.
30. FN (1879a), p. 481.
31. FN to Chatfield, January 1888, BL Add. Mss 45807, fols 248–9, draft.
32. FN (1879e), pp. 417–419.
33. FN (1879e), p. 421.
34. FN (1879e), p. 425.

35. FN (1879e), pp. 421–422.
36. FN (1879e), p. 422.
37. FN (1879e), p. 424.
38. FN (1879a), pp. 489–490.
39. FN (1879d), pp. 536–537.
40. Gidumal (1892), p. viii.
41. FN to Ripon, 29 October 1890, BL Add. Mss 43546, fol. 249.
42. FN to the Joint Secretaries, 16 February 1891, *Quarterly Journal, PSS*, July 1892, vol. XV, no. 1, *Proceedings*, p. 11.
43. FN to the Joint Secretaries, 16 February 1891, *Quarterly Journal, PSS*, July 1892, vol. XV, no. 1, *Proceedings*, p. 12.
44. *Our Indian Sisters. A Quarterly Magazine published by the Baptist Missionary Society*, London, July 1886, p. 98.
45. Review of Education, 1886, Calcutta, 1888, p. 282.
46. Balfour and Young (1929), p. 33.
47. Billington, M.F. (1895), *Women in India*, London: Chapman & Hall, p. 89. For a critical assessment of the contribution of the Dufferin Fund, see Harrison (1994), pp. 90–97.
48. FN to Lady Dufferin, January 1886, BL Add. Mss 45807, fol. 216, draft.
49. Cook (1913), vol. 2, p. 370.
50. FN to Sutherland, 27 November 1885, BL Add. Mss 45758, fols 195–6.
51. Morris, H. (1906), *The Life of John Murdoch, LLD*, London: The Christian Literature Society for India, p. 111.
52. Murdoch, J. (1881), *Education in India: a Letter to the Marquis of Ripon*, Madras: C.K.S. Press, Verpery.
53. Murdoch, J. (1881), *England's Duty to India: a Letter to the Marquis of Hartington*, Madras: C.K.S. Press, Vepery.
54. FN to Murdoch, 6 July 1886, BL OIOC, Mss Eur A 192.
55. Morris (1906), p. 218.
56. Morris (1906), p. 220.
57. Government of Bombay, Public Records, General No. 101, 20 January 1888. In Florence's private papers there exists a copy of the book full of health care advice for rural Indians. See Nightingale Papers, 1858–94, BL.
58. FN to Wedderburn, 9 December 1896, BL Add. Mss 45814, fols 42–45.
59. FN to Murdoch, 27 June 1897, as quoted in Morris, 1906, p. 219.
60. FN to Pedder, 19 November 1885, BL Add. Mss 45807, fols 183–8.
61. In November 1893, Mary Scharlieb gave a paper on the supply of medical aid to the women of India, in the central Conference of Women Workers held in Leeds, in the session on Indian Women. A few other women delegates from India were also present at that conference. Nightingale Papers 1858–94, BL.
62. Balfour and Young (1929), p. 30.
63. FN to Scharlieb, 1 December 1887, BL Add. Mss 45808, fol. 5.
64. Scharlieb, M. (1924), *Reminiscences*, London: Williams & Norgate, pp. 46–48.
65. *Speeches Delivered in India by the Marquis of Dufferin and Ava, 1884–1888*, Calcutta: J. Murray, 1890, London, p. 248.
66. Billington (1895), p. 248.
67. FN to Scharlieb, 20 February 1888, BL Add. Mss 45808, fols 41–42. Kadombini Ganguli joined the Calcutta Medical College in 1883, and

graduated in medicine and surgery in 1888. She also worked for the Dufferin Fund as a doctor.

68. FN to Wedderburn, 9 December 1896, BL Add. Mss 45814, fols 42–45.
69. FN to Wedderburn, 9 December 1896, BL Add. Mss 45814, fol. 42.
70. FN to Wedderburn, 26 June 1896, BL Add. Mss 45813, fols 210–212, draft.
71. FN to Ghose, 19 May 1896, BL Add. Mss 45813, fols 199–200, draft.
72. FN to Franklin, 24 March 1897, BL Add. Mss 45814, fol. 133.
73. Cook (1913), vol. 2, p. 403.
74. FN to Babbington Smith, 10 November 1896, BL Add. Mss 45814, fols 4–11, draft.
75. Gokhale to Joshi, 16 April 1897, as quoted in Patwardhan, R.P. (ed.) (1968), *The Select Gokhale*, New Delhi: Maharashtra Information Centre.
76. Ranade to Wedderburn, 19 March 1897, as quoted in Nanda, B.R. (1977), *Gokhale: the Indian Moderates and the British Raj*, Oxford: Oxford University Press, p. 90.
77. Wedderburn to Gokhale, 6 May 1897, Gokhale Papers, 579-1, NAI, New Delhi.
78. FN to Gokhale, 15 June 1897, File no. 382-1, Microfilm, Servants of India Society, Gokhale Institute, Pune.
79. FN to Franklin, 1897, BL Add. Mss 45814, fols 183–84.
80. Nanda (1977), pp. 102–117.
81. Patwardhan (1968), p. 40.
82. Patwardhan (1968), p. 40.
83. Gokhale to [?], 2 August 1897, draft, Gokhale Papers, File no. 382-2, NAI, New Delhi. The addressee of the letter was not identified, and from the personal tone of the letter it seems likely that it might be Wedderburn.
84. Mrs Wedderburn to Gokhale, 6 February 1911, File 579-150, 1-406, Microfilm, Servants of India Society, Gokhale Institute, Pune; Wedderburn to Gokhale, 10 January 1911, Gokhale Papers, 579-146, 1-399, p. 4, NAI, New Delhi.
85. Patwardhan (1968), pp. 385–386.
86. Ratcliffe (1923), pp. 125–126.
87. Aga Khan (1954), *World Enough and Time*, London: Cassell & Company, pp. 33–34.
88. Aga Khan (1954), pp. 53–54.
89. FN, private notes, 5 July 1898, BL Add. Mss 45827, fols 194–196.
90. FN, private notes, 5 July 1898, BL Add. Mss 45827, fols 192–196.
91. FN (1896), pp. 359–60.

CHAPTER TEN

A Private Endeavour in Public Health

The question that inevitably arises in one's mind in assessing Florence Nightingale's Indian work is: what exactly did she do, apart from writing innumerable letters and memoranda to various individuals in power and occasionally publishing articles on India? As we know, she never went to India in spite of several invitations she received from people like Sir Charles Trevelyan or Dr Pattison Walker. She never toured the country like Mary Carpenter, or agitated in person on location for social reforms or liberal legislation. Whatever she did, she did from her bedroom by writing letters. When viewed from this angle, her achievements for India would certainly appear insignificant, her success pallid, and some biographies of Florence Nightingale, such as Lytton Strachey's and more recently F.B. Smith's, have certainly made this point.[1] It is only when viewed in the broader perspective of nineteenth-century colonial imperialism that the value of her contribution in sanitary and other reforms in India can be fully understood.

There are some tangible contributions that Florence made in the history of Indian sanitary reforms that no one could quibble about. One such reform was army sanitation. Her initial objective was the improvement of the health of the British soldiers in India. Here, she successfully achieved what she had set out to do. The high death rate of British soldiers in peacetime India was drastically reduced, and by 1900, a few years before her death, it was almost negligible. The expressed hope in 1863 was that the improved sanitation of the barracks would eventually lead to a possible mortality rate of 20 per thousand, but the rate of success was more than that. In 1900, the mortality rate of British soldiers was only 15.6 per thousand.[2]

At Florence's initiative and continuous pressure on the Viceroys and Secretaries of State, the living standards of the soldiers were also improved. Spacious barracks were built, cantonments were made more salubrious, clean drinking water was supplied, proper drainage was laid, the soldiers' diet was improved, recreation facilities were provided, and the soldiers' sexual health was maintained with the help of the Contagious Diseases Act and the Lock Hospitals. Some of these improvements spilled over to benefit the *sepoys* as well. The death rate of Indian soldiers decreased considerably, though not at the same rate as of the British soldiers. There was also improvement in their accommodation and hospital facilities. In later years, at the end of the century, the canteen system for the *sepoys* was introduced.

The introduction of a system of keeping statistical records of mortality for the civil and military population was another important contribution Florence made in Indian sanitary history. As a keen medical statistician, she always insisted on the need for keeping such records. Both in her *Observations* and *Suggestions*, she placed considerable emphasis on this point. Her initial priority was of course the British Army in India, but she did not ignore the necessity of keeping such records for the general public. In her letters and memos to the Viceroys and published articles on India, she continuously pointed out that no one knew how many natives died of preventable diseases or in famines. The official memoranda written by the Sanitary Commissioners showed how much importance was given to her insistence on the collection of vital statistics for the civil population, in spite of the fact that they were not often able to act accordingly.[3]

The registration of deaths in the Indian Army was properly implemented during John Lawrence's viceroyalty in the 1860s, and subsequently the vital statistics of European soldiers as well as of the *sepoys* were scrupulously included in the yearly sanitary reports of the Government of India. These reports showed a gradual progression of army health over four decades which was often described as 'most satisfactory' or 'very favourable'. Only in 1889–90 was army health compared unfavourably with that of previous years, because of the prevalence of venereal diseases among the British soldiers.[4] The health of the native army was also monitored regularly and was often described in the reports as 'satisfactory' or 'favourable'. The impact of venereal diseases was always less on the *sepoys* for one reason or another, though they continued to suffer from fever and enteric ailments.

In spite of Florence's insistence and official acknowledgement of the need for keeping records of vital statistics of the general population, progress in this area was conspicuously slow. The task was enormous and there was no suitable Government infrastructure to carry it through. Lack of funding added to the difficulties. The District Commissioners often admitted that without central funding from the Supreme Government such work would not be possible.[5] The registration of death, and later the registration of birth, was slowly introduced to big cities like Calcutta, Bombay and Madras, and subsequently spread to small towns and their suburbs. But the results were often inaccurate and incomplete. The Sanitary Commissioners, who were entrusted with the responsibility of keeping such records, passed it on to the local municipalities and local boards. They in turn depended on local police, village *patels* or *chowkeedars* to furnish such information. These lower strata of indigenous workers neither had the education nor the expertise to gather such information, nor was there any training scheme for them. Besides, ordinary people looked on them with suspicion and often considered that registration of birth and death was only a preliminary to further taxation.[6] As a result, the scant information that was gathered even up to the end of the century was not reliable. It was observed in the sanitary report of 1891–92 that the registration of births and deaths, relatively speaking, was still in its infancy in India. In the towns, some progress had been made but not in the rural tracts and there was 'a great variety in the efficiency of the performance of this duty'.[7] Even in as late as 1911, when the All India Sanitary Conference took place in Bombay, it was admitted that the collection of vital statistics was still unsatisfactory due to lack of funding, reluctance of people to co-operate and the inefficiency of the village *patels*.[8]

The introduction of modern nursing and employment of female nurses in India were two other significant contributions of Florence. Although her initial attempt to introduce female nursing in 1865–67 did not come to fruition during Lawrence's administration, her ideas and suggestions were later taken up, as we have seen, by Lord Napier, the Governor of Madras. He introduced her ideas for fully trained professional nurses in Madras and gave them his official support. That was, in a sense, the beginning of modern nursing and midwifery, and the Government's acknowledgement of the need for female medical education in India, in which Madras became the pioneer city.[9] The credit also goes to the Surgeon-General Dr Edward Balfour of Madras, who gave much importance to the idea of medical care of women by women. Initially, only Anglo-Indians, Eurasian and Christian women went for such training, but soon they were followed by other Indian women, Hindu, Muslim and Parsi. When in other big cities of India such medical education and professional training were not available to women, Madras opened its doors for them and the era of Indian medical women began.

Similarly, some thirty years after Florence had suggested female nursing in military hospitals in India, her ideas were implemented at the initiative of Lord Roberts during the viceroyalty of Lord Dufferin. As was mentioned earlier, Catherine Grace Loch, the superintendent of the newly-arrived nurses, implemented some of Florence's ideas in the management of nursing and took particular interest in training Indian hospital orderlies as had been suggested by Florence during Ripon's administration. The employment of female nurses in army hospitals also opened another door, which would one day allow Indian women to get in. Indian women started to work in military hospitals during the First World War, which was only four years after Florence's death.[10] The impact of the introduction of female nursing in general and military hospitals in India was more than the eye could see. It was a step forward in the fight for equal rights and opportunities for Indian women in that sector, and the credit for it certainly goes to the lady who gave a prestigious position to the 'Mrs Gumps' of nineteenth-century England.

Florence's involvement with Lady Dufferin's enterprise to provide medical care for Indian women who were in *purdah* was also significant. This was one project in public health care in British India that was not remotely connected with the army, and Florence played an important role in it by organising people to write sanitary primers essential for training Indian midwives, nurses and hospital auxiliaries at the basic level of medical care. The Dufferin project enabled Indian women to qualify as medical professionals and later to be employed as medical practitioners. When Florence started her Indian work in the 1860s, there was not a single Indian female doctor trained in Western medical practices. But during Florence's lifetime, the number of Indian women studying for medical degrees and certificates rose enormously. The yearly sanitary reports showed that by 1901, 13 women were studying medicine and health care in the Calcutta Medical College, 52 in the Agra Medical School, 26 in the Madras Medical College and School and 45 in the Grant Medical College of Bombay. With this, the need to import medical women from abroad to India declined gradually.[11] It must be said that Florence was not alone in this venture of introducing Indian women to modern medical education and training. There were many others in Britain and India who were equally involved in it. But this development was due in no small measure to Florence's efforts and continuous lobbying over the years.

In evaluating her success, it appears that the army sanitation was a relatively easy task for Florence. After the Crimean crisis and the subsequent appointment in 1857 of the first Royal Commission to investigate the health of the British Army, setting up the second Royal Commission for the Indian Army in 1859 was comparatively easy. This was possible because both the British Government and the general public were ready for it. Naturally, sympathy went to the soldiers in India, particularly after the bloodbath of the mutiny. The actual process of forming a working committee, choosing suitable members who would be interested both in sanitation and in India, gathering information from the Indian army barracks, preparing the report, writing the *Observations*, publishing and publicising it, and finally implementing the Commission's recommendations through John Lawrence, were all fraught with difficulties as we have seen, but they were not insurmountable.

Army sanitation was a specific task within a limited sphere and with definite guidelines. Above all, it had official blessing. Lawrence, in spite of his financial difficulties, found ample funds to secure most of the army sanitary reforms as wished by 'Miss Nightingale'. What was not completed in his time, successive viceroys saw to. Although Florence was a hard task-mistress, and often an outspoken critic of the Viceroys for failing to achieve the goal laid out, the Viceroys themselves, Lawrence, Mayo, Northbrook, Ripon, Dufferin and Lansdowne, all kept the army interest intact in their minds. They did not fail to understand that the British Army was the backbone of the Empire and that one needed 'healthy' soldiers to maintain the Empire. Particularly after 1857, the number of British soldiers in India was increased dramatically and consequently the health and sanitation of the army there became a major issue. This was why, in spite of her teething troubles with the Royal Commission, Florence did not face much resistance in introducing sanitary measures for the army.

There is no doubt that at the beginning of her Indian work, Florence did share the general idea that India would have to be kept by means of a healthy occupying force. But soon she moved away from that. The nine-teenth-century idea of 'exporting civilisation' took its place, and civilisa-tion to her was sanitation – sanitation for both army and civilian popula-tions. The Empire would be saved, she thought, not by 'healthy' soldiers, but by the goodwill of the healthy and prosperous natives. There would be no need for an army anymore. That was why it was essential to improve the quality of life for ordinary Indians. Florence, like many nine-teenth-century utilitarian liberals, considered India as Britain's moral responsibility. She felt that Britain could justify its presence in India only by doing good for the Indians. However, in comparison with army sanita-tion, the introduction of sanitary reforms for the people of India proved to be a far more difficult task for her. Here, she faced two crucial problems, which in her initial naivety of Indian affairs she did not anticipate. One was the sheer size of the problem. The country was vast, the population immense, and years of wars, colonial exploitation and regressive adminis-tration had left the country in such a destitute state that the problem was not just one, sanitation, but many. It was truly, as she described it, 'a hundred-headed hydra'. The other problem she faced was the absence of correct political attitude needed to confront such a situation, and this was the greatest hurdle on her way.

There was always a cosy misconception among the nineteenth-century British administrators that Indians as such were apathetic and indifferent towards sanitation. They did not appreciate the value of a clean environ-ment, and tended to foul their surroundings. Their personal hygiene was not in question, but their sense of communal hygiene was very much in doubt. As Mark Harrison said, the British administrators considered Indians very much as part of the sanitary problem.[12] This attitude was evident in the Royal Commission's report on the sanitary state of the British Army in India, in which the native bazaars and dwellings were considered as the 'reservoirs of dirt and disease', and official reports and memoranda in India contained similar references. John Lawrence, in his private letters to Florence, often mentioned Indian apathy towards sanitation.[13] John Strachey, the President of the Bengal Sanitary Commission wrote: 'Attempts to force such measures (sanitary) upon people who cannot appreciate their value will defeat their own object unless made with great caution and discretion.' At the same time, he admitted that: 'There is no reason for supposing that the people of this country have any special dislike to sanitary improvements.'[14]

There was no denying that Florence in her earlier writings sometimes referred to the lack of sense of communal hygiene in India. But she never fully succumbed to the theory of Indian indifference towards sanitation. Since the days of her collecting materials for the Royal Commission's report, she considered such a theory as a 'European excuse'.[15] She always argued that health ignorance and apathy could only be removed by health education. Where there was apathy, her logical mind tried to look for an explanation. One could not ask a person to observe sanitary rules if he did not stay alive to do so.[16] As to the question why they could not stay alive, she found the answer in British policies in India.

It is necessary to bear in mind that in British colonial history, India was a place where 'a few' confronted 'many'. India was never a white settlers' country as some other parts of the world became at that time. The idea of large-scale immigration to India was never encouraged by the Board of Directors of the East India Company or later by the Crown after the take-over, as was done in the cases of Australia, Canada or South Africa. The idea of the strategic benefit of such an enterprise was floated now and then, but it was never considered as a viable proposition. It was generally believed that the climate of the country, apart from the hill stations, was not conducive to the European constitution. 'Climate was a central feature of European existence in India, so much so that it became the single most important resource for the explanation of cultural and racial differences.'[17]

However, there was more to this than mere climatic and environmental issues. It should be noted that throughout the British period in India, no encouragement was given to the 'poor whites' to emigrate to India, nor were shiploads of 'social outcasts' sent there to find a new life. The Europeans who had the misfortune of becoming a vagrant or destitute in India were promptly arrested and put in the workhouse. If they failed to retrieve their fortune within a reasonable time, they were deported at the State's expense by the earliest available boat.[18] At an earlier period of history, even the missionaries were not freely allowed in India. The East India Company earnestly tried to restrict the entry of the missionaries to India until 1813, when with the renewal of the Company's charter such restrictions were removed.[19] The result of such policies was that only a handful of Britons and other Europeans lived in India.[20] Apart from planters, traders and entrepreneurs, and some skilled workers in the jute mills and the railways, the only other Britons were Government officials and their families, and soldiers. From the perspective of this small white community, India was a vast estate to be enjoyed by those fortunate few who were there, and it was considered that the influx of poor whites would only lower the prestige and authority of the Raj.[21] As Hutchins put it, they lived like a middle class aristocracy 'in a manner well above the station from which they had sprung in England'.[22]

The latter half of the nineteenth century was also a time when the British sense of racial superiority was at its height.[23] From that height, when these 'pseudo-aristocrats' viewed Indians, most of them, particularly the Bengalis whom they had to reckon with, appeared as miserable examples of human species – small, dark, thin-limbed, huddled together in their poverty, and dying in famines and epidemics in millions.[24] Yet such a situation should not have been unfamiliar to the British administrators. They already had their own 'great unwashed', the purveyors of dirt and disease in the big cities of England where many lived in similar degrading poverty with resultant diseases.[25] As Roy Porter wrote: 'The submerged classes crammed sardine-like into the slums of Whitechapel, Clerkenwell and St. Giles'.[26] This situation continued well into the nineteenth century until various reform acts improved the living conditions of the slum dwellers in Britain. As we know, it was possible to introduce public health and sanitary measures for the urban poor of Britain. Why then did not similar reforms take place in India? Why was the progress of civil sanitary reform so slow? These were the questions Florence continuously raised in all her writings about India, and the answer to them of course lay in the political context of the time. In recent years, a number of well-researched books have been written on British colonialism and public health in India, which have dealt with this question from different perspectives.[27] It is interesting to see how many of them echoed what Florence had said more than a century ago about administrative incompetence and indifference.

Since the mutiny of 1857, the British administrators had adopted a deliberate policy of not interfering with the customs and religions of the Indians in case it would trigger another revolt. However, they included civil sanitation within the customs and religious practices of Indians. Both the Supreme and the provincial governments used this excuse again and again whenever the question of taking measures for civil sanitation arose. It was a 'convenient rationalisation for state inertia and financial stringency'.[28] In as early as 1868, J.M. Cuningham, while officiating as a Sanitary Commissioner, wrote: 'It seems to be a hopeless task to attempt by means of legislation to force on so large a population occupying so vast a continent reforms which involve, it may be said without exaggeration, a radical change in their everyday habits and customs to which they cling with a reverential persistence partaking largely of superstition.'[29] Even where it was possible to interfere, the Government was reluctant to do so as that was considered as politically inexpedient. As Kiernan said: 'Where alteration of Indian customs for India's own benefit was in question ... there was cautious prudence instead of peremptory decree' and practically 'any government action, outside the sphere of revenue, sacred to British needs, could be construed as interference with religion.'[30]

Though the philosophy of apartheid was never an official policy in India, the *de facto* racial segregation that was there was also a clue to the question of why civil sanitary reform was so slow and partial. The British administrators who were the main decision-makers at central and local levels, with the exception of a very few, never had any sense of identity with India or the Indians. The two communities, segregated by every possible contingency, had no meeting point. There was nothing to bridge their social difference. The reciprocity of cultural minds that existed in the early part of the eighteenth century, or before the mutiny, gradually disappeared in the late nineteenth century. Florence was painfully aware of this: 'As a rule, natives are as slow to understand our actions as they are quick to observe them. They cannot in the least trace the connection between what we do or say, and what we think or intend, or wish in doing or saying it.'[31]

Had there been a large white community settled in India, the attitude of the British authorities would certainly have been different. This community would have shared some of the sanitation problems with the Indians, and the administrators could not have used the excuse of the apathy of the populace. It was not Indian indifference towards public health that curtailed the progress of civil sanitary reforms; it was the lack of political will on the part of the British administrators that made them hesitant to take effective public health measures. They were keen to follow the Royal Commission's recommendations regarding army sanitation, but their enthusiasm faltered whenever the question of civil sanitation arose. Florence had to work within this colonial context and persuade these reluctant officials to act.

The sanitary reforms that started in India in 1864 were, as we know, focused on the army; military interest was the primary guiding factor. Civil sanitation was relevant where it affected the army and the European community. Thus time was not wasted in cleaning up the surroundings of the army barracks and the native bazaars and dwellings in the cantonment areas. Similarly, in big cities, areas where most of the Europeans lived were provided with proper drainage, clean water and waste removal facilities. There is a general presumption in the writing of modern historians that when Calcutta was provided with filtered water from Falta in 1870, all the inhabitants of the city received the benefit of it. On the contrary, as Beverley pointed out in his census report, the supply of filtered water did not exceed seven million gallons daily, a quantity that was not enough to meet the requirements of the town.[32] Most of the Indian residents of the town had to wait for their share of piped filtered water. However, for their benefit, 511 hydrants were scattered around the town so that native householders could queue up to collect filtered Ganges water. The same happened with the drainage system. In the sanitary report of 1876, William Clark's underground drainage scheme for Calcutta was praised for producing a most marked sanitary improvement in the city: 'The effect on health is made very apparent by comparison of the death rates in the Northern and Southern divisions of the city, in the latter of which the drainage details have been more exclusively carried out than in the former.'[33] The southern division was of course where the Europeans lived and the drainage work remained incomplete in the northern native part of Calcutta. This also provoked an angry response from the Health Officer of Calcutta, not because he was concerned about the high death rate in the northern part of the city, but because he feared that the insanitary conditions in the north could affect the salubriousness of the white enclave in the south:

> I am opposed to drainage works as carried on at present which are in general more injurious than beneficial. Progressive work in one section of the town to be completed before another portion is undertaken would in my opinion, have a direct action on the localities in which they are executed and unless the minor sewers are rapidly constructed, and their action extended to the portions inhabited by the poorest classes of the community, I fear that the sanitary state of the town will become worse every day.[34]

Even by 1876, as Beverley admitted in his census report, large areas where the natives lived were still not connected to the main drainage system and the supply of filtered water needed enlargement and extension. He wrote: 'No one, I am convinced, who has seen what the Native town really is would wish to see the good work discontinued until the Augean stable has been completely cleansed.'[35] The situation did not change much in the following decade. In July 1884, a large number of Calcutta residents sent a petition to the Lieutenant-Governor of Bengal, asking for an inquiry into the sanitary conditions in the town.[36] This at least showed that Indians were not endemically indifferent to their environment as was often claimed in official reports.

It was not just Calcutta; in almost everywhere in India civil sanitary progress was extremely slow in providing the two basic essentials of public health: filtered water and a proper drainage system. The sanitary reports from 1868 to 1894 were full of phrases like 'plans were drawn up for early execution of drainage', 'survey operations in progress', 'a scheme for water supply is in progress', 'a project for drainage was sanctioned', or 'no special sanitary work of any magnitude was executed'. Whatever progress was made was mostly either in the army cantonment areas or in the vicinity of the European quarters and, as in the case of the *sepoys*, some of the benefits of the sanitary improvement of course spilled over into the native area. Even in as late as the 1940s, the visual difference between the 'Sahib' areas and the Indian areas in big cities and towns remained palpable. The first had its straight leafy avenues, spacious housing and all kinds of civic facilities, whereas most of the Indian areas were overcrowded with little or no civic facilities, a feature which was repeated throughout the British Empire, particularly in Africa and Asia.[37] 'In every Asiatic City where Europeans have settled there have generally arisen, side by side, what are called a "White and Black Town."'[38]

In spite of Florence's continuous demand to know what was done or not done for 'the community at large', the official reaction was always nonchalant and ambivalent. From Lawrence to Lansdowne, Salisbury to Cranbrook, Cross and Kimberly, a lot of excuses were always given. Time and time again it was repeated to her that sanitary progress in India must be slow, the people of the country were not interested, and there was no cash in the till. In contrast to this, there was little hesitation in spending Imperial funds for war purposes. Considerable sums were also spent in lavish *Durbars*. But money always ran out when the question of providing clean water for the rural community arose. The Viceroys were in India for only a short period of time, and they often wanted to make their mark in something big like the Bhutan War, the Afghan War, the annexation of Upper Burma, pushing the frontier with a forward policy or countering the prospect of a possible Russian threat. They had to tackle other internal issues as well such as army reorganisation, the introduction and later repeal of the Vernacular Press Act, tenancy reforms in Bengal, coping with Anglo-Indian racism over the Ilbert Bill and, later on, countering the rising tide of Indian nationalism. Sanitation for the community was never on the list of priorities. During the four decades of Florence's involvement with India, whatever was done for the people of India regarding sanitation was done by default.

Florence's initial suggestion of creating a central sanitary executive for the whole country was never pursued. Even the newly born Sanitary Commissions of 1864, which were only advisory and consultative bodies, were soon abandoned and replaced by Sanitary Commissioners during

Lawrence's viceroyalty.[39] Florence wanted the Government to use the skill and expertise that had worked in Britain. But most of the Sanitary Commissioners appointed in India had no experience or training in urban or rural sanitation. They were 'of lower stamp', as Florence described them. Their salary was poor, and the work unattractive. In the name of saving the Imperial fund, Lawrence reduced their number as well as their salaries.[40] Lawrence also asked the District Commissioners and Collectors to provide their own funds for local sanitary work, which they unanimously rejected as an unworkable proposition.[41]

The Sanitary Commissioners were responsible for sanitation of vast areas of the country, but did not have any executive power. Their duties included touring and investigating outbreaks of epidemics, advising on health matters, and reporting and collecting vital statistics which, considering the enormous size of the presidencies, was difficult for one person to do effectively. But the key question was never sanitation. As Cuningham said: 'The mere sanitary question cannot be considered apart from its bearing on finance or apart from the general policy of the Government.'[42] Ripon, during his viceroyalty, tried to make the job attractive, but was not able to proceed far. During that time, whatever work was undertaken was carried out by ordinary engineers, despite Florence's plea to the Government to appoint proper sanitary engineers. The same thing happened with other Viceroys as well. More or less all of them wanted to put the sanitation of the country on the right footing, but, as Florence said, changes and more changes were made. Whatever work was done was done in a piecemeal fashion, never in a structured way.

By July 1888, the Government of India had established Sanitary Boards in each province. The idea, launched by Dufferin, was faithfully executed by Lansdowne.[43] These Boards consisted of a Sanitary Commissioner and a Sanitary Engineer, as Florence had initially asked for. But by this time most of the Indian towns and districts had local municipalities, and district or Taluka boards. They were responsible for the sanitation of their respective areas, such as for drainage, water supply, hospitals and dispensaries, and in some cases education as well. The Sanitary Boards were supposed to oversee the work of these organisations and, if necessary, to advise them. Florence was delighted to see that the Sanitary Boards were given some executive power, but she was doubtful about the efficacy of such power without proper funding.[44] Although the Government promised some financial help, the local municipalities and district boards were supposed to raise their own funding by levying local taxes, but many of them did not have even this power. Where they did, the poor rural population was not able to pay. Florence suggested that the village organisation or the *panchayats* should have the power to spend the money raised by such taxes for their own village conservancy. But, the power to spend was left in the hand of the 'Sahib' Collectors. Florence knew that the streets where the Collector would pass would be swept clean, but not the back alleys.

The sanitary boards continued to exist up to the end of the Raj, but their role remained more or less consultative, and the little executive power they had was hardly ever used. On average, they held a couple of meetings a year, and continued to 'advise' the Government and the local bodies and were rarely concerned with matters regarding village sanitation.[45] In the course of time, a system of keeping records of sanitary work in a village inspection book was introduced, which was 'found to be of considerable value'. When Florence came to know about this, she commented in her usual fashion: 'Village Sanitary Inspection Book invaluable, if carried out.'[46]

Over the years, systems like vaccinating the population and keeping statistical records of births and deaths were slowly introduced, and hospitals and dispensaries were established. But the focus was never on the villages where most of the Indians lived. They remained in the same abyss of ignorance, poverty and squalor as before. The Government sanitary reforms hardly reached them. One Sanitary Commissioner commented sarcastically that there might not be drainage in the villages, but there were other ways of keeping the villages clean. Thanks to the heat and dry atmosphere, 'together with the bountiful provision of nature in the matter of scavengers, quadruped and biped, feathered and plumeless, effect much in the way of counteracting the otherwise inevitable results'.[47]

Some historians are of the opinion that sanitary legislation as happened in nineteenth-century Britain was never a viable option for India. India was too big an area to be policed, and there were not sufficient trained people to ensure its enforcement.[48] There is some truth in this argument, if one considers the vastness of the country and the remoteness of some rural areas. Even then, keeping a supervisory control over public health might have been a difficult but not an impossible task. From 1857 onwards, the colonial government in India had consolidated its position strongly and there was no internal or external threat to that position as such in the latter part of the nineteenth century. The country was by that time politically policed even up to the remote rural areas, and there was no reason why such control could not have been extended, if wished, in improving public health. The British administration, in order to counter international criticism for failing to prevent cholera in India, was able to look after the pilgrims' health in their sea voyages to Mecca, or in big religious gatherings within the country such as the Magh Mela in Hardwar. They could have done similar things, if not in all, in at least some rural areas of India. Florence observed correctly that there was no plausible reason in failing to adopt similar stringent rules and regulations to improve rural health.[49]

As for the insufficiency of trained personnel, that was a direct result of British policies pursued up to the very end of the Raj. It was obvious that the rural health of the vast tracts of India could only be monitored by Indian personnel, that is, Indian doctors and medical attendants. But Indian participation in health care was considered as suspect. Not only was interference with religion and custom used as an excuse for inaction, but also throughout the British period Indians were considered as untrustworthy. They could not be relied upon with any responsibility whatsoever. In the eyes of the British administrators most of the Indians were lazy, dishonest and corrupt. They did not have the same moral standards as the British and, unless they were supervised by British administrators, it was feared that they would misuse their power. Cuningham wrote in 1868 on the question of appointing Indian agents to carry out sanitary improvements at the local level that there would always be a danger that they would use their authority to cause injustice and oppression. An Indian sanitary inspector would have favourable opportunities for extortion: 'I do not hesitate to say that if such agents were appointed throughout the country they might cause very serious discontent among the people. I am therefore of opinion that the time has not yet come when they should be appointed.'[50]

The Indian Medical Service and Indian doctors could have played a positive role in this situation. But the Indian Medical Service was not 'Indian'. Its members were mostly army doctors, all European, with little interest in rural health. They also kept the service exclusive by insisting on a very high standard for Indians to qualify as doctors.[51] Those Indians who were successful in qualifying as doctors were often treated as substandard second-class doctors by the Indian Medical Service, and a high proportion of them became general practitioners. Throughout this period, the academic dispute among medical men regarding the cause of epidemics, such as cholera and its spread, was rife. Most of the members of the Bengal Medical Service as well as Florence herself believed in the miasmic theory and insisted on the need for a clean environment. The supporters of the contagion theory of disease were still limited in number and their alternative ideas provoked immense hostility among the establishment. This professional dispute between two schools of thought also overshadowed any effort for rural sanitation.[52]

It was sometimes alleged that ordinary Indians, especially the rural community, did not accept Western medicine.[53] They allegedly rejected the health policies of the Government. There might be some truth in this argument in the sense that the concept of Western medicine was alien to the rural communities, and the fear of the unknown and ignorance played an important role in it. But this was not universal, as the popularity of the Dufferin Fund work showed. Though the Fund's work was aimed at the *purdanashin* women, the ones who benefited the most from it were the poorer women from the lower strata of society. The alleged fear of Western medicine obviously did not stop them from receiving Western medical care. The gradual increase in the number of vaccinated people in the country also showed that aversion towards Western medicine was breaking down. The sanitary report of 1883–84 actually recorded that people's faith in European medical science had increased.[54] The British Government in India also discouraged the development of indigenous medicine, which was prevalent in the country. Nor did they try to educate the general public in Western health care, as Florence continuously suggested. Had there been such policies, any public apathy could have been dispelled earlier as had happened in Britain. It was only at the end of the century that the Government started to talk about health education in rural areas. Florence had to work in the midst of this indifference of the establishment throughout the four decades of her involvement with India.

The most significant achievement of Florence in her Indian work was, however, not sanitation, army or civil, but to give a voice to the people who lived in the villages, the peasants, the *ryots*, who constituted almost 80 per cent of the population. Throughout her involvement with India, Florence continuously wrote and published about the conditions in which the Indian peasants lived, and drew the attention of the British public to the real situation that existed in India. Through her powerful writings, she portrayed a picture of rural India: how British apathy and incompetence failed to confront famines in India, how British land policy had taken away the customary rights of the *ryots* on their land, how the British legal system had failed to save the *ryots* from being exploited by the *zemindars* and moneylenders and, finally, how the British education system had left the *ryots'* children in the darkness of ignorance and illiteracy.

It must be said that Florence was not alone. Many others in Britain and India had tried to draw public attention to the conditions of the Indian peasants. But Florence was unique in the sense that she was the one with whom Viceroys and Secretaries of State conferred. The Viceroys privately sent her reports from India and sought her advice. The India Office and the War Office officially sent her Indian sanitary papers right up to the very end of her life. The Secretaries of State always asked her to brief them by writing a quick memorandum, and she did this many times. Sir Bartle Frere asked her to write memoranda for Lord Mayo so that Mayo could orient himself towards Indian sanitary reforms. Lord Cross, the Secretary of State, asked her to write comments on Dufferin's idea of sanitary boards, and she obliged him. Although she never held any official position, she was in a way a part of the establishment. She was almost like a resident critic or feature writer for the Government, and what the administrators failed to see she pointed out for them with her list of more viable and effective suggestions. Her personal relationship with the Viceroys and the Secretaries of State put her in a unique position of being the 'Governess of the Governors' in the real sense of the term. It also underlines what a determined individual without any real power could aim to achieve.

Yet she always held radical anti-establishment views. She often acted as the Government's conscience and their voice of reason. Like a political journalist, she wrote to embarrass the Government so that they were obliged to take some action. She used her reputation, her political acumen and her sanitary know-how to put pressure on the Government to recognise their failures and acknowledge their responsibilities. The skills she used to achieve her goals could provide lessons for any contemporary political lobbyist. There is no doubt that Florence was one of the most outstanding and influential spokespersons for ordinary Indians in nineteenth-century Britain. Her efforts were humanitarian, visionary and politically expedient.

Florence understood from the very beginning that the problems of the Indian peasants were not social or environmental; they were political. Social problems and environmental catastrophes certainly were there, but it was the political situation that had kept the Indian peasants in such a pitiful state. Her apparent failure to bring reasonable sanitary reforms for the Indian community within a reasonable time had made her search for the real cause that existed. Her writings from 1870 onwards clearly showed the logical development of her understanding of the Indian situation. She again and again pointed out that famine was expensive, and the large sum of revenue spent on famine relief could easily be spent on preventive measures such as irrigation. But as we know, irrigation was practically ignored for almost half a century on the grounds that it was non-remunerative, and other imperial priorities such as railways took over. As said before, it was from the beginning of the twentieth century, from the viceroyalty of Lord Curzon, that administrators began to pay more attention to irrigation and famine-preventive measures, and finally, after 1947, irrigation projects received the attention they deserved in a country like India. Surprisingly, many of the post-independence irrigation projects were undertaken in areas where Florence more than half a century earlier had said such work should be done.

The logical development of Florence's ideas did not allow her to stop just with famine and irrigation. In the course of time, the 'high priestess of sanitation' gradually moved to the path of a political agitator and became involved with the Bengal Land Tenancy issue, and it seems inevitable that her sympathy would go to the *ryots* and not to the *zemindars*. Consistently over the years she warned the British Government that if the situation did not change, the *ryots* would not wait for the Secretary of State. There would be uprisings in India as had happened in Europe. Her knowledge of working class movements in Britain, Germany and France dictated her to anticipate similar events in India. Florence was not wrong, as a number of peasant revolts did take place in nineteenth-century India. However, the political leadership in India did not come from the proletarians, but from the English-educated middle class.

Although Florence continuously agitated for the *ryots*, it has to be admitted that she had no contact at that level. Her Indian contacts were all middle class educated men, the *Bhadralok*. However much these men were interested in the plight of the *ryots*, sanitation of the rural communities was not their main concern. In some cases, as happened in the Bengal Land Tenancy situation, the issue was often against their class interest. The associations and organisations Florence was in touch with were also headed by these middle class men. It was therefore understandable why some of these associations were not always enthusiastic about working in the villages. In some cases, of course, associations like the Poona Sarvajanik Sabha or the Indian Association did agitate for the peasants' interests, but their overall aim was somewhat different. They saw their role as one of political lobbying and were more keen to put pressure on the Government to take action on a specific issue than to go to the villages to teach the rural community how to clean their environment. Their method of work was to publish articles in their associations' proceedings, present memoranda to the colonial Government, organise meetings, send deputations to the Viceroy, and if necessary make trips abroad to present India's case to the British Members of Parliament. These men were politicians, not sanitarians, and the associations they led were political organisations. They were more involved with the economic drain from the country than with the actual drains of Calcutta, Bombay or Poona. By 1885, the main concern of the Indian leaders was to work towards the Indianisation of the administration, looking after India's political interest and finally consolidating India's political will. In the context of India's cultural, religious and linguistic heterogeneity, they preferred to keep social questions outside the sphere of national political struggle. Unfortunately, like their political masters, they also put civil sanitation within such social questions.

By the 1880s, Florence painfully realised that sanitary civilisation could not be exported to India without a positive approach from the British administrators, and India needed Indianisation for her progress. So she became, as was noted before, an ardent supporter of Ripon's decentralisation policy for local government, and sharing power at local level with Indians. In this matter, the racist uproar caused by the Ilbert Bill incident was an eye-opener for her. Her liaison with Indian leaders in the late 1880s and early 1890s emerged from her search for a positive approach towards India. This led her to support the foundation of the

Indian National Congress and to encourage Indian delegates to spread their message in England so that the British people would know what was happening in India. This was also the reason why, in 1891, she wanted Indian leaders to attend the International Congress on Hygiene and Demography and to speak for themselves.

To a certain extent, Florence succeeded in creating public opinion and awareness both in India and in England. She certainly inspired people like Runchorelal Chotalall of Ahmedabad, B.M. Malabari of Bombay and Dayaram Gidumal of Sindh. It is also worth noting that although social issues were initially kept outside the sphere of the Indian National Congress, later, at Ranade's and Malabari's initiative, the National Social Conference was organised as a sister association of the Congress to discuss social problems.[55] And much later, a young Indian barrister called M.K. Gandhi introduced ideas like Florence's regarding village education and rural sanitation in his *Gramodyog* project.

Florence's main handicap in her Indian work was that she had to depend on others to deliver the goods. As Vicinus and Nergaard said: 'Nightingale was the engine that drove the machinery of sanitation, since she could not be the machinery that performed the work.'[56] The manner in which she worked through official channels created problems for her. She herself could not initiate any work. 'I never did anything except when I was asked,' she once said. 'I am more like a donkey than an explorer – that is, saddled and ridden away at a moment's notice.'[57] Florence had to wait for the Governor-Generals or Secretaries of State to be asked to write reports, memoranda, suggestions for female nursing or barrack improvement, or to provide advice about how to go about Indian sanitary work. As we know, she was responsible for writing a large section of the voluminous Royal Commission reports, the *Suggestions*, and part of the early sanitary reports. Yet it is difficult to find her name mentioned anywhere except where she specifically wrote something under her own name.

Florence's work was of course limited by the fact of who she knew; who were her contacts in India or Britain at particular periods of time. When she was lucky enough to have an obliging Viceroy, like Lawrence or Ripon, she had a favourable wind for her sails, but when Lytton and Salisbury were in power her work faltered. Similarly, her contacts in India also determined to which part of the sub-continent her attention and efforts would turn. Thus at the beginning of her Indian work, in 1864–69, during Lawrence's administration, her contacts were Dr Hathaway, Dr Pattison Walker, members of the Bengal Social Science Association and Lawrence himself, all centred on Calcutta, the capital of British India. Consequently, Florence's attention went there. At the latter part of her Indian work, her contacts were from the Bombay and Poona regions, and included Wedderburn, Dadabhai Naoroji and B.M. Malabari. It was not surprising, therefore, that she would be involved with the Bombay Village Sanitation Act and establish rapport with various associations in western India. This did not mean, as has been suggested sometimes, that she hopped around from subject to subject, area to area, without concentrating on one area, or getting involved with one subject. On the contrary, the focus of her attention always followed a logical path of development and when it changed, it changed as dictated by that logic.

Florence was not a social reformer; she did not want to change Indian society. As we know, she disliked the tag of being a philanthropist. All her life she avoided publicity and shunned limelight as was evident from her manner of returning home at the end of the Crimean War.[58] Personal fame or recognition was never her aim. As Cook said: 'She had a consistent and perfectly sincere shrinking from every form of popular glare and glory.'[59] Her aim was to initiate sanitary reforms for ordinary Indians and she took such steps as she thought necessary to achieve that. If that made her involved with issues such as famines, irrigation and land tenancy, so be it. Her private letters to various people of course often revealed her anguish and anger at the slowness of Indian sanitary progress and the inefficiency of the powers that be, but most of the time she preferred to work through the official channels. It was only when they failed to perform to her expectations that she established contact with Indians. Yet, in all her efforts, she kept herself more or less in the background. This was probably why in recent studies on British public health policies in India her name was only mentioned in passing, or omitted entirely.

Florence herself was depressed about her Indian work and its lack of overt success. As mentioned earlier, she kept in touch with events in India up to the very end of her life. It was not easy for a semi-recluse and housebound person like her to have that interest going for such a long time, almost 40 years. But she had a sense of destiny about her Indian work and was totally dedicated to it. She considered her work as services to God. However, Florence was limited by her social circumstances and the way she chose to work. If her achievements were not immediately apparent it was because of the colonial mechanism through which she worked and on which her success depended. And that followed its own logic, which she could do little to alter. As Vincente Navarro said, the major cause of death and disease in the poor parts of the world is not lack of resources, but a pattern of control over resources in which the majority of the population have no control.[60] This was certainly true about British India, and however influential the power of 'the Governess' might have been, it was not enough to loosen that control.

Notes

1. Smith (1982); Strachey, G.L. (1942), *Five Victorians*, London: Reprint Society
2. *Imperial Gazetteer of India*, 1907, (New Edition), vol. 1, Oxford: Clarendon Press, pp. 527–528.
3. Major Malleson's Memorandum, 2 June 1866, BL Add. Mss 45782, fols 212–218.
4. *Report, Sanitary Measures in India, 1889–90*, p. 1.
5. *Report, Sanitary Measures in India, 1870*, p. 104.
6. *Report, Sanitary Measures in India, 1876*, p. 5.
7. Report, Moral and Material Progress of India 1891–92, p. 367.
8. Proceedings, First All India Sanitary Conference held in Bombay, 13–14 November 1911, Parliamentary Papers 1912–13, vol. LXII, pp. 102–109.
9. Parliamentary Papers, 1876, vol. LVI, p. 279.
10. Wilkinson (1958), p. 11.
11. *Report, Sanitary Measures in India, 1900–1901*, p. 33–34.
12. Harrison (1994), p. 48.
13. Lawrence to FN, 7 April 1865, and 17 June 1866, BL Add. Mss 45777, fols 64, 79.
14. Government of Bengal, Judicial Proceedings, No. 620, October 1865; Strachey to the Secretary, Government of India (Home), 5 September 1864.
15. FN (1863a), pp. 81–82.
16. FN (1874a), p. 63.
17. Harrison (1999), pp. 92–110.
18. Arnold, D. (1979), 'European orphans and vagrants in India in the nineteenth century', *Journal of Imperial and Commonwealth History*, vol. VII, no. 2, pp. 104–127. Arnold has argued that there were some poor whites in India, but the description that he gave of these poor whites does not make them 'poor' in the same sense as rural Indians were, that is, living a hand-to-mouth existence.
19. Mehrotra (1971), p. 33. See also *The Bengal Mission – a History*, (1892), London: The Church Missionary Society, p. 4, footnote.
20. According to the 1901 Census there were 89 000 Eurasians and 170 000 Europeans, including Britons, living in India, and the total population of the country was 294 000 000. See Ballhatchet, (1980), p. 6.
21. Arnold, D. (1983), 'White colonization and labour in 19th century India', *Journal of Imperial and Commonwealth History*, vol. XI, no. 2, p. 148.
22. Hutchins, F.G. (1967), *The Illusion of Permanence*, Princeton, Princeton University Press, p. 108.
23. Ballhatchet (1980), p. 6.
24. Sinha, M. (1995), *Colonial Masculinity, the 'Manly English Man' and the 'Effeminate Bengali' in the Late Nineteenth Century*, Manchester: Manchester University Press, pp. 1–32.
25. Harrison (1994), p. 48.
26. Porter, R. (1991), 'Cleaning up the Great Wen: public health in eighteenth century London', in Bynum, W.F. and Porter, R. (eds), *Living and Dying in London*, London: Wellcome Institute for the History of Medicine, p. 63.
27. See Pati, B. and Harrison, M. (2001), *Health, Medicine and the Empire: Perspectives on Colonial India*, New Delhi: Orient and Longman; Arnold, D. (1993), *Colonizing the Body, State Medicine and Epidemic Disease in Nineteenth Century India*, Berkeley: University of California Press; Arnold,

D. (1985), 'Medical priorities and practice in nineteenth century British India', *South Asia Research*, vol. 5, no. 2, pp. 167–183; Jeffery, R. (1988), *The Politics of Health in India*, Berkeley CA, and London: University of California Press; Ramasubban, R. (1988), 'Imperial health in British India 1857–1900', in MacLeod, R. and Lewis M. (eds), *Disease, Medicine and Empire, Perspectives on Western Medicine and the Experience of European Expansion*, London, New York: Routledge, pp. 38–60.

28. Arnold (1985), p. 173.
29. Cuningham, J.M., Notes on the Sanitary Inspection and Sanitary Executive Service Proposed for India, 26 October 1868, BL Add. Mss 45777, fols 176–183. See also: Hume, J.C. (1986), 'Colonialism and sanitary medicine – the development of preventive health policy in the Punjab 1860–1900', *Modern Asian Studies*, vol. 20, no. 4, p. 718.
30. Kiernan, V.G. (1969), *The Lords of Human Kind*, London: The Cresset Library, p. 38.
31. FN (1879b), July, p. 495.
32. Beverley (1876), p. 56.
33. *Report, Sanitary Measures in India, 1876*, p. 29.
34. Report of the Health Officer of Calcutta, 1874, in *Report, Sanitary Measures in India, 1876*, p. 120.
35. Beverley (1876), p. 60.
36. Report, Moral and Material Progress of India, 1884–85, p. 71.
37. See King, A.D. (1976), *Colonial Urban Development, Culture, Social Power and Environment*. London: Routledge and Kegan Paul.
38. Beverley (1876), p. 39.
39. Military Despatch, Nos 462–463, 21 October 1865, *Memorandum, Sanitary Measures*, 1867, p. 9.
40. Government of India, Home (Public), A88-101, Governor General's Minute, Consultation Paper 2, 9 January 1866, NAI.
41. Government of Bengal, Judicial Proceedings, Nos 145–146, 9 November, 1865, WBSA.
42. Cuningham, J.M., Notes on the Sanitary Inspection and the Sanitary Executive Service Proposed for India, 26 October 1868, BL Add. Mss 45777, fols 176–182.
43. Report, Moral and Material Progress in India, 1891–92, p. 374.
44. FN's report to the India Office, September 1868, BL Add. Mss 45808, fols 247–252, draft.
45. Hume (1986), p. 721.
46. FN to Babbington-Smith, 10 November 1896, BL Add. Mss 45814, fol. 4, draft.
47. Report, Moral and Material Progress of India, 1891–92, p. 373.
48. Harrison (1994), p. 87.
49. FN to Lawrence (undated), 1868, BL Add. Mss 45777, fol. 172, draft. See also FN to Ripon, 12 August 1881, BL Add. Mss 43546, fol. 178.
50. Cuningham, J.M., Notes on the Sanitary Inspection and the Sanitary Executive Service Proposed for India, 26 October 1868, BL Add. Mss 45777, fols 176–182.
51. Jeffery, R. (1979), 'Recognizing Indian doctors: The institutionalisation of medical dependency 1918–1939', *Modern Asian Studies*, vol. 13, no. 2, pp. 301–326. See also Arnold, D. (2000), *Science, Technology and Medicine in Colonial India*, Cambridge: Cambridge University Press, pp. 61–65.
52. Hume (1986), p. 722.

274 FLORENCE NIGHTINGALE AND THE HEALTH OF THE RAJ

53. Arnold (1985), pp. 178–179.
54. *Report, Sanitary Measures, 1883–84*, p. 27.
55. Seal (1968), p. 295; Heimsath, C. (1964), *Indian Nationalism and Hindu Social Reform*, Princeton: Princeton University Press, pp. 176–204.
56. Vicinus and Nergaard (1989), p. 10.
57. Cook (1913), vol. 2, p. 429.
58. Cook (1913), vol. 1, pp. 303–304.
59. Cook (1913), vol. 2. p. 431.
60. Navarro, V. (ed.) (1982), *Imperialism, Health and Medicine*, London: Pluto Press, p. 7.

A Chronology of Florence Nightingale's Indian Work

1820. Born in Florence, Italy.

1854–56. Involved with nursing in the Crimean War.

1857–58. Worked for the first Royal Commission with Sidney Herbert. Wrote *Notes on Matters Affecting the Health, Efficiency and Hospital Administration of the British Army* (1857) with an appendix on India. Liaised with E. Chadwick and H. Martineau to publicise the Royal Commission's report.

1859–62. Worked for the second Royal Commission on the sanitary state of the army in India. Wrote a questionnaire, sorted the evidence gathered, chose members for the working committee, prepared the *Report* and wrote *Observations* (1862). Collaborated with Sidney Herbert, Lord Stanley, Dr Sutherland and Dr Farr for publication, and with Chadwick and Martineau to publicise the report.

1863. Worked for the appointment of the Sanitary Commissions in India. Established rapport with Sir John Lawrence, exchanged ideas with him about barrack improvement and the choice of personnel for Indian Sanitary Commissions. Defended the Royal Commission's report in the face of criticism. Wrote *How people May Live and Not Die in India* (1863) for the Social Science Conference in Edinburgh.

1864–68. Corresponded and collaborated with Lawrence in India about army sanitary organisation; wrote *Suggestions, in Regard to Sanitary Works for Improving Indian Stations* (1864); liaised with the India Office and the War Office for prompt action; wrote a Memorandum to answer Dr Leith's criticism on behalf of the Barracks and Hospital Improvement Commission, and *Suggestions on a System of Nursing for Hospitals in India* (1865) in collaboration with Sir John McNeill; liaised with Mary Carpenter, Dr Hathaway, Dr Pattison Walker and Lord Napier in India on the progress of public health in India; started to make unofficial contacts with Indians (1867); wrote *Memorandum on Measures Adopted for Sanitary Improvements in India up to the end of 1867* (1868); lobbied Lord de Grey and Sir Stafford Northcote for military and civil sanitary reforms in India.

1869–70. Collaborated with Sir Bartle Frere. Wrote a Memorandum on Indian sanitary measures for Lord Mayo, and the introduction to the *Report on Measures Adopted for Sanitary Improvements in India, 1868,* (1869). Accepted honorary membership of the Bengal Social Science Association; wrote an Address to the members on Indian sanitation, which was included in the *Report on Measures Adopted for Sanitary Improvements in India, 1869–70;* wrote *Sanitary Progress in India* (1869–70).

1871–73. Wrote *Observations on Sanitary Progress in India* (1872); worked with the Sanitary Department in the India Office. Became involved with famine, irrigation and the poverty of people in India; wrote *Life or Death in India, with an Appendix on Life or Death by Irrigation* (1873) for the Social Science Conference in Norwich; finished the proof copy of *The Zemindar, the Sun and the Watering Pot as Affecting Life or Death in India* (1873–74); liaised with Lord Northbrook and Lord Cranborne about military and civil sanitation in India. Started to focus more on the poverty of the people than on sanitation.

1874–76. Alliance with Sir Arthur Cotton to fight for irrigation in India. Lobbied Lord Salisbury (Cranborne) for irrigation canals; became involved in the railway vs. canal dispute; published 'Irrigation and means of transit in India' (*Illustrated London News*, 1874).

1877–79. Focused on famine, the *ryots* and irrigation; tried to build up public opinion in Britain about India's plight; published 'The famine in Madras' (*Illustrated London News*, June 1877), 'The Indian Famine' (*Daily Telegraph*, August, 1877), 'The united Empire and the Indian peasant' (*Journal of the National Indian Association*, 1878), 'The people of India' (*The Nineteenth Century*, 1878), 'A water arrival in India. By a Commissioner' (*Good Words*, 1878). Became involved with land tenancy issues in Bengal, and rural education; corresponded with P.K. Sen; published three articles, all titled 'A missionary health officer in India' (*Good Words*, 1879), 'Co-operation in India' (*Journal of the National Indian Association*, 1879), three articles, all titled 'Irrigation and water transit in India' (*Illustrated London News*, 1879), three articles, all titled 'Can we educate education in India to educate men?' (*Journal of the National Indian Association*, 1879); liaised with Gladstone to promote agricultural banking in India.

1880–84. Continued to agitate for tenancy reform in Bengal; wrote 'The Dumb shall speak and the Deaf shall hear, or the Ryot, the Zemindar and the Government' (*Journal of the East India Association*, 1883), 'Our Indian Stewardship' (*The Nineteenth Century*, 1883), 'The Bengal Tenancy Bill' (*The Contemporary Review*, 1883). Worked for Native Army Hospital Corps and village sanitation with Ripon; supported Ripon's reforms; liaised with Gladstone and the Queen for Ripon. Established rapport with Lord Dufferin.

1885–88. Liaised with W. Wedderburn, A.O. Hume, Dadabhai Naoroji; supported the Indian National Congress. Received Indian delegates abroad, helped them to publicise their cause. Corresponded with Lord Dufferin on sanitation. Focused on female health education in villages.

Worked for Lady Dufferin's project to get sanitary primers written, established contact with John Murdoch, Dr Mary Scharlieb, Manmohun Ghose and others for suitable books. Worked for a judicious Bombay Village Sanitation Bill; established contact with the Poona Sarvajanik Sabha and the Bombay Presidency Association. Helped Lord Roberts to select nurses for army hospitals in India. Corresponded with Catherine Grace Loch, the first lady superintendent of the army hospitals in India.

1889–92. Established contact with Lord Lansdowne through Benjamin Jowett; criticised the idea of Sanitary Boards in India. Wrote a Memorandum for Lord Cross. Worked on the amended draft of the Bombay Village Sanitation Bill with the Poona Sarvajanik Sabha and the Bombay Presidency Association; lobbied in favour of an Indian Committee in the International Hygiene Congress; invited Indian delegates to take part; offered them hospitality at Claydon; organised a Memorandum to be sent to the Secretary of State regarding village sanitation. Publicity in the journal *India*. Wrote an introduction on rural health education to Malabari's biography (1892).

1893–96. Published *Health Lectures for Indian Villages* (1893) and *Health Missioners for Rural India* (1896) in *India*. Liaised with Wedderburn and Malabari. Advocated rural health education using women health workers; wrote 'Village Sanitation in India' (1894), *International Hygiene Conference*, Budapest.

1897–98. Continued to receive Indian sanitary papers from the India Office for her comments; met M. Bhownaggree, Dinsha Wacha, G.K. Gokhale and the Aga Khan; continued correspondence with nurses in India and some Indian acquaintances.

1906. Declined to receive sanitary papers any more.

1910. Died on 13 August, at the age of 90.

Glossary

ABWAB special additional assessment on land

ADI GANGA the 'Original Ganges'; specifically Tolly's Nala (canal) in Calcutta

ANGLO-INDIAN British and other Europeans living and working in India, or who had worked in India

BABU, BABOO title, specifically referring to English-educated middle class Bengalis

BHADRALOK English-educated middle class, specifically Bengalis

BHEESTIEWALLA water-carrier; the man who delivers water in a bag made of animal skin

BRAHMIN a high-caste Hindu, a priest

BRAHMO SAMAJ nineteenth-century religious association and movement in Bengal to reform Hinduism, led by Raja Ram Mohun Roy

BUSTEE working class settlement in a town

CHETTIES trading caste in South India

CHITPAVAN Brahmin from Deccan

CHOWKEEDAR watchman, village policeman

CHOWKEEDARI village police centre

CHUMAR low-caste person who works with animal skins

COOLIE hired labourer

DURBAR Court, public levee, of Indian princes and British Viceroys

EURASIAN person of mixed European and Indian parentage (nineteenth-century expression)

FAIRAZI Muslim religious sect

FAKIR Muslim mendicant

GHAT steps leading to water

GOMASTAH agent of a zemindar

GRAMODYOG village reform movement led by the Indian Nationalist leader M. K. Gandhi

HINDOOSTAN India

IJARADAR a type of landholding sub-tenant

JIHAD holy war

KABULIYAT and **PATTA** contract documents between a zemindar and his peasants

KALI Hindu goddess

KANUNGO Government official who supervised and registered the signing of the Kabuliyat and patta; local land registrar

KHUS-KHUS vegetable matting for making tatties

LAL BAZAAR a brothel

LINGA refers to the Hindu god Shiva, as well as to sexual organs

LUMBERDAR a registered revenue-paying cultivator

MADRASSA Muslim religious school

MAHALBARI a land revenue system

MAMLUTDAR a native officer in charge of a talook or sub-division of a district (word used in western India)

MANG, MEHTAR, MHAR sweeper or cleaner, belonging to an untouchable caste

MOFUSSIL provincial administrative areas (as distinct from large towns or cities)

MOULAVI Muslim religious teacher

PANCHAYAT village organisation for arbitrating village disputes, typically with five members

PANDIT Sanskrit scholar

PARSEE, PARSI member of the Zoroastrian community from Persia (Iran) settled in western India

PATEL village headman (western India)

PATHSHALA village primary school

PATNIDAR type of landholding sub-tenant

PATTA see Kabuliyat

PUJA act of religious worship or offering (Hindu)

PURDAH, PURDAH NASHIN middle class Indian women who do not appear in public in front of men; women in veil

RAJ, The RAJ kingdom, sovereignty; the British Empire in India

RYOT, RAIYAT peasant, smallholder, cultivator

RYOTWARI form of land tenure system imposed by the British in southern India

SABHA an assembly, society

SALAMI payment to landlord, often illegal

SANYASI Hindu ascetic or holy man

SEPOY native Indian soldier

SOWCAR, SOWKAR moneylender (Deccan)

TALOOKDAR native officer in charge of a talook, an estate or subdivision

TATTIES screen made of khus khus, usually soaked in water to cool rooms in hot weather

VAKEEL, VAKIL lawyer

WAHABI Muslim sect; followers of Abdul Wahab

ZEMINDAR a landholder

ZEMINDARI system of landholding

ZENANA women; womens' quarters in an orthodox Indian household

Some Important Personalities and Correspondents Relating to Nightingale's Indian Work

Dr Elizabeth Garrett **Anderson** (1836–1917). First English woman to obtain a medical degree; feminist, fought for women's right to enter the medical profession; established a dispensary for women in London (later renamed the Elizabeth Garrett Anderson Hospital, now defunct); correspondent.

Surendranath **Banerjee** (1848–1925). Barred from Indian Covenanted service in 1874; co-founder of the Indian Association; politician, involved in India's freedom movement; President of the Indian National Congress; member of the Bengal Legislative Council.

Lord William **Bentinck** (1774–1839). Governor-General of India (1828–35); famous for the Education Act of 1835 and abolition of the Suttee system.

John Drinkwater **Bethune** (1801–1851). Educationist, founder of Bethune school for girls in Calcutta (1849) previously known as the Calcutta female school.

M.M. **Bhownaggree** (1851–1933). Barrister, MP (1895 and 1900), supported by the Tories as a parliamentary candidate.

Dr Elizabeth **Blackwell** (1821–1910). Born in England; emigrated to the USA but returned in 1868; first woman doctor in the USA; feminist, medical practitioner.

Ananda Mohon **Bose** (1846–1906). Barrister, co-founder and Secretary of the Indian Association; member of the Bengal Legislative Council; President of the Indian National Congress.

John **Bright** (1811–89). MP; member of the British India Society, supported India's cause.

Dr J.L. **Bryden** (1833–80). Civil Surgeon in the Bengal Presidency; believed in the airborne theory for spread of cholera; wrote a number of cholera reports included in the Sanitary Reports from India.

Sir James **Caird** (1816–92). Agriculturist; member of Indian Famine Commission; correspondent.

Lord **Canning** (1812–62). Governor-General and the first Viceroy of India (1856–62); earned the name 'Clemency Canning' for showing leniency towards the Indians taking part in the mutiny of 1857.

Lady Charlotte **Canning** (1817–61). Vicereine; helped Florence to get a job in Harley Street Hospital and later to recruit nurses for Crimea; correspondent.

Mary **Carpenter** (1807–77). Unitarian philanthropist; took an active part in the reformation of neglected children, founded a Ragged School and reformatories for girls in Bristol; follower of Raja Ram Mohun Roy; visited India four times and agitated for female normal schools, juvenile delinquents, and prison reforms in India; co-founder of the Bengal Social Science Association (1867); one of the founders of the National Indian Association, which promoted social contact between Indians abroad and the Britons; correspondent.

Edwin **Chadwick** (1800–90). Social reformer, journalist, sanitarian; led the public health movement in England; a collaborator of Florence, helped her to publicise the Royal Commission's report; wrote articles on Indian Army sanitation; correspondent.

Narayan Ganesh **Chandavarkar** (1855–1923). Lawyer, editor of *Indu Prakash*, social reformer; visited Britain in 1885 as a delegate of Poona Sarvajanik Sabha and the Bombay Presidency Association to lobby British MPs, and met Florence.

Runchorelal **Chotalall** (1823–98). Pioneer of the modern Indian textile industry; President of the Ahmedabad municipality; worked for water works and drainage system in Ahmedabad; member of Bombay Legislative Council; correspondent.

Lord Randolph **Churchill** (1849–94). Tory Secretary of State for India (1885–86).

William **Clark** (1821–1880). Civil engineer, responsible for the drainage of Calcutta; correspondent.

Lord **Cornwallis** (1738–1805). Governor-General of India (1786–93, 1805); introduced 'permanent settlement' in land tenancy in the Bengal Presidency.

Sir Arthur Thomas **Cotton** (1803–99). Royal Engineer, worked for various irrigation projects in India; a vociferous spokesperson for public works in India; collaborated with Florence for irrigation in India; correspondent.

J.M. **Cuningham** (1829–1905). Surgeon-General and Sanitary Commissioner in India; member of the Army Sanitary Committee; correspondent.

Henry Louis Vivian **Derozio** (1809–31). Eurasian poet; teacher in the Hindu College; inspired the Young Bengal Movement, lost his job for 'corrupting young minds'.

William **Digby** (1849–1904). Journalist, editor of *The Madras Times*; Secretary of the National Liberal Club in London.

Lord **Dufferin**, 1st Marquis of Dufferin & Ava (1826–1902). Viceroy of India (1885–89); passed Bengal Tenancy Act; the Indian National Congress was formed during his viceroyalty; correspondent.

Lady Hariot **Dufferin** (1843–1936). Vicereine, founder of the Dufferin Fund; collaborated with Florence to produce sanitary primers; correspondent.

Sir Ashley **Eden** (1831–87). Lieutenant-Governor of Bengal (1877–82); member of the Secretary of State's Council (1882); the Calcutta Eden Hospital for women and children was founded in his honour.

Dr William **Farr** (1807–83). Medical statistician; collaborated with Florence in writing the Royal Commission's report and helped in her subsequent work for India; correspondent.

Dr Thomas **Farquhar**. Surgeon to the Viceroy; criticised Florence's arguments concerning sanitation in India in 1867.

Sir Bartle **Frere** (1815–85). Governor of Bombay (1862–67); member of the India Council (1867–77); Chairman of the Sanitary Committee at the India Office; correspondent.

Naoroji **Furdoonji** (1817–85). Social reformer; shareholder of *The Bombay Times*, famous for sacking its editor Dr George Buist for writing inflammatory comments about the Indians during the mutiny of 1857.

Captain Douglas **Galton** (1822–99). Permanent Under-Secretary, War Office; involved with army sanitation; Florence's confidant and correspondent; married her cousin Marianne Nicholson.

Dr Kadombini **Ganguly** (1861–1923). First Bengali woman to become a doctor; worked in the Dufferin Fund Hospital; later went to Edinburgh and Glasgow to obtain further medical qualifications.

Lalmohun **Ghose** (1849–1909). Barrister; went to England (1879) to lobby for the repeal of the Vernacular Press Act, the Arms Act and raising the age limit in the Indian Civil Service examinations; stood as a parliamentary candidate from Deptford but lost. Was involved with the Indian Association; met Florence in 1885. Later became President of the Indian National Congress.

Manmohun **Ghose** (1844–96). Barrister; brother of Lalmohun Ghose, President of the Indian Association; active in the Indian National Congress; correspondent.

William E. **Gladstone** (1809–98). Liberal Prime Minister, famous for the repeal of the Vernacular Press Act in India; correspondent.

Gopal Krishna **Gokhale** (1866–1915). Academic, journalist, politician; edited the *Quarterly Journal of the Poona Sarvajanik Sabha* (1887–95); a moderate in the Indian National Congress; founder of the Servants of India Society; met Florence in 1897.

Sir M.E. **Grant-Duff** (1829–1906). MP, Under-Secretary of State for India (1868–74); Governor of Madras (1881–6). His wife, Lady Grant-Duff, helped Florence to find suitable authors to write health primers in vernacular languages.

Sir John **Hall** (1795–1866). Surgeon in India; Inspector-General of hospitals in Crimea; clashed with Florence about nursing and her role in Crimea.

Lord **Hartington** (1833–1908). Secretary of State for India (1880–82).

Dr Charles **Hathaway**. Secretary to Sir John Lawrence, the Viceroy; correspondent.

Sidney **Herbert** (1810–61). Met Florence in 1847–48, developed an admiration and friendship; Secretary at War during Crimea crisis; sent Florence and her nurses to Crimea; worked with her in two Royal Commissions as Chairman. His wife Elizabeth Herbert helped Florence to get her job in Harley Street Hospital and to recruit nurses during the Crimea Crisis; correspondent.

Allan Octavian **Hume** (1829–1912). Civil Servant in India; founder of the Indian National Congress, and the journal *India*.

Sir Courtney Peregrine **Ilbert** (1841–1924). Law Member of the Viceroy's Council (1882–86), famous for handling the Bengal Tenancy Act and the Ilbert Bill; correspondent.

Benjamin **Jowett** (1817–93). Master of Balliol; a life-long correspondent and confidant of Florence; supported her Indian work; her adviser and script reader.

Arthur Seymour **Keay** (1839–1909). Banker, writer, MP; sympathetic to India's cause; supported the Indian National Congress.

Aga Khan (1875–1958). Hereditary Imam or spiritual leader of the Ismaili sect of Shia Muslims; under the influence of Pheroze Shah Mehta supported moderate Indian Nationalism; later became the president of All India Muslim League; met Florence in 1898.

Lord **Lansdowne**, 5th Marquis of (1845–1927). Student of Benjamin Jowett; Under-Secretary for War (1880); Viceroy of India (1889–94); correspondent.

Lord John **Lawrence** (1811–79). Achieved fame for bravery during mutiny; Chief Commissioner and later Lieutenant-Governor of Punjab; gave evidence to the Royal Commission; Viceroy of India (1864–69); introduced sanitary reforms into the Indian Army; member of India Council; correspondent.

Catherine Grace **Loch** (1854–1904). Superintendent of the first batch of English nurses appointed to the military hospitals in India; updated training for Indian hospital orderlies; correspondent.

Rev. James **Long** (1814–87). Missionary, social reformer, writer, social scientist; founder of Bengal Social Science Association; famous for Nil Durpan Trial; correspondent.

Lord **Lytton** (1831–91). Viceroy of India (1876–80); infamous for the Vernacular Press Act.

Behramji Merwanji **Malabari** (1853–1912). Social reformer, poet, editor of *The Indian Spectator*; famous for agitating against child marriage and enforced widowhood; friend of Mary Carpenter and Florence; correspondent.

Sir Louis **Mallet** (1823–90). Member of the India Council (1872–74); Permanent Under-Secretary of State for India (1874–83); a confidant of Florence; correspondent.

Dr James Ranald **Martin** (1793–1874). Surgeon in the Bengal Medical Service, practised in Calcutta; wrote Fever Hospital Report; gave evidence to the Royal Commission; member of the Army Sanitary Committee; well known for his book *A Brief Topographical and Historical Notice of Calcutta*.

Harriet **Martineau** (1802–76). Unitarian, political journalist, feminist, leader writer of *The Daily News*; led agitation against the Contagious Diseases Act; published articles on the Indian Army; collaborated with Florence for publicity; correspondent.

Lord **Mayo** (1822–72). Viceroy of India (1869–72); tried to reform agriculture and introduce local government in India; correspondent.

Dr J. **McNeill** (1795–1883). Assistant Surgeon on the East India Company's Bombay establishment; went to Crimea for inspection with Col Tulloch; their report was unpopular in the War Office; Florence's confidant, collaborator and one of her strongest allies in her Indian work; correspondent.

Pheroze Shah **Mehta** (1845–1915). Politician, barrister, judge; member of the Indian Legislative Council; member of the Bombay Presidency Association.

John Stuart **Mill** (1806–73). Utilitarian philosopher, MP; worked for women's suffrage; a correspondent and reader of Florence's manuscripts.

Peary Chund **Mitra** (1814–83). Student of Derozio; Secretary of the Bengal Social Science Association; writer, social activist.

Madam **Mohl** (Mary Clarke) (1793–1883). Family friend, Florence and her sister spent holidays with her in Paris; correspondent.

Salem Ramaswami **Mudaliar** (1852–92). Lawyer, politician; went to England as a delegate from the Madras Mahajan Sabha (1885); met Florence; later member of the Indian National Congress.

John **Murdoch** (1819–1904). Christian evangelist; went to Colombo as a teacher (1844); author of suitable books for native Christians; Secretary of the Christian Vernacular Education Society in India; correspondent.

Dadabhai **Naoroji** (1825–1917). Businessman, politician, MP (1892–95); founder of the East India Association; President of the Indian National Congress; correspondent.

Lord **Napier** and Ettrick (1819–98). Governor of Madras (1866); interested in sanitation; introduced female nursing to Madras; correspondent.

Sir Stafford **Northcote** (1818–87). Secretary of State for India (1867); correspondent.

Kristodas **Pal** (1838–84). Editor of *The Hindoo Patriot*; Secretary of the British Indian Association; member of Bengal Legislative Assembly and Indian Legislative Council.

Vasodeo Balwant **Phadke** (1845–83). Clerk; organised the famine-stricken peasants of Deccan into an unsuccessful uprising against the Government; imprisoned for life in Aden, where he died.

Charles **Plowden**. Clerk; sent sanitary papers to Florence from the India Office; correspondent.

Mahadev Govind **Ranade** (1841–1901). Lawyer, politician; member of the Bombay Legislative Council; judge, social reformer, editor of the *Quarterly Journal of the Poona Sarvajanik Sabha*; founder of the National Social Conference.

Lord **Ripon** (de Grey) (1827–1909). Liberal politician; Under-Secretary for War (1859), Secretary for War (1863), Secretary of State (1866), Viceroy of India (1880–84) where he was famous for his progressive reforms; correspondent.

Lord F.S. **Roberts** (1832–1894). Field Marshal; Commander in Chief of the Indian Army during Dufferin's viceroyalty; introduced female nursing to army hospitals in India.

W.R. **Robertson**. Principal, Madras Agricultural College; Superintendent of the Government farm; correspondent.

Raja Rammohun **Roy** (1772–1833). Social reformer, educationist; led the anti-suttee movement in Bengal; served in the East India Company; founder of the Brahmo Samaj; died and buried in Bristol.

Lord **Salisbury** (Cranborne) (1830–1903). Conservative politician; Secretary of State for India (1866, 1874–75), Prime Minister (1885, 1886, 1895); anti-irrigation and pro-railway in India; correspondent.

Dr Mary **Scharlieb** (1845–1902). Medical practitioner in Madras; a pioneer of Indian female medical education; correspondent.

Keshab Chandra **Sen** (1838–84). Social reformer; one of the leaders of the Brahmo Samaj; educationist; friend of Mary Carpenter.

Prasanna Kumar **Sen** (1850–?). Lawyer, writer; member of the Brahmo Samaj; was involved with the Indian Association and the land tenancy reform agitation in Bengal; correspondent.

John **Slagg** (1849–89): MP; President of the Manchester Chamber of Commerce.

Lord **Stanley** (Derby) (1826–93). Colonial Secretary (1858); chaired the second Royal Commission after Sidney Herbert's death; approved appointment of Indian Sanitary Commission (1859); correspondent.

John **Strachey** (1823–1907). Lieutenant-Governor of North-West Frontier Province; member of Viceroy's Council; President of Bengal Sanitary Commission.

Dr John **Sutherland** (1808–91). Member of two Royal Commissions; worked with Florence in writing reports; Florence's devoted confidant and correspondent.

Kashinath Trimbak **Telang** (1850–93). Social reformer, judge; member of the Bombay Legislative Council and Bombay Presidency Association.

Sir Charles **Trevelyan** (1807–86). Governor of Madras (1859); Finance Minister (1862); educationist; supported Florence's Indian work; correspondent.

Colonel A. **Tulloch** (1801–64). Went to Crimea to report on the conditions in the army hospitals; a confidante of Florence.

Badruddin **Tyabji** (1844–1906). Barrister, politician; member of the Bombay Legislative Council and the Bombay Presidency Association.

Sir Harry **Verney** (1801–94). Liberal MP; initially wanted to marry Florence, but after her refusal married her sister Parthenope; devoted to Florence; entertained Indian guests at Claydon House; correspondent.

Iswarchandra **Vidyasagar** (1820–91). Social reformer, educationist; agitator for widow marriage in Bengal.

Dinsha Edulji **Wacha** (1844–1936). Businessman, journalist; member of the Bombay Presidency Association and active in the Indian National Congress; met Florence in 1897.

Sir William **Wedderburn** (1838–1918). Civil servant in India; Judge of Bombay High Court; founding member of the Indian National Congress (with A.O. Hume); educationist; helped to found the Florence Nightingale Fund in India, and journals such as the *Voice of India*, and *India*; correspondent.

Bibliography

Archival sources and official documents

British Library (including Oriental and India Office Collection), London, UK
  Dufferin Papers (OIOC).
  Lawrence Papers (OIOC).
  Nightingale Correspondence and Miscellaneous Papers (BL Add. Mss and OIOC).
  Ripon Correspondence (BL Add. Mss and printed papers).
National Archives of India, New Delhi, India
  Dadabhai Naoroji Papers.
  Gokhale Papers.
Jawarhalal Nehru Memorial Library, New Delhi, India
  Servants of India Society Press Clippings.
  Gokhale Papers.
  Dadabhai Naoroji Papers.
Servants of India Society, Gokhale Institute, Pune, India
  Gokhale Papers (microfilm).

Official documents and pamphlets

Bengal Tenancy Bill: a Speech into the Legislative Council of the Governor General by Courtney Peregrine Ilbert, 2 March 1883, Simla: Government Central Branch Press.
General Order by the Governor-General in Council, No. 87 of 1864 (1870), *Gazette of India*, L 99.
Government of Bengal, Judicial (Home) Proceedings, 1861, 1865.
Government of India (Home) Famine Commission Reports, 1860–61, 1866, 1880, 1898, 1901.
Government of India (Home, Public) Proceedings, 1866.
Imperial Gazetteer of India (1907), Oxford: Clarendon Press.
Memorandum: Sanitary Measures in India, 1867, 1868.
Moral and Material Progress in India, 1884-85, 1891-92.
Parliamentary Papers, 1876, vol. LVI; 1912–13, vol. LXVII.
Reports: Sanitary Measures in India, 1869–70, 1870, 1876, 1883–84, 1889–90, 1900–01.
Review of Education in India in 1886 with Special Reference to the Report of the Education Commission (1888), Calcutta: Bureau of Education.

Royal Commission Appointed to Inquire into the Sanitary Condition of the Army (1858), *Report of the Commissioners Appointed to Inquire into the Regulations affecting the Sanitary Condition of the Army, the Organization of Military Hospitals, and the Treatment of the Sick and Wounded: with Evidence and Appendix*, London: HMSO.

Royal Commission on the Sanitary State of the Army in India (1863), *Report of the Commissioners*, London: HMSO.

Government of India (1867), *Report of the Commissioners Appointed to Enquire into the Famine in Bengal and Orissa 1866*, Calcutta: Government of India.

Other primary sources

The Speeches of the Native Members in the Governor Generals' Legislative Council on the Bengal Tenancy Bill (1883), Calcutta.

Report of the Debate on the Bengal Tenancy Bill at the Annual Meeting of the British Indian Association, 5 April 1883, Calcutta: Hindoo Patriot Press.

Bombay Presidency Association, *3rd and 4th Annual Reports* 1887, 1888, 1889.

India, (London), 1892, 1896.

Proceedings of the Bethune Society (Calcutta), 1859–60, 1862.

Proceedings of the British Indian Association (Calcutta), 1853, 1861, 1864, 1866.

Proceedings of the Calcutta Municipal Corporation, 1864.

Proceedings of the Poona Sarvajanik Sabha (Bombay), 1879, 1880, 1892.

Transactions, Bengal Social Science Association, (Calcutta) 1867, 1870.

Voice of India (Poona), 1883, 1885, 1887.

Our Indian Sisters. A Quarterly Magazine published by the Baptist Missionary Society (1886), July.

Speeches Delivered in India by the Marquis of Dufferin and Ava, 1884–1888 (1890), Calcutta and London: J. Murray.

The Bengal Mission – a History (1892), London: The Church Missionary Society.

The Local Opinions on the Criminal Procedure Code Amendment Bill 1883 (n.d.). Reprinted from *The Englishman* [Calcutta].

Secondary and other sources

Acharya, S. (1992), *The Changing Pattern Of Education In Early Nineteenth Century Bengal*, Calcutta: Puthipustak.

Adhikari, S.K. (1990), *Vidyasagar and the New National Consciousness*, Calcutta: Vidyasagar Research Centre.

Aga Khan, His Highness the (1954), *World Enough and Time*, London: Cassell & Company.

Ambirajan, S. (1978), *Classical Political Economy and British Policy in India*, Delhi: Vikas Publishing House.

Anon (1859), 'Lodging, food and dress of soldiers', *The Contemporary Review*, **105** (January), 155–176.

Anon (1861), *The History of the Nil Durpan, with the State Trial of the Rev. J. Long of the Church Mission*. Reprinted from *The Englishman*, Calcutta, July 30 1861, Calcutta.

Anon (1889), *Lord Salisburys 'Black man'*, Lucknow: G. P. Verma & Brothers Press.

Arnold, D. (1979), 'European orphans and vagrants in India in the nineteenth century', *Journal of Imperial and Commonwealth History*, **VII** (2), 104–127.

——— (1983), 'White colonization and labour in 19th century India', *Journal of Imperial and Commonwealth History*, **XI** (2), 133–158.

——— (1985), 'Medical priorities and practice in nineteenth century British India', *South Asia Research*, **5** (2), 167–183.

——— (1993), *Colonizing the Body, State Medicine and Epidemic Disease in Nineteenth Century India*, Berkeley: University of California Press.

——— (2000), *Science, Technology and Medicine in Colonial India*, Cambridge: Cambridge University Press.

Bagal, J.C. (1953), *History of the Indian Association*, Calcutta: Indian Association.

Baird-Smith, R. (1861), *Report on the Famine of 1860–61*, Calcutta: Government of India, Home Department.

Bajwa, S. (1965), *Kuka Movement*, New Delhi: Motilal Banarasidas.

Balfour, M.I. and Young, R. (1929), *The Work of Medical Women in India*, London: Oxford University Press.

Ballhatchet, K. (1980), *Race, Sex, and Class under the Raj*, London: Weidenfeld and Nicolson.

Banerjee, A. (1995), *Finances of the Early Raj: Investments and the External Sector*, New Delhi: Sage.

Barnes, M. (1940), *The Indian Press*, London: George Allen and Unwin.

Beverley, H. (1868), 'Statistics of agriculture in Bengal', *Transactions of the Bengal Social Science Association*, **2** (2), 143–166.

——— (1876), *Report on the Census of the Town of Calcutta, 1876 taken on the 6th April 1876*, Calcutta: Bengal Secretariat Press.

Bhatia, B.M. (1972), *Famines in India*, Delhi: Asia Publishing.

Billington, M.F. (1895), *Women in India*, London: Chapman & Hall.

Booth, A.J. (1869), *Robert Owen – the Founder of Socialism in England*, London: Trübner & Co.

Bosworth Smith, R. (1883), *Life of Lord Lawrence*, London: Smith, Elder and Co.

Bradshaw, A.P. (ed.) (1905), *Catherine Grace Loch – a Memoir*, London: Henry Frowde.

Brock, M. (1993), *The Great Reform Act*, London: Gregg Revivals.

Buckland, C.E. (1901), *Bengal under the Lieutenant Governors*, Calcutta: S.K. Lahiri & Co.

Campbell, G. (1893), *Memoirs of my Indian Career*, London: Macmillan & Co.

Carpenter, M. (1868), *Six Months in India*, London: Longman, Green and Co.

Chanda, M.K. (1987), *History of the English Press in Bengal*, Calcutta: K.P. Bagchi and Co.

Chandavarkar, N.G. (1887), *English Impressions Gathered in Connection with the Indian Delegation to England during the General Election of 1885*, Bombay: Radhabai Atmaran Sangoon.

———— (1910), 'Florence Nightingale: the heroine of the 19th Century', *Subodh Patrika*, 21 August (copy in Servants of India Press Clippings, NMML).

Charlesworth, N. (1982), *British Rule and the Indian Economy, 1800–1914*, London: Macmillan.

Chatterjee, B. (1992), *Trade, Tariffs and Empire: Lancashire and British Policy in India*, Oxford: Oxford University Press.

Chattopadhyay, G. (ed.) (1978), *Bengal: Early Nineteenth Century. Selected Documents*, Calcutta: Research India Publication.

Chaudhuri, S.B. (1955), *Civil Disturbances during the British Rule in India 1765–1857*, Calcutta: The World Press Ltd.

Chotalall, R. (1892), 'The Sanitation of the City of Ahmedabad in the Bombay Presidency', in Shelley, C.E. (ed.), *Transactions, 7th International Congress of Hygiene and Demography*, XI, London: Eyre & Spottiswood, pp. 166–168.

Coats, T. (ed.) (2000), *Florence Nightingale and the Crimea 1845–55*, London: The Stationery Office.

Cook, E. (1913), *The Life of Florence Nightingale*, 2 vols, London: Macmillan.

Cook, S.B. (1993), *The Imperial Affinities*, London: Sage.

Cotton, A. (1854), *Public Works in India: Their Importance with Suggestion for their Extension and Improvement*, London: Wm.H. Allen & Co.

———— (1875), *Irrigation in India: an Address in Reply to the Marquis of Salisbury, 26 February, 1875*, Manchester: Guardian Letter Press.

—— (1880), *Reply to the Report of the Committee of the House of Commons on Indian Public Works*, Dorking: R.J. Clark.

Cowan, M.G. (1912), *The Education of Women in India*, Edinburgh & London: Oliphant, Anderson & Ferrier.

Dalyell, R.A. (1867), *Memorandum on the Madras Famine of 1866*, Madras.

Datta, K.K. (1970), *Anti-British Plots and Movements before 1857*, Meerut: Meenkshi Prakashan.

Dennis, B. and Skilton, D. (1987), *Reform and Intellectual Debate in Victorian England*, London: Croom Helm.

Dutt, R.C. (1874), *The Peasantry of Bengal*, Calcutta: Thacker, Spink & Co.

—— (1897), *England and India. A Record of Progress During a Hundred Years 1785–1885*, London: Chatto and Windus.

—— (1901), *Indian Famines: their Causes and Prevention*, London: P.S. King & Son.

—— (1902), *The Economic History of British India*, London: Kegan Paul, Trench & Trübner.

—— (1904), *The Economic History of India in the Victorian Age*, London: Kegan Paul, Trench & Trübner.

Eyler, J.M. (1979), *Victorian Social Medicine*, Baltimore: Johns Hopkins University Press.

Fitzgerald, R. (2001), 'Clinical Christianity: the emergence of medical work as a missionary strategy in Colonial India', in Pati, B. and Harrison, M. (eds), *Health, Medicine and Empire: Perspectives on Colonial India*, New Delhi: Orient and Longman, pp. 88–136.

Flinn, M.W. (1976), 'Medical services under the new Poor Law', in Fraser, D. (ed.), *The New Poor Law in the Nineteenth Century*, London: Macmillan.

Fox, F.W. (1879), *On Reform in the Administration of India*.

Ganguli, B.N. (1965), *Dadabhai Naoroji and the Theory of Drain*, London: Asia Publishing House.

Garthorne-Hardy, A.E. (ed.) (1910), *Garthorne Hardy, First Earl of Cranbrook. A Memoir*, London: Longman.

Ghose, J.M. (1930), *Sanyasi and Fakir Raiders in Bengal*, Calcutta: Bengal Secretariat Book Department.

Gidumal, D. (1888), *The Life and Life Work of Behramji M. Malabari*, Bombay: Education Society of Bombay.

—— (1892), *Behramji M. Malabari: a Biographical Sketch*, London: Fisher and Unwin.

Gillion, K.L. (1968), *Ahmedabad – a Study in Indian Urban History*, California: University of California Press.

Gopal, S. (1949), *The Permanent Settlement in Bengal and its Results*, London: Allen and Unwin.

—— (1953), *The Viceroyalty of Lord Ripon, 1880–1884*, Oxford: Oxford University Press.

—— (1965), *The British Policy In India*, Cambridge: Cambridge University Press.

Gourlay, J. (2001), 'Medical women and female medical education in nineteenth century India', in Bagchi, J. et al. (eds), *Education and Empowerment: Women in South Asia*, Calcutta: Bethune School Praktani Samiti, pp. 117–138.

Hare, A. (1893), *Story of Two Noble Lives*, London: George Allen.

Harris, D.G. (1923), *Irrigation in India*, London: Oxford University Press.

Harrison, M. (1994), *Public Health in British India: Anglo-Indian Preventive Medicine 1859–1914*, Cambridge: Cambridge University Press.

—— (1999), *Climate and Constitutions*, New Delhi: Oxford University Press.

Heimsath, C. (1964), *Indian Nationalism and Hindu Social Reform*, Princeton: Princeton University Press.

Hickey, J.A. (ed.) (1780), *Bengal Gazette or Calcutta General Advertiser*, Calcutta.

Hobhouse, A. (1883), 'Native Indian judges; Mr Ilbert's Bill', *The Contemporary Review*, 43 (June).

Hope, E.R. (ed.) (1900), *General Sir Arthur Cotton – his Life and Work*, London: Hodder & Stoughton.

Hume, J.C. (1986), 'Colonialism and sanitary medicine – the development of preventive health policy in Punjab 1860–1900', *Modern Asian Studies*, 20 (4), pp. 703–24.

Hunter, W.W. (1875), *The Life of Lord Mayo*, London: Smith Elder and Co.

—— (1892), *A Study in Indian Administration: Bombay 1885–1890*, London: H. Frowde.

Hutchins, F.G. (1967), *The Illusion of Permanence*, Princeton: Princeton University Press.

Hyndman, H. (1878), 'The bankruptcy of India', *The Nineteenth Century*, XX (October), pp. 585–606.

Indian Economic and Social History Association (1969), *Indian Economy in the Nineteenth Century: a Symposium*, Delhi: Hindustan Publishing Corporation.

Jeffery, R. (1979), 'Recognizing Indian doctors: the institutionalisation of medical dependency 1918–1939', *Modern Asian Studies*, 13 (2), 301–326.

—— (1988), *The Politics of Health in India*, Berkeley, CA and London: University of California Press.

Kiernan, V.G. (1969), *The Lords of Human Kind*, London: The Cresset Library.

King, A.D. (1976), *Colonial Urban Development, Culture, Social Power and Environment*, London: Routledge and Kegan Paul.

Kling, B.B. (1966), *The Blue Mutiny. The Indigo Disturbances in Bengal, 1859–1862*, Calcutta: Firma KLM Private Ltd.

Knorr, K.E. (1944), *British Colonial Theories 1570–1850*, Toronto: University of Toronto Press.

Leith, A.H. (1864), *Report on the General Sanitary Condition of the Bombay Army*, Bombay.

Levine, P. (1994), 'Venereal disease, prostitution, and the policies of Empire: the case of British India', *Journal of the History of Sexuality*, **4**, 579-602.

Long, J. (1862), *Five Hundred Questions on Subjects Requiring Investigation in the Social Condition of Natives of India*. Calcutta.

—— (1865), *History and Politics. Russia, Central Asia and British India*, London.

—— (1866), 'Social science in England and social science for India', *The 8th and 9th Annual Reports of the Family Literary Club*, Calcutta.

—— (1870), *Village Communities in India and Russia*, Calcutta.

Maclean, W.C. (1870), 'Miss Nightingale on theories of disease', *The Lancet*, **2** (29 October), 618–619.

MacPhail, J.M. (1905), *A General Survey of Medical Missionary Work in India*, Calcutta: The Indian Medical Missionary Association.

Malabari, B.M. (1896), 'Health missioners for rural India; a rough scheme for consideration', *India*, September.

—— (ed.) (1887), *Infant Marriage and Enforced Widowhood in India: a Collection of Opinions and Letters Received by B.M. Malabari*, Bombay: Voice of India.

Martin, J.R. (1847), *A Brief Topographical and Historical Notice of Calcutta with a Sketch of the Rise and Progress of Sanitary Improvement in the East Indies*, London.

Mathur, L.P. (1972), *Lord Ripon's Administration in India*, New Delhi: Chand & Co.

Mazumdar, R.C. (1962), *The History of the Freedom Movement in India*, Calcutta: Firma K.L. Mukhopadhyay.

Mehrotra, S.R. (1971), *The Emergence of the Indian National Congress*, New Delhi: Vikas Publishing.

Midwinter, E.C. (1968), *Victorian Social Reform*, London: Longman.

Mitra, S.C. (1902), *Iswar Chandra Vidyasagar, a Story of his Life and Work*, Calcutta: New Bengal Press.

Mitra, S.M. (1911), *The Life and Letters of Sir John Hall*, London: Longmans Green & Co.

Morris, H. (1906), *The Life of John Murdoch, LLD*, London: The Christian Literature Society for India.

Mukherjea, A. (1880), *The Proposed New Rent Law for Bengal and Behar*, Calcutta.

Murdoch, J. (1881), *Education in India: a Letter to the Marquis of Ripon*, Madras: C.K.S. Press, Verpery.

———— (1881), *England's Duty to India: a Letter to the Marquis of Hartington*, Madras: C.K.S. Press, Verpery.

Nanda, B.R. (1977), *Gokhale: the Indian Moderates and the British Raj*, Oxford: Oxford University Press.

Natesan, G.A. (ed.) (1918), *Speeches and Writings of Sir W. Wedderburn*, Madras: Natesan & Co.

Navarro, V. (ed.) (1982), *Imperialism, Health and Medicine*, London: Pluto Press.

Nightingale, F. (1858), *Notes on Matters Affecting the Health, Efficiency and Hospital Administration of the British Army Founded Chiefly on the Experience of the Late War*, London: Harrison & Sons.

———— (1859), *A Contribution to the Sanitary History of the British Army during the Late War with Russia*, London: Harrison & Sons.

———— (1863a), *Observations on the Evidence Contained in the Stational Reports Submitted to her by the Royal Commission on the Sanitary State of the Army in India*, London: Edward Stanford.

———— (1863b), *How People May Live and Not Die in India*, London: Victoria Press.

———— (1864a), *Suggestions in Regard to Sanitary Works Required for Improving Indian Stations; Prepared by the Barrack and Hospital Improvement Commission, 1 July 1864*, London: Eyre and Spottiswoode.

———— (1864b), *How People May Live and Not Die in India*, London: Longman, Green, Roberts, and Green.

———— (1865), *Suggestions on a System of Nursing for Hospitals in India*, London: Eyre and Spottiswoode.

———— (1869–70), 'Remarks on the present aspect of the sanitary improvement in British India', *Report, Sanitary Measures in India, 1869–70*.

———— (1870a), 'Letter to the Editor', *Lancet*, 2 (19 November), 725.

———— (1870b), 'Letters to the Secretaries', *Transactions, Bengal Social Science Association*, IV, xiv–xv, 1–8.

———— (1873), *The Zemindar, the Sun and the Watering Pot as Affecting Life or Death in India: The Zemindary System as Affecting Life or Death in India* (proof copy), BL Nightingale Papers, 1858–1894.

———— (1874a), *Life or Death in India, with an Appendix on Life or Death by Irrigation*, London: Spottiswoode and Co.

———— (1874b), 'Irrigation and means of transit', *Illustrated London News*, 65 (August), 99.

———— (1874c), 'Irrigation and means of transit', *Journal of the National Indian Association*, September, 45.

———— (1878a), 'The united Empire and the Indian peasant', *Journal of the National Indian Association*, June, 90.

—— (1878b), 'The people of India', *The Nineteenth Century*, **XVIII** (August).

—— (1879a), 'Can we educate education in India to educate men?', *Journal of the National Indian Association*, September, **105**.

—— (1879b), 'A missionary health officer in India', *Good Words*, July, August and September, pp. 492–96, 565–71, 635–40.

—— (1879c), 'Co-operation in India', *Journal of the National Indian Association*, May, **101**.

—— (1879d), 'Can we educate education in India to educate men and women?', *Journal of the National Indian Association*, October, **106**.

—— (1879e), 'Can we educate education in India to educate men?', *Journal of the National Indian Association*, August, **104**.

—— (1883a), *The Dumb Shall Speak and the Deaf Shall Hear, or the Ryot, the Zemindar and the Government*, London: East Indian Association.

—— (1883b), 'The dumb shall speak and the deaf shall hear, or the ryot, the zemindar and the Government', *The Journal of the East India Association*, **XV**, 163–210.

—— (1883c), 'The Bengal Tenancy Bill, October 1883', *The Contemporary Review*, **44**, 599–602.

—— (1883d), 'Our Indian stewardship', *The Nineteenth Century*, **XIV** (December).

—— (1887), 'Letter to the Editor', *Voice of India*, **V** (4), 183.

—— (1889), 'Letter', in *Bombay Presidency Association, 3rd and 4th Annual Reports 1887, and 1888*, Bombay.

—— (1892a), 'Letters to the Joint Secretaries', *Proceedings, Poona Sarvajanik Sabha, Quarterly Journal*, **XV** (July).

—— (1892b), 'Introduction', in Gidumal, D., *Behramji M. Malabari: a Biographical Sketch*, London: Fisher and Unwin.

—— (1893), 'Health lectures for Indian villages', *India*, 1 October.

—— (1894a), 'Village sanitation in India', in Gerlöczy, Z. (ed.) *8th International Congress of Hygiene and Demography*, **2**, Budapest.

—— (1894b), *Health Teaching in Towns and Villages: Rural Hygiene*, London: Spottiswoode & Co.

—— (1896), 'Health missioners for rural India', *India* (December).

—— (1991), *Cassandra and Other Selections from Suggestions for Thought*, Poovey, M. (ed.) London: Pickering and Chatto.

Oddie, G.A. (1979), *Social Protest in India: British Protestant Missionaries and Social Reforms 1850–1893*, Delhi: Manohar.

Palit, R.C. (ed.) (1882), *Speeches and Published Resolutions of Lord Ripon, Viceroy in India*, Calcutta: J.W. Thomas.

Pati, B. and Harrison, M. (2001), *Health, Medicine and the Empire: Perspectives on Colonial India*, New Delhi: Orient and Longman.

Patwardhan, R.P. (ed.) (1968), *The Select Gokhale*, New Delhi: Maharashtra Information Centre.

———— (ed.) (1977), *Dadabhai Naoroji Correspondence*, Bombay: Allied Publishers.

Pickering, G. (1974), *Creative Malady*, London: George Allen and Unwin Ltd.

Porter, R. (1991), 'Cleaning up the Great Wen: public health in eighteenth century London', in Bynum, W.F. and Porter, R. (eds.), *Living and Dying in London*, London: Wellcome Institute for the History of Medicine.

———— (1994), *London: a Social History*, London: Hamish Hamilton.

Pulling, F.S. (1885), *Life and Speeches of the Marquis of Salisbury*, London: Sampson Low & Co.

Quinn, V. and Prest, J. (1987), *Dear Miss Nightingale: A Selection of Benjamin Jowett's Letters to Florence Nightingale*, Oxford: Clarendon Press.

Ramasubban, R. (1988), 'Imperial health in British India 1857–1900', in MacLeod, R. and Lewis, M. (eds), *Disease, Medicine and Empire, Perspectives on Western Medicine and the Experience of European Expansion*, London, New York: Routledge.

Ratcliffe, S.K. (1923), *Sir William Wedderburn and the Indian Reform Movement*, London: Allen and Unwin.

Richey, J.A. (ed.) (1920), *Selections from Educational Records*, New Delhi: National Archives of India.

Roberts, Lord (1905), 'Introduction', in Bradshaw, A.P. (ed.) *Catherine Grace Loch – a Memoir*, London: Henry Frowde.

Roy, P.C. (1883), *The Rent Question in Bengal*, Calcutta: M.M. Rakhit.

Saint Clair, W. (1887), *John Laird Mair Lawrence, A Viceroy of India*, London: Hamilton, Adams & Co.

Sarkar, H.C. (1910), *The Life of Ananda Mohun Bose*, Calcutta: A.C. Sarkar.

Scharleib, M. (1924), *Reminiscences*, London: Williams & Norgate.

Seal, A. (1968), *The Emergence of Indian Nationalism: Competition and Collaboration in the late Nineteenth Century*, Cambridge: Cambridge University Press.

Selanders, L.C. (1993), *Florence Nightingale: an Environmental Adaptation Theory*, London & Thousand Oaks, CA: Sage.

Sen Gupta, K.K. (1974), *Pabna Disturbances and the Politics of Rent, 1873–1885*, New Delhi: People's Publishing House.

Sen, K.C. (1871), 'The improvement of Indian women', *Transactions of the Bengal Social Science Association*, V, 8–12.

Sen, P.R. (ed.) (1937), *Florence Nightingale's Indian Letters*, Calcutta: M.K. Sen.

Seymour Keay, J. (1883), 'The spoliation of India', *The Nineteenth Century*, **LXXVII** (July).

Sharp, H. (ed.) (1920), *Selections from Educational Records*, New Delhi: National Archives of India.

Shelley, C.E. (ed.) (1892), *Transactions, 7th International Congress of Hygiene and Demography, London, August 1891*, vol. **XI**, London: Eyre & Spottiswoode.

Shiman, L.L. (1992), *Women and Leadership in Nineteenth Century England*, London: Macmillan.

Singh, H.L. (1982), *The British Policy in India*, New Delhi: Meenakshi Prakashan.

Sinha, M. (1992), '"Chathams, Pitts, and Gladstones in Petticoats" – The politics of gender and race in the Ilbert Bill controversy, 1883–1884', in Chaudhuri, N. and Strobel, M. (eds) *Western Women and Imperialism – Complicity and Resistance*, Bloomington and Indianapolis: Indiana University Press, pp. 98–116.

——— (1995), *Colonial Masculinity, the 'Manly English Man' and the 'Effeminate Bengali' in the Late Nineteenth Century*, Manchester: Manchester University Press.

Smith, Dr D. *Causes of Epidemic Fever at Present Prevalent in Lower Bengal.*

Smith, F.B. (1982), *Florence Nightingale. Reputation and Power*, London: Croom Helm.

Southgate, D. (1962), *The Passing of the Whigs, 1832–1886*, London: Macmillan.

Srivastava, H. (1968), *The History of Indian Famines and Development of Famine Policy, 1858–1918*, Agra: Sri Ram Mehra & Co.

Stephens, M.D. and Roderick, G.W. (eds) (1983), *Samuel Smiles and Nineteenth Century Self-help in Education*, Nottingham: University of Nottingham, Department of Adult Education.

Stokes, E. (1959), *The English Utilitarians and India*, Oxford: Clarendon Press.

Stone, I. (1984), *Canal Irrigation in British India: Perspectives of Technological Change in a Peasant Economy*, Cambridge: Cambridge University Press.

Strachey, G.L. (1942), *Five Victorians*, London: Reprint Society.

Taylor, B. (1983), *Eve and the New Jerusalem*, London: Virago Press.

Thomson, D. (1950), *England in the Nineteenth Century, 1815–1914*, Harmondsworth: Penguin Books.

Trevelyan, C.E. (1838), *On the Education of the People of India*, London: Longman, Orme, Brown, Green, & Longmans.

Tripathi, D. and Mehta, M. (1990), *Business Houses in Western India*, New Delhi: Manohar Publications.

Veith, S. (1990), 'The recluse: a retrospective health history of Florence Nightingale', in Bullough, V., Bullough, B. and Stanton, M.P. (eds), *Florence Nightingale and her Era: a Collection of New Scholarship*, New York: Garland.

Vicinus, M. and Nergaard, B. (1989), *Ever Yours, Florence Nightingale. Selected Letters*, London: Virago.

Walkowitz, J.R. (1980), *Prostitution and Victorian Society: Women, Class and the State*, Cambridge: Cambridge University Press.

Watts, S. (1997), *Epidemics and History – Disease, Power and Imperialism*, Boston: Yale University Press.

Wedderburn, W. (1878), *The Village Panchayet – a Remedy for Agrarian Disorders in India*, London: East India Association.

—— (1880), *Agricultural Banks for India*, Reprinted from *The Bombay Gazette*.

—— (1883), 'The Poona Raiyat's Bank: a practical experiment', *Journal of the East India Association*, **XV** (July).

—— (1913), *Allan Octavian Hume: Father of the Indian National Congress, 1829–1912*, London: Fisher Unwin.

—— (1914), 'Florence Nightingale on India', *The Contemporary Review*, **105** (No. 580).

Whitcombe, E. (1972), *Agrarian Conditions in Northern India*, Berkeley, CA: University of California Press.

Wilkinson, A. (1958), *A Brief History of Nursing in India and Pakistan*, Madras: Trained Nurses Association.

Willie, J. (1867), 'The Foreign Policy of Sir John Lawrence', *The Edinburgh Review*, **255** (January), 1–47.

Wolf, L. (1921), *The Life of the First Marquis of Ripon*, London: John Murray.

Woodham-Smith, C. (1950), *Florence Nightingale, 1820–1910*, London: Constable.

Zaidi, A.M. (ed.) (1988), *The Grand Little Man of India; Dadabhai Naoroji: Speeches and Writings*, New Delhi: Indian Institute of Applied Political Research.

Index